Becoming: Transformative Storytelling for Education's Future

Edited by Laura Colket,
Tracy Penny Light and
M. Adam Carswell

This book is part of the *Transformative Imaginings: Critical Visions for the Past-Present-Future of Education* Series
Series Editors: Tricia M. Kress and Robert Lake

DIO Press International Editorial Board:

Karen Anijar-Appleton, University of Arizona, USA, *Emerita*
Rochelle Brock, University of North Carolina, Greensboro, USA, *In memorium*
Robert Carley, Texas A & M University, USA
Barry Down, Murdoch University, Australia
Paula Andrea Echeverri Sucerquia, Universidad de Antioquia, Colombia
Venus Evans-Winters, African American Policy Forum, Planet Venus Institute, USA
Henry Giroux, McMaster University, Canada
Ivor Goodson, University of Brighton, UK, *Emeritus*
Winthrop Holder, New York City Department of Education, USA, *Retired*
Awad Ibrahim, University of Ottawa, Canada
Myunghee Kim, Soonchunhyang University, Korea
Peter McLaren, Chapman University, USA
Ann Milne, Kia Aroha College Community, New Zealand
Marta Soler-Gallart, University of Barcelona, Spain
Juha Souranta, University Tampere, Finland
Sandra Vega Villareal, Instituto de Pedagogia Critica, Mexico
Galia Zalmanson Levi, Ben Gurion University & Hakibbutzim College, Israel

This edited volume was completed in the midst of the 2020 pandemic. As we and our contributing authors wrote the words contained in this book, our world lost 1.26 million people to the virus. Every day, we continue to lose to more and more people to COVID-19. We see this as a political disaster, as much as it is a medical disaster. We dedicate this book to everyone we lost to COVID-19. Many of those deaths could have been prevented. We hope their stories will be passed on through future generations.

From Laura:
This book is dedicated to my two curious and kind boys. As you grow older, I hope that your curiosity and kindness will lead you toward a deep understanding of and commitment to justice and equity. And one day, when you are older, I hope the stories in this book will help you in your journey.

From Tracy:
My mother was my first storyteller. She shared traditional children's stories but also lots of stories about our family and our history. My current work in storytelling is largely reflective of her efforts to ensure we knew about our past to understand who we are. As I get older, I recognize the deep importance of this and the importance of weaving storytelling into my own teaching and learning practices. I dedicate this book to her.

From Adam:
I dedicate this book to the teachers of my past, present, and future—both formal and informal—who've had such a profound influence on shaping who I have become as an educator, leader, husband, father, and human being.

ISBN 978-1-64504-141-2 (Paperback)
ISBN 978-1-64504-142-9 (Hardback)
ISBN 978-1-64504-143-6 (E-Book)

Library of Congress Control Number: 2021938989

Printed on acid-free paper

© 2021 DIO Press Inc, New York
https://www.diopress.com

All Rights Reserved

No part of this work may be reproduced, stored in a retrieval system, or transmitted in any form or by any means, electronic, mechanical, photocopying, microfilming, recording or otherwise, without written permission from the Publisher, with the exception of any material supplied specifically for the purpose of being entered and executed on a computer system, for exclusive use by the purchaser of the work.

Table of Contents

Foreword... vii
    Sharon M. Ravitch
Preface... xv
Acknowledgments xvii
Introduction: Critical Storytelling as a Tool to Support Educators through a Continual Process of Becoming 1
    Laura Colket and Tracy Penny Light

Part I: Claiming Identity

1. Unheard Stories: How Honoring and Acknowledging My Experiences Shape Me as a Teacher 11
    Browning Neddeau
2. Hometraining 17
    Raheem Jackson
3. Unlearning Evangelicalism: What a Poor Education Taught Me 27
    Lucas F. W. Wilson
4. Written on the Mind: Emotional Imagination in Storying and Re-storying Learner Identity And the Formation of Critical Pedagogies 35
    Sharon Ravitch & Janay Garrett

Part II: Border Crossing

5. The Stories We Carry and the Ones We Let Go: Casual Carcerality in School 63
    Melissa Kapadia
6. Snippets from a Nomadic Educational Autobiography 75
    Talar Kaloustian
7. Journey Across an Educational Divide.................................. 103
    Eliana Elkhoury
8. Toward My Educator Identity 117
    Talia Guttin

Table of Contents

Part III: Anti-colonial Ways of Being

9. Awakening Enquiry, Assisting Discovery: My Journey as Learner and Teacher 129
   Antonia MacDonald

10. A Piece of Glass 155
    Shaakira Raheem

11. A Stranger in My Own Country 165
    Thembelihle Brenda Makhanya

12. Beyond the Shadows of My Educational Experiences: Bridging the Gap through Reflexivity 181
    Debbie Devonish

Part IV: Social Class, Politics and Education

13. "Education is something that can never be taken away from you!" 199
    Theresa Conefrey

14. They Named Me Candy: An Unlikely Academic Success 213
    Candyce Reynolds

15. A Political Education in Community Wealth and Transformative Learning 225
    Sonja Taylor

16. The Many Layers of My Life: How My Relationships Shaped Me 237
    David B. Ross

Part V: Changing Pedagogical Practices

17. Finding Your People: A Co-storied Critical Autoethnography 255
    Kathryn Coleman, Clare McNally and Brian Martin

18. A Vet's Journey Out of the Cave 289
    Rohini Roopnarine

19. From Boredom to Discovery: Storytelling as a Tool for Teaching and Learning Science 299
    Andrew Sobering

20. As I Grew Up: A Narrative Reflection with Colleagues' Responses 317
    Kathleen Yancey

21. Uncovering and Examining Three Distinct Paths to Educational Leadership 331
    Laura Colket, Tracy Penny Light and M. Adam Carswell

Conclusion: Re-storying Education for Future Generations 349
Laura Colket and Tracy Penny Light

About the Editors and Contributing Authors 361

Foreword

by Sharon M. Ravitch

"We live inside an unfinished story."
—Rachel Held Evans

Stories are how people understand the world—they have power to constrain, liberate, destroy, repair, create, teach, heal, and transform. Stories change in form and focus, time and place, meaning and process. Storytelling is as old as humans; it is the heart of many cultures, religions, families, and communities, the foundational building block of psychology and counseling, the cornerstone of schooling and education. Stories shape life, learning, and people's sense of self and what is (im)possible. Stories convey the real and the imagined, sometimes merging them to illuminate what is possible. There is transcendent power in stories and transformative possibility in learning how we have been storied, that we can re-story ourselves and the world as we learn into who we are becoming. The transformative possibility of stories and storytelling lives in our storying and re-storying of our experiences, in building counter-narratives to grand narratives that deficitize and dehumanize. The possibility lies in the ways we engage stories to give ourselves voice and to listen, to imagine and work for justice and peace, authentic connection, and ethical interdependence.

Becoming: Transformative Storytelling for Education's Future offers a look into some of the deeply generative and restorative possibilities of storytelling in education, the transformative promise it holds for resonant and culturally responsive schooling, teaching, and learning. Chapter authors share emergent stories of how teaching and learning connect through stories, illuminating how reflexive storytelling processes shape their teaching philosophies and inform their pedagogical choices and approaches. Their stories portray and evince the powerful nature of critical re/storying as critical pedagogy, ways of working to co-construct the conditions in which students can intentionally story and re-story themselves, each other, and the world through learning how to re-story their own education and broader life experiences with authentic, intentional, and critical self-understanding.

Stories and storytelling are powerful for all students, helping them learn to engage in inquiry, reflection, and meaning-making-portals into their own interpretive processes and the experiences and perspectives of others. While in some educational circles storytelling is new, educators must be clear in naming and lifting up the long oral traditions of many indigenous peoples, communities, tribes, and cultures. Storytelling is increasingly centralized in the education of traditionally minoritized communities as a tool to center their wisdoms, to affirm and contest false narratives of their history, and to ground and foment critical consciousness and political resistance (Khalifa, 2018). As Brayboy (2005) shares, "many indigenous people have strong oral traditions… stories remind us of our origins and serve as lessons for the younger members of our communities; they have a place in our communities and in our lives" (p. 439). In relation to societal narratives of deficit, counter-storytelling can serve as an analytical tool for challenging dominant narratives and dominating stories by foregrounding the stories of marginalized people and communities (Solórzano & Yosso, 2002). Similarly, testimonios are first-person accounts, a form of narrative inquiry used by Latinx peoples as a tool to center their knowledges, insights, and histories, to share and affirm collective, group, and individual experiences. Rosales Montes and Peynado Castro (2020) draw on El Ashmawi et al. (2018) as they explain: "Through our testimonios, we explore our lived experiences and bear witness to advance our own liberation, build bridges to reclaim and produce a collective account that is told by us and that is centered on our agency to overcome oppressive barriers" (para. 5). Storytelling is a deeply generative approach to learning, it provides powerful opportunities to build third spaces (Bhabha, 2004) of identity expression, affirmation, and preservation for all learners, and can be particularly powerful when focused on re-storying, testimonios, counter-storytelling, and counter-narratives in BIPOC (Black, Indigenous, People of Color), LGBTQ, disability, and trauma-informed communities given the resonance of stories and the dire need to push back on dehumanizing grand narratives and the harmful policies, programs, and pedagogies they uphold.

Critical pedagogy grounds the generative and regenerative ways that stories and critical literacy support the cultivation of agency and advocacy for self and community. Across these and the great range of approaches to storytelling are desires for learning and growth, resiliency, self-learning, relational learning, and world-learning. Stories are a pedagogical portal into critical and resonant inquiry, insight generation and knowledge production, identity and history affirmation, and the cultivation of agency and critical transformation—personal, group, community—into ever-widening spheres of influence and connection. Stories help us to see how the personal is political (Hanisch, 1970), and help us to dismantle deficit thinking and the ways we take this in/on ourselves and project it onto other people and groups (Valencia, 2010). Stories, across time and place, can be positioned as vital processes for *undoctrination* from socialized knowledge hierarchies and logics that constrain possibility (Ravitch, 2020). Stories are an embodied invitation into our own and each other's critical consciousness (Freire, 1973) and to our liberated being and becoming (Ravitch, 2020).

Storytelling is an intentional approach to cultivating intra- and inter-personal awareness and compassion for self and others, learning about our storied lives in relation to the experiences and stories of our interlocutors. Intentional storytelling processes—which include a range of approaches to sharing and listening to individual and group stories—helps us make deeper and wider (i.e., more critical) sense of our lives, the rootedness of our ideologies and beliefs, and the historical and contextual moorings of our current emotions, beliefs, and stances. Storytelling helps people create the conditions for critical examination of our belief systems and the broader social, cultural, political, and structural forces and narratives that shape them (Solórzano & Yosso, 2002). Storytelling offers a means of learning, confirming, and contesting reality, building and preserving community, and conveying knowledge, values, beliefs, and emotions; it allows us to engage in grounded and contextualized self-reflection and to become constructively critical of self *and* society and self *in* society (Khalifa, 2018; Stevenson, 2014).

Salman Rushdie (1991) offers us the liberated understanding that, "Those who do not have power over the story that dominates their lives—the power to retell it, rethink it, deconstruct it, joke about it, and change it as times change—truly are powerless, because they cannot think new thoughts" (p. 480). The powerful hold that stories can have on us—as individuals and groups—must be explicated and interrupted so that education can be enacted as a practice of freedom (hooks, 1994). Through intentional storytelling processes, people learn to identify, reflect on, examine and re-examine experiences, histories, and values (Khalifa, 2018). And further, to explore and challenge the meaning, authenticity, and validity of the information they have, to reflect on assumptions, actions, and inactions to identify root motivations and contextual mediators. Further intentional storytelling processes help learners examine how context and history inform thought and behavior patterns in both visible and tacit ways (Solórzano & Yosso, 2002).

Storytelling is a powerful tool for learning and growth because the process of telling stories in intentional, reflexive, and relational ways helps us to co-create the conditions to identify, consider, and work ongoingly to understand our own ways of being, and over time, to make sense of the familial and broader social, cultural, educational, and ideological contexts that shape us through the ways that we interpret our experiences in the world as that changes over time (Nakkula & Ravitch, 1998; Stevenson, 2014). This includes the ways that we internalize and take on others' projections, transferences, and subjective value hierarchies as if they are "the truth of us" and make them our own story of self; they become laid down in our embodied memory as our own hierarchies. As Chimamanda Ngozi Adichie (2009) offers in *The Danger of a Single Story*, "Many stories matter. Stories have been used to dispossess and to malign. But stories can also be used to empower, and to humanize. Stories can break the dignity of a people. But stories can also repair that broken dignity."

Our educational and familial socialization conditions us to believe in a storied version of our self—a byproduct of our *emotional imagination*—the meeting place of the cognitive, creative, and reflexive dimensions of the human psyche (Ravitch, 2020). Imagination is a cognitive process of mental functioning that invokes psychological imagery; at its core, imagination involves how we conceptualize, take in, create, and envision possibilities. Building on this broad definition of imagination, our *emotional imagination* shapes how we visualize, make meaning of, and understand ourselves *and* the world and ourselves *in* the world—through the nexus of complex feeling-webs that shape our thoughts which shape our emotions—all in simultaneous and recursive loops, seemingly without effort and usually without being noticed or consciously processed. Emotional imagination is a vital growth and healing concept—our emotions shape our thought patterns and vice versa—they are inextricably linked and mutually reinforcing aspects of human consciousness, memory, and being.

The idea of having an emotional imagination is particularly salient to building a sense of personal and collective agency, which we can do through cultivating an actionable understanding of how to unlearn and relearn (i.e., change and build) our storied selves and the thought patterns, internal dialogues, and behaviors that these impositions-as-stories-of-us bring and reinforce over time. The concept of emotional imagination helps to conceptualize how experience is indexed as it is being transformed into memory (i.e., a process that goes through both the limbic and adrenal systems in specific ways that are important to discern and understand in order to do this work most effectively (Richo, 2019), how thought patterns shape both in-the-moment and over-time meaning-making, self-understanding, and the ways we write who we think we are on our minds because of who people told us we are were/are (Ravitch, 2020).

Our emotions shape our thoughts, including as fodder for the formation of limiting thoughts and cognitive distortions that, when identified and challenged, can be consciously reckoned with and processed to resolution. These limiting thoughts, as false beliefs that cause inner and outer misattunements, can be reshaped to create liberating possibilities to change our thought patterns and re-imagine and feel ourselves anew. In re-storying, we intentionally name and explicitly learn to identify and explore the emotional register of specific experiences through conscious storying and re-storying (Ravitch, 2020). We do this with ourselves and through dialogic engagement—a heuristic for intentional thought partnership, critical dialogue and support that invites relational and perspectival deepening of critical learning and contextualized self-reflection (Nakkula & Ravitch, 1998; Ravitch & Carl, 2020). In doing so we can challenge past experiences and narratives of self in terms of how false beliefs (e.g., "I'm not smart" or "I'm selfish if I don't take care of everyone else first") have been formed through repeated messaging, often through the veil of transference and projection, which is implanted in our psyches as fact and filter during our developmental years. These facts and filters are then re-used and re-experienced over the course of our lives through continued projection and transference; this unless interrupted and engaged with loving and compassionate attention to aspects of our shadow side (i.e., that which is suppressed because it was deemed problematic or threatening), our ego, and our early experiences (Richo, 2019). Engaging our emotional imagination with curious and loving attention is vital to cultivating a daily, and over time, a durable sense of inner and relational possibility—to imagine ourselves now and imagine ourselves forward in healthier, more authentic and agentic ways that are an outgrowth of imaginatively uncovering and then working directly with our feelings as they are—attached to our memories of past experiences and living within us in our consciousness, our thoughts and feelings, and our frames and sieves for viewing and experiencing the world (Ravitch, 2020).

Our emotional imagination is a nexus of the intrapsychic processes of taking in, interpreting, and making sense of the people, circulations of emotions and values as well as specific familial ones, and socially constructed meanings messaged to us in both direct and indirect ways over time. In this sense, the value sets of others are taught to us as stories of us, as us, and become implanted in us as an introject—an unconscious, idealized mental image of adults in our lives whose stories of us as youth had more weight than our emerging stories of ourselves (Ravitch, 2020). These stories, phrase by phrase, image by image, subjective value by subjective value (disguised as objective values), become our storyboard—our vision of self and sense of our identity now and in the future—a byproduct of the interactions around us, the actions done to and around us as well as not done for us, and the people with whom we identify and relate, to such a significant-though-unconscious degree that it takes considerable intention and constructively critical self-reflection to first learn to identify, and then learn how to work to uncover and constructively address, in our thoughts, feelings, and behavior patterns (Ravitch, 2020). This is agentic self-literacy that leads to more inner and lived freedom, an ever-growing practice of growing compassion for self, in relationship, for community/ies, and for the world. Ultimately, this process of reflection, understanding, and addressing internalized, socialized values through storytelling, leads us to re-story and recast ourselves and our intersectional identities to and with ourselves and then to and in the world in ways that are bespoke, authentic, and agentic (Stevenson, 2014).

Storytelling is one method to practice in the intentional process of becoming practiced in recasting and resolving experiences and aspects of one's identity and self-in-the-world (Stevenson, 2014), an entry point to engaging with and cultivating one's emotional imagination with agency. Reading stories through the prism of critical intersectional inclusivity (Pak & Ravitch, 2021) means considering representation and addressing marginalization within and across identity dimensions within a relational ecosystem of interdependent care for teachers and students. This is vital to their sense of safety and engagement, and to a sense of belonging to communities of interdependent concern, justice, and care (hooks, 2003)—to their becoming.

In these times of global chaos and radical flux in students' lives, families, and communities, educational processes must foreground storytelling as knowledge production, learning and healing strategy, and as an approach to community and social justice. The work of transformative education centers on dialogic engagement with youth that focuses on, and emerges from, their stories and those of the people around them—including their teachers—which pushes into power dynamics and humanizes pedagogy. Storytelling was the past of education—squashed by positivism, neoliberalism, and standardization—and, as this book illuminates, *storytelling is the future of education*—evincing and supporting critical intersectional inclusivity (Pak & Ravitch, 2021) in education and schooling as we work for justice and peace. We must do so in the spirit of Muriel Ruckeyser's (1968) words "My lifetime listens to yours" (p. 18)—with radical compassion, criticality, and shared unwavering commitment to equitable transformation.

References

Adichie, C. N. (2009). *The Danger of a Single Story*. TedTalk.
Bhabha, H. K. (2004). *The Location of Culture*. Abingdon, OXON: Routledge.
Brayboy, B. M. J. (2005). Toward a tribal critical race theory in education. *The Urban Review*, 37(5), 425–446. https://doi:10.1007/s11256-005-0018-y
El Ashmawi, Y. P., Sanchez, M. E. H., & Carmona, J. F. (2018). Testimonialista pedagogues: Testimonio pedagogy in critical multicultural education. *International Journal of Multicultural Education*, 20(1), 67-85.
Freire, P. (1973). Education for critical consciousness. New York, NY: Seabury Press.
Hanisch, C. (1970). The personal is political. In S. Firestone & A. Koedt (Eds.), *Notes from the second year: Women's liberation: Major writings of the radical feminists* (pp. 76–78). New York, NY: Radical Feminism.
Held Evans, R. (2018). *Inspired: Slaying giants, walking on water, and loving the Bible again*. Nashville, TN: Thomas Nelson.
hooks, b. (2003). *Teaching community: A pedagogy of hope*. New York, NY: Routledge.
hooks, b. (1994). *Teaching to transgress: Education as the practice of freedom*. New York, NY: Routledge.
Khalifa, M. (2018). *Culturally responsive school leadership*. Cambridge, MA: Harvard Education Press.
Nakkula, M. J. & Ravitch, S. M. (1998). *Matters of interpretation: Reciprocal transformation in therapeutic and developmental relationships with youth*. San Francisco, CA: Jossey-Bass.
Pak, K. & Ravitch, S. M. (2021). *Critical Leadership Praxis: Leading Educational and Social Change*. New York, NY: Teachers College Press.
Ravitch, S. M. (2020) Flux Leadership: Leading for Justice and Peace in and Beyond COVID-19. *Perspectives on Urban Education*.
Ravitch S. M. & Carl, M. N. (2020). *Qualitative research: Bridging the conceptual, theoretical, and methodological*. (2nd Ed.). Thousand Oaks, CA: Sage Publications.
Rosales Montes, I. & Peynado Castro, L. (2020) Finding Hope, Healing and Liberation Beyond COVID-19 within a Context of Captivity and Carcerality. *Perspectives on Urban Education*.
Rukeyser, M. (1968). Käthe Kollwitz. In *The speed of darkness*. New York, NY: Random House.
Rushdie, S. (1991). One Thousand Days in a Balloon. *The New York Times*.
Solórzano, D. G. & Yosso, T .J. (2002). Critical race methodology: Counter-storytelling as an analytical framework for education research. *Qualitative Inquiry*, 8(1), 23-44.
Stevenson, H. C. (2014). *Promoting Racial Literacy in Schools: Differences that Make a Difference*. New York, NY: Teachers College Press.
Valencia, R. R. (2010). *Dismantling contemporary deficit thinking: Educational thought and practice*. New York, NY: Routledge.

Preface

The idea for this book grew out of our collective interest in storytelling as a powerful and transformative process. We wanted to explore the ways that stories can be used to amplify how power and privilege are embedded in the work we do in educational settings and the ways that some stories are traditionally silenced in these spaces. This book project (and our wider efforts at the Center for Research on Storytelling in Education) aims to create space for diverse groups of educators to reflect on their own stories through an *archaeological dive* into the ways that they experienced and continue to experience educational systems. Our hope was that by sharing our stories, we might collectively gain deeper insights into the ways that privilege and oppression are complicated, situational, and intertwined to identify opportunities for creating more transformative and liberatory spaces for teaching and learning that recognize the importance of valuing all stories and perspectives.

When we began this process, we could not have anticipated that much of our work together would happen amid a global health crisis. The COVID-19 pandemic starkly illuminates the medical, political, social, cultural, and educational inequities that exist in our world today. Storytelling can help us to better understand our diverse experiences—we have found our shared storytelling helpful for making human connections during an isolating time. The simple act of sharing stories can help us to process our powerful emotions. Most importantly, it can help us to learn from our experiences and the experiences of others (Colket, 2009; Colket, 2020).

As editors, we are deeply aware of our own privilege and power as we've undertaken this project. We have approached this process with an inquiry stance aimed at enabling us to learn from the diverse experiences of our colleagues while also recognizing the importance of surfacing our own stories as a way to grow as educators. As Brené Brown notes, it is important to "write what you need to read" (Brown, 2018, p. 5). We believe that the stories in this book are what all educators need to read. Most importantly, we hope this book is a call to action to surface your own stories in the service of fostering more equitable, inclusive, and accessible learning spaces.

Acknowledgments

From all the Editors:
We acknowledge the Windward Islands Research and Education Foundation (WINDREF) who supported our idea for the creation of a Center for Research on Storytelling in Education (CRSE), and who have provided incredible support in our efforts to secure research funding, which will enable a conference (supported by The Spencer Foundation) to further the efforts begun here. Dr. Sara Rabie, our Department Chair, has also been incredibly supportive of this work and of all our work and we know she will be one of the first people to take up this work in her own teaching and leadership.

From Laura:
I first want to acknowledge all the educators who have positively impacted me throughout my time as a student. As will be seen in Chapter 18, my time as a younger student was often challenging and not in productive ways. Luckily, I did have positive learning experiences as well, although those were mostly as an adult. I would not be the educator or academic that I am today if it had not been for my time as a doctoral student at the University of Pennsylvania, Graduate School of Education (PennGSE). My time at PennGSE not only exposed me to research and theory that helped me to make sense of my past educational experiences, but it also helped me to develop a philosophy of teaching and research that would inspire me to continue in the field. There were three classes that had a particularly profound impact on me: Dr. Sharon Ravitch's Qualitative Modes of Inquiry, Dr. Susan Lytle's Practitioner Inquiry, and Dr. Shaun Harper's Critical Race Theory. What I learned in each of those classes, I have carried with me at every step of my career. Sharon Ravitch is deserving of a particular acknowledgement, as she went on to become my mentor, dissertation chair, colleague, co-teacher, and most importantly, my friend. Another colleague, mentor, and friend I would like to acknowledge is Dr. Ron Scapp, as he encouraged me when I originally shared my ideas

for this book. Without his initial encouragement, I am not sure if this book would exist. Finally, I want to acknowledge my co-editors, Tracy and Adam. I could not imagine going through this process with anyone else. The two of you helped make this process joyful and meaningful. Thank you for helping to make this dream a reality.

From Tracy:

I feel so privileged to have had the opportunity to read the stories and learn from all the contributors to this book. Their enthusiasm for storytelling and the collaborative process has been truly inspirational and without their efforts, this volume would not have come to fruition. I am also thankful to the many teachers I've experienced throughout my learning career and those I have yet to encounter. We can learn something from everyone and everything we connect with, even when those connections seem less than positive. Finally, I want to acknowledge my two co-editors, Laura and Adam. Rarely do we get to work with people who are transformative in our lives, just by being themselves. It is such a gift to work with you both and I've learned so much from you.

From Adam:

When I reflect on the learning experiences that have now become my story, I feel grateful to those who brought joy and authenticity to learning. As a child and young adult, my educative experiences seemed to ebb and flow based on how successful (or not!) my teachers were in engaging a somewhat reticent learner. Thank you to those teachers who took the time to get to know me—to ignite my curiosity and trick me into learning! As an adult, I came to understand that learning took place beyond the walls of a school. Thank you to my mentors, friends, colleagues, and family who inspired me to learn, who challenged me to explore beyond my comfort zone, and who encouraged me to persevere through failure and setbacks. Finally, thank you to my co-editors, Tracy and Laura, who have taught me so much while working together that I wonder if I might get a tuition bill. It's truly been a pleasure becoming a part of your stories.

Introduction

Critical Storytelling as a Tool to Support Educators through a Continual Process of Becoming

Laura Colket & Tracy Penny Light

Anthropologist Mary Catherine Bateson (1989) aptly notes that "storytelling is fundamental to the human search for meaning" (p. 34). Stories help to create human connection and serve as powerful tools to support us in deciphering cultural norms, events, experiences, and realities (Clandinin & Connelly, 2000; Mládková, 2013; Ricoeur 1991). Through stories, we can come to better understand ourselves, our communities, and our broader social, historical, and cultural milieu. Critical storytelling (like critical theory and critical pedagogy) pushes us to interrogate and re-imagine the systems we inhabit and the cultural norms we embody (Barone, 1992; Ellis, Adams & Bochner, 2011; Solórzano & Yosso, 2009). When understood and utilized as an educational tool, critical storytelling becomes a profound meaning-making process that results in personal growth, professional learning, and organizational transformation. Storytelling therefore becomes "not...a place at which to arrive, but...a place to begin inquiry" (Gallagher, 2010, p. 52). When educators take an inquiry stance toward their practice, they are better positioned to develop and maintain equitable and transformative educational practices (Cochran-Smith and Lytle, 2015).

Brazilian educator, philosopher, and critical pedagogue, Paulo Freire, talks about the "unfinishedness" of human beings, and he argues that we are always "in the process of becoming" (2007/1970, p. 84). As Freire explains, "The unfinished character of human beings and the transformational character of reality necessitate that education be an ongoing activity" (p. 84). He argues that conscientization is developed through an ongoing engagement with reflection and action. As Freire explains, "Knowledge emerges only through invention and reinvention, through the restless, impatient, continuing, hopeful inquiry human beings pursue in the world, with the world, and with each other" (2007/1970, p. 72). American philosopher Maxine Greene (1995) likewise argues that critical consciousness develops when "teachers and learners find themselves conducting a kind of collaborative search, each from his or her own lived situation" (p 23). She models this sentiment when she says: "I am forever on the way" (p.1).

We believe that all educators should always be on their way, always in a process of becoming. In other words, educators should be iteratively learning about and refining their teaching practice, whether they are new or experienced educators. Marilyn Cochran-Smith and Susan Lytle argue that an inquiry stance is the most powerful form of professional learning because it creates important opportunities for developing more socially-just approaches to education. As they describe, when educators adapt an inquiry stance toward their practice, they develop:

> …[A] worldview and a habit of mind—a way of knowing and being in the world of educational practice that carries across educational contexts and various points in one's professional career that links individuals to larger groups and social movements intended to challenge the inequities perpetuated by the educational status quo. (2015, p. viii)

When educators maintain an inquiry stance toward their practice, stories are not simply stories, but they are fuel for personal, professional, and organizational transformation.

This book provides a framework for educators to make critical connections between their stories of learning and their stories of teaching to enhance their ongoing professional growth, specifically with an aim toward creating more equitable and inclusive educational institutions and learning environments. In this book, we argue that educators and educational leaders are particularly well positioned to learn and grow through critical storytelling because of their direct experience in the field since childhood. Educators' past learning experiences are often reflected in their teaching and leadership practices and philosophies, whether they are conscious of it or not. When educators spend the time critically reflecting on their past learning experiences in relation to their current practices and philosophies, they open the space for personal, community and organizational growth. The stories contained in the chapters of this book demonstrate the power of this intentional inquiry.

This is not, and should not be, an easy process. If we feel entirely safe and sit comfortably with storytelling, we are not pushing ourselves toward critical storytelling and counter-storytelling, and we lose the power to create transformative change. Counter-storytelling, a pillar of Critical Race Theory, is a tool for surfacing and highlighting the stories and realities of marginalized people that are typically hidden, ignored, or distorted by the dominant narrative (Delgado & Stefancic, 2001; Solórzano & Yosso, 2009). This book draws on counter-storytelling because both the teaching profession and leadership studies have mainly been shaped by White, cisgender, heterosexual, Eurocentric/American, socio-economically advantaged perspectives and experiences. In this book, we aim to de-center such stories. Stories that are marginalized in society and in the field more broadly are not marginalized in this book, and the role of identity in learning and teaching is a central focus of the stories told here. While we have not excluded stories from people who exist in the center, we attempt to shatter that center by including a broad range of stories from people embodying a wide spectrum of identities.

The chapters in this book are written by educators who exist within and across various social locations and who have all committed to creating more equitable, culturally-sustaining (Paris, 2012), transformative, liberatory (hooks, 1994), and engaging educational experiences for their students. The authors engage with topics such as anti-colonial praxis, social class and social policy, anti-racist pedagogy, de-humanizing curriculum, re-storying, and innovative pedagogical practices. As a collective, the authors' stories surface important complexities, distinctions, and commonalities across their lived experiences of learning and teaching.

The stories in this book create both windows and mirrors (Botelho & Rudman, 2009) for educators exploring this process of becoming. This book is intended for educators and educational leaders from a variety of contexts, whether they are teaching children or adults, in formal or informal settings, and regardless of the subject area, the level, the location, or the cultural milieu. The strategies and stories presented in this book are useful for brand-new and well-seasoned educators alike. This book could be read by an educator on their own, in a community of practice with educators from similar or different spaces, for coursework in a degree program, or as a shared text within one institution as they engage in collaborative professional learning. This first chapter provides an introduction and framing for the practice of critical storytelling for professional learning. The final chapter discusses the themes that emerged from the stories in this book as we consider what can be learned by looking within and across the experiences and perspectives of educators coming from a range of institutional, social, and cultural contexts. The chapters included within are grouped into sections based on general themes, but there are cross-cutting themes that connect across the sections as well.

This book represents an example of the ongoing process of becoming through structured inquiry. As a compilation of critical and collaborative inquiries from educators, all in different moments in their process of becoming, this book can be considered a tool for conscientization for the authors and the readers alike. Throughout this edited volume, current educators and educational leaders engage with their past, present, and imagined futures through storytelling by sharing and exploring their experiences of learning and teaching. This book was guided by three main goals: (1) to compile a broad range of personal narratives about learning and teaching in order to better understand both diversity in experience and commonalities; (2) to better understand the connections between people's experiences as learners and their experiences as teachers and educational leaders; and (3) to offer a collection of narratives about learning and teaching to support the professional growth of educators and educational leaders.

The Writing & Reading Process

In each of the included chapters, the authors engage in what we describe as an *archeological dive* into their past educational experiences in order to relate those experiences to their current teaching/leadership practices and future professional aspirations. Each chapter represents the author's exploration of their personal educational experiences, illustrating the ways in which they have sifted through the layers of their own histories to make meaning of, and to reflect on, how they (and others) can become more critically engaged and transformative educators. Using an autoethnographic approach (Ellis, Adams & Bochner, 2011; Starr, 2010) and drawing on counter-storytelling (Delgado & Stefancic, 2001), intersectionality (Crenshaw, 1989), and critical reflection (Brookfield, 2010), this edited volume includes authors who move beyond simply telling their stories to understanding the broader significance of those stories by analyzing them in their social, historical, and cultural milieu (Adams, Holman Jones & Ellis, 2015; Ellis & Bochner, 2000; Maréchal, 2010; Plummer, 2001). Autoethnographic research is much like narrative research in that it is a qualitative method based in storytelling. However, while narrative research involves a researcher creating or co-creating the narrative of their participants through the collection of data (often through in-depth semi-structured interviews), autoethnographic research consists of the researcher creating and telling their own stories. As a research method, autoethnography can be used by practitioners as a tool for professional learning and improving practice (Berci, 2007; Davis, 1996; Elbaz-Luwisch, 2010), and as such, it is an ideal method for supporting the ongoing process of becoming.

As a collaborative process, this book enabled chapter authors to read and listen to each other's stories while serving as "critical friends" (Bambino, 2002) through the writing and editing process. The process leveraged the power of dialogue which is, as American theorist and activist bell hooks explains, "…one of the simplest ways we can begin as teachers, scholars, and critical thinkers to cross boundaries, [and traverse] the barriers that may or may not be erected by race, gender, class, professional standing, and a host of other differences" (1994, p. 130).

As editors of this volume, we believe that the dialectical nature of storytelling is one of the most powerful elements of the process; in other words, storytelling not only involves both the act of creating and sharing one's own stories, but also authentically listening to *and* hearing (Delpit, 2006) the stories of other people. This dialectical process can transform both the perspectives and actions of those involved, ultimately supporting us in creating more equitable environments for teaching and learning (Colket, Garrett, Shaw, 2020).

As you read through the stories in this book, we invite you to continually ask questions, embrace any discomfort you feel, dive into stories that feel familiar, as well as those that feel unfamiliar, and consider how reading the stories of these educators might impact your practice as an educator and/or educational leader. We also invite you to consider what you might learn by engaging in an *archeological dive* on your own, and/or in collaboration with other educators. If you are interested in engaging in the process yourself, you are welcome to use the same guiding prompts that we provided for the contributing authors in this book:

1. Please write an educational autobiography in which you reflect on critical incidents in your experience as a student in relation to literature and theory about teaching and learning. In doing so, please consider the following questions:

   - How did those defining moments shape you as a learner?

   - Are you able to identify an arc or any themes in your experience?

   - What roles have your various social identities played in shaping your educational experience?

   - What role did the contexts in which you were learning shape your experience?

   - How did your broader social/cultural/political sphere shape your educational experiences?

   - What main struggles did you face as a student?

- Did you have any resources, supports, people or strategies to help you overcome those struggles?

- What are you most proud of when you look back on your time as a student?

- What are you most surprised or concerned about?

- If you were to go back to talk to your teachers now, what would you tell them about how to better support you as a learner?

2. Please write about your teaching or leadership philosophy. In doing so, please reflect on the following questions:

- What are your key beliefs about teaching/leadership?

- What literature and/or theory supports your beliefs?

- What specific strategies do you draw on that align with your key beliefs?

- What critical incidents have shaped your beliefs and practices?

3. Please write a critical reflection about your experience thinking through these aspects of your teaching and learning experiences.

- What connections, themes, contradictions or new understandings emerged for you through this writing process?

- What implications might this have for your practice?

Importantly, we want to acknowledge that there are many ways to use critical storytelling as a tool for professional growth. The process we outline above is simply one approach. For example, you do not have to connect your stories to the broader literature. For us, this made sense because (a) we believe that connecting personal experiences to research and theory can help people to make sense of their own experiences, practices, and beliefs in more profound ways; and (b) we were curious to know what kinds of literature educators from a range of positionalities would use to help them make sense of their experiences. If you can make connections between your experiences and the broader literature, we encourage you to do so, and to reflect on your meaning-making process throughout. While we believe this enhances the experience, it is not necessary. Another modification you could consider making is the medium and format of your story. Your story does not have to be written. You could tell your story orally, you could create a video, you could draw your story, or make a collage. You could alternatively (or additionally) turn your story into a graphic novel, or act it out. Seemingly simple, yet powerful options could be generating a three-word or six-word story (e.g., what three words would you use to describe your experience as a learner?) and then share how and why you chose those specific words.

The possibilities for storytelling are endless, so we encourage you to explore, to be creative, and to reflect on the affordances and constraints of different approaches. If you try multiple approaches, consider which approaches felt most and least powerful to you. Which were most and least challenging, and why? And if you were to facilitate this experience for other educators, what approaches would you suggest to people and why? How might you structure this process differently?

As you dive into this process, whether you are telling or listening, writing or reading, creating or observing, we invite you to engage with a curious mind. We invite you to see storytelling as a tool in your ongoing process of becoming. Through this critical inquiry, we hope you will re-examine and re-imagine what your teaching and leadership practices can and should be, and what education more broadly can and should be. As Maxine Greene reminds us, "It is simply not enough for us to reproduce the way things are" (1995, p. 1). Storytelling can help us to interrupt harmful patterns and practices and can be a spark for much-needed transformation.

References

Adams, T. E., Holman Jones, S., & Ellis, C. (2015). *Autoethnography: Understanding Qualitative Research*. New York: Oxford University Press.

Bambino, D. (2002). Redesigning professional development: Critical friends. *Educational Leadership*, *59*(6), 25-27.

Barone, T. E. (1992). Beyond theory and method: A case of critical storytelling. *Theory into practice*, *31*(2), 142-146.

Bateson, M. C. (1989). Composing a life. New York: Grove Press.

Botelho, M. J., & Rudman, M. K. (2009). *Critical multicultural analysis of children's literature: Mirrors, windows, and doors*. Routledge.

Brookfield, S. (2010). Critical reflection as an adult learning process. In: Lyons N. (eds), *Handbook of Reflection and Reflective Inquiry*. Boston: Springer.

Clandinin, D. J., & Connelly, F. M. (2000). *Narrative Inquiry: Experience and Story in Qualitative Research*. John Wiley & Sons, Inc.

Cochran-Smith, M., & Lytle, S. L. (2015). *Inquiry as stance: Practitioner research for the next generation*. Teachers College Press.

Crenshaw, K. (1989). Demarginalizing the intersection of race and sex: A black feminist critique of antidiscrimination doctrine, feminist theory and antiracist politics. u. Chi. Legal f., 139.

Delgado, R. and Stefancic, J. (2001) *Critical race theory: An introduction*. New York: New York University Press.

Delpit, L. (2006). Other people's children: Cultural conflict in the classroom. New York: The New Press.

Ellis, C., Adams, T., & Bochner, A. (2011). Autoethnography: An Overview. *Forum: Qualitative Social Research*, 12 (1), Art 10.

Ellis, C., & Bochner, A. (2000). Autoethnography, Personal Narrative, Reflexivity: Researcher as Subject. In, N. Denzin & Y. Lincoln (Eds.), The Handbook of Qualitative Research (2nd ed.) (pp. 733-768). Thousand Oaks, CA. Sage.

Freire, P. (2007/1970). *Pedagogy of the oppressed*. New York, NY: The Continuum International Publishing Group Inc.

Gallagher, K. M. (2011). In search of a theoretical basis for storytelling in education research: Story as method. *International Journal of Research & Method in Education, 34*(1), 49-61.

Green, M. (1995). *Releasing the Imagination: Essays on Education, the Arts, and Social Change.* San Fransisco: Jossey Bass.

hooks, b. (1994). *Teaching to Transgress*. New York: Routledge.

Maréchal, G. (2010). Autoethnography. In A. J. Mills, G. Durepos & E. Wiebe (Eds.), *Encyclopedia of case study research* (Vol. 2, pp. 43–45). Thousand Oaks, CA: Sage Publications.

Mládková, L. (2013), Leadership and Storytelling. *Procedia – Social and Behavioral Sciences.* 75 (2013), 83-90.

Plummer, K. (2001). The call of life stories in ethnographic research. In P. Atkinson, A. Coffey, S. Delamont, J. Lofland, and L. Lofland (Eds.), *Handbook of ethnography* (pp. 395–406). London: Sage.

Ricoer, P. (1991). Myths as a Bearer of Possible Worlds. (Dialogue with Richard Kearney). In Ricoeur, P. *Reflection and Imagination*, ed. Mario J. Valdes. New York: Harvester Wheatsheaf, 1991.

Solórzano, D. G., & Yosso, T. J. (2002). Critical race methodology: Counter-storytelling as an analytical framework for education research. *Qualitative inquiry, 8*(1), 23-44.

Starr, L. J. (2010). The use of autoethnography in educational research: Locating who we are in what we do. *Canadian Journal for New Scholars in Education, 3*(1), 1-9.

Part I

Claiming Identity

1

Unheard Stories

How Honoring and Acknowledging My Experiences Shape Me as a Teacher

Browning Neddeau

Browning Neddeau ndezhnekas. Chico, California ndoch bya nesh je Hollister, California edayan. Bodewadmi ndaw. Browning Neddeau my name is. I come from Chico, California but I am originally from Hollister, California. I am Potawatomi. Elders remind me to introduce myself in my tribe's language. As a public-school educator, I work in a system that is grounded in assimilation and oppressing voices from historically marginalized populations. The public education system is built around constructed labels. It was not until recently that educational professionals, broadly defined, centered assets over deficits and celebrated a rainbow of identities. I am excited about sharing future, inclusive educational spaces with emerging scholars. As a Potawatomi, Jewish, and gay man, my lived experiences required me to be resilient and to remember that my work honors the seven generations before and after my time. Below, I reflect on critical incidents in my experience as a student in relation to literature and theory about teaching and learning.

K-12 Education

I was raised in a small agricultural community with a handful of public elementary schools, two public middle schools, and one public high school. The community also included a few countryside schools to reach students living in more rural parts of the county. The community had a large population of Spanish-speaking households and families that immigrated to the United States of America. During winter breaks, some students would leave school to return later in the spring because their parents worked as farm laborers and moved with the industry needs. My father was a high school music and English teacher and my mother was an elementary school teacher. It was not until about the 1990s that the community started welcoming big corporations into the town for business, with few earlier exceptions.

I was reminded of my identities from a very young age in formal schooling. Student comments about being gay, my grade one teacher telling my parents that I needed a stronger male figure in my life that was not so artsy, and historically inaccurate teaching of Native American peoples in the classroom (grades three, four, five, 10, 12), all were reminders of society's misconceptions and how the educational spaces at the time perpetuated misconceptions. In my early elementary years, I became an expert at code-switching, moving between differing situational rules or procedures, to fit into societal expectations.

As Erikson (1994) described regarding cultural implications of development, certain cultures may need to resolve the stages in diverse ways based upon one's cultural and survival needs. For instance, in kindergarten, I came home with a vest made out of a brown paper grocery bag and some poster paint prints. School taught me that this is how Native Americans dressed (past tense) and how Native Americans looked (also past tense). It was puzzling because many generations of my Potawatomi family were alive at the time, and none of us wore brown paper grocery bags with poster paint prints for clothing. Deloria (1998) discussed the history of "playing" Indian and how generations perpetuated such practices and shaped society's understanding of Native American identity, both politically and culturally.

In grade three, a paraprofessional/classroom aide in the school asked me to demonstrate Native American dancing to my peers. As I did, she encouraged me to look for bear tracks. This confused me because I was not taught that my people looked for bear tracks while dancing. I was taught that we stand tall to dance and are strong and pride-filled. I dance for my ancestors.

My middle- and high-school years were filled with involvement in the performing arts and politics. I served as the drum major of the marching band in middle and high school and played trombone in multiple ensembles. In middle school, I was elected as the student body president. During my high school years, I volunteered to call voters during election seasons and participated in campaigns that served the community. In my telephone calls to voters and conversations in canvasing for political campaigns in neighborhoods, I learned about the lived experiences, hopes, and frustrations of community members. Conversations became more about capacity-building rather than getting a particular message to community members. During this time, I realized the importance of community in making change and how I could funnel my extroverted personality to better my community. I rallied support for initiatives that served the community in meaningful ways.

Higher Education

I relocated to a big city from my small agricultural town, where I earned a Bachelor's degree at a public institution before moving to another densely populated city to earn my Master's and Doctoral degrees at a private institution. During my undergraduate studies, I quickly learned about the role of student organizations on university campuses and sought to join organizations that reflected my identities. I discovered the Jewish Student Union and became involved in the group, eventually moving into the roles of vice-president and co-president. I searched for Native American student organizations but did not find one. I noticed lesbian, gay, bisexual, transgender, queer, questioning, intersex, asexual, ally, pansexual, fluid (LGBTQQIAAPF) student organizations at the universities and became friends with an individual in one of the LGBTQQIAAPF student organizations. This individual helped me gain a sense of belonging and assurance of place in higher education. In general, I think student organizations helped me visualize a sense of belonging on campus whether I was aware of this or not at the time.

In retrospect, my undergraduate studies was a time of trying to find a sense of belonging and purpose in community outside of my hometown. It was also a time where I gained a heightened awareness about the erasure of my identities in privileged settings, such as university environments. Shotton, Lowe, and Waterman (2013) underscored how students that identify as Native American are "omitted from the curriculum, absent from the research and literature, and virtually written out of the higher education story" (p. 17). I learned that *survivance* (Vizenor, 2009) meant a continuation of stories; for me, this required conformity to societal understandings while also challenging myself to accept my identities as authentically and uniquely me.

I earned my Master's and Doctoral degrees at a private, religious institution. Up until this point, my educational journey had taken place in public schools. My entry into a private university setting—moreover, a religious institution—provided me with an entirely new perspective on education that I had not lived. The extensive library resources, small class sizes, and a small cohort of peers all differed from my previous educational experiences. I recall my studies at the private institution as the first time that I clearly acknowledged my privilege. As I toured campus, I noticed the exceptional resources I had access to and the support systems that were available. While in graduate school, I had an exchange with a peer that elevated my awareness of the privilege I held at the institution. I specifically recall a peer suggesting to me that her prior educational experiences made her above others in our cohort. My retort was, "And yet we are all sitting here together now." This was one of my first exchanges in education where I had to specifically call out privilege, making me more aware of the privilege that I hold.

Disrupting Settler-Colonial Practices in Education

Experiences guide our understanding of the world in which we engage, persist, and live (Dewey, 1934; King, 2005). It is from my lived experiences that I arrived at my teaching and learning choices. My experiences shape the pedagogical approaches I make in the courses I teach and in the spaces I occupy as a learner. Through time, my research on teaching and learning has sought to elevate a re-imagining of curriculum and instruction to best honor the prior experiences of the students. I seek to increase student engagement through meaningful learning experiences where students can make personal connections to content.

As a student, I experienced invisibility and ignorance, and the inaccurate storytelling of my people. To succeed in academia, in general, I had to conform to unwritten, yet cookie-cutter expectations for success. To overcome struggles, I depended greatly on my sense of agency and a very close group of friends. I would not be the person I am today without my friends. Institutions of higher education offered support that I accepted, but the support did not improve my challenges related to society's acceptance and understanding of my identities.

If I were to go back to speak with my teachers now, I would thank them for their service in education as longevity in the profession requires flexibility and reflectivity. I have been successful in my educational journey through colonized educational spaces because of their coaching in these spaces. My teachers did their jobs dutifully as the educational system is set up to do. I would also invite my former teachers to be more culturally responsive to alternative ways of knowing and doing. As teachers, we need to place more value on our students' personal stories instead of underscoring a scripted education. I would ask them to join me in disrupting the settler-colonial practices in education that value a Eurocentric narrative over the multiple narratives that create the dynamic community in which we live and thrive. Centering our conversations on being effective and reflective teachers could help frame the missing pieces in educational practices. Lastly, I would offer my former teachers the opportunity to pilot the curriculum I created to honor Native American perspectives across the curriculum, welcoming their feedback once they teach the lessons. I hope that the lessons would provide the teachers insights on how to better support students from diverse backgrounds, including students like me.

Part of supporting students in their learning is to foster a sense of belonging in the curriculum and the classroom. To disrupt settler-colonial practices in education, we must first peel away the layers of what we notice and observe to better understand where we can improve curricular decisions. My current research, titled the "I See Me! Project," challenges people to reflect on their educational journey and critically analyze curriculum in their classroom. More specifically, the person engaged in the project documents how much they do and do not see themselves in the school-adopted curriculum's images and graphs. After analyzing their findings, the person is asked to create a lesson plan that stresses their identity(ies). Encouraging my former teachers to participate in the "I See Me! Project" might give voice to otherwise silenced voices in the curriculum. Such exercises could be a starting point for acknowledging settler-colonial practices in education and how disrupting the practice needs to be intentional. The exercise also provides teachers with time to reflect on lived experiences and how such experiences shape their teaching and learning choices of today.

Reflecting Back to Shape the Future

I survived settler-colonial practices in education. This does not mean that future generations need to face the same challenges. I know I am a part of changing the narrative in education. When I look back on my time as a student, I am most proud that I survived walking in at least two worlds: my identities and settler-colonial. LaFromboise, Coleman, and Gerton (1993) described the idea of walking in two worlds without compromising a sense of cultural identity as bicultural efficacy. The public and private educational systems I experienced were constant reminders that I needed to be an advocate for myself, including my identities and ancestors. I walked in a world that challenged my being. In an ever-changing world, I faced discrimination because of my sexual orientation and genocide of my people. I did not stand idly by. Instead, I took these moments as opportunities to grow and carve my own path for curricular reform and refinement to help future generations.

It causes great pause to reflect on others whose educational journeys do not honor their identity(ies). How can learning spaces be more inclusive and inviting instead of oppressive and binary? How many stories are lost or unheard in classrooms around the world due to ignorance or fear? I am concerned that the stories unheard are the ones that hold the keys to fully understanding the world in which we live.

As I reflect on the process of thinking about my educational autobiography in relation to my teaching philosophy, I realize it is necessary to acknowledge our lived experiences and leverage our lived experiences as entry points for others to learn and grow. For example, settler-colonial practices in education can only change if such practices are identified. Writing my educational autobiography was, at times, difficult because it forced me into uncomfortable spaces with memories that I wished not to relive; memories that the general human tendency is to avoid. My students attempt to skirt uncomfortable or difficult conversations. I encourage them to acknowledge their feelings as justified and grow. Writing my educational autobiography required me to have a conversation with my own uncomfortability with self-encouragement to grow. As an educator, I have practiced being reflective in my work. Yet, writing my educational autobiography alongside my teaching philosophy was a new and informative approach to better understanding my authentic self as a professional educator.

To hear unheard stories, we must create learning spaces that invite knowledge keepers to the table. Uninterrupted, uninterpreted, unabridged, raw, authentic stories that help society make better sense of the world by connecting the silos in which the busy world unabashedly operates. Through opportunities to share unfiltered stories, people can better understand their neighbors, community, and the world. We can be better teachers when we hear the full stories.

References

Deloria, P.J. (1998). *Playing Indian.* New Haven, CT: Yale University Press.
Dewey, J. (1934). *Art as experience.* New York, NY: Penguin Group.
Erikson, E. (1994). *Identity and the life cycle.* New York, NY: W.W. Norton & Company.
King, T. (2005). *The truth about stories: A native narrative.* Minneapolis, MN: University of Minnesota Press.
LaFromboise, T., Coleman, H.L.K., & Gerton, J. (1993). Psychological impact of biculturalism: Evidence and theory. *Psychological Bulletin, 114*(3), 395-412.
Shotton, H. J., Lowe, S. C., & Waterman, S. J. (2013). *Beyond the asterisk: Understanding Native students in higher education.* (H. J. Shotton, S. C. Lowe, & S. J. Waterman, Eds.) (1st ed.). Sterling, VA: Stylus Publishing, Inc.
Vizenor, G. (2009). *Native liberty: Natural reason and cultural survivance.* Retrieved from https://ebookcentral.proquest.com

2

Home Training

Raheem Jackson

Educational Autobiography

The teaching that Grandma did at home rarely coincided with the classroom content I encountered in primary and secondary school, but it supplemented my formal education. Grandma taught, emphasized, and continuously reinforced the importance of "home training": a respectfulness and social etiquette typically taught at home. Many of her Southern codes of respect instilled a sense of deference to her authority and set expectations for how we would conduct ourselves and represent her in the community. Many of her teachings effectively silenced us as children. She preached the value of "be[ing] slow to speak and quick to listen." "Children are to be seen and not heard" acted as one of those idioms I now view with a bit of disdain.

Grandma taught us a great deal of academic information as well. She explained the historical narratives and significance of the foods that we ate. She shared stories with us about her childhood and our family, providing our family's perspective of historical events that we learned about through movies or school. The cultural and historical knowledge she provided cultivated a sense of pride and confidence, but it was minimally useful in the classrooms that rarely asked for or valued that knowledge. The soft-spoken, reverential, and meek temperament that emerged from her "home training," however, ended up being essential for my academic successes during primary and secondary school. My behavior garnered the most positive attention from educators and community leaders.

Of course, my teachers and school leaders praised my effort and my academic performance. Yet, the disproportionate attention that was afforded to my behavior gives me pause and reveals the salience of my Grandma's painstaking efforts to make sure that I remembered my "home training." I love my teachers and the people in the community for seeing me. If I could tell them anything now, though, I would ask that they validate me in my own right.

Instead, they often implicitly and explicitly compared and contrasted me to the other Black boys in my peer group and community. "You are such a good, respectful young man," "You're going to be somebody," and "Your grandmother did such a great job raising you" lose value when they are consistently preceded or followed by some iteration of, "I wish a little more of you could rub off on [some student of color]." Teachers, parents, and other students differentiating me from other Black boys became sources of racial stress and anxiety for me. To be clear, this was not the overrepresented phenomenon of a Black student navigating accusations that they "act White." Instead, this was a very astute observation from early on: meeting behavioral expectations could garner as much or more praise as my academic successes and that Black boys were discursively and actually the disproportionate targets of classroom behavioral management.

I recall being placed in "gifted classes," tracked for upper level and Advanced Placement high school classes during primary school, which made the fascination with my enactment of my Grandma's particular codes of respect so much more significant. I remember the classrooms at my public schools in rural North Florida feeling rather segregated. The more advanced the class, the more disproportionately represented the White students were in the class. Here, I feel compelled to problematize this as one of the dynamics that I, as an educator, commit to disrupting. Even as a student, I felt that it warranted an intervention. The processes for tracking students into the programs must have been biased. There must have been ways to make the classes more accessible to different students. How else could you explain it without some indictment of Black students, communities, and cultures? Tracking is a system that is often used in schools to place students on different "tracks" (which might be different classes or even entirely different programs within a school). As an adult, I now know that research has found tracking systems to be biased and detrimental to students of color and low-income students, as they are disproportionately placed in lower tracks. It is noteworthy that I felt this, even as a young student (Modica, 2015, p. 77-81).

Nevertheless, I was always the only or one of two Black students in my academic classes of twenty to twenty-five students throughout primary and secondary school. Moreover, very few Black educators were charged with shaping my learning experiences at school. I waited until my junior year of high school to have my second Black teacher in an academic discipline. Sadly, I would not experience sitting across from a Black male teacher in an academic classroom until my second year of undergraduate as a declared Black Studies major. There was, however, a sizable Black adult presence at my schools. Black men coached me during athletics, and I saw Black adults overrepresented in the dining and custodial staffs of each of my campuses in rural North Florida. In addition to a dearth of Black educators and educators of color, I never once had an African American History class available during the entirety of my primary and secondary school experience.

During my undergraduate career, my Black Studies and Sociology majors provided the first explicit and intentional spaces—academic spaces—to extensively learn *my* histories. The Black Studies department offered a myriad of courses that centered and uplifted Black experiences, scholarship, cultures, and histories. They helped explain, corroborate, and reflect on my realities in a way that no academic class had done before. For example, I explored code-switching within African American communities for the capstone project of my research methods course. Prior to the project, I understood code-switching as a term that partly described my daily routine: communicating naturally with my Black family and friends, then speaking differently in my classroom spaces. I understood it as a tool to navigate the harsh reality that attitudes toward how I spoke at home ran the gamut from dismissive to outright offensive.

While doing the project, I learned that even the *term*, code-switching, reflected extremely different attitudes toward our way of speaking in my household. The term implied a switch between two *distinct* language systems: African American English (AAE) and Standard American English (SAE) (2001, Wyatt, p. 273). Some deny that AAE exists in a legitimate way that warrants such a distinction between it and SAE (2001, Mufwene, p. 24-34). Nevertheless, I found joy in research that illustrated AAE as a cultural treasure with observable peculiarities and a historical context worth noting. I relished every moment that I got to share my learning, discussing the nuance of arguments that African American English developed as a result of mixing African language traditions with the English language, for instance (Dillard, 2008, p. 54-69; Mclaren, 2009, p. 101). I felt empowered. My inquiry equipped me with language and knowledge to better understand and celebrate something else that I shared with my family and communities. Most importantly, I began to think about when and how I would employ code-switching in a new way that made me feel more in control of how I navigated the world.

I had never considered myself an avid reader, but the sheer amount of Black authors on the syllabi intrigued me. I read Octavia Butler's *Kindred*, C.L.R. James' *Black Jacobins, Souls of Black Folk* by W.E.B. Dubois, and more in the introductory Black Studies course alone. I loved reading *The Coldest Winter Ever* by Sistah Souljah, as well as Terry McMillan's *Disappearing Acts* and *Waiting to Exhale* in "Black Women's Narratives and Counternarratives." Yet, I found myself struggling to contribute meaningfully to the classroom discussions of the book. Before I enrolled in that elective course and "Women Writers of Africa and the African Diaspora," no one ever explicitly instructed me to center the voices and experiences of Black women as I discussed or thought about any issue of concern to Black people. Thus, I had never seriously interrogated my complicity in some of their harmful experiences. At the time, the mere epiphany that I had never explicitly done so resonated, even though it was embarrassing.

As I previously discussed, I was adept at succeeding in classroom spaces that were led by White teachers. However, Professor Redding and Professor Drabinski's syllabi reflected genuine respect for and value of Black History and culture. That differentiated them from the White teachers I grew accustomed to before college. In fact, Drabinski's "Black Panther, Black Power" course partly inspired me to propose an elective History and Social Science course I teach at my current school. Using many of the same texts that I first read in his class, I offer an introduction to twentieth-century Black intellectual and social movements to interested students. It is a humble supplement to our school's core curriculum and Black History Month programming that eerily paralleled the one I received in primary and secondary school: an annual, perfunctory overview of enslavement, abolition, and the Civil Rights Movement from 1954-1965.

I concluded my undergraduate experience by dedicating my senior honors thesis, "Remember Your Home Training: Black Masculinities and Black Men's Lives in Context," to my grandmother and mother. I interviewed other Black men in four-year institutions who were raised in female-headed households. Their counternarratives complicated or subverted the notions that discursively blame single Black women for toxic Black masculine behaviors or obscure our moments being nurtured by Black men in our communities (Allen, 2016, p. 1832). My thesis advisor, Professor Cobham-Sander, helped me make sense of my life and the men's experiences in nontraditional families without using a deficit model. She implored me to refrain from approaching my inquiry with a view of their households and family structures as inherently lacking (a male presence or biological father). Instead, I sought out their understanding of their family structure's importance in their lived experience, remaining open to the strengths and values that they attributed to their home contexts. It was one of the most rewarding experiences of my life; now, helping students uncover the possibilities of their scholarship to be transformative for them, their peers, and our communities fuels my passion for education.

The faculty of the Independent School Teaching Residency program at the University of Pennsylvania made a concerted effort to value and cultivate that passion. During a graduate school assignment, I wrote the following sentence that still mostly captures how empowering and enlightening my postsecondary educational experience was: I write, teach, and exist from the love of and dedication to folks who are systematically impeded from garnering "prestige." My experiences—both joyful and hurtful experiences—inform my practice. I hope to provide learning experiences for students that mirror those that I received in my postsecondary contexts. Conversely, I avoid simply reinforcing or ignoring the structural problems that I observed intuitively as a student, such as de facto segregated classrooms or a Eurocentric curriculum.

Educational Philosophy

I prioritize wellness first, skills, and then content. bell hooks (1994) insists that "'[t]o teach in a manner that respects and cares for the souls of our students is essential if we are to provide the necessary conditions where learning can most deeply and intimately begin" (p. 13). If students feel disempowered, hopeless, anxious, fearful, or vigilant, then they are not well enough for the optimal teaching and learning experience. Unfortunately, our schools and classrooms often perpetuate race-class-gender hierarchies, causing or intensifying those aforementioned feelings. Therefore, developing and maintaining an anti-sexist, anti-racist social justice framework is integral to my teaching and classroom management (Hackman, 2005). Predominantly White, elite, independent schools have been the setting of the entirety of my young teaching career. The racial and class makeup of the campuses, the inherent exclusion embedded in selective admissions, and the hefty price of tuition renders a social justice education lens particularly potent in my current educational context.

bell hooks (1994) and Christopher Emdin (2016) both illustrate how educational experiences can marginalize students, validating my own subjective insights on the matter. For example, hooks (1994) begins *Teaching to Transgress: Education as the Practice of Freedom* with a powerful contrast of her learning experiences before and after integration. At the all-Black Booker T. Washington elementary school, she remembers Black women nurturing her intellect and preparing her for an anti-racist struggle; after integration, she and her peers were continuously reacting to White teachers' lessons, assumptions, and actions that reinforced racism and racist stereotypes (p. 2-3). Emdin (2016) argues that Black youth and young people with marginalized identities have historically had an imperial relationship with the United States. It is imperative, then, that we as educators actively disrupt the imperial relationship that these students may have with our schools.

Emdin (2016) offers cosmopolitanism as one approach to effectively do so. He describes this as: "an approach to teaching that focuses on fostering socioemotional connections in the classroom to build students' sense of responsibility to each other and the learning environment" (p. 105-106). Attention to students' sense of connectedness to their learning environments informs the importance of social-emotional development within my working educational philosophy. I make clear to students a number of skills that provide the basis for upholding what will be our nonnegotiable community norms: taking and valuing multiple perspectives, empathizing, identifying emotions, and self-advocating. Of course, this is a complicated and messy process. Still, I find the focus on cosmopolitanism particularly useful when there is conflict between students and there is a potential to alienate one or both of them. Like the importance of research and analytical skills, social-emotional skills also play an integral role in student learning and engagement with content.

I do not intend to disregard the importance of content for student development with my working philosophy and priorities. Rather, my approach to teaching derives from a basic acknowledgement of the grave importance that content traditionally plays in a students' educational experience. In fact, the content and curriculum that students encounter may alienate students or render them disinterested, pessimistic, antagonistic, or hopeless. For example, finding primary source documents with minimal to no Eurocentrism, xenophobia, or blatant hate speech to teach history and social sciences presents a nearly impossible challenge, in every unit. Moreover, each primary source may elicit a myriad of responses from students that range from apathy to distress. Distress compromises genuine and effective learning.

With that being said, I also recognize that many of the factors that impact student learning lie outside of my control. External factors such as tuition rates as well as financial aid and enrollment decisions determine which students will have access to my classroom. That recognition is one of many things that makes a social justice teaching stance especially difficult, and often renders me pessimistic and disillusioned. It requires an advocacy that continually requires facing patterns, systems, traditions, and inequities that I do not have the power to individually change.

I rely on a mantra, "next play mentality," that I adapted from my time as a football player at Amherst College to sustain my commitment to enacting my working philosophy as an educator. This mantra is shorthand for a particular disposition and work ethic that Coach Mills instilled in me. It entails approaching each play, regardless of the last play's outcome, with the same mentality and approach—a clean slate. I truly believe that mantra and that lesson transcends the game of football and applies to my work in schools. Perhaps, a "next *day* mentality" might be more appropriate without the specific football context. Nevertheless, it is imperative to materializing the just and equitable spaces in our schools that I often envision.

Reflection

The scarcity of Black male teachers, who make up about two percent of the teaching workforce, adds to the responsibility I feel to enact my working educational philosophy. Both educators and laypeople share their unsolicited convictions about which educational settings "need" me most. During my first month at my current school, a coworker asked why I accepted the teaching and coaching roles. Before I could answer, she proclaimed, "these kids don't need you here." That was our very first encounter. Her statement and others frequently remind me that many people feel that my work has substantially less value than it might if I taught at a school that primarily serves students of color.

Others, on the contrary, frame the novelty of my existence as a Black male educator in predominantly White independent schools as the integral factor that gives my work meaning. Teachers, especially, emphasize the importance of my presence to the students of color who are navigating these schools that often were not founded with the intention of educating them. Moreover, I am continuously reminded that—for some students—I am one of the only intimate interactions with a Black professional that they have as adolescents. Although I rarely find clarity about which educational setting is best for me, people's perceptions of my role make clear the sheer gravitas of the racialized context that shapes my decisions and actions as a teacher.

Being one of only a few educators of color often leaves me feeling highly visible, isolated, and burned out. This tokenism, in addition to enacting a social justice framework for my teaching, is exhausting. I often feel as though the lack of numerical representation creates another dimension of obligation to actively participate in faculty diversity and equity task forces and working groups, diversity programming, affinity groups, etc. I am one of two Black teachers at my current school. I understood from the outset that it was very likely that I would be asked to sponsor the affinity group for Black students, for instance. I spend a great deal of time listening to students talk about their on-campus experiences and observations. These discussions regularly happen outside of scheduled class time and events. The students generally deduce that I am willing to listen to and discuss how they perceive systems of oppression operating in their lived experiences from my involvement in the aforementioned programs.

With that being said, Jermaine Gassaway (2017) identifies at least five deterrents for Black men in the field of education: lack of respect within the field, lack of career advancement, diminution of financial sustainability, demanding workloads, and typecasting into disciplinary roles (p. 66). With the exception of typecasting as a disciplinarian, I can attest to the realities and significance of those disincentives. Those deterrents compound the exhaustion and frustrations that result from the racialized context that defines my work. Still, the occasional thought of leaving the education field evokes intense feelings of guilt because I take the responsibilities seriously that educating as a Black man entails. It is a peculiar paradox.

However, I understand that I stand on the shoulders of giants and that I am not alone in what I experience. Other Black educators and educators of color have done great work in similar school contexts in the past. A number of them are change agents in schools currently. I try my best to find strength in what my mentors and role models meant to me as a young student and student-teacher. Coach Shepphard demanded that I *"be better"* than him after I affectionately told him that I wanted to be *like* him. His words, along with his serious tone and demeanor, take on new meanings as I find myself in the position of advisor, coach, or teacher. Now, I understand that his retort represented a duty to us as student-athletes and mentees to inspire us to surpass what his role in our lives as a coach made us conceive as possible for our own futures. Each time that a student has insisted that they would like to be like me, I carefully respond with my own iteration of "don't be like me. Be better than me." Each opportunity has brought me joy, at least temporarily.

I also continue to seek guidance and mentorship from faculty members who were influential in my life, drawing strength from their wisdom and empathy frequently. For example, James Greenwood was the Director of Multicultural Education at an independent school when I first met him. He insisted once that I need only to worry about reciprocating his mentorship and guidance in the future, by similarly uplifting and advocating for others as he did for me. His continued support and mentorship of me acts as both a reminder of that moment and an indication that he still has concern for my wellness. Thus, I find the ability to provide for others what he and so many others provided for me. Most importantly, I remember and value the importance of my "home training."

References

Allen, Quaylan. (2016). Tell your own story: manhood, masculinity and racial socialization among black fathers and their sons. *Ethnic & Racial studies, 39*(10), 1831-1848.

Dillard, J. L. (2008). A Sketch of the History of Black English. Southern Quarterly *45*(2), 53-86.

Emdin, Christopher (2016). *For White Folks Who Teach in the Hood… and the Rest of Y'all Too: Reality Pedagogy and Urban Education.* Beacon Press.

Gassaway, Jermaine. (2017) Unopened Books: Multiplying the 2%. Jermaine Gassaway.

Hackman, H. W. (2005). Five essential components for social justice education. *Equity & Excellence in Education, 38*(2), 103-109.

hooks, bell (1994). *Teaching to Transgress: Education as the practice of freedom.* Routledge.

Modica, M. (2015). My Skin Color Stops Me from Leading: Tracking, Identity, and Student Dynamics in a Racially Mixed School. International Journal of Multicultural Education, *17*(3), 76-90. doi:http://dx.doi.org/10.18251/ijme.v17i3.1030

Mufwene, Salikoko, (2001). What is African American English?, In Sonja L Lanehart (ed) *Sociocultural and Historical Contexts of African American English* (pp. 21-51). John Benjamins Pub. Co.

Wyatt, Toya. (2001). The Role of Family, Community, and School in Children's acquisition and maintenance of African American English, In Sonja L Lanehart (ed) *Sociocultural and Historical Contexts of African American English* (261-280). John Benjamins Pub. Co.

3

Unlearning Evangelicalism

What a Poor Education Taught Me

Lucas F. W. Wilson

When I first began my studies at Liberty University, a religious institution of the evangelical persuasion, I was searching for answers on how to reconcile my faith with my sexuality. As a young, gay man in a conservative faith tradition, I thought I had to choose between loving Jesus and loving men. And when it came to such "decisions," as if one could simply choose one's orientation like how one chooses what's for dessert, God always took the cake, so to speak. Since in the evangelical faith tradition, binary thinking is the modus operandi and the either/or reigns supreme, I considered it my cross to bear to reject a constitutive part of who I am—my sexuality—in favor of a God I was told hated homosexuality. So, attending Liberty, the world's largest evangelical university, seemed like the obvious choice, especially, in no small part, because of their gay reparative "therapy" program.

I thought that attending Liberty and going through reparative therapy would help rewire that which was "wrong" with me and would thereby set me straight (pun, indeed, intended). Such specious therapy did not work, and yours truly is still thoroughly gay—surprising, I know. However, I went through their reparative therapy program during all four years while receiving an immersive education in religious and political conservatism. Though I officially majored in English, it is perhaps more accurate to say that my time at LU more so taught me what it means to be a Republican and a Southern Baptist—though I have come to find out the two categories are often synonymous in certain parts of the U.S. Despite having adopted a conservative identity for my teenage self, as a young man from Toronto, Ontario, Canada, there was still much to learn vis-à-vis U.S. conservatism. From the time I received extra credit to attend an NRA-sponsored forum on concealed carry laws to listening to conservative politicians invited to speak during our thrice-weekly chapel services, I received a thorough tutelage in what it meant to be an American evangelical.

As for my time in the classroom, my experience cannot be defined, as one may expect, by critical thinking, intensive study, or challenging theory. Instead, rote memorization, regurgitation of the "correct" evangelical answer (which was, more often than not, simply "Jesus" or "the resurrection"), and the championing of evangelical doctrines defined the education I received at Liberty. I blindly put faith in my professors, as I did in my pastors, trusting that they knew better than I and that if they were able to make it through secular universities and remain people-of-faith, I must be in good hands. The circumscribed paradigm they helped me construct restricted the realm of possibility for me as a young gay man and reinforced the narrow world I thought I had to inhabit as a "Bible-believing" Christian. The school's foundational theology, which more accurately can be defined as its driving ideology, told me what was supposedly possible and what was therefore impossible. As James Berlin (2008) helpfully suggests, "ideology defines the limits of expectation" (p. 120), and I was taught that a different way of being and operating other than as a "straight" man was simply not in the cards. For "[i]deology always carries with it a strong social endorsement, so that what we take to exist, to have value, and to be possible seems necessary, normal, and inevitable—in the nature of things" (Berlin, p. 120). But, thankfully, graduate school taught me otherwise.

After I left Liberty without any conclusive answers on how to negotiate my desire to know God with my desire for men, I entered graduate programs first at McMaster University and then at Vanderbilt University on a mission to figure out how to be holy while being wholly myself. Looking back now, I can see that I needed answers to my questions about the relationship between faith and sexuality and new habits of mind even to begin thinking through such questions. Yet, before I became comfortable with my sexuality and before I realized that I am preceded by—to adapt a phrase from scripture—a "great cloud of [gay] witnesses," I first had to dismantle not only the content of what I was taught at Liberty but the evangelical *framework* that undergirded essentially all of what I had learned. At the time, though now it is quite clear, I did not realize that I needed an almost complete overhaul of how I approached and thought through others' ideas, works of literature, and the world around me.

By way of example, when I first began my MA at McMaster University back in my native province of Ontario, I had to submit my proposal for my Master's thesis, and it was rejected not once. Not twice. No, not three times. Not four, five, or six times. As a matter of fact, it was rejected *seven* times before being accepted on my eighth attempt because of its lack of focus, clarity, coherence, and argument—something that I attribute to the poor education I received at Liberty.

After the sixth proposal was denied, my thesis supervisor suggested that I read his work on the novel on which I was writing my thesis. In my utter desperation to draft a successful proposal while reading his work, I began to dissect how he approached the text and how he constructed *his* argument so I could, in turn, approach *my* argument in a similar manner. One long and tearful November night in my office, with the generous assistance of one of my good friends and former colleagues, I finally drafted an improved proposal that was accepted by my thesis committee.

At the time, it was important for me to persist, for me not to quit, because I wanted to prove to myself I was capable of writing a successful proposal and, eventually, a successful thesis. Despite how my professors were recurrently confused by the work I handed in for the first few months of my MA, I had faith that my dearth of academic success was not because of a lack of ability but, rather, a lack of training. I began thinking to myself: *How could I have graduated from my undergrad at the top of my class, yet now be so far behind? How was I able to succeed as an English major at Liberty, yet barely be able to follow the basic arguments presented in the academic articles assigned to me here at McMaster?* I felt—for the first time since being in a math class—clueless "in the face of the [seeming] impenetrability of the academic world," as Gerald Graff (2008) puts it (p. 32). I came to realize there were significant gaps in my knowledge and I had not been exposed to academic conversations and conventions of which my classmates had been cognizant since early in their undergraduate careers. I wondered how my experience might have been different if I had been privy to such conversations and conventions, that is, had I been trained at a university that didn't shelter its student from topics that diverged from its doctrines. But I refused to allow my lack of training to determine my academic trajectory. Instead, as it became clear that crafting a successful thesis proposal was a sink-or-swim moment, I knew I had to deep-dive into academic thought and argumentation in order to succeed.

Through this pivotal experience (or, more accurately, through this profound *struggle* [or, even more accurately, through this true *debacle*]) with my master's thesis proposal, I learned the vital importance of not only peer-review but also of mimicking successful scholars' stylistic choices to inform my own writing style. David Bartholomae's (2008) notion of "inventing the university," speaks precisely to my experience at McMaster. Bartholomae posits:

> The student has to appropriate (or be appropriated by) a specialized discourse... [She or h]e has to invent the university by assembling and mimicking its language while finding some compromise between idiosyncrasy, a personal history, on the one hand,

and the requirements of convention, the history of a discipline, on the other hand. He must learn to speak our language. (p. 3)

Indeed, my experience at McMaster of "assembling and mimicking" the language of the university while negotiating (that is, largely, though not completely, throwing out) what I had been previously taught, along with the new discourses I was encountering, was an experience that most students undergo in their freshman year of their undergrad. But for me, it was a crash course in academic literacy during my first semester in grad school.

This frustrating and daunting thesis proposal ordeal laid the foundation for me to begin mimicking other academics' modes of argumentation to develop my own voice and my own arguments. It was made clear that my scholarly approach was not working out and that I needed a strategic plan to find a seat at the academic table. I knew that unless I was intentional and systematic in my approach to this work, I would most likely flunk out—especially given how my professors did not have the time to offer one-on-one, step-by-step tutoring to bring me up to speed about topics that, without question, should have been covered in my undergrad. As I read scholarly and creative articles and books, and as I listened to my professors convey their arguments in their own ways, I began to note the rhetorical strategies and sentence formulations they used. In fact, I made what came to be an eight-page Microsoft Word document titled "Good Words!" with not only vocabulary words from class readings that I had to look up (e.g., "agentic," "simulacrum," "Occidental," and the eight-page list goes on) but also syntactical constructions that would later function as formulas for me to employ in my own writing (e.g., "_____ finds expression in _____," "_____ offers us pause," etc.). As I diagrammed the styles and methods of argumentation of others, along with experimenting with syntactical construction, diction, and modes of argument in my own writing (e.g., through the academic essay, through narrative, etc.), I began to develop a way of writing that succinctly and clearly put into words my thoughts.

I began adopting their stylistic choices and shedding binary approaches to topics as I embraced a more complex worldview, which was reinforced and encouraged by conversations with my colleagues and professors. As I slogged through the fields of literature and literary criticism, these habits of mind I was developing began to transfer, slowly but surely, into how I worked through my understanding of sexuality and faith. Indeed, the arduous groundwork I laid in claiming my academic literacy later equipped me with the ability to realize and articulate the narrow limits of my former paradigm.

This is not to say, however, that I wholesale rejected every aspect of my former approach to the world around me. In fact, from my time in church and my four years at Liberty, I retained a strong desire to entertain questions of ethics and morality. Though the *content* of what I believed to be ethical and moral dramatically began to change, my *desire* to access, think about, and live out "the good life" remained consistent. Contrary to holding fast to the same ethical or moral system of evangelicalism of my former years, I learned in Divinity School at Vanderbilt how to dismantle said system and its constitutive parts, that is, to critique the basic ethical and moral tenets that form the basis of evangelicalism. These ethical and moral tenets—the Golden Rule, for instance—became the tools that I used to critique evangelicalism's undergirding moral hypocrisy, along with its ethical (and intellectual) shortcomings. Drawing upon such ethical and moral tools and putting them to their proper use, I began to deconstruct the hegemonic structures of conservative religiosity in order to work my way out. Instead of using these tools to reinforce the paradigm that I had previously adopted blindly, I used them, along with the developing ability to think critically, to emancipate myself from the restrictive position of being a gay man in a conservative religious tradition. Today, this groundwork that was laid has afforded me great confidence and relief after years of hiding in the closet alone without the tools to liberate myself. To put it mildly, the growing pains of graduate school were tremendous, but the result was that I was able to articulate my ideas, both within and without the academy, with a much higher degree of success.

My immense difficulty with bridging the gap between my poor education at Liberty and the rigorous instruction I received at McMaster and Vanderbilt—and eventually at Florida Atlantic University—was foundational for how I introduce my students to academic writing and how I teach them to articulate themselves. Just as it was difficult for me "to speak not only in another's voice but through another's code" (Batholomae, p. 22), it is often uncomfortable and sometimes stressful for my students when they begin to write academically. But the discomfort and stress that frequently accompanies the learning curve associated with university writing is, in small quantities, something that I have found to be productive in creating confident and competent writers. As Graff (2008) reminds us, "Given the inherent difficulty of academic intellectual work, some degree of cluelessness is a natural stage in the process of education" (p. 33). Many of my students do not anticipate the level of work successful writing entails, and when they receive a low grade on their first rough draft—or again on their first final draft—they come to me somewhat panicked. Through this panic, as it was the case for me at McMaster, students begin to take seriously the work required to write well. Many students, after their early- and mid-semester period of panic, begin to apply what I introduce in class and are able to draft, bare minimum, *clear* prose that are a direct result of said panic.

But for me, the greatest fruit of my labor, that is, the most rewarding part of holding my students to a high standard of excellence, has always come at the end of the semester, when one or two students (or sometimes more but, up until this point, never fewer) begin to work "self-consciously to claim an interpretive project of their own, one that grants them their privilege to speak" (Batholomae, p. 24). These students begin to write differently, diverging from their former "naïve" or "everyday" prose, and in doing so, develop a style of writing that allows them to express themselves with self-possession and eloquence, even if it is at times still somewhat difficult to do (Batholomae, p. 23). The expectation that Bartholomae upholds—of the academy not bending to students but instead of students conforming to the academy—is one that I champion *in the classroom*, and a large number of my students rise to the occasion. Here, I emphasize *in the classroom* because, as I always tell my students, we learn how to approach subjects academically and to write for the academy because once we know the "rules" and "principles" (that is, academic conventions and standard best practices), we can later break them. In other words, I expect my students to enter into academic discourse so that they can employ such discourse when needed and depart from it when it does not suit their purposes.

How I teach my students to navigate and switch between academic and non-academic modes of communication successfully is a direct function of my experience of translating what I have learned from the academy for my conservative friends and family. I had to explain to them my beliefs not in scholarly prose but in *their* terms, using *their* vocabulary, thereby first "employing" the university conceptually and then "putting it aside" when it was no longer helpful in the name of discussing matters of faith and sexuality, encouraging them to think critically, to think otherwise, and to think for themselves about the LGBTQIA+ community.

My personal progression in and through academia has allowed me not only to communicate with success through the written word but has further enabled me to express myself verbally, which has indeed shaped my pedagogical method. My original goal to find a way to articulate my lived experiences as a gay man and as a Christian was indeed achieved, though I now no longer identify as the latter. I nonetheless continue to think through the relationship between faith and sexuality, as well as ways to engage others in such important conversations, through my scholarship. Indeed, as I engage critically with matters of thought, language, and argument, I realize more and more the importance of clear communication and effective persuasion. With the myriad political challenges that the U.S. (along with Canada) continues to face and with the host of prejudices that hinder the lives and livelihoods of minority folk around the continent, like those of non-normative sexual orientations in conservative religious traditions, I believe there to be an ethical imperative placed upon me to ensure that my students learn to argue and articulate themselves for the betterment of their communities. I seek to give my students "access to forms of intellectual capital that have a lot of power in the world" (Graff, p. 39). Even if we must undergo moments of stress or a period of growing pains to achieve it, the ability to communicate and to communicate *well* is imperative in the political climate in which we currently live.

Reflecting on my learning journey, as it relates to my teaching philosophy, has only reinforced my thinking about the value of stories in education. Of course, my personal experience of struggling through graduate school informed my teaching, but I have found that sharing my experiences from both undergrad and grad school with my students has proven to be effective for several reasons. First, I think it humanizes me as their instructor. I used to be greedy for my professors' personal anecdotes—for stories that fleshed out the person at the front of the classroom, for stories that offered me entrance into the life of someone who held my respect and high esteem, and for stories that offered real-world connections to what we were learning in class. And offering personal stories about my educational experience now, I believe, facilitates in this humanization process. Second, it furnishes my students with a clear apologia as to why I hold them to such high standards and why I refuse to water down my expectations in the name of "making life easier." I explain to them that almost none of my professors required even semi-quality work from me in my undergrad, and I wish someone had. In response, I maintain high standards to ensure they are not cheated out of a proper education like I was. Third, and arguably, (much) more importantly, offering stories from my educational journey helps students realize they are not the only ones who have struggled in navigating the often disorienting waters of higher education. I can serve as an example of one who was, in a semester, able to learn how to rise to the expectations of his professors. If I can do it, I explain to them, they surely can, too. More often than not, they come to find the tools to begin writing their own stories of academic success in my class and beyond.

References

Batholomae, D. (2008). Inventing the university. In T. R Johnson (Ed.), *Teaching composition: Background readings* (pp. 2–31). Bedford/St. Martin's.

Berlin, J. (2008). Rhetoric and ideology in the writing class. In *Teaching composition: Background readings* (pp. 117–38). Bedford/St. Martin's.
Graff, G. (2008). *From* clueless in academe. In *Teaching composition: Background readings* (pp. 32–58). Bedford/St. Martin's.

4

Written on the Mind

Emotional Imagination in Re-storying Learner Identity and the Formation of Critical Pedagogies

Sharon M. Ravitch & Janay M. Garrett

Introduction

"Trust me, I'm telling you stories.... I can change the story. I am the story."

—Jeannette Winterson, *Written on the Body* (1994, p. 118)

We are the stories we tell, with all of their nuance, complexity, and temporality. Over time, as we discuss in this chapter, we can learn to become agentic in storying and re-storying our experiences and narratives of self, as Winterson's words powerfully evince. In this sense, we can change our stories to be evermore liberating in ways more aligned with our authentic selves. In this chapter, we draw on the framing from the foreword of this book as we share and reflect on critical incidents from our own education experiences. We discuss how these incidents shaped our individual teaching philosophies and our shared approach to critical pedagogy in a doctoral course we teach on qualitative inquiry. This chapter is intentionally poly-vocal since we currently work as a teaching team. It explores and juxtaposes our K–12 and higher education schooling experiences in terms of how the stories told to us by educators turned into the stories we told ourselves about ourselves, thus shaping our sense of self as learners, our sense of our identities in the world, and the relationship of this to our educational trajectories—imagined and real. Through the prism storying and re-storying, Janay shares her education story from the lived experience of presumed incompetence as a Black and Chicana woman in predominately White educational spaces, and Sharon shares her education story of simultaneous visibility and invisibility as a White Jewish girl growing up in a traditional Jewish home and religious school, both with constraining gender scripts and invisible social contracts that included ignoring underlying mental health issues in family and community. The power of stories to define us as learners (and people) and then the transformational power of re-storying ourselves (and each other through critical pedagogy) is both figural and generative throughout this chapter.

In reflexively narrating our stories with attention to the individual ways that our early and ongoing educational experiences shape how we have come to imagine ourselves as learners and then as teachers, and by weaving our stories and our re-storied self-narratives together as an equity-focused educational bricolage, we share our learner-identities-in-process, and offer insight into the ways that our feelings, needs, ideas, struggles, and strengths were often unseen and unmet in school. We narrate the ways that we experienced deltas of support and a dearth of positive learner attribution in school in terms of what we interpreted and internalized about ourselves as people and learners within confusing and often intimidating educational milieux. In so doing we offer intimate portraits of how we have re-storied—made and remade more critical, loving, and emancipatory meaning over time—of ourselves as learners in relation to our bespoke processes of coming into critical consciousness (Freire, 1970; 1997; hooks, 1994; 2003) about ourselves and the world, and how other people's stories of us became written on the mind (Winterson, 1994)—internalized as a constraining narrative of self, an introject of limitation and deficiency.

In this chapter, we analyze critical moments from our distinct educational histories, which leads to a reflexive dialogue about ways we have transformed our individual and shared learning experiences into a hopeful and loving critical pedagogy for teaching and learning (hooks, 1994; 2003). Through examining critical turning points we experienced from early schooling through graduate school, narrating our stories from a reflexive perch attentive to re-imagining one's learner self, we share how we have made meaning and use of our emergent stories of self as learner and, further, how reflexive re-storying processes shape our teaching philosophies and collaborative pedagogical approach to a doctoral-level research course we co-teach. Given our stance on re-storying as a form of critical pedagogy, we work to co-construct the conditions in which we and the doctoral students we teach can consider re-storying ourselves through learning to re-frame and re-index our own life and learning experiences with ever-more critical insights generated by equity-focused reflexivity that engenders critical self-knowledge and understanding. The chapter weaves the concepts of emotional imagination, re-storying, re-framing and re-indexing experience as a reflexive, person-centered RECAST learning process (Stevenson, 2014) that help us to build a set of teaching and learning practices supported and actualized by an inquiry stance in/on our practice (Cochran-Smith & Lytle, 2009) and based in the principles and practices of critical pedagogy (Khalifa, 2018) and critical leadership praxis as an ethic of teaching, learning, education, and schooling (Pak & Ravitch, 2021).

Repairing Educational Ruptures: Critical Feflexivity as a Path to Healing (Janay Mae Garrett)

In periods of internal dissonance, when I feel stuck and am struggling to create or imagine, I turn to those with whom I feel safest—my family. Most often, this is my husband James, my mama, or my stepdad, who I affectionately call "Pops." Other times, I connect with my little-big sister who I dubbed 'Bub,' long ago. On lesser occasions, I call my biological dad, Mack. The nature of our relationship has always been complicated—a natural consequence of his extended absences. I recall my dad being most present in the earliest years of my life. *His* story of me then, is crystallized by those years we spent the most time together. In this way, my dad is able to remind me of the power of my childhood ambitions and how I continue to manifest those dreams in my adult life. In discussing my educational history, my father's stories of me are an important emotional tether, as they are imbued with messages of pride, confidence, and joy—messages that inform my healthy self-talk or help me transform harmful narratives of self.

One such story my father loves to tell, is of our third Christmas eve together. Each time he tells the story, he chuckles—I picture his smile and hear his voice in my head, clear as day. "We had opened all the gifts and I expected to find you playing with one of the many toys you got that year. I turned around, and you were in a giant chair, reading a book. I knew then you were a special kid." Each time he tells this story, I feel reconnected to my younger self and am reminded that I was always fascinated by the creation of other worlds and engrossed in the production of knowledge.

My early love for learning extended to my general excitement to attend school when it came time. My mom was intentional in her school choices, actively selecting schools and educators she felt would satisfy my intellectual hunger and deepen my learning capacity. Although we have never discussed this explicitly, as an adult now well-versed in the educational landscape of my hometown, I know she selected schools in wealthier, predominately White neighborhoods, as *those* schools were historically well-resourced and consistently outperformed others throughout the city. My mama's intentions were unfortunately marred by my repeatedly painful interpersonal experiences with peers and adults as a Brown girl in White schools.

In the following section, I share a few selected scenes and critical incidents in my K–12 schooling history that I have come to describe as *educational rup-*

tures, or moments that upended my expectations and imaginations of self and others. I also reflect on my reactions to those experiences as precursors to my culminating critical turning point and resultant pursuit of critical self-awareness as a path to healing. I explore how my process of reflexivity and learning, propelled me towards actively cultivating an identity as an activist scholar and how it continues to shape my teacher pedagogy and educational philosophy.

Prior to my third-grade year, I had the privilege of being taught by mostly women of color educators who were both compassionate and invested in my total wellness as their student. Those first few years in school are indexed in my mind as exciting, rigorous, and full of creativity—this early educational socialization set me up to believe in schooling as a site of possibility. Over time, I held this in tension with experiences that left me feeling like schools were, in fact, sites of symbolic violence and racial hostility.

Third grade, 1997
At the start of each class, we were expected to submit our homework to a wire basket near the entrance before sitting in our assigned seats. One particular morning, as my teacher was checking the previous night's homework for completion, she loudly announced that I did not, in fact, turn in my work and I would need to change my index card color from green to red on the class discipline chart (a visible chart displaying students' classroom ruptures and proximity to increasing punitive action) by the end of class. Shocked, both because I completed my work the night before and also because I had undoubtedly turned in my work, I protested, emphatically defending myself, but just shy of telling my teacher that she was wrong. She continued to accuse me of lying, insisting that my homework was not in the basket and I should simply tell her the truth. I riffled through the papers, panicked, not finding my work the first time around. I tried again, to find my work with someone else's name at the top. A White male student who was also my bully, had pulled my homework out of the pile, erased my name and written his name over because he forgot to do his work. Despite the harm I felt in this interaction, there was no acknowledgement of the mistake nor accountability taken by the teacher. She simply operated as if nothing happened—adding insult to injury, the male student was encouraged and offered support to complete his work in class, a markedly different approach than my public shaming. In this early formative memory, the burden of proof fell on me, the child and student. It hurt that she did not believe me. It was infuriating and scary to be a child defending myself to a teacher who, in my eyes, held the power. I interpreted and indexed this as

a racial moment, feeling disappointed and disillusioned, I spent the rest of the school year unravelling my expectations of her and self.

Seventh grade, 2001
My next strongest memory of rupture comes from a conversation with my seventh-grade honors math teacher, who was also a White woman. In this class, I excelled far beyond most of my peers and was "on track" to begin honors math classes at the high school (across the street) a year early, during my eighth-grade year. In order to enroll in classes at the high school, we needed the advanced approval of our current math teacher, a guardian and an academic counselor. During a one to one meeting, I recall seeking my teacher's advice, perhaps looking for affirmation that I was indeed, capable. Contrary to my expectations, she strongly suggested I enroll in IMP (interactive mathematics program) courses, because the curriculum was designed to consider "real world" applications of math through word-based problems about daily routines or common experiences—her rationale was that she believed the work would be "easier" for me. Angry, frustrated, and confused, I asked her what she meant by *easier*—though I do not remember how she responded, I knew what she meant. I took the course descriptions and enrollment materials home to my mom. I told her I preferred to take honors math, not IMP, and she quickly encouraged me to enroll in the class *I* wanted to take and that would challenge me most. I quietly rejected the advice of my math teacher and instead enrolled in algebra honors math, continuing on this "advanced" math track through graduation. I returned to her classroom for a casual visit at the end of every school year (from then on) to inform her that I was thriving, *still*. In the final months of my senior year of high school, I was offered admission to Princeton University—she was one of the first people I visited that day to share the news. Although this might seem like a taxing process, for me, it was always exhilarating—my courageous way to subvert what I believed to be a limited imagination about my future.

11th grade, 2005
In my junior year of high school, I enrolled in AP English along with three other AP courses. Our teacher, who also happened to be a White woman, was a firm (and I learned in conversations with her as an adult, quite caring) educator who at the time, lacked a critical lens around race and class. Due to this lack of criticality, I often found myself in the position of forced discomfort, engaged in the emotional labor of explaining to my wealthier White peers why people like me are not often in AP classes (e.g., inequities originating in classism and racism, rather than a lack of competence). In one specific instance, I recall

openly sharing in class how it felt to be one of the few Black *and* Chicana students who also did not have expendable money to pay for AP exams (I was in multiple AP courses, each exam ~$90 USD). Disclosing this truth came not from a place of trust in my relationships with classmates, but rather self-advocacy, necessitated by being pressed to register without a consideration of potential barriers. I resented having to share this information publicly, feeling like it should have been my teacher's responsibility to think critically about the course requirements and how expectations may be inaccessible for some of her students. I also expressed then and in future discussions that it felt unfair to link our final grade in the course to our AP exam scores at the end of the school year. My classmates and teacher responded with silence. I did not take up the topic again, exhausted by the emotional labor it required—nor did she seek any resolve between us. There was no change made to the course policies or expectations. Perhaps considering it helpful, she suggested I apply for fee waivers instead, never broaching the conversation about racial or economic inequity in advanced education courses.

In each of these moments, I felt underestimated, isolated, and abandoned by many of my educators. As a youth, I took these moments of rupture between myself and my teachers quite personally. Most often, I reacted to these moments with a vigorous internal and unspoken commitment to prove said educators wrong, even if might take *years*, through continued academic excellence and a silent, strong resolve (an approach I now consider to be steeped in internalized notions of respectability as it relates to academic achievement). While this was one form of resistance that yielded positive performance outcomes, it was not without harmful developmental and psychological consequences, including a lingering imposter syndrome, a constant dance of seeking approval/aiming to prove myself, and an implicit belief that I had to learn to navigate systems of power alone, because I could not rely on my teachers/mentors to have high expectations for my future.

Princeton University, 2006
As a young adult, it was difficult to situate these experiences in a broader context because I, too, lacked a certain criticality and language about my gendered and racialized experiences. I struggled to heal from these earlier academic ruptures, limiting *myself* as an undergraduate student through a reluctance to connect with most faculty—a projection of sorts that engaging with them more regularly would leave me feeling incompetent, incapable or unworthy. To counter strong feelings of unbelonging and fear, I poured myself, my time, and my emotional labor into strengthening student-led Black affinity groups. It was through

campus community engagement and student leadership that I discovered I had a knack for organizing others towards collective social change. These student organizations were also spaces for critical, informative and reflective ongoing dialogue about racial politics and identity development, which helped me move forward in the midst of ongoing racial trauma at Princeton. It was not until my graduate education at California State University Long Beach (2015) however, that I began to learn about and latch on to critical theories and discourses around education, race, class and gender. Learning about Black feminist epistemologies (Collins, 2002), critical pedagogy, the practice of dialogical engagement (Freire, 1970) and a broader scholarly tradition of critique was nothing short of liberating. I was twenty-four years old when I learned that my experiences were not isolated, *microaggressions* were real, and that my exhaustion, sadness, anger, and confusion was valid (Solórzano, Ceja, & Yosso, 2000).

Reflections on Re-indexing Experience and Imagining Forward
It would take many years before I was able to critically reflect on my own evolving positionality and apply these critical lenses to my story of self—an effort to re-interpret and re-index my educational experiences alongside new knowledges. I learned not to interpret these moments as simply small, isolated incidents, but rather consider my resistance, even now as an emerging scholar in academia, as "Black feminist memory work [which] extends a long lineage of Black women subversively creating alternatives that defy the body-numbing demands of the death and decay-inducing knowledge production normalized in academia" (Ohito, 2020. P. 7). In this way, this critical reflexive process, for me, has been an honest unearthing of grief and anger as it relates to my expectations of self and others, in hopes that doing so will help me imagine a way forward "to creatively *re*-member…in order to increase the heart's capaciousness and capacity for compassion" (Ohito, 2020, p.7).

Documenting the process of remembering, reflecting, and re-indexing educational ruptures is a relatively new process for me. Although difficult, intentionally and consciously engaging in this process has helped me to name the ways I have performed vulnerability as both student and educator, while in actuality, being selective and protective over when to engage in *shared vulnerability* (Perez Huber, 2019)—a direct result of many unmet educational and personal life ruptures. Critical reflexivity for me then, is a pathway to healing, recognizing that alongside these critical incidents I have just as many memories of validation and affirmation, grounded in the stories of me that were rooted in love. These love stories, originated with and from a strong squad of family, friends, peers, and mentors that continues to grow to this day. Working towards healing, I am critically self-aware of the ways these experiences and my indexing of them, parlay into my teaching philosophy and consequently my capacity to operate from a place of trust, love, and compassion as opposed to distrust, protectiveness, and fear.

Re-framing and Re-indexing Experiences as Self-development (Sharon Meir Ravitch)

Re-storying is a generative intra-psychic and inter-personal process that enables us to identify, reckon with, reframe, and move beyond the often-unrealistic and harmful myths and assumptions that have come to shape our hopes and life choices, to re-index past experiences and conceptualizations of self that have not and do not fit us as we truly are and that do not serve us well. This kind of intra-psychic growth process—learning to re-index experiences and re-understand self through new frames and with new skills—constitutes a powerful process-approach to building healthy thinking and choice-making, to cultivating happiness through self-liberation from harmful social constructions turned inwards as cognitive distortions and false beliefs that can rule our inner lives and corrode healthy relationships if not identified, explored, and thoughtfully attended to with compassionate resolve and a commitment to unlearning. They are a path forward into a healthier, less burdened, and more authentic and agentic version of self (Ravitch, 2020).

In this section, I trace the history of my adaptations to my childhood realities and socialization as a young White, Jewish girl in a fairly traditional Jewish family and Jewish school in the United States. This storying of my lived experience across educational moments is part of a conscious effort to examine how my own psychological adaptations to childhood realities, including significant family trauma, have caused me to subconsciously create and maintain tacit theories about myself as a learner and knower, and thus to index an array of working assumptions about teaching, learning, and schooling. These tacit theories, which resided in people's stories of me and then resided in me—the ways that I took on and internalized those stories—became the unconscious grounding for my story of myself. This then shaped my own transferences and projections in the world—I have grown to see over time, for example, that I interpreted student learning needs through the filter of my own learning needs, that is, how I would want to be taught as a younger, anxious version of myself.

This unconscious and impositionally implanted introjection was interrupted as I began to view myself more critically—both as a gendered and raced Jewish White woman raised in a cultural and educational milieu and family system that, among many wonderful and loving things, was heavily gendered in ways that set me up to assume a stance of over-functioning and doing emotional labor for others without recognition or reciprocity. Moreover, I now have unpacked the ways that it led me to believe that I was only a good daughter—and therefore a good and worthy person—if I made myself and my needs as small as possible. This set of hard-won realizations and unfoldings[1] was the result of engaging in focused self-development work on my anxiety and its sources within, and on rewriting my family's narrative and my role within it through an intentional self-development pathway of coursework, groupwork, dialogic engagement, and therapy (Meg Turner, Lecture, Harvard University, February 11, 1994). The work of shifting my self-narrative through actively and ongoingly working to re-story past experiences and grand narratives of who I am (i.e., Sharon is a dutiful daughter, Sharon is a giver, Sharon is a mini Eyshet Chayal, which is Hebrew for Woman of Valor[2]) with present understandings, facts, and insights, and with compassion for myself, has been the most liberating work I have done in my life, both personally and as a professor, thought leader, and researcher. Re-storying is not just a lofty concept, it is a liberatory pedagogy. It is a portal.

Fifth Grade, 1980

A near-fatal high-speed car crash on our way home from a Purim celebration at our synagogue, Tifereth Israel, when I was in fifth grade, changed my life and my family forever. I was dressed as Queen Esther, I was 10. My sister Elizabeth was 13 (dressed as Vashti) and my mother, Arline, was 41. We were driving home when a car crashed into us head-on at top speed on the highway. My mother's head went through the windshield, and she was critically injured and on her deathbed for months, then endured years of life-threatening surgeries, and even

---

1 Rainer Maria Rilke's unfolding related to aspects of ourselves that remain hidden, often even to us, and that conceal parts of us, limiting our ability to live authentically and in reciprocal relationship with ourselves and others. In his poem, "I Am Much Too Alone in This World, Yet Not Alone," Rilke wrote, "I want to unfold. Nowhere I wish to stay crooked, bent; for there I would be dishonest, untrue" (p. 17).

2 Eishet Chayil is Hebrew for "Woman of Valor." It's a passage from the Book of Proverbs (Chapter 31:10–31) read each Friday night at the Sabbath meal; it is considered the highest attribution a Jewish woman can be given: "A woman of valor, who can find? Her value is far beyond rubies. Her husband's heart trusts in her and he shall lack no fortune. She repays his good, but never his harm, all the days of her life. She seeks out wool and linen, and her hands work willingly. She is like a merchant's ships; from afar she brings her sustenance….She rises while it is still nighttime, and gives food to her household….She senses that her enterprise is good, so her lamp is not extinguished at night. She puts her hand to the distaff, and her palms support the spindle. She spreads out her palm to the poor and extends her hands to the destitute. She fears not snow for her household, for her entire household is clothed with scarlet wool….Well-known at the gates is her husband as he sits with the elders of the land….Strength and splendor are her clothing, and smilingly she awaits her last day. She opens her mouth with wisdom, and the teaching of kindness is on her tongue. She anticipates the needs of her household, and does not eat the bread of idleness. Her children rise and celebrate her; and her husband, he praises her: "Many daughters have attained valor, but you have surpassed them all. False is grace, and vain is beauty but a God-fearing woman, she should be praised…." This is said weekly on Sabbath, thius becoming written on my mind as the feminine ideal—until I re-storied myself and broke free from an imposed axiology and reductive axiology. Bespoke reinvention is everything."

now has significant health issues. This reality, embedded as it was within my own familial and social system, shaped my life and schooling experiences in ways that were both visible and invisible at the time, but that I now see as incalculably formative in harmful and diminishing ways that I had to unlearn through focused self-development and therapy. In my family and little Jewish world growing up, this situation was the final seal on the implicit deal of becoming my mother's primary caretaker, as well as her nurse, cheerleader, and the person who managed her affect for her since she had untreated depression and an anxiety disorder and since we were psychologically enmeshed and codependent (as were many of the Jewish mother-daughter dyads I saw in my youth, something I am currently thinking and writing about). And so, this became an unquestioned reality that shaped each hour of each day which over time morphed into how I saw myself, the world, and possibility—it was who I became.

Middle School, 1982-1985

Looking back, I can see how taking on the role and ultimately the identity of selfless caretaker was harmful to my development in middle and high school, which included anxiety-filled days of feeling responsible for my mother's happiness and health, guilty whenever I was not taking care of her, and blaming myself for not knowing how to do so while also being a young person with my own identity and aspirations. My identity in my family and at school, which felt like an extension of my family, kept me from feeling smart, competent, and worthy of real academic attention or goals.

My mother's narrative became mine in some ways—she didn't go to college and got married and raised her children and so would I. Even as I got used to a new normal with a mother with a disability who was hospitalized for months at a time, and even while so many people loved me so very much, looking back, it's clear that I had no real academic supports and that no one saw in me someone who should be taken seriously intellectually. My mother's own educational trajectory plays in here since she struggled in high school and did not go to college and since I identified so strongly with her as an Eshet Chayil and aspired to fill her exact footsteps.

I learned quickly that I was there to take care of my mother, and the worst part is that my teachers and the principal routinely *praised me for it*. They repeatedly told me what a good daughter I was, how selfless I was (as if that is a good thing…), that I was "training to be an Eshet Chayil," that my "place in heaven will be secured" by my caretaking acumen. And since they storied me this way, they didn't notice me. They didn't see that I was flailing in school, and so they did not offer help or even observe that I didn't take care of myself and was not engaged or connected to school or the kids in it. They passed me along with B's and C's which I came to understand through my peers were "pity grades." I learned little in my classes, and no one noticed or cared. I was anxious every. single. day. I applied their stories to myself—their stories became myself—and I defined myself by how much I could take care of others and learned to disavow and invisibilize my own needs. Worse yet, I learned to deficitize, judge, and shame myself for even having them.

I realized in the middle of seventh grade that no one really cared if I succeeded academically, it was not even on the radar, they did not seem to see me as a capable student like the other students. No one ever asked how I felt about not doing well in school (except my best friend, Deborah, who tirelessly tutored me to no avail since the force of my learned helplessness proved too formidable for her desire to uplift me out of my mediocrity). The teachers, who acted and felt like aunties to me in my Jewish school, just felt bad for me, so they'd check in with me awkwardly every few weeks to see if I was ok, make sad eyes at me or hug me when asking about my mother's health, bake me sufganiot on Chanukah, and just give me a pass on everything academic—meaning anything even remotely challenging or anything I didn't make an effort on was fine with them because my mother was always in the next health crisis. They acted like, given these issues, why would they hold me accountable? And, after all, they set their expectations so low for me academically, so I too figured I would graduate high school and get married and raise children and either not go to or not finish college. Stories have the power to wither parts of us. Or to prevent us from growing in the first place.

High School, 1986-1989
In high school, I thought the teacher behavior of academically ignoring me was awesome (read *easier*) and I leaned into it hard. While it felt good then, this caused harmful accumulated learning opportunity costs and a poor self-image. I was missing key areas of knowledge and sets of academic and life skills that my peers around me clearly had—this realization started in early high school and was in full force throughout college. It was an experience of feeling on the outside looking in academically, wondering why my peers all knew what to do in class, how to study, how to behave and how to pace themselves, to prepare for and take tests, to manage stressful situations, and so on. I did not have this information: my sister and I are the first two women in our family to go to college and our parents were not directly engaged in our education though they were conceptually supportive of it—so my teachers' stories of me seemed like *the* story of me as a learner. After all, I conferred dominance onto my teachers

and so their lack of faith in me as a student translated into me assuming and internalizing their view of me and then quietly opted out of my own learning. Back to the students around me—they all seemed so calm and they could think about their futures without being overcome by anxiety. My anxiety had emerged as a real problem, meaning it was harder to manage on the outside. Some stories speak through our bodies, they call us to our own attention, they are as Winterson avers, written on the body.

Temple University, 1990-1993
While in my freshman year of college (1989) at Tel Aviv University I could hide behind my foreignness to the Middle Eastern college system and university norms, once I got to Temple University for sophomore year, it quickly became clear that I was rather ill-equipped for college, for effective studying and test-taking, and that I had not developed many life skills to help me navigate my new realities. I was placed into remedial writing and math in my first semester, which confirmed to me that I was deficient as a student, and as a person (i.e., "the stories of me were right, I am not intelligent…"). Things started off rough, and I considered dropping out and going the route my mother did that year itself.

During these years, I learned I was anxious in ways that were not identified in my little Jewish world and school—the fish doesn't know it's in water much like Jews don't know we're anxious since we have elevated anxiety numbers on index due to what's called a Founder Effect—a major ramification of the Nazi internment and extermination of Jews—which has forever changed the Jewish genetic pool, creating exacerbated rates of depression, anxiety, schizophrenia, and reproductive cancers in Ashkenazi Jews[3] (Kedar-Barnes, 2008). In my socialization experience, anxiety is often not noticed, it is the water in which many Jewish families swim since inter-generational trauma is written on the body across time and across bodies (Winterson, 1994). I was anxious and lost, and it took a few close friendships and the arrival of a dedicated mentor, Dr. Norbert Samuelson (Zichrono L'vracha), to show me that I was smart and worthy of a college degree and a mentor, to see that I could make it through college and even thrive.

The moment that Professor Samuelson (a Judaic Studies scholar, which I mention because it was a corrective experience to have a critically engaged Jewish teacher take interest in me) chose to take me under his wing, my en-

---
[3] Ashkenazi Jews originated in Eastern Europe. Sephardic Jews are from the areas around the Mediterranean Sea, including Portugal, Spain, the Middle East, and Northern Africa. Roughly 72% of Jews have Ashkenazi ancestry, and 28% are of Sephardic ancestry, according to The Hebrew University Genetic Resource. Understanding that Jews are indigenous to the Levant is vital to debunking contemporary mythologies that Jewish Israelis are colonizers of our native land, Palestine (Ashkenazi Jews, n.d.).

tire educational experience transformed, my world opened up, and I began to blossom. I credit Dr. Samuelson for being the first person who viewed me as an academically capable and intelligent (not just sweet or nice or thoughtful) person with valuable ideas, someone who was curious and could be stretched intellectually. And I credit him also with caring enough to connect me with Dr. Laura Levitt, a Jewish feminist scholar, who introduced me to critical social theory and who created the conditions for me to begin to develop and cultivate my critical thinking and writing skills and, in so doing, to reimagine myself as a person, student, and as a writer. This is when I first felt what it was like to be seen and storied as a capable learner—and to have someone create and hold the space for us to co-construct learning that was bespoke to me and reciprocal— she valued my ideas and experiences!

Simultaneously I had the tremendous fortune of enrolling in a service-learning course with Dr. Nancy Hoffman, and that is when my whole sense of my future exploded! I can see now that Nancy—who was Jewish and my mother's age but went to college and got her doctorate and was such a different universe of woman for me—showed me by her very being that Jewish women can be intellectual and serious academics as well as family oriented and nurturing; our engagements were a kind of academic and intellectual re-parenting in retrospect. My emotional imagination was affirmed and revivified! Some stories grow you by supplanting old constraining ones with new versions that are full of authentic possibility. These stories that other people opened up for me helped me grow into a passionate, budding scholar, a young woman who felt smart and capable and who could have an identity outside of caretaker and people-pleaser. I have been, am, and will be forever grateful to these people who saw things in me that I had not seen in myself yet. These teachers didn't know the old stories of me and they saw me anew. They opened doors in my mind, led me in, and helped me feel safe even as they pushed me forward. Looking back, I can see that the ecosystem of my education growing up shaped my view of self in ways that made me think I was deficient. Powerful unlearning and re-seeing.

In my case, re-storying myself meant re-storying the world. Not just my world, but the world. As I now teach across all topics I teach, White people are raised in a sea of racism but act like the fish in water—and our psyches and perspectives on the world are deeply distorted by it. For me, it was not until my senior year of college that my White entitlement worldview was challenged. It happened in a course when I watched a White male professor speak in class about his research with what I would later learn is a deficit orientation towards Latinx populations and a White savior complex. Fortunately, he was challenged by Latinx students in the class, though I would later come to learn that the professor whose course it was should have stepped up and not put them in the situation to do that emotional labor. Seeing how agentic my Chicana classmates were when I was 20 and still in my racialized privilege bubble was watershed for me; this experience continues to teach me different lessons as I reflect on it over decades and situations. It has shaped my understanding of the importance of speaking truth to power, the responsibility for the professor or person in charge to call out racism and discrimination as well as microaggressions that play out in class, the need for me as a White woman to identify, understand, and be accountable to my privileges and entitlements even as I struggle with anti-Semitism and anti-Zionism in complex ways in my professional and activist life, and about the power of deficit orientations and minoritization to limit access to growth and possibility, even within ourselves and of course more broadly. This was a radical moment of interruption and unlearning that continues to teach me about the possibilities of agentic, constructively critical dialogic engagement, dialectics of mutual influence, and reciprocal transformation (Nakkula & Ravitch, 1998).

One major lesson of this experience is that I learned that for my peers of color, the erasure and violence done to them and their communities by researchers and the education system—historically and to the minute—was the driving force of their courageous actions of challenging and countering the stories this problematic and deficitizing researcher told. Further, in retrospect I think a lot about how my attribution of authority to this White professor as deserving respect is itself a hugely culturally and contextually mediated relationship to power and authority stemming from my own socialization. In the moments of teaching that remind me of this interruptive learning experience of my own, I reflect on how my limited purview shaped such a deep lack of knowledge and understanding of experiences outside my own narrow life experience. This created for me, as I see it do for my students and peers, a kind of discriminatory myopia (Ravitch, Reflection Memo, October 18, 1994). This educational experience was so powerful that it induced a new kind of politically oriented empathy and radical compassion which helped me to work on cultivating my own critical understanding of the world through a lens of equity, structural racism, and intersectionality. This became the focus of my work as a graduate student and practicing school counselor and continues in various forms to this day.

Reflections on Re-indexing Experience and Imagining Forward

I have reframed notions of myself as a learner (and more broadly) by first identifying, and then working to understand, the range of ways that my learner self was understood and performed across contexts and key moments in my education. I believe that we are often unclear about our self-perception and self-presentation because we do not tend to see ourselves accurately in terms of how our social identities matter and play out, how our behaviors stem from our unconscious understandings of self, thereby leaving our unexamined parts and social constructions that we have internalized flapping in the proverbial wind. Through sharing these stories of moments and patterns of conflict and connection, I share ideas about becoming more conscious, thoughtful, and intentional about working to understand and story myself more accurately across relationships and contexts. The concepts of learning to re-story situations and re-index experiences serve as powerful tools for more intentional and healthy thinking and choice-making, for happiness and liberation from harmful social constructions and cognitive distortions that quietly rule our inner lives and, therefore, corrode healthy possibilities if not identified, explored, and thoughtfully attended to. Our emotional imaginations can help move us forward powerfully if we are attuned in intentional and generative ways.

I have learned the liberatory value of mindful engagement with my emotional imagination in relation to formative and ongoing life experiences—the positive and negative ones that have helped me to create my voices of shame, blame, guilt, and fear—in ways that help me to understand how to identify, listen to and actually hear, be curious about, rather than judgmental of, and to work through the parts of me, my self-talk, and my choices and behaviors that no longer serve me well, that are a part of old stories that have constrained me and made me feel afraid, less than, on the outside (Ravitch, 2020). I am always working towards a more spacious consciousness, a more deeply receptive sensibility that creates the conditions for me to engage my emotional imagination, to stand in my strength, with more clarity and kindness towards myself and those around me. With a spirit of possibility and an understanding that we can come to re-envision our own narratives—both internal and external—to rewrite our life stories with more possibility and agency, to reframe re-index our experiences, write new scripts for ourselves and others, and engage models and metaphors that are increasingly liberating, that help move us forward in our life-journeys with a fuller and more accurate sense of self. I work from this as an ethic and I work to create the conditions with my students for these things to play out. And I want to create the conditions in which my students have the opportunity to see themselves anew, pushing into social and familial and structural constructions of reality. The concept of post-traumatic growth—the growth that is cultivated by building inner resources and emerging stronger from our trauma experiences—has been powerful in my journey and is becoming foregrounded in my teaching in important ways.

This self-reimagination has radically shifted me as a person and educator—my pedagogy has changed significantly as a result of ongoing work on my perspective-taking skills and emotional clarity and health. This clearing work helps me to have the skills and insights necessary to be able to co-create the conditions for freedom of learning within inquiry structures, freedom in which we can co-build a thoughtful (if at times quiet) attention to mental health issues and trauma—individual and inter-generational—as well as to interpersonal issues such as group dynamics, transference and counter-transference, imposter syndrome and how it surfaces in groups, the imposition of White fragility and privilege, the ways that social class and caste play out in groups, and so on. It has only been through engaging in thoughtful, ongoing reflection and dialogic engagement on myself and my teaching individually and in community/ies that I've been able to realize the degree to which I've projected my own anxiety-ridden experience of K–12 through college and graduate school onto the experiences of the students I teach. In so doing, I am inaccurately interpreting them and their needs and wants and speaking to anxiety they might not even have: a projection of my deficit orientation towards myself cultivated in my early schooling years onto them, unknowingly. As a way to tell how I have come to more complexly understand, story, and re-story myself as a learner, I share critical moments from my educational experience—key pieces of an ever-evolving story about how my educational experiences shaped my sense of self, my sense of the (im)possibilities in my own life, my relationship to my own and others' trauma and mental health issues, and my understanding of the role of power and inequity in human dynamics and relationships as well as in relation to identity and intersectionality as it shows up in teaching, learning, loving, and living.

For me, this learning was about comprehending the power of social constructions, paradigms of thought, and educational socialization processes as central to how we come to view, understand, and story ourselves. The key is to learn how to more critically interpret what is messaged to us, both implicitly and explicitly, as we grow up and get schooled. In focus in my narrative is invisible anxiety (in its Jewish American urban Philadelphia cultural context of the '70s and '80s) and how that speaks to, as I re-story myself, the ways that mental health issues were ignored and overlooked within cultural familiarity and our specific cultural context. Looking back I see how this relates to the ways that culture-based gender scripts and expectations meant that my lack of academic or intellectual engagement never showed up or got addressed, not ever in my K–12 schooling (which is also in part generational as an almost 50-year-old woman in the United States). And further, how all of this is mediated by social class differences between me (first generation of women in my family to go to college) and the other kids at school (largely second or third generation college-going families with inter-generational wealth), was shame-inducing and deeply socially and academically marginalizing even within my own cultural identity group. Yet, as I see now, my White privilege meant that even with this academic neglect, I had a financial safety net as I figured out my needs, issues, goals, and so on. That is a deeply important mediating factor that cannot leave my consciousness as I teach about anything, since I teach from that social identity, and it matters to every way that I construct meaning in my courses.

Through these experiences, I learned about many important aspects of human development, including the role of projection and transference in life, and then specifically in teaching and learning. It is vital to recognize that, and how, people project onto us and each other based on biases and socially constructed beliefs and how we often internalize transferences and projections onto us in education contexts given asymmetrical power relations. We explore how socialization, tacit beliefs and assumptions, socialized axiologies, and implicit biases shape these experiences and how assets-based re-socialization is deeply liberating. I have also spent time reflecting on the lack of criticality about equity, identity, and deficit orientations in my own education and in the education of most of my peers, especially my White peers who did not get this learning at home or in their own educational experiences. Learning about criticality, social identities, and my Whiteness is a central part of cultivating a more critically conscious and authentic and humanizing and relational emotional imagination. This is at the heart of my personal and professional learning and development, and it has become central to the way that I conceptualize, design, and teach courses and do research, connect with my students, advise, and so on.

Engaging the Emotional Imagination in/for Critical Pedagogy

> Education either functions as an instrument which is used to facilitate integration of the younger generation into the logic of the present system and bring about conformity or it becomes the practice of freedom, the means by which men and women deal critically and creatively with reality and discover how to participate in the transformation of their world. (Shaull R., 2000, p. 31)

Freire's quote from *Pedagogy of the Oppressed* evinces the way that we each and together conceptualize education, teaching, and learning; it informs how we think about and develop the courses we teach and how we co-create the conditions for transformative re-storying to happen within the learning process. In this final section, we highlight some of the ways that our education experiences have shaped our current pedagogical stances, values, and approaches.

We see meaningful connections across our stories as we dialogically explore the horizontals across our experiences, such as the invisibility of ongoing, ever-evolving family trauma, our stealthy, conciliatory coping mechanisms and how these were gendered and raced, and how we continue to work to dismantle the belief systems and false narratives that lead us and our peoples to ways of being in the world that no longer serve us well as women (and perhaps never did). In sharing our stories of learning and of being storied as individuals, and of learning to re-story ourselves as learners and through the process of co-teaching a doctoral-level qualitative inquiry course, a new kind of embodied critical pedagogical understanding and connection has emerged in ways that reflect Muriel Rukeyser's (1968) words, "My lifetime listens to yours."

As a teaching team, we know the vital importance of living into this kind of critical-relational-listening as an ethic of our collaboration and as the driving force of our teaching and mentoring of graduate students. We work to move from re-storying ourselves as learners to co-constructing learning spaces for and with our students. This collective development process is based on the belief that co-constructed healing stories have the power to create durable learning through corrective experience and healing. We end with discussing how our styles and beliefs meet in our own graduate classroom.

For Janay, the central aspects of my teaching philosophy and approach include that:

- I must resist the notion that degrees and positions of institutional power confer expertise; as such, I work from the stance that we are all experts of our own experiences, as modeled by my mentors and extended to my students and mentees, and that expertise is vitally important to our learning community.

- I lead with critical care and intention to demystify the academy. I do so through being transparent wherever possible, including in the sharing of resources and by prioritizing building relationships first through a process of *shared vulnerability*, courageously being my most authentic self while inviting others to do the same (Pérez Huber, 2019).

- I resist the notion that knowledge should reside with me only, or that my thoughts are necessarily novel; I do so by offering to share resources, encouraging others to exchange knowledge/information, finding ways to extend knowledge creation beyond the academy, and seeking/initiating opportunities for our work to be collaborative.

- I aim with intention to highlight, center, and name the voices not reflected/present in our discourse and move towards thinking critically about what is missing and how it might currently shape our bodies of knowledge—this is done not just in discourse, but in course materials (like the syllabus or guest speaker invites), as well as my own self work as an individual, learner, and researcher.

- I actively practice and model "Affection, Correction, Protection" (Stevenson, 2014) in my discourse, feedback, and mentorship—this looks like seeking to understand students as a first measure, often through dialogical engagement, affirming *and* critiquing with care and protecting others through my actions as it relates to the learning community (e.g. confidentiality, addressing harm, advocating on behalf of students).

For Sharon, the central aspects of my teaching philosophy and approach include that:

- My teaching philosophy and approach is deeply embedded in pedagogies of critical hope, critical consciousness, and critical love (Freire, 1970; hooks, 1994, 2003) as well as radical compassion and loving kindness for each and all of my students (Richo, 2019).

- I work from the stance that everyone is an expert of their own experience which means that everyone has valid and valuable knowledge and, further, that we must disrupt knowledge hierarchies. In this paradigm, we are all teachers and learners who can constructively challenge and critique each other. This serves to interrupt traditional power dynamics and asymmetries including that we question the hegemonic codification of the academic texts we read and of expertise as a whole.

- I work from a view that the binary of "expert" and "learner" is based on a false Western construction that places knowledge above emotions and values. Conferring dominance onto so-called experts is an outgrowth of White supremacy in the United States, which must be disrupted. This includes actively questioning and disrupting taken-for-granted assumptions about hierarchies that situate epistemology over axiology, Western over all else, transactionalism over transformation. I teach how and why binaries are reductive as an entry point into broader issues of socially constructed valuations of knowledge.

- Taking an inquiry stance on my practice means that I reflect on myself in a range of ways that help me show up in learning spaces as a learner not a knowledge dropper or expert, it means that learning is viewed and approached as a meeting place of our beliefs and ideas as well as our knowledges so that we can de-construct and re-construct teaching, learning, and the socialized nature of knowledge together.

- I work from and speak about a multiplicity of locals, i.e., that local knowledge = local knowledges. This means that not only is local knowledge valid, but must be engaged and centralized in order to inform local discourses, policies, and practices. Moreover, local is not a monolith, there is always a range and variation of people in any group—this is an argument for, among other things, a critical and receptive understanding of intra-group variation (Ravitch & Carl, 2020).

- Course discussions must attend to a range of embodied understandings of intra- as well as inter-group variability and challenge socialized notions of diversity to resist essentializing people and groups. This is a component of emotional and cultural intelligence, which is equal in importance to other kinds of intelligence and which we need to question and develop in community with compassion and criticality.

- As a White, heterosexual, able-bodied, upper-middle-class woman, I position myself as a thoughtful, reflexive, and humble ally with BIPOC (Black, Indigenous, People of Color); I try to know my place and work with my power to validate and amplify non- and anti-dominant knowledges, value systems, points of view, and experiences without virtue signaling or reinscribing impositional and performative allyship.

- As a White academic with incredible social capital and power I must work to continuously interrupt and address racism, sexism, microaggressions, and deficit orientations with clarity, calm, and kindness (i.e., not shaming people so they can learn) while not tolerating bad behavior and White fragility (i.e., assiduously challenging discriminatory views and assumptions as they emerge in the group).

- I must address inequities and microaggressions that arise in a group of students during a course session *in the group* so that I model authentic rather than performative ally-ship in terms of being constructively critical and not being complicit by passing on my responsibility to intervene and teach. This helps to show and model how a White person can resist imposing and acting out our own White fragility (even through inaction).

- I work from a perspective that I, like White people in general, need to step back and do racial literacy work and identity-based learning on my own time and with proactive fidelity because I am attuned to BIPOC's being expected to do emotional labor for White people, the ways White people tokenize BIPOC in predominantly White spaces, and so on. This all stems from ongoing work on my racial literacy and the ways I try to teach racial literacy no matter what else I am teaching.

- There must be pedagogical attunement and sensitivity to a range of possible mental health issues, imposter syndrome experiences and projections, and trauma in any given classroom. That means that I need to understand trauma-informed pedagogy and to think of trauma complexly and contextually. Identifying and honoring the resilience and creativity of individuals and groups that have experienced trauma is vital as is including concepts of post-traumatic growth (Ravitch, 2020).

- We all misinterpret each other and are misunderstood all the time. Assuming this as a reality of life creates openings for self and relational understanding through consistently looking for how we misunderstand, engage in transference, and project onto others as well as how we impose expectations onto communication (Nakkula & Ravitch, 1998). I try to model this as a pedagogical approach in a range of ways including how I engage with students' questions to check for understanding.

- I teach explicitly in every class (no matter the course topic) about the importance of understanding how identity factors influence our misunderstandings of self and others. We do this by examining ourselves through the lenses of our implicit biases, prejudices, assumptions, and ideologies. This is key to understanding the layers of misunderstanding and projection in learning and life more broadly.

- Reflections on our implicit biases, relationship to intersectional systems of oppression, and social locations cause a reckoning with uncomfortable truths. Viewing discomfort as an impactful pedagogical tool for learning (Boler & Zembylas, 2003) is vital. Critical inquiry leads to the recognition that we all contribute to hegemonic constructions of difference, which can cause anger, grief, disappointment, and resistance. I have moved into a clearer understanding of pedagogies of discomfort and how and when they make sense and when they shut down learning. Shame is very real in many people's learning experiences past and present and so I am ever-attuned to this reality as the person with the most power in the room. Shame is never a productive emotion and so creating a classroom ethos free of fear of shame is vital as we endeavor to challenge ourselves and each other to grow and learn.

- I need to learn in each class, from each student, where I am missing the mark or overstepping or not speaking truth to power adequately. I open myself up to feedback in a number of ways. For example, I share that I am working on my ableist and non-binaried language and invite students to correct me even mid-sentence because I believe that words generate meaning and that I am harming people with the ways I falter on this as a role model, teacher, and researcher.

- Finally, and centrally, I have moved into working from a perspective on so-called safe spaces as an outstretch of White supremacy that becomes instantiated and normalized in groups and institutions. I believe in brave spaces as a way to re-create norms that are more organic and validating to everyone and less Whitewashed and violent to BIPOC (Arao & Clemens, 2013). Brave spaces refer to a set of communication and process norms that invite authentic, ongoing, and critical dialogue around issues that are challenging to discuss but are important for a group or organization's development. Brave spaces require leader bravery as well as ongoing modelling so that groups can discuss issues that live at the heart of education in ways that go a layer deeper than what is typically discussed given that these "safety" rules serve to uphold White male middle class values and norms of communication (Ravitch & Carl, 2019). We work to create Brave Space norms on the first day of class and ongoingly, and this is marked in a number of ways including in the course requirements on the syllabus.

We bring our individual experience, beliefs, and values to our approach as a teaching team. Our shared philosophy on the generativity of critical pedagogy and the importance of critical teaching and learning through a relational inquiry stance shapes the learning environment we co-create with our students and each other. We come together as a teaching team with an authentic and deeply shared desire to support students even as we believe we must challenge them to interrogate their own identities and positionalities in ways that can be trying and anxiety-producing but, ultimately, we believe, liberating. In the course, we work to create conditions where we are positioned as and can experience ourselves as experts and learners, which extends from our shared axiology, and which opens up new kinds of learning for us as well as the students.

Our course has an expressed focus on equity and identity formation at the systemic, social, interpersonal, and psychic levels as well as its enactments within the course. As one example, we work to intentionally integrate the research of scholars and practitioners of color in course readings and with speakers as well as within weekly course discussions and assignments with a focus on how identity, values, and macro and micro-sociopolitical and socio-economic forces and contexts shape research. As another example, we work to create the conditions in which we and our students can share thoughts, ideas, feelings, and the work of individuals and communities that are marginalized and essentialized in ways that speak to academic and broader hegemony in order to interrogate this together. And we work assiduously to develop and amplify the ideas of all of our students, whom we see through an asset-based framework. Our stance on power dynamics and brave classroom spaces works to undo certain positions and impositions of power; it interrupts and rearranges our relative positions of power in many ways, which allows us to lean into our respective knowledges and experiences with ease and to model a receptive sensibility and a specific kind of agentic kindness and compassion.

Re-written on the Mind

Written on the Body re-imagines love without the socially constructed registers of gender identity, gendered roles, and gendering norms. To interrupt cognitive and emotional hegemony, i.e., the ways that our hearts and minds—our emotional imaginations—are colonized by constructions of gender, Winterson (1994) not only reimagines, but importantly entirely re-stories love beyond the socially constructed binaries that constrain human conceptualizations and experiences of love. This exegesis of the emotional imagination is apt given our deep rootedness in Freirean and hooksian theory, wherein love is central to the pursuit of education for critical consciousness, of individual and collective liberation. As Freire (1970) imagines it, "[L]ove is an act of courage, not of fear, love is a commitment to others. No matter where the oppressed are found, the act of love is commitment to their cause—the cause of liberation" (p. 97). For us, pedagogical love and the emotional imagination come together in the storying and re-storying of ourselves, each other, our students, education, and the world—critical pedagogy, at its heart, is about a love of humanity that pushes us forward through embodied questioning and through shared re-writing on the mind with critical hope.

References

Anderson, R. E., & Stevenson, H. C. (2019). RECASTing racial stress and trauma: Theorizing the healing potential of racial socialization in families. *American Psychologist, 74*(1), 63.

Arao, B. & Clemens, K. (2013). "From Safe Spaces to Brave Spaces: A New Way to Frame Dialogue around Diversity and Social Justice." In Lisa M. Landreman. Sterling (Ed.), *The Art of Effective Facilitation: Reflections from Social Justice Educators* (pp. 135–150).VA: Stylus Publishing.

Ashkenazi Jews. The Hebrew University. http://hugr.huji.ac.il/AshkenaziJews.aspx.

Boler, M. & Zembylas, M. (2003). Discomforting truths: The emotional terrain of understanding differences. In P. P. Trifonas (Ed.), *Pedagogies of difference: Rethinking education for social justice* (pp. 10-136).

Cochran-Smith, M., & Lytle, S. L. (2009). *Inquiry as stance: Practitioner research for the next generation.* New York, NY: Teachers College Press.

Collins, P. H. (2002). *Black feminist thought: Knowledge, consciousness, and the politics of empowerment.* New York, NY: Routledge.

Delgado, R., & Stefancic, J. (2001). *Critical race theory: An introduction.* New York, NY: New York University Press.

Ohito, E.O. (2020). Some of us die: A Black feminist researcher's survival method for
creatively refusing death and decay in the neoliberal academy. *International Journal of Qualitative Studies in Education*, DOI: 10.1080/09518398.2020.1771463

Fontanella-Nothom, O. (2015). *Teacher perspectives on raising issues of race and racism when educating young children.* California State University, Long Beach.

Freire, P. (1997). *Pedagogy of the heart.* New York, NY: Continuum.

Freire, P. (1970). *Pedagogy of the oppressed.* New York, NY: Continuum.

Gorski, P. C. (2019). Fighting racism, battling burnout: Causes of activist burnout in US racial justice activists. *Ethnic & Racial Studies, 42*(5), 667-687.

Gutiérrez y Muhs, G., Niemann, Y. F., González, C. G., & Harris, A. P. (2012). *Presumed incompetent: The intersections of race and class for women in academia.* Boulder, CO: University Press of Colorado.

hooks, b. (2003). *Teaching community: A pedagogy of hope.* New York, NY: Routledge.

hooks, b. (1994). *Teaching to transgress: Education as the practice of freedom.* New York, NY: Routledge.

Kedar-Barnes, I., Rozen, P., Shohat, M. & Baris, H.N. (2008). Genetic disease in the Ashkenazim: Role of a founder effect. John Wiley and Sons Online Library.

Khalifa, M. (2018). *Culturally responsive school leadership.* Cambridge, MA: Harvard Education Press.

Nakkula, M.J. & Ravitch, S.M. (1998). *Matters of interpretation: Reciprocal transformation in therapeutic and developmental relationships with youth.* San Francisco, CA: JosseyBass.

Pérez Huber, L. (2019). Moving beyond ethicality: Humanizing research methodologies with
Undocumented students and communities. *UndocuScholars Policy and Research Brief Series.* University of California Los Angeles.

Pak, K. & Ravitch, S.M. (2021). *Critical Leadership Praxis.* New York, NY: Teachers College Press.

Ravitch, S.M. (2020) Flux Leadership: Leading for Justice and Peace in & beyond COVID-19. *Perspectives on Urban Education.* Special Back-to-School Pandemic Issue. Fall 2020.

Ravitch, S.M. (2020) Flux Pedagogy: Transforming teaching and leading during coronavirus. *Perspectives on Urban Education, 17*(4). 18-32.

Ravitch S.M. & Carl, N.M. (2020). (2nd Ed.) *Qualitative Research: Bridging the Conceptual, Theoretical, and Methodological.* Thousand Oaks, CA: Sage.

Ravitch, S.M. (2020). "Storytelling, relational inquiry, and truth-listening." BlogPost Sage MethodsSpace, March 2020.

Ravitch, S.M. & Carl, M.N. (2019). *Applied research for sustainable change: A guide for education leaders.* Cambridge, MA: Harvard Education Press.

Richo, D. (2019). *Triggers: How we can stop reacting and start healing.* Berkeley, CA: Shambhala Press.

Rilke, R. M. (2001). (A. S. Kidder, Trans.). The book of hours: Prayers to a lowly god. Evanston, IL: Northwestern University Press.

Rukeyser, M. (1968). *The speed of darkness.* New York, NY: Random House.

Shaull, R. (2000). Foreword. In P. Freire, Pedagogy of the oppressed 30th anniversary edition (M. Ramos, Trans.) (pp. 28-34). Continuum. (Original work published 1967)

Solórzano, D. G., & Yosso, T. J. (2002). Critical race methodology: Counter-storytelling as an analytical framework for education research. *Qualitative Inquiry, 8*(1), 23-44.

Solórzano, D., Ceja, M., & Yosso, T. (2000). Critical race theory, racial microaggressions, and campus racial climate: The experiences of African American college students. *Journal of Negro Education*, 60-73.

Stevenson, H. (2014). *Promoting racial literacy in schools: Differences that make a difference*. New York, NY: Teachers College Press.

Winterson, J. (1994). *Written on the Body*. New York, NY: Vintage International.

Part II

Border Crossing

5

The Stories We Carry and the Ones We Let Go

Casual Carcerality in School Settings

Melissa Kapadia

This is a story I carry with me. I tell it repeatedly. It is central to who I am. *I'm smart, but I was never good. I made it out, but I wasn't supposed to.* This chapter is about the stories we carry and about what is needed for us to let those stories go. It asks, in what ways do education spaces shape our narratives about ourselves as learners and as people? What roles can educators play in helping us to unlearn the stories we have carried?

Educational Autobiography

I Was Never a Good Student

I learned that I was a bad student fairly early in life. I was born an Indian citizen in the United Arab Emirates. A product of an interfaith marriage, I began my life with many teachers and many self-stories. I attended two different Indian schools in the UAE, but truth be told, I was not the most engaged young student. I moved too slowly through my homework. I often completed it poorly. I brought home bad report cards. I was flighty, day-dreamy, disengaged. From my recollection, my brothers were "smarter" and "better" students than I had been. I was a disappointment in a variety of ways. In the collective family memory, I was a "kind" and "gentle" kid, but I was not "smart" or "quick."

Despite this, my literacy and learning life at home was quite rich. My mom had taught us to read and write before we entered pre-school. My parents took us to the library to borrow comics and books. We listened to a lot of music as a family, exploring many genres and vocalizing our individual tastes. We had a keyboard at home, on which I learned to play and eventually to make music. On weekends, my dad made blank booklets out of printer paper for us to turn into zines. This life was so vastly separate from the one I had at school. It's unclear to me if I felt fragmented then, or if it is only through memory that those worlds seem fragmented to me now.

There is a story I have been told many times by my mom about my bringing home a bad report card on my fifth or sixth birthday, and being punished for this with a slap in the face. In retrospect, it's unclear to me if I was as devastated then as I would eventually become by the knowledge that I was "stupid" and "slow," and a poor student. I have no deep recollection of what I felt then, just that this was an idea that was reinforced by my teachers, my mother, and my siblings. I am sure I knew what words like "stupid" and "slow" meant. I am sure I knew they weren't good.

These designations, though linked to school performance, became markers of my full being. That brings me to a primary truth I hope to thread throughout this chapter: schools are carceral spaces (Wun, 2017).

At the most fundamental level, we know this is true because we live in a carceral world. What I mean by this is that we live in a world that likes to punish. Broadly, carcerality is the belief that a person who does not fit within social norms—or what Annamma (2015) has described as an "unwanted body"—deserves punishment for their poor fit. And so, when I say schools are carceral spaces, I do not mean to imply that they are more carceral than others.

Families, for example, can also be carceral spaces. When a child gets punished for a bad report card, their parent is extending the carcerality of one institution (school) into another (family). When I was punished for my poor grades at that very young age, it confirmed and validated a story I was already familiar with by that point: *I was never a good student.*

We moved to the US in 1991, when I was in the third grade. Although not without its own set of challenges, our new school, an international elementary school, was a place where I thrived. In the fourth grade, my teacher introduced us to journaling, and so from that point on, I began to record my experiences and feelings—and my journals, spanning from 1993 to the present day, are archival resources I can now use to trace the origins and trajectories of my self-stories.

Critical Moments

As I began to plan for this chapter, I thought about critical moments in my education and, interestingly, carceral moments with specific teachers stand out to me so clearly even after all these years. So, here, I tell the stories of three critical incidents that shaped my experiences in schools and my understanding of educational spaces as carceral ones.

MRS. T was my third grade teacher. She was the first teacher I had in the US. Our class was filled with young immigrant students from a variety of places and with many different levels of English language proficiency. Somehow, I became Mrs. T's star student. She loved me and I liked being the teacher's pet. I was obedient, gentle, and a proficient English speaker, despite being very fresh off the boat. At the same time, Mrs. T did exhibit some problematic behaviors, many of which came from her lack of knowledge of cultural norms or practices beyond the US. For example, she didn't know that Indian students tend to use alternative spellings that derived from British English, so my spellings of certain words were simply deemed "wrong" without any clarification or nuance. That said, she was known as quite a successful teacher, who had a positive impact on countless students. And I was slowly becoming an excellent student, not just in my academic performance, but also in my moves to assimilate to American expectations: by the end of that year, my Indian accent had been masked by a practiced American one; by the following year, my legal name would be changed to Melissa.

Many years later, Mrs. T retired and the elementary school, which was celebrating a milestone anniversary, decided to honor her with a teaching award. By then, in my early 20s and a newlywed, I planned to attend the celebration with my then husband. We drove about two-and-a-half hours to my old school. We were young and wore bright, mismatched clothes. At that time, I was fat and had pink hair. Although I didn't expect her to remember me, I was excited to see Mrs. T after so many years, to tell her about the impact she'd had on me, about my plans to pursue a doctorate, and about my work as a community educator.

But when we saw each other, Mrs. T was rude to me and my husband, and wouldn't make time to talk with us. I can't know her reasons for doing this. It's possible Mrs. T was overwhelmed by all the students who had come to see her. It's possible that she was aging and embarrassed by her bad memory. It's also possible that in her mind, a fat person with pink hair did not fit her idea of a model brown person and that I no longer presented as a "good student" in her eyes. Then again, maybe the look she gave us wasn't one of disgust, as we had read it. Maybe it was something else entirely. For me, this interaction was a reminder that no matter my prior role as Mrs. T's "star student," I could not maintain that "good student" status.

MS. J. In the seventh grade, I had a Social Studies teacher named Ms. J. She was odd and geeky, but vibrant and very silly—as a teacher, I imagine I probably resemble her much more than any other teacher I've had. She had a nervous rambling quality that I, too, have developed as an adult. Unlike my international elementary school, the middle school in this area used a tracking system. By this point, I must have been a high-achieving student and had tracked into the "Accelerated" classes in my grade. This meant I was no longer in classes with my neighborhood friends, but was primarily in all-white classes with students from a higher wealth background than mine. I imagine my accent, name, and tracking placement also well-disguised my immigrant status.

Ms. J began every class period with a quiz. On this particular day, the quiz was about US mountain ranges. I knew nothing about US geography or mountain ranges, but this was the day Ms. J called on me. When I told her I didn't know the answer to the quiz question, she responded, "Of course you do." And we had a very awkward back-and-forth in which she insisted that if the answer wasn't such-and-such mountain range, it had to be something else that I must know. I insisted I didn't know. My classmates, many of whom were my friends, were silent, avoiding any engagement with this uncomfortable back-and-forth. I was embarrassed and ashamed. The two years I spent in this school and in those classrooms were marked by many moments just like this one. Despite being marked as a "good student" via the tracking system, I experienced near constant shame and feelings of unpreparedness. I was plagued by reminders of my "stupidity" and a constant awareness that everyone around me knew I was "too stupid" to be in class with them. This particular moment was a reminder to me of the precariousness of my "good student" status: it took just one moment of seeming unpreparedness to remove that identity.

But Ms. J definitely didn't want this. In fact, she must have realized at some point that it was very likely a student who had only been in the country for three or four years may not have ever received a lesson on mountain ranges. At some point later that year, she approached me and asked if I had any interest in sharing with my classmates some facts about my home country. Accepting her invitation, I brought in pictures, coins, and other artifacts from the UAE, which I shyly shared with my classmates, answering questions while being filled with nervousness that this would be another moment showcasing how little I knew. Ms. J was gracious, encouraging, and engaged through my presentation. In retrospect, it's likely that this was a critical incident for Ms. J as well.

MR. B AND MS. M. In eighth grade, I was again the new kid, this time in an even wealthier school, though one in which there were many kids of color in the higher tracks. Ms. M was a young teacher (possibly a student teacher) who was co-teaching a half-year elective. Ms. M was friendly with some of the students in the class; it was clear she knew them, either through family or through synagogue. One day, some students were loudly making fun of my clothing, which was clearly cheap and not branded. Ms. M overheard them and giggled along, winking at them.

Later that same year, I had forgotten a worksheet at school one evening, and asked a friend if we could work on the homework together over the phone. She agreed. Our plan was to talk through all of the questions together and collaborate on the answers, which she would write down and I could copy onto my worksheet at school the next day. We had both enjoyed the reading and had fun doing the assignment together. The next day, Mr. B saw my friend and me in the lunchroom together. He grabbed my worksheet out of my hand and scolded me for "copying someone else's work." When I tried to explain that we had worked on the assignment together the night before, he dismissed me, loudly and publicly embarrassed me in front of others in the lunchroom, and walked away. Later that day, in Ms. M's class, I had no worksheet to hand in, and I received a zero on the assignment.

I'm not sure why this last incident sticks in my mind. By that point, I was firmly settled in the narrative that I hated school and it wasn't for me. Maybe I remember it because even though it wasn't for me, I had enjoyed the assignment and was excited about the work before being reprimanded for "cheating." I don't think I felt ashamed or stupid this time; I knew I had done the assignment and I felt good about the answers. What I was feeling was abandonment, the knowledge that people assumed the worst of me, and the frustration that I was being removed from engaging in an activity or conversation I had been excited about. In other words, in prioritizing rules and punishment, Mr. B had taken away an opportunity for me to engage and learn with my classmates.

The Work of Retelling

Retelling these incidents is not particularly healing for me. Even years later, a teacher myself now, I feel a familiar shame and frustration when I write these stories. These were moments in which I wasn't "good enough." At the same time, these stories do not necessarily define my education narrative. My experiences with schooling have also been lovely, revelatory, engaged, and positive. So, I wonder, is there some freedom in telling these specific stories? Does writing them down help in letting them go? Or does putting them in print and allowing them to be read by others only make the shame more real, and make the above statements more true? Don't they confirm that ever-present story, that I was never a good student?

If so, what does it mean to be a bad student? Are bad students also bad people? Are bad students even bad learners? Or are bad students ones who don't fit with social expectations of students in a particular learning environment, "unwanted bodies" in a system that would work better without them? Who dictates those expectations? This is at the heart of carcerality. When social spaces, cultural environments, schools, teachers, and other students craft norms around student expectations, students who enter those spaces without meeting those norms are automatically punished, often simply for being who they are.

This broad reading of carcerality may seem to overlook or devalue systemic carcerality and the use of schools as systems to enforce it; salient examples in recent US history include reservation schools (Crow Dog, 1990; Lomawaima, 1993; Margolis, 2004), conversion camps (Johnston & Jenkins, 2004), and the school-to-prison pipeline (Alexander, 2010; Wald & Losen, 2003; Wun, 2017). These are tangible, violent, and legal ways that schools and teachers have reinforced systemic carcerality. My intention here is not to devalue the impact of systemic carcerality but to point to the ways that carcerality behaves as more than simply a practice; it is a mindset and a belief system, one often so invisible to enforcers and recipients alike that we forget that it is absurd to be punished simply for existing. And it is equally offensive that our first response to any kind of breach of social norm is punishment. When education spaces default to punishment, they reinforce a broad culture of carcerality.

So, when I write that schools are carceral spaces, I am thinking both about their important role in upholding and supporting formal institutions of carcerality and about their roles as purveyors of casual, everyday carcerality. The casual ways that schools shame and punish students shape students' sense of self; these daily practices support the creation of self-stories that are guided by carceral belief systems. It is inevitable that these self-stories and critical moments can cause students to go through schooling with many levels of fear and lack of trust. If these are the primary feelings students experience when in education spaces, students are less likely to experience education spaces as ones in which they can thrive, experience success, or feel free. Those stories we carry may become integral to who we believe ourselves to be, but many of them also put us in an ongoing battle with schools, which is especially harmful when schools are significant determiners of our future success.

How Do We Teach in Carceral Spaces?

My practice as an educator has been shaped by a deep and well-developed dislike for education spaces. I understand, of course, that teachers are human and imperfect. We bring our own biases and trauma into the classroom; and we are products of our cultural, familial, and national environments, shaped by the ideologies of those worlds. So, it's inevitable that I, too, have enacted everyday carcerality and created circumstances in which my students have felt shame, mistrust, and a lack of safety. If schools are carceral spaces, then teachers become enforcers of carcerality, whether conscious or unconscious, and both systemic and "casual." Given this, a question that has dictated the bulk of my experiences as an educator is: how do I make this space less carceral for my students and for myself?

Reading the work of Mary Crow Dog and bell hooks has helped me to imagine the potential of education spaces as ones that engage learning as a practice of freedom. Both Crow Dog (1990) and hooks (1994) have described their early learning experiences (which took place in community environments) as ones that engaged their whole selves, helped them build relationships with community members, taught them key cultural values and practices, and reinforced their individual worth and value to their communities. These learning experiences took place early in their lives. For Crow Dog (1990), this was her experience in her Lakota community prior to being moved to a government-mandated Indian boarding school[1]. For hooks (1994), this was her experience in a segregated Black school prior to being moved to an integrated, predominantly white school.

Both writers have described the ways education spaces were intrinsically tied to their sense of self. When educators were community members interested in children's lived experience and well-being, the practice of learning brought with it a kind of joy and freedom. When educators were people who viewed children as "other," education spaces became carceral: the children's home languages, physical appearance, world views, personal experiences all became markers of their innate carcerability. Learning, let alone joy, could no longer be prioritized by the children because they had to focus on self-protection. They had to focus on survival. The history of formal education spaces is marked by their violence; in the US, this violence has primarily been directed toward Black and Native students, queer and trans students, students with disabilities and illnesses, and undocumented students.

Educators must take as a premise that our students have experienced education spaces (and likely family and community spaces) as carceral ones. This is only further emphasized by institutional carcerality, i.e. students whose identities (racial, citizenship, gender, and so on) are treated as criminal in the broader institutional landscape experience carcerality as an inherent part of their daily existence (Wald & Losen, 2003). If education spaces are inherently carcer-

[1] Although field and popular discourse are currently moving away from the term "Indian" and toward terms like "First Nations" and "Indigenous," I use "Indian" here with respect to the author's voice and historical accuracy. Notably, Mary Crow Dog (1990) uses the term "Indian" as a self and community descriptor in her writing, as has been common among activists in the American Indian Movement (AIM). Further, Indian boarding schools were government-mandated and not established or supported by Indigenous communities.

al, our jobs as educators (or mentors, or leaders) is to create spaces in which students are not treated as devoid of past trauma or shame (Dutro, 2013). We must assume that students bring with them harmful self-stories that other education spaces have reiterated, validated, and confirmed. If our goals are to create spaces in which those who are learning from or with us can feel safe, make mistakes, and pursue liberation, we cannot ignore the ways students' prior education experiences have created barriers not only to their current learning but also to their very ability to exist as their whole selves. We must not take for granted that schools have enforced a value model that forces students to measure their own worth as intrinsically tied to their education performance, at times stripping them of any external value or personhood. This is a heavy burden for students to bear.

We must take as a further premise that by virtue of our positioning as teachers, we are an extension of the carceral hand. Even on our best days, when we have built significant trust with our students and have shown them that we see them as complete and flawed human beings, even when we have shown them our own flaws and struggles, we still represent authority and we must not take this representation lightly. This means that no matter how much work we do to de-carcerate our education spaces, our opinions of our students (or their perceptions and beliefs about what we think of them) will shape and reinforce the stories they carry about themselves.

Knowing this, we can never view education spaces as ones that are welcoming or nurturing just by virtue of their existence. That is not the objective reality of education. It would be dishonest and a disservice to students who have been traumatized from their time in education spaces. Nor can we view education as a simple practice of learning new things from people with expertise (Freire, 2000). That is not actually the job of educators. To assume this would be to treat ourselves, our students, and our learning spaces as one-dimensional.

If we take the work of teaching (and its intrinsic ties to the violent histories of schooling) seriously, education should be about unlearning the things that have harmed us. Education as liberatory practice asks us to let go of the stories we have carried. As educators, our primary objective should be to help our students excavate these harmful self-stories, commit to the lifelong work of letting these stories go, and craft new self-stories that will serve them in their personal work, work that goes beyond the confines of the classroom.

Critical Reflection: Where Do We Go from Here?

I have struggled to identify as a teacher because of the story I have carried from a very young age that schools simply aren't for me. How could a person be a teacher when they had never been a good student? That said, as a lifelong learner, imagining education as the practice of freedom has been a liberating process—the idea itself seemed to confirm so much of how I'd experienced learning in my own life: schools were places of trauma where I could do nothing right; and yet outside of schools, I was learning and creating constantly. Here, I share a few brief explorations that have reminded me of the importance of committing to work that (a) considers casual carcerality and harm as inevitable parts of the human experience, (b) takes the challenge of education as liberatory seriously, and (c) attempts to offer spaces in which people can unlearn or let go of the harmful self-stories they carry.

Challenging Carceral Norms

Naming one's positionality can be particularly useful in classroom spaces; in activist spaces, for example, meetings can often begin with introductions that include naming one's access needs. So, as a chronically ill and immunocompromised person, my naming practice likely began out of necessity rather than out of any kind of intentional pedagogical plan. However, once I began teaching college freshmen, I realized that their living in close quarters and resultant increased likelihood of illness meant I had to begin my classes with warnings about my being immunocompromised. Naming the potential harm they could do to me and my health shifted the responsibility of wellness into one of collective community care.

Because of this initial warning, students became comfortable asking questions like, "How's your health?" Similarly, they became comfortable sharing their own health and access needs. Naming my illness meant they could name theirs, and they could ask for accommodation. Over time, I have noticed that these initial conversations have led to students being more open about their needs regarding mental health, chronic illness, and learning disabilities. When my students and I are open about our access needs, we are rejecting the ways that schools as carceral spaces punish disability, illness, and difference. This is not a perfect system, but it poses anti-carceral possibilities.

Possibilities for Collective Unburdening

Given my earlier descriptions of schools as unwelcoming spaces, it should be no surprise that testing this philosophy and integrating it into teaching practices has been easier to do in out-of-school spaces. In my 20s and early 30s, I began to organize in leftist Asian spaces, including creating workshops and learning series that centered pan-Asian American experiences. Some of these learning environments were collaboratively built with the goals of exploring non-hierarchical learning and engagement. As queer, feminist, and anti-carceral spaces, these learning environments challenged educators and learners to confront not only individual trauma but also collective trauma. Creating learning experiences for high school-aged immigrant youth dealing with school violence, queer South Asian and Indo-Caribbean youth, and Asian American women has helped me to rethink and re-envision the possibilities for community healing; it has further opened up conversations about collective carcerality and the ways that community learning can offer us opportunities to unburden ourselves of false stories together.

These Stories Never Leave Us; This is Ongoing Work

As a writing coach, I have often been hired by private clients who are well-established professionals returning to school for advanced degrees. These people hire me for support in learning how to write for their fields and programs. The work is traditionally very individualized, focused on specific writing and reading competencies. Because of the ongoing nature of this work and the one-on-one learning environment, I end up bearing witness to a significant number of harmful self-stories, sometimes ones the students have never told anyone.

In the early days of doing this work, I was often surprised by what I heard. These were successful people, well-established in their fields, earning significantly more than I was in my profession, and yet they carried harmful beliefs about themselves that were shaped by experiences they'd had in elementary school. For example, one client believed she was a terrible writer because of a third- or fourth-grade teacher, who had told her she would never be good at grammar. Often, these clients retell these stories in such a matter-of-fact way because the stories have become intrinsic to who they are. They often warn me that they will frustrate me: "I've heard great things about you, but I want you to know, I'm simply not a good writer. Please don't think it's your fault if I never get better."

The work here is not to make a better writer; it's to help the student unlearn the idea that bad writers exist, and eventually, to unlearn the personal narrative that they are bad writers. This is painstaking work, and it should not be taken lightly. At times, when I observe my students—if I'm lucky and they give me a glimpse at their whole selves, I can see that none of their harmful self-stories are true. My work involves so much effort in supporting their unlearning, and I am so focused on that goal, that I at times forget to acknowledge how painstaking *their* work is. Whereas I am tasked with supporting their unlearning, they are tasked with the actual labor of unlearning. And that work is brutal and unending.

In Closing

As educators, if we are serious about making learning spaces "safe," we cannot pretend our biases don't exist, nor can we pretend that the world is not a deeply biased and harmful place. We cannot treat our classrooms as pristine and devoid of pain and hurt, or places where students are supposed to leave their worries at the door. By the time our students get to our classrooms, it is likely they have received some negative messaging about themselves as learners or as people. It is likely that they bring shame into their classrooms. It is likely that we perpetuate this shame, or create classroom environments that are breeding grounds for pre-existing shame. This should be an ongoing focus for educators in every setting.

It is important to note that educators do not have the right to students' stories. In my classes, I am happy to open spaces for sharing, but I am also adamant that sharing is not a requirement. Participation grades should never be based on the amount of personal stories shared because pedagogies that center healing should encourage students to *excavate*, that is, unearth for their own benefits; they should not ask students to *share*, that is, unearth for others' benefit.

Initially, I had written that when it came to harmful self-stories, there was nothing our students could not heal from. However, this concept does not apply to teachers' inevitable role as purveyors and enforcers of systemic carcerality. Students whose identities are treated as criminal and students who are most affected by institutional carcerality require our protection. So, while we can forgive ourselves for the times in which we've defaulted to carceral thinking, our work cannot focus on self-forgiveness; it must focus on protection and harm reduction.

While many of our classroom behaviors and belief systems are deeply embedded, our commitment to unlearning them must include relieving ourselves from our own carceral mindsets. This requires that we invest energy into excavation. We have to keep asking ourselves: How do I craft spaces of healing; how do I perpetuate trauma (including systemic trauma); and what do I need in order to heal from my own trauma (in other words, what do I require in order to let my own harmful self-stories go)?

References

Alexander, M. (2010). *The new Jim Crow: Mass incarceration in the age of colorblindness.* The New Press.
Annamma, S. (2015). Disrupting the carceral state through education journey mapping. *International Journal of Qualitative Studies in Education, 29*(9), 1210-1230.
Crow Dog, M. (1990). *Lakota woman.* Grove Press.
Dutro, E. (2012). Towards a pedagogy of the incomprehensible: Trauma and the imperative of critical witness in literacy classrooms. *Pedagogies: An International Journal, 8*(4), 301-315.

Freire, P. (2000). *Pedagogy of the oppressed*. Bloomsbury.
hooks, b. (1994). *Teaching to transgress: Education as the practice of freedom.* Routledge.
Johnston, L.B. & Jenkins, D. (2004). Lesbians and gay men embrace their sexual orientation after conversion therapy and ex-gay ministries: A qualitative study. *Social Work in Mental Health (4)3*, 61-82.
Lomawaima, K.T. (1993). Domesticity in the federal Indian schools: The power of authority over mind and body. *American Ethnologist, 20*(2), 227-240.
Margolis, E. (2004). Looking at discipline, looking at labour: Photographic representations of Indian boarding schools. *Visual Studies, 19*(1), 72-96.
Wald, J., & Losen, D.J. (2003). Defining and redirecting a school to prison pipeline. New Directions for Youth Development, *99*, 9–15.
Wun, C. (2017). Not only a pipeline: Schools as carceral sites. *Occasional Paper Series, 2017*(38), 1-5.

6

Snippets from a Nomadic Educational Autobiography

Talar Kaloustian

The Big Picture

Mine is a complicated educational autobiography: I attended nine schools in five different countries (six different cities) by the time I was 18 years old. I lived through war, experienced constant interrupted schooling, faced multiple new languages that were not my native one, and all while dealing with a family situation that would seem odd to many—but was the only normal that I knew—in which I saw my father just a couple of times a year. And no, I was not an army brat. And yes, identity crisis is my middle name. And thank goodness, we had a good sense of humour and were able to make light of rough times. Before getting into the nitty-gritty of my educational trajectory, I must explain what education stands for in my family.

One constant (among very few others) that has always governed much of my family's direction, decisions, status, and standing is that *we* are an *educated* family. Being educated, and the very field of education itself has been my family's *habitus* (Bourdieu, 1990) for centuries, a symbol of hope, a pathway representing freedom. Bourdieu's *habitus,* "a durable, transposable system of definitions" (p. 53) is initially acquired in the home by a child as the result of the conscious and unconscious practices of the family, and continued throughout the child's schooling in primary, secondary, and tertiary educational institutions. In other words, a habitus is the way of thinking that includes lifestyle, values, dispositions, beliefs, expectations, history, and memory. According to the many stories my parents told us, we—my two older sisters and I—came from a long line of educated people. People who, against all odds, had made it through school and even university, despite being persecuted throughout history. My grandparents, having survived the Armenian Genocide, went on to earn masters and doctoral degrees in the fields of education, literature, and linguistics; they garnered love and respect from the thousands of students they taught; my great-grandparents, as well, attended schools and placed great value on the freedom that education could provide; all of my aunts and uncles have multiple degrees and hold professorship positions in higher education; my parents were able to complete their primary schooling and bachelor's degrees in the midst of not one, but *two* wars that ravaged Lebanon. In continuing the tradition of this defining family characteristic, education, both my older sisters and I hold doctoral degrees. We have mostly lived an upper-middle-class life on a middle-class budget, but our monetary wealth was not our worry: we had that education ace up our sleeves and that would open up doors for us.

I guess I have always felt, or rather known, that we have value of some sort, a status, because we come from a long line of degree-carrying *heroes*. Our entire way of being embodies our history, a history of people my sisters and I had never met but whom we were taught to hold in the highest esteem. The profundity of Bourdieu's explanation of habitus as "… the active presence of the whole past of which it is the product" (Bourdieu, 1990, p. 56) is very much a part of the narrative of our lives. Our degrees have always been and still are our currency, and our education, our reputation. Our ultimate capital. This is how I internalized it, and still do, albeit it with some conflicted feelings about my arbitrarily random good fortune to have been born into this habitus.

A Quick "Educational Background"

As I noted earlier, mine is a complicated educational autobiography. War in Lebanon was the primary reason for the many moves in my earlier years, back and forth between Lebanon, Cyprus, and Saudi Arabia. Subsequent moves were often randomly decided upon, and these I delve into as I walk you down parts of my educational memory lane. But through it all, Beirut was the home

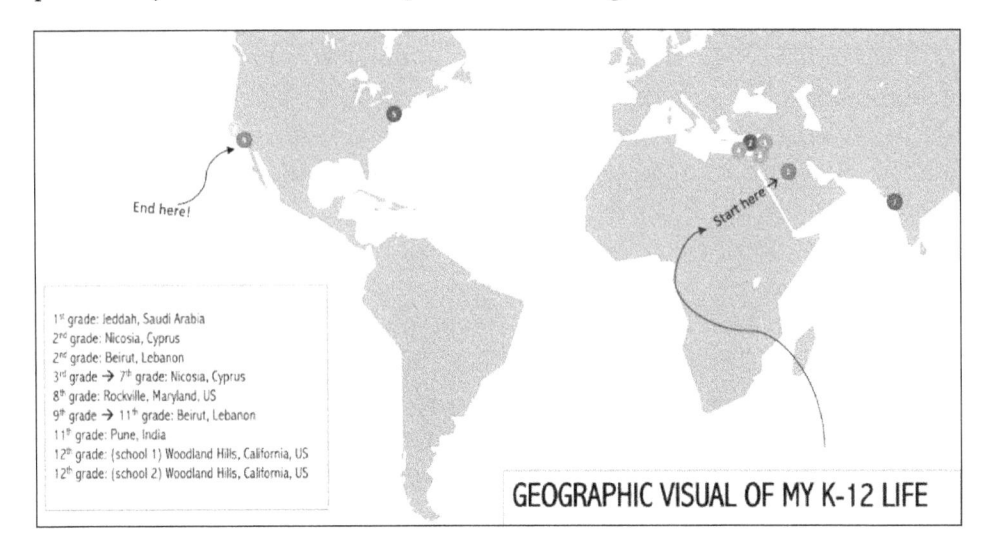

1st grade: Jeddah, Saudi Arabia
2nd grade: Nicosia, Cyprus
2nd grade: Beirut, Lebanon
3rd grade → 7th grade: Nicosia, Cyprus
8th grade: Rockville, Maryland, US
9th grade → 11th grade: Beirut, Lebanon
11th grade: Pune, India
12th grade: (school 1) Woodland Hills, California, US
12th grade: (school 2) Woodland Hills, California, US

GEOGRAPHIC VISUAL OF MY K-12 LIFE

base, the homestead, the force whose pull never weakened. No matter where we lived—and at one point, each of my family members lived on a different continent—we held Beirut in our heads, our minds, our hearts, in our very being, as the center of our universe.

Now, a visual of my geographic movement until I graduated from high school. Hopefully, this will serve as a helpful reference as I reflect on the critical educational moments that have impacted me in my journey thus far.

Let me note that this background is key to even my investigation into my educational trajectory and the events that shaped me. As I have reflected on my schooling over the years, what I have realized is that my K–12 experiences shaped me first and foremost as a student, second as a researcher, and third as a teacher. The running theme of "new school year, new school" on an almost yearly basis made me an excellent student. I knew how to start anew. I knew the value of reading instruction, reading social cues, reading culturally defined facial expressions; I knew how to interpret intonations and body language. This must have been a survival strategy, to survive all the newness. I suppose, now, that I was a qualitative researcher without even knowing it. It was not a rarity for me to start my new school in the middle of the school year, or a few weeks into the new term, but I would eventually thrive in each new academic setting grades-wise and time and time again friends-wise. I could always look like I knew what I was doing by purposely imitating what "locals" were doing. Graduate school taught me that all those years, I was engaging in legitimate peripheral participation (Lave & Wenger, 1991) in a *new* community of practice on a regular basis; I would start at the periphery of any given community as a newcomer, and eventually make my way to the heart of the community, quickly taking on the role of "old timer" and, in fact, even contributing to the cycle of inviting in and initiating new members. Graduate school also taught me that I was building up my funds of knowledge (Vélez-Ibáñez & Greenberg, 1992)—all the experiences, skills, knowledge, and world views that would help me navigate the new communities I was being thrust into.

Moments that Impacted Me (K-12)

Nicosia, Cyprus: Six years old, going on seven

By the age of six, I had already attended four different schools in three different countries. I had already experienced being the "new" person so many times. Still, all I wanted was to fit in—something a little bit impossible to do when nobody around me (except for my family) was like me culturally, linguistically, and in so many other ways—and even then, with my wildly different schooling from my sisters', I felt different from them, too. Even our accents in English are different from each other's! I've just always constantly aware of being *really* different and internalizing that different-ness as lacking.

According to Dewey (1916), a primary function of a school is to serve as "an escape from the limitations of the social group in which [one] was born, and to come into living contact with a broader environment" (Dewey, 1916, p. 24); I revere Dewey's work and regard him as one of the greatest educational thinkers/philosophers of all time; I agree with him that "the adult" educator must help the "immature" student by intentionally creating an environment for the student to learn in different ways. In my case, however, the "beyond the limitations of the social group [into] which [I] was born" was an ever-shifting landscape—country-wise, language-wise, weather-wise, you name it; it was confusing and left me feeling incomplete. More than that, since I always felt like I was playing catch-up, I was left with the feeling that I would never "arrive," that I would always be a step behind.

One of the first times I experienced this in a visceral way—this feeling of incompleteness, this feeling of not being good enough—was when I was about to begin attending a British school in Cyprus called Falcon School. I look at this as a critical educational moment because it set the educational expectation tone—in terms of what others expected of me, and what I expected of myself—for the rest of my academic life. We had just escaped the war in Lebanon for the second time, halfway through my second grade. I finished out the year, and I must have taken a placement or entrance exam of some sort at some point because I remember having to do summer school; apparently, I was very much behind in Math and English. Big surprise. And yet, it *was* a big surprise, a surprise filled with acute shame. I remember feeling an agonizing shame every day that I went to summer school to catch up on Math and English. I came from an educated family, and here I was, failing at the most basic of subjects, so much so that I needed to actually go to summer school? What about my heritage? Wasn't academic success in my actual blood? How did it come to this? How was I suddenly in a remedial summer program? Was there something wrong with me? As it turns out, such a thing does not have to signify the end of the world. Through conversations with my sister who is in the field of early childhood education, I've since learnt that it is not at all uncommon for children with interrupted schooling to experience "behindness" (my own made-up word) and overall gaps in education: the terminology for this is *students with interrupted formal education* or SIFE (Decapua, 2010).

SIFE refers to a situation in which a student's education is interrupted during the school year due to several factors such as civil unrest, war, and migration. Check, check, and check. Unlike many categorized under SIFE, however, I was not the first in my family to go to school, or graduate from school. We had stable family income that allowed for a private school education with my lovely teachers to private music lessons. I did not fit the "typical" SIFE profile and as far I recall, my behindness was not ever explicitly explained away by the geographic instability. But in my six-year-old mind, I must have advanced the hypothesis that I was greatly lacking, and I vowed that I would never allow myself to be relegated to such a position again, geographic instability be damned.

Rockville, Maryland: 12 years old

The next critical point in my education was not so much a moment as it was a transformative period. After I finished seventh grade in Cyprus, my family made the unexpected decision to move to the US—or rather to just stay in the US when we had been visiting with relatives one summer. I went from a small, British private school, which all in all, from Kindergarten to Seventh Form (sort of like 13th grade) had around 1000 students (if that), to an enormous public middle school that had triple the number of students in only three grade levels. I was to be in the eighth grade. The stark contrast between Falcon School in little Cyprus, and Julius West Middle School in the greater DC area was blinding.

As much as I had seen in the world at the tender age of 12, this was completely foreign territory to me. I had just had a relatively stable five years in one geographic location, in one cozy little school (and even until today, I have not lived in one place for more than five consecutive years. Cyprus was the last time I had that type of stability, and thank goodness I have at least that). Now I was on a different planet: thousands of lockers, an enormous campus, hundreds of students wearing their hair in so many different ways, wearing make-up, wearing flips flops—flip flops!—and oh my goodness, the uninhibited loudness. Students were loud. Teachers were loud. The gym was loud. The cafeteria was like a scene from a movie, a space buzzing with student chatter and an excited energy: with rows of tables filled with students of all races; with a lunch line where students could get pizza, hotdogs, burgers and fries; with teachers walking around, keeping the peace; with loud fliers for school events plastered all over the walls; with nasally announcements made over the PA system. So many sounds and colours that stimulated all my senses. I was coming from a private school where I had worn a uniform; where I had worn my hair in a specific way with no colourful scrunchies or anything (hair ties and the like could only be black, or the colour of our hair as my headmaster very matter-of-factly made clear to me when she caught me with an orange hair tie once); where make-up was not allowed; where recess was spent at a small tuck-shop; and where flip-flops had *not,* under *any* circumstances, been allowed. Such a visual and aural messiness was antithetical to the neat discipline that I was socialized into, not only in my school world, but as well in my home world (my father's unfortunate obsession with perfection is the umbrella under which my mum, sisters, and I had to operate, even while he lived in an entirely different country, and even with our contact with him existing mostly as a phone call here or there). Kapadia (2020 from this same section in this book), in reading an earlier draft of this chapter, put forward a critical question here: In what ways do school and home cultures socialize our ideas of what school is/who we are/how we should be when we're at school? This is a surprisingly obvious question, and yet, I had never given much thought. It is something that I will explore going forward, but suffice it to say, my educational habitus was always changing, always throwing me curve balls, engulfing me into new communities of practice, new ways of socialization. On the other hand, my home habitus remained almost static in terms of our priorities—family first, school second, music third. It also remained static in terms of expectations of "respect" toward anyone older than you, with "respect" never being defined beyond "no talking back to your elders;" "no challenging the word of your elders;" and "do what you're told to do."

So, back to Julius West—clearly, I was in shock: culture shock (Agar, 1994). In the literature, culture shock has been identified by many names: *acculturative stress* (Berry, 1997), *intercultural stress* (Ward, 2001), *language shock* (Agar, 1995), and *culture fatigue* (Oberg, 1960). Sam and Berry (2006) delve into the nuances of all these different terms, but essentially, culture shock is a negative experience in the process of one's acculturation. No matter the terminology or the stages—I was definitely in a new and uncomfortable state of being. The biggest shock of all was the power dynamics between adults and kids, specifically between teachers and students. At the time, what I saw was a lack of deference—that "respect"—on the part of students toward their teachers; what I mean is, the way teachers and students interacted with one another was quite different from teacher–student interactions I was used to. I saw an attitude in students, an individualism that I had not before experienced. They seemed brazen and unabashed, speaking to teachers as though they were adults themselves, "talking back" to teachers, and challenging "the word of our teachers." Now, I am not sure if this is the transitional age at which such a thing happens, or if it is cultural—at the time, it was simply so shocking to me that I just attributed it to culture.

Later on in my life, as I began my work in intercultural competence and pragmatics, the focus of my doctoral dissertation, I came across Hofstede's (2009) famous (or for some, infamously reductionist) cultural dimensions, one of which is power dynamics, what he calls the power distance index (PDI). This is defined as "the extent to which the less powerful members of organizations and institutions (like the family) accept and expect that power is distributed unequally" (Hofstede, 2011, p. 8). This perspective toward cultures—looking at them through the lens of ranges resonated with me enormously and immediately took me back to my days at Julius West. I always assumed younger people were inherently less powerful members of any group because that is what I grew up with in my home, and in all the schools that I had attended up until that point. But from my 12-year-old eyes, I saw far less of a hierarchy. Despite my shock, or maybe as a result of it—I'm not entirely sure—I suddenly became "brazen" myself in the way that I made conversation with the principal on the day that he walked me around the school. The principal was walking *me* around the school, not walking my mum. I was being treated like an adult! In all of my former schools, I had been socialized in a strictly hierarchical system that did not necessarily show appreciation or give value to younger voices (although, maybe they had and I'd been too preoccupied to notice?). In any case, at Julius West, I learned to thrive. Similar to Neddeau (2020, Section 1 of this book), who had to navigate between different cultural roles, I can say that I began developing nuanced expertise, with the ability to "mov[e] between differing situational rules or procedures," joining the "brazen" culture at school, and falling back into "different" culture mode at home.

Maybe because I had never seen such a robust library; maybe because I had the opportunity to learn the trombone, the bass, and the bass guitar; maybe because there were so many resources that I felt like a kid in a candy store; or maybe because I was a fascinating foreign little oddity for the teachers who took an interest in me—whatever the reason, I learned to find my voice for the first time, to indulge in my many interests, and to shine as my bloodline had intended for me to do. Something inside me had clicked. At the age of 12, going on 13, despite the initial shock of the move and the dramatic lifestyle change, I experienced an academic confidence that quite possibly carried me through the next several radical environmental changes that I lived through. So for that year at least, there was no more behindness for me. I'd arrived.

Beirut, Lebanon: 13 years old

One short year found me in Beirut again. This was yet another unexpected move. The Maryland move was planned for the long term, but family circumstances and ongoing financial setbacks led us back to a home that was ours. In a city that was ours. Beirut. It was just my mum and me. My sisters were in college, my dad was in Saudi Arabia, things had calmed down in Lebanon, and a quick decision was made to move back to the homeland. These three teenage years were wonderful, and I can write entire books about the impact they had on me, my friendships, my music, and my academics. What stands out most from my three years at Broumana High School, though, was the relationships that I forged with my teachers—Ms. Massad, Mr. Habib, Ms. Karen, Ms. Houda, Mrs. Nasr: their dedication to my educational pursuits and success is a critical point in my journey. These are the teachers who recommended that I apply for a prestigious scholarship to a United World College (UWC).

In brief, the United World College mission is to bring young minds from all over the world together to champion peace and intercultural understanding. At the time, there were only 10 UWCs, and a student selection committee had been formed in Lebanon; one of the committee members was a teacher at my school, Mrs. Nasr. While I had never had Mrs. Nasr, as one of my teachers, we knew each other, and she, together with a few other teachers, took the time to prepare me for the application and interview process. It is important to note that at the time, we did not have college counselors to help us through any such process—these teachers went above and beyond in their quest to prepare me for the rigorous application process. I will never forget the kindness that these teachers offered me, taking the time to give me feedback on my statement of purpose; staying after school to do mock interviews, checking in with me to ensure that I felt prepared for the multiple rounds of interviews ahead of me. Together with mine, their efforts paid off: of the four scholarships being awarded to Lebanese students that year, I was awarded the one to attend Mahindra United World College of India (MUWCI, informally referred to as "myoo-kee"). These teachers not only contributed to my confidence as a young adult, but they also literally shifted my educational trajectory from remaining in Lebanon to going on an adventure in India.

Village Khubavali, Pune, India: 16 years old
At MUWCI, I existed in a state of warring self-beliefs: the first, that I was more than prepared for this rigorous academic work, that I had been armed with all the things I needed to manage the workload, live away from my mum, develop friendships among the 200 16-to-20 year-olds from over 75 nations, on top of a mountain in the middle of nowhere, and to be the top of my class. The second self-belief was that this was too much for me, that I was no longer the big fish in a small pond, and that I would never fit in with all these geniuses around me. I

represented my country, Lebanon, but I barely spoke the national language: I believed I was a fake. Even during our campus football (soccer) "World Cup," I supported the North Americas team, and not the Middle East team. And the third belief was that by hook or by crook, I would make it. I knew myself, I knew how to learn, I'd had more life experiences than anyone at that age, and a national committee had chosen *me* out of hundreds of other Lebanese students. I have had such warring self-beliefs at other stages in my life. Still, it was not until I was well into my 20s that I learnt about the psychological phenomenon called imposter syndrome, that feeling of "incompetence" and of "deceiving others about one's own abilities" (Langford & Clance, 1993). And come to think of it, I wonder if this was what I was fighting against as a six-year-old girl in pigtails, going to summer school in Cyprus. While I am sure that the imposter inside me grew insidiously over the years as a result of hundreds, if not thousands of small moments that easily generated self-doubt, it felt to me that I was always just shy of "having arrived." Even after my "thrive-ful" (my own made-up word again) year at Julius West under my belt, moving again to Lebanon, and then again, this time to India, I felt exposed and vulnerable. I retook up the war with that imposter within me as I tried to disguise it, overcome it, and rationalize it away.

One space at MUWCI where this tension within me felt so raw was my English Literature class. This is the critical moment I focus on here. I was 16, going on 17, and my teacher was 22: a young woman from England with uninhibited energy, a winning smile, and a youthful sincerity. Charlotte was phenomenal. There were maybe nine other students in the class with me, and together, we crushed it (thanks fam, for teaching me that phrase). We read, analyzed, critiqued, and rebelled against several non-traditional (for high school) books that year with Charlotte at the helm: we read Manuel Puig's *Kiss of the Spider Woman*, about two cellmates in an Argentinian prison; we tore apart Garcia-Marquez' *Chronicle of a Death Foretold*, marveling at the inevitability of the death, and the clever non-linear telling of the story; we argued over Sethe's attempted murder of her own children in Toni Morrison's *Beloved*. It was a life-altering course. Charlotte valued every single one of our opinions, views, and insights; she worked with us in creating knowledge and instilling confidence. We poured over texts, carefully weighing the evidence to support our views, and she would acknowledge, dissect, and challenge our stance. She encouraged off-the-beaten-path thinking, pushing us to voice our dissents.

I will never forget the day when we were reading *The God of Small Things* by Arundhati Roy, and in an expression of protest against the very idea of love laws, we ended up on our feet, chanting loudly, "Fuck! The! System! Fuck! The!

System!" over and over again, righteously banging our fists on our desks, and shamelessly making our feelings known to anyone within earshot. The course was liberating. Charlotte was allowing us to exist in a realm that I, at least, had never known. A realm where the refinement and decorum that to me *defined* education was altogether thrown out of the window (there is that changing educational habitus again). What a thrilling wave I was riding. I remember going back to my room after class and thinking to myself, "Am I in a cult? Should I be here? Is this actually school? Do I belong here?"

Along with the exhilaration, though, I felt a sense of revulsion. I felt like I was too good for this space. The world of teaching and learning I had known had no space for four-letter words. But, perhaps I was being let in on something that only the enlightened knew? I didn't know if I was the imposter anymore, or if the school was the imposter, if my teacher was the imposter, or if my peers were the imposters. I was all over the place—I even felt guilt for being someplace I was sure my parents would disapprove of because of this unmannerly, this crass incident. This was just such an entirely different version of the educational habitus they or I had ever known.

As it turns out, there is more than one way of "doing school," and banging my fists on a table, shouting out obscenities was one. Cue Freire (1998), not in terms of the obscenities, but in terms of a dialogic pedagogy that allows for a construction of knowledge and individual growth through unjudged interactions. This incident revealed a new way to view "education," one in which judgment is antithetical to the very essence of learning. On that day, a seed was planted. A seed that would eventually grow into a sort of subconscious guiding light in my role as a teacher, that education is the act of creating a safe space that frees minds of inhibitions, with the ultimate goal of generating growth in knowledge and confidence in both learner and teacher.

Los Angeles, California: 17 years old

Due to personal reasons, I was unable to complete my two years at MUWCI, and one short year later found me in Los Angeles for my senior year of high school. I moved in with my oldest sister who had just relocated there herself, and I embarked on yet another journey. Here, the critical educational moment was actually a critical interaction with a principal that impacted my entire senior year. I was at my ninth school in the unexpected position of attending a tiny Armenian school in San Fernando Valley ("the Valley"). I started about three weeks into the school year, and if Charlotte at MUWCI had taught me to embrace rebellion, the teachers at this little school pretty much quashed my zeal for any growth, let alone any tendency to push boundaries.

To begin with, even my attending Manoogian-Demirdjian (an Armenian school in L.A.) as a senior was problematic for the school; the principal met with me and tried to kindly, if not condescendingly, explain that he would not advise me to attend the school since I was brand new, that he feared I would not fit in with all the students who had known one another since Kindergarten. Let me reiterate that this was *the principal* who was trying to push me away. The principal's words scared me—if this school didn't take me, what would end up happening to me? The desperation I felt resulted from the weeks leading up to that day. Prior to attending the Armenian school, I had enrolled at a local high school; when the counselor at the public school saw that my transcripts were from countries like Lebanon and Saudi Arabia and India, she claimed that she was unable to confirm the integrity of these documents and promptly changed my status to ninth grade. (Interestingly and confusingly, Mrs. Kassem was married to an individual from Lebanon, so I sort of thought she would have my back. But no). I was almost 18 at this point. My mum and I scrambled for about a week, and I was all set to attempt completing four years of high school in two years by attending the public high school's ninth grade, and taking as many night courses at the local community college as possible—but then, magically, the Armenian school came into the picture.

So, here is what I was grappling with: I had left my school in India under less than pleasant circumstances, I was not seen as a legitimate senior at the public school, and I was not welcome at the Armenian school, among my very own people. Challenge accepted.

In a one-two punch, my mum name-dropped her father's—my grandfather's—name, Onnig Sarkissian, one of the great educators at this very school. This "benevolent"[1] principal did an about-face mid-sentence and accepted me into the school. My mum, the daughter of one of the most beloved educators in the 1950s–1970s Armenian community, had never name-dropped anyone before, ever. Name-dropping was not the way for people of our educated class: merit was; hard work was. But we had reached a desperate point. The principal had me arbitrarily write an essay about an arbitrary topic, "My Best Friend," to ensure that I could write a coherent essay in the English language. He finally "allowed" me to take an AP English class, but any other higher-level courses were out of the question because I was a new senior, and he was "unsure" about how I would handle the environment.

Once again, for the ninth time I had to do this whole song and dance to prove myself credible, trustworthy, and respectful, and this and that and here and there. The culture shock, again, was exhausting. This was a different cul-

---
[1] A little word play – the organization behind this school is called AGBU: Armenian General Benevolent Union.

ture shock though: I had just left an incredibly liberal and progressive school in the middle of nowhere, where 200 kids (their parents and families in faraway lands) had ruled the school. I was about to start the new school year in a small K–12 Armenian private school, where students had known each other from Kindergarten and most social events at school were Armenian-centric. Students had to wear uniforms and act "respectfully" (the definition that I was taught growing up) toward their teachers and parents. It was a small community where everyone knew each other. So, I had to prove myself. And prove myself I did, both academically and socially, while also working after school and over the weekends. I took only one AP course on a probationary period of three months before I could be trusted to handle this course—English literature—and the rest of my courses lacked the challenging content I craved; they included Astronomy (for those students who couldn't hack it in Physics), and basic Armenian for heritage speakers (who couldn't be trusted to take a higher language level). At the end of the year, I took *several* AP exams despite my preparation and did famously. I say this because I still sometimes feel the need to prove myself. I did it and I did it in spite of the restrictions that were placed on my learning. Doing well in these APs was my *Pretty Woman* "BIG mistake" moment. It just ate at me that I *wanted* to take more challenging courses, I *wanted* to study and excel, I *wanted* to learn! And I had the capacity for all of it.

The powers that be—one sixty-something-year-old individual whose decision-making capacity I seriously question—decided to put me in my place. My place was a "lower" standard. My place was supervised, a small box, the outside world of which I was not privy to. Why? Because I was a new senior in a school where *everyone* had known everyone *else* since they were toddlers, or at *least* since eighth grade. Because I was an unknown. Because I was starting a new school during senior year. What blasphemy! I still don't get the logic. Are your students, or worse yet, your teachers not able enough to know how to deal with—gasp!—a new student?

Why this is such a key moment in my educational trajectory has to do with the impact it had on my confidence. It singlehandedly undid years of self-motivation and confidence-building. I began to lose the war to the imposter within me. Was I really of such little value that I wouldn't even be welcomed into a school filled with my Armenian brothers and sisters, a school that is meant to represent the unity of the Armenian people, the Armenian Diaspora? I should have been invited to join the school merely based on the fact that I am Armenian: after all, this was an Armenian General Benevolent Union (AGBU) school, built to unite and assist the 11 million Armenians living outside of what is today Armenia, the Armenian Diaspora that was cultivated as a result of genocide, of holocaust. How the principal—*the principal*—tried to turn me away was deeply hurtful. Where was the kindness that so many of my teachers had shown me over the years? Where was the burning fire to reach students, teach and nurture them, and watch them grow? Why was I not important enough? And was I just not Armenian enough? Over the next eight or nine months, I just kept telling myself that it would soon all be over and I would start afresh in college.[2] Indeed it did end, and I was able to start afresh, but this time on my terms.

Moments that Impacted Me (post-K–12)

My educational trajectory after high school continued taking all sorts of unexpected twists and turns. I will spare you another map, but suffice it to say, it was just as geographically "exciting" as my K–12 years. The main difference between my K–12 life and post-K–12 life, however, was that I was able to exercise far more agency than I had ever been able to before in deciding where I would go, what I would study, and how I would achieve the goals that I set for myself. In a recent therapy session, I think I may have come to a new realization: that unfamiliarity was the only familiar I knew, and I sought it out relentlessly.

San Diego, California: 18 years old

My undergrad years were incredible. This entire period in my life is such a critical one due to the way in which it empowered me and rebuilt my confidence in myself. Unlike before, nobody singled me out to question my academic credentials or ability; I had the freedom to take whatever courses I wanted to take; I took part in any extracurricular activities or projects that I wanted to take part in. Unlike in my home life, or in a couple of my previous schools, I was in a realm where I could exercise *a lot* of agency. The imposter remained, but it was a lot quieter than it had been in a while.

At the University of California, San Diego, the weather was always perfection, we were on a quarter system, and the world was my oyster. It was like my utopian educational habitus. Our tuition policy was an excellent one: pay for up to four classes per quarter and take more if you wish to *for no charge*! I took full advantage of this situation. Since we were on the quarter system, I was taking at minimum, 16 courses a year. Sure, some of them were "easy" music performance courses, for example, but I was living it up taking so many courses, double-majoring, minoring, studying abroad in Paris and Cambridge,

---
[2] I should add, here, that despite my disappointment about my academic life, I had some lovely, kind and funny teachers; also, my social life was wonderful. It is thanks to my close-knit group of 6 friends that I am still close to (and one of whom walked me down the aisle!) that I was able to find enjoyment in my final year of high school.

doing a DC internship quarter, working at the campus gym and various other offices, and having a blast. To me, *this* was what education was about. It was about growing and being allowed to grow—I hit the ground running with that growth. I was acculturating myself into this new environment; I was engaging in a way that mattered to me; I was participating in a meaningful way (Bochner, 2006; Cook, 1970; Dewey, 1916; Menard-Warwick, 2005).

My efforts were paying off; I was being recognized for my good work, both academically and professionally. On graduation day, I led the graduation march, and my role model Dean of Student Affairs, Ashanti Houston-Hands, honoured me with a speech about my accomplishments. Most of all, I was proud to be recognized in front of my parents, my sisters, my friends, and my professors. I was continuing my ancestors' and family's tradition of academic excellence. This moment represents a personal victory, and I still turn to it when the imposter within me even tries to rear its ugly head.

Prague, Czech Republic: 22 years old

After completing my undergrad, I went down an unexpected path once more: I moved to Prague with just a few dollars in my pocket to teach English and "find myself." I had changed my mind about going to law school, and instead found that I wanted to continue exploring the world. I took a month-long *Teaching English as a Foreign Language* (TEFL) course to be a part of the force that brought the post-Cold War Czech Republic into the privatized and English-speaking world of business. Pete, our TEFL instructor, was one of the greatest teachers I'd ever had in any subject until that point, and more intense than any teacher I had known; he gave teaching his *all*. His whole facial expression, body movement, focus, and drive were magnetic. This chain-smoking, Keith Richards lookalike absolutely reinforced my belief that teaching is about the student. What he taught me, though, was how a teacher's unflinching commitment to nurturing his student makes space for a student to respond in kind and give *her* all.

Here is what I mean. Pete was tasked with teaching us a language that was new to us all: Japanese. The goal was to demonstrate, through active modeling, that a student could learn the target language even when the teacher only used that target language to communicate. In other words, he was allowing us to experience total immersion in a way that many of our future students would also be experiencing. Not once in our weekly sessions did Pete use English, and yet we learnt so much. He used every resource he could; he drew pictures, repeated words, pointed at himself, pointed to students, made intense eye contact, jumped and ran around class, got in our faces, used gestures to elicit responses *in* Japanese from us, handed out sheets with pictures and words in Japanese—and our exasperation at not having "control" (in terms of understanding what the hell was going on) did not dissuade him one bit. As awkward as it got with Pete pretending not to understand what we were saying in English, with him getting in our faces, trying to hold our gaze, making us contort our mouths into unfamiliar shapes, eventually that awkwardness simply did not matter. He knew that as long as he kept putting in all the sincere effort that he was putting in, we would eventually get it. And we did. My friends Sutko and Allison and I still use those Japanese phrases with one another a decade and a half on. And he was kind, too. He hung out with us, gave us his time, his tips, his advice not just on the topic of teaching English, but also in general, about navigating Prague. Each of us had just moved there and none of us knew the language or the streets or anything. He was there for us on more than one level. Intense, sincere, funny, kind guy.

I have carried Pete's teaching with me ever since that course. My students most likely think, at least initially, that I am a nutcase because I am just as intense in the classroom as I remember Pete being. I know of some of my students' first languages, and that can certainly come in handy. Still, for the most part, I do not suppress my fervor for achieving connection and understanding through my physical, theatrical, and linguistic antics. There need be no suppression; my goal is to reach the student.

Philadelphia, Pennsylvania: 25 years old

I never knew that my career would take me down the teacher path. I did not even know that there was such a thing as a master's degree in TESOL—Teaching English to Speakers of Other Languages. I ended up on this path, though, when I felt the need to reevaluate my life goals after being rejected from several political science master's programs (poli sci focusing on international relations had been one of my majors). When I discovered TESOL, I jumped at it because I knew that I had so enjoyed teaching English in the Czech Republic.

One of my first master's courses, Sociology of Language, was taught by Anne Pomerantz, my future dissertation chair and one of the best teachers I have ever had. It is here that I experienced a critical shift in my understanding of my own identity. Mori's (1997) *Polite Lies: On Being a Woman Caught between Two Cultures* opened my eyes to a whole field on identity crises. In her memoir, Mori describes one identity associated with the Japanese language, and an almost opposite identity associated with the English language. She is able to make a clear distinction in her two identities based on language. Up until this course, I had felt as though I were a cultural fraud: if anyone asked me where I was from, I would say I am Lebanese—and I would be thinking, "but my Arabic is by far the weakest of the languages that I speak, and I am not even Lebanese by blood. Plus, I had only really lived in Lebanon for six years."

Other times, depending on audience, I would say I am Armenian. Still, my linguistic repertoire (Gumperz, 1965) in Armenian—the ability to communicate in various contexts e.g., academic language, informal language—is limited to the social linguistic scape. I can converse with family in Armenian about topics like movies or chores, but not about politics or religion. And even still, I find the need to throw in words, phrases, and discourse markers from other languages. How about claiming I was Armenian? I had only been to Armenia once in my life. So, I could say I am American? After all, I had lived in the U.S. more than any other place (if you added up all the time I had spent in Maryland, Los Angeles, San Diego, DC and Indiana) by the time I was in my master's program. English was my "best" language, but if you heard me talk, you would think I was pretending to be something or someone I am not. I have an unidentifiable accent that I have been told sounds Irish, British, French, Greek, and who knows what else. I also get a lot of, "Oh, so I sense an accent? Where are you from? What languages do you speak? How do you know English? How do you speak it so well? Where did you learn it?" And frankly, I do engage in linguistic accommodation (Giles, 1991) sometimes with purpose, and others without realizing, so that does throw a little wrench into people's calculations about the origins of my accent and all the assumptions that come with not being part of the dominant and "Standard" accent. I imitate accents. Without necessarily meaning to. But it does also happen to be one of my party tricks. Could I claim I am Cypriot, because nowhere else had I lived for five straight, stable years? And because my childhood home is Cyprus? Then again, I don't speak Greek at all (apart from a few words), although I do feel very much at home when I hear Greek, or people speaking in Greek, or people speaking in English with a Greek accent! (And yes, I do realize I am complicit in the generation of assumptions that are entirely based on accents I hear. What can I tell you? I'm a walking contradiction). There is no place for someone of my mixed up, meshed identities, in this equation. Language knowledge is competing with geographic movement; geographic movement is the competing perceptions of me; perceptions of me are competing with my identity; and full circle, my identity is competing with my geographic location.

When I began writing a reaction paper to Mori's memoir, I think I finally started realizing that I did not *have* to be bound by linguistics or geography, or any other prescribed imagined communities. I realized that I could pick and choose and live out my identity with no justification. This was indeed a critical moment in my educational trajectory. For so many years, I had felt like I did not have a clean framework within which to build and proclaim my identity; but now, I was learning, I had the power to develop my *own* framework. I did not have to settle for a pre-defined category of identity. I could create my own. I had become empowered with a choice of identity.

Philadelphia, Pennsylvania: 26 years old
A final critical educational moment that I must share occurred during my doctoral studies. The lesson came not from a professor or a book, but one of my very peers. To cut a long story short, I learnt that one of my cohort mates did not think me a suitable partner for group work because, as I later found out, "English isn't even her first language." While it pains me to have to include anything about this individual in my writing, I must do so because it is at that moment that the identity I had created and proclaimed for myself crumbled. (Such a fickle thing, confidence, and how unkind the mind). It appears that the empowerment I had felt was still rather weak and vulnerable to even the most inane utterances. I have, thus far, spoken quite frankly about what education has meant to my family and me, and how it has sown what I can only call a sort of elitism within me—although, let it be noted that the elitism was never directed at others, only toward myself (this logic works for me right now). I only held myself to what I believed were important standards in my family, history, and imagined history. I had struggled with believing myself to be worthy. And somehow, hearing about a comment like this from a peer was blindingly hurtful. I cried for days by myself. It was almost as if this individual had summoned the imposter from within me. I guess I had assured myself that at least within the realm of the "educated world," I would be safe from such ignorance. I just never would have believed that someone at this point in their studies, at an ivy league school, and at the Graduate School of Education at that, could embody such a high level of ignorance.[3] Kapadia (2020, Section 2 of this book) and Taylor (2020, Section 4 of this book) in reading one of the first drafts of this chapter, talked about the low-visibility acts of exclusion all around us, which in my opinion is a scary level of discriminatory practice due to its seemingly innocuous nature. This is one but one example of this precise concept.

When I started my doctoral program, I had some insecurities about how I would be perceived in terms of my ability to converse in a "code" that was unfamiliar to me, a code not in terms of a language that could be categorized as English, French, Arabic, Hindi, or Czech, but rather in terms of a language

---
3 In the end, by the way, I ended up doing my project with my best friend Nina; with Nina, I felt not one ounce of inferiority, only empowerment, because she is just that cool.

of author's/researcher's/scientist's names, educational philosophies, guided research, eras in pedagogical orientation, and so much more. I was acutely aware of my lack of knowledge of pretty much anything in anthropology, linguistics, educational pedagogy, qualitative research, you name it, and I do know that I held back in my classes initially that very first semester.

That was one of the first times in a long time—perhaps since my last year of high school—that I felt that special kind of lack of control; it is the type of "control" that has to do with familiarity or lack thereof, where the newness, without delay, triggers that adrenaline—a rush that both invigorates you and paralyzes you with self-doubt. The imagined imposter within me was back. But after spending weeks, if not months, brooding over my perceived humiliation, I reasoned and acted the imposter away. I did what I had already done many times in new communities of practice: I read instructions, I read social cues, facial expressions, and body language; I learnt to identify rhetorical moves in the texts we read, and I emulated them. In other words, I imitated what the locals were doing in the same way I had done as a six-year-old in Cyprus; the same way I had done as a twelve-year-old in DC; a thirteen-year-old in Beirut; a sixteen-year-old in India; a seventeen-year-old in the Valley; an eighteen-year-old in San Diego; a twenty-two-year-old in Prague; a twenty-five and twenty-six year old in early grad school; and still in many more moves that I have not even mentioned here. I observed like the good researcher that I had become purely as a result of the need to adapt and survive, and even thrive. I have kept that imposter at bay, but it is still there, lurking. And while I used to think that that was a bad thing, Reynolds (2020, Section 4 of this book) noted in an earlier draft of this chapter that *her* imposter kept her on her toes. I am now learning to see my inner imposter as a check on the actual Talar; an ally—but one to be reckoned with.

Teaching Philosophy

As detailed above, my life has been largely shaped by exposure to cultures and languages that are different from my own: my life experiences have greatly shaped the manner in which I relate to people—culture—and interact with them—language. Perhaps unsurprisingly, in the classroom, my life experiences also shape my teaching philosophy that emphasizes openness, a solid organizational structure that is flexible to change as needed, a genuine air of mutual respect, understanding, and most of all, kindness. I want my students to experience and feel pride; and I want my students to feel confident and worthy. My ultimate goal is to contribute to my students' intellectual growth and personal development—particularly as it pertains to confidence and independence—and strengthened communicative skills, no matter where they are and who they interact with. For me, as Mark Van Doren states, "the art of teaching is the art of assisting discovery (1959)." I see this sentiment echoed by my peers throughout the chapters of this book as well.

Learner Goals

In striving to meet these goals as a teacher, I am not unaware of my students' own goals. Often, these revolve around the explicit pursuit of high grades that rest on the consumption of knowledge. While recognizing that pursuit of high grades is a common goal—as I was socialized in a system of rewards and punishments, be it in the form of grades, degrees, or publications and rejections—I place emphasis on students' a priori knowledge and unique personal experiences when building on course content. Being open to and recognizing my students' funds of knowledge helps me create a meaningful learning environment. I am very much a disciple of Dewey's constructivist approach. For example, I implement reflection and expectation assignments at the beginning, middle, and end of a term in all my classes. This tool helps illuminate what students already know, while also demonstrating to the students that I value their background and their needs. Ultimately, like Charlotte, my English teacher in India, I seek to impart a sense that I am willing to give my students the space they might need to comfortably communicate their thoughts, fears, and expectations related to their own learning goals.

Having already related some of the key moments in my life as a student, my teaching approach probably comes as no surprise. I spent so much of my early childhood, pre-teen, and young adult years trying to prove myself as worthy, or at least as merely having *some* value. No one really asked me, though, how I felt, what I thought, what I expected, what I wished to do in terms of school and schooling. That was very much the case not only in school, but also at home. As I think back now, on my years as a student, I realize that this was probably a cultural thing, not only in terms of the teacher teaching the "empty vessel" paradigm (Piaget & Cook, 1952) adopted in the majority of K–12 education and college education learning institutions around the world, but also in terms of my family culture. With my parents having to endure the realities of war and geographic dislocation, there was no space to ask us three daughters how we felt about this or that. They were the adults, and we were the children, full-stop. We were expected to one day choose what we wished to study in college and where, they would support us in any way in that endeavour, and that was all there was to it. (The way this reads makes it sound way worse than it was - it wasn't).

Today, I mostly teach English as a Second Language (ESL) at an urban community college, and I see plenty of similarities in this adult/child, and teacher/student balance—or rather *im*balance—in my students' lives. My students bring with them hope and dreams; but they also bring pain, shame, and guilt. While I did not plan, when I first became a teacher, to be this benevolent savior of my students' souls, I have grown into a role that prioritizes valuing each student for who they are, and every one of my students knows it. Rohini's (2020, Section 5 of this book) reference to Brookfield (2015) is a good reminder that learning is an *emotional* experience. One of my undergraduate students even just brought this up only the other day. Learning is an emotional experience. Learning is not free of our conscious, agentive minds, just as teaching is not; I approach my students with this very much in mind.

Approach to Teaching

Now, while I am confident in my students' goals, there are times when my confidence as a teacher is challenged. In my classroom, I strive for an atmosphere of respect, to maintain an air of openness, and to give students "power" over the direction of a course (Cochran-Smith & Lytle, 2009; Freire, 1998). However, striking the right balance between being open yet "in charge" while meeting learner expectations daily with different student populations can be a challenge. Half a decade ago, I gained greater insight into how fragile this balance can be. I was teaching Brazilian mid-career English teachers in an action research course and, in alignment with action research goals, as well as my own, I gave students an opportunity to provide feedback halfway through the term; I did so with some trepidation as I had begun to sense some dissatisfaction among the students whose ages ranged from 25 to 60 (I was 29 at the time). One group of students told me in sum and substance that they had lost confidence in my ability to teach them anything of value and they felt frustrated and lost with the course material. Though I had sensed some discontentment by this group of students, I was not expecting such feedback. It affected me deeply—especially since I fully believed I was teaching a life-changing course that would encourage initiative, independence, and fulfillment. Ironically, exploring Freire's pedagogy of freedom (1998), a pedagogy focusing on the democratization of the "classroom" written by my students' fellow countryman, did not hit home in the way that I had hoped for it to do.

Following this event, I began to reevaluate my concept of "openness" particularly related to learner goals and learner expectations of course content *and* guidance. While trying to be open to students' thoughts, ideas, questions, and requests and attempting to build on them, did I perhaps overlook the importance of being authoritative? Are the two necessarily mutually exclusive concepts? And—notwithstanding the fact that a course such as this required *them* to take charge—wouldn't telling them what to do stifle their independence and critical thinking skills? In exploring such questions, I recognized that I had overlooked student expectations and learning styles with bias toward my own goals and expectations: the students required me to actively "teach" them (albeit through the empty vessel paradigm) the material and provide a more explicit framework of guidance.

Fortunately, I initiated changes halfway through the semester. After crying my eyes out for a quick ten minutes between classes, I taught the next class and rested over the weekend before going into class on Monday to face the students and discuss the oral stoning I had undergone. I claimed my vulnerability to them, and apologized for not giving them the more guided approach they were looking for. They too, apologized for the manner in which they had expressed themselves. We came to an understanding: We would reflect on this incident and use it to investigate each of our teaching philosophies. Of course, I took on a more active role as a teacher, but I also made it clearer to students that they were accountable and responsible in this type. I share this one experience because it demonstrates the importance of balancing teaching philosophies and student expectations regularly and in all teaching contexts. Thus, while my approach to teaching continues to value openness, a solid organizational structure and air for mutual understanding, respect, and kindness, I now actively and explicitly—through additional questions on reflection and expectation assignments—seek and gauge the extent to which I can allow myself to be open and authoritative in this delicate matter of assessing what will be best for my students.

As for my teaching approach with regards to cultural sensitivity and fluency, I have lived in many different types of places with people of many different ways of life; so I feel at ease with my ability to connect with my students on many levels—cultural, linguistic, sociolinguistic, paralinguistic (all the non-verbal communication that accompanies spoken language)—while also ensuring that I do not make any intercultural blunders. Although if I did (and I have), my students would tell me that I did (and they have), and would ensure that I understood what the bungle was and how to prevent it from happening again (yes, again, they did and I did). My rich exposure to very different people, religions, cultures, foods, languages, group dynamics, from a young age has prepared me for intercultural understanding and navigation, and culture-switching (in the code-switching sense).

Integrating Teaching and Research

I am a naturally very curious individual. I have always loved school, and I love learning new things that are completely different from my own field of study. In that sense, then, I think I have one extremely important quality of researchers: genuine curiosity. Additionally, I have come to believe in the power of qualitative research. Digging into lived experiences sends a message that individual voices matter, and can impact larger-scale endeavors. As I finally begin to settle into my identity as a practitioner, I have begun to devote more time to my current academic interest—English Language Learner (ELL) student experiences. However, in part, due to many rejections from peer-reviewed academic journals, I have come to see that for now, perhaps, I fit better in the world of narratives and storytelling, worlds where jargon, the number of references I have, and subjectivity—aka "scientism" (Macedo, 1998)—do not indicate a lack of rigor, expertise, or overall value. Again, this speaks to my growing confidence in deciding who and what I represent and when.

Critical Reflection

When I first learned of this opportunity to write about my own educational autobiography, I was filled with excitement to put into words the many diverse experiences that have shaped me into the person I am today. I did not anticipate, though, the almost visceral reaction to transporting myself through time and memory. In writing this narrative, I have relived joys and anxieties, triumphs and fears, validations and disappointments. Indeed, as Yancey (2020, section 5 of this book) notes, "We do not learn from experience. We learn from reflecting on experience" (Dewey, 1993, p. 33). This opportunity to reflect on key incidents in my own growth as a student, and the impact of this growth on my growth as a researcher and a teacher, has led me to discover and learn about the critical role that kindness has played in my life.

Throughout my quite chaotic educational journey, I have felt moments of acute shame but also moments of deep empowerment. The moments of shame, blame, and unworthiness do force their way into my consciousness here and there, but the power they exert is diminishing, and the frequency with which they appear is, as well. Instead, I have more often begun to think of the light that my many teachers—whether or not they knew what I was carrying within me—shined on me, bringing me out of my confused clouds, with their kindness. It always amazes me that when people ask me who has stood out most out of the hundreds of teachers that I have ever had, what pops into my mind is kind eyes and welcoming smiles. In all of the instability and confusion that surrounded me, my teachers' kindness is that I point to as having been the source of my own growth as a person, and as a result, of my growth as a conscientious and confident student. Yes, I have always clearly been very different. My name is the first dead giveaway; I never really spoke "fluently" the languages around me; my accent was always an elusive trait that people would ask me about and try to analyze and categorize, while my accent itself kept shape-shifting, to use mythological verbiage, and accommodating the changing influences around it; my culture at home was never ever a continuation of the culture of the schools I attended; my holidays were different from those of the Lebanese, Cypriot, British, and American students around me; we had zero extended family in any of the countries we lived in; and my family was not a typical nuclear family with a two-parent household. And yet, whether or not they saw how I felt different, I know that it is thanks to my teachers and their small kind acts, kind words, and overall attitude of kindness that I made it through the many schools I attended.

An even bigger revelation throughout this educational, autobiographical journey, is the role my mum has played. The kindest person that I have ever known in my life is Maral Sarkissian Kaloustian—my mum. I have learned from her what kindness is, what it looks like, and what it means, not only through her interactions with me, but also through her naturally warm and kind tendencies toward everyone. She has a subtle, almost magical way of connecting with people, making sure they feel they are a part of whatever she is in on; it is a wonderful thing to witness my mum's kindness. I have always known that she is kind, but her wit, her humour, her laugh, her life-of-the-party personality are what first pop into my mind when I think of her. But now, I am flooded by thousands of memories of thousands of her kind acts, both big and small; pure kindness, with no inhibition. In going on this autobiographical journey down educational memory lane, I see, now, things in a new light. I see, now, that in every new community I ever entered, I sought out kindness: I purposefully sought out people with kind eyes, welcoming smiles, and a nurturing demeanor. I don't think that all these teachers to whom I am forever grateful were naturally drawn to me; I think *I* was the one who was drawn to *them*. I was looking for kindness anywhere I could find it because I knew that it would bring me comfort, safety, protection, and most of all, mental peace at a time when environmental instability reigned supreme in my life. Whenever my mum offered me her sweet gestures, all the confusion of my life would fade away and be replaced by warmth, a protective shield. This is what I have always sought. As I come to this realization, I feel myself getting choked up.

Only now do I see a connection between the kindness I sought and the kindness I offer my students. So many of my evaluations by students mention the word "kind." I have often thought about my role with my students as one of "orienter" (a made-up word) or guide; I know what my students have the capacity for, and I believe I create a guiding space for them that builds their confidence and pushes them to reach their potential. But I have never thought of the adjective "kind" as a defining characteristic. As I reflect on my own experiences as a student, I cannot help but see the parallel in what a special few of my teachers did for me and what I do for my students. I make time for my students, give them warm words of motivation, validate their concerns, check in with them outside of the classroom, text with them, and do many other things that contribute to their sense of belonging in their foreign environments. My ESL students especially tend to describe their experiences in my courses as ones that make them feel like they are part of a community, and even more so, a family. Interestingly, I have only just learned that the etymological root of kind is related to "kin"—perhaps that is a coincidence. Still, it does shed new light on my understanding of kindness and its role in my teaching. As I think out loud for a moment, I begin to understand kindness as a manifestation of familiarity and trust. In theory, these are also characteristics that are very much associated with family or those who represent family— people you know well and people you can count on and trust. And to me, it would seem that with familiarity and trust comes a need to *give* things of value—be they in the form of words, time, services, or material things—without expecting anything in return. Kin and kind are related etymologically. Very cool.

In all of my studies and research, not at all did I come across anything related to kindness in education; I can imagine that this is a topic of great import in psychology, and ostensibly, it would fit in with any literature on building rapport. I have taken philosophy courses centered around concepts such as happiness (the closest conceptual abstraction to the kindness that I can think of). In education, the kindness piece is not discussed much, but I think it should be. Perhaps one reason it isn't, as Douglas (1966) suggests, is that kindness is one of those concepts that can be categorized as "matter out of place" especially within the domain of education. Maybe, as Rowland (2009) writes, "it can suggest a sentimental and unrigourous approach" (p. 207). Whether that be the case at this or any other juncture in my life is inconsequential. Kindness works. Sincerity works. And my students benefit from this in ways that I sometimes only learn about when my students, years after I have seen them or taught them, contact me to thank me for giving them space where they felt good about themselves. I am so grateful to them for reaching out and letting me know that what I am doing is working.

If I could talk to my former teachers today, specifically those who helped me on my journey in a more meaningful way than they could ever have imagined, I would say:

Thank you. Thank you for caring.

You may never have realized what a huge thing your smiles, your kindness, and your care was for a little girl, a pre-teen girl, a teenage girl, and a young adult from "not here." It's not even the subject matter you taught, but the kindness and sincerity with which you taught it. Decades later, I now do the same with my students, who just happen to be "not from here-ers," just like I was.

On Tuesday, August 4, 2020[4], an explosion that registered 3.3 on the Richter scale, which was felt by friends in Cyprus 150 miles away, all but obliterated my beloved Beirut. The third-largest explosion that our human species has ever seen. The largest non-nuclear explosion. The damage is unfathomable. The plight of hundreds of thousands of people is unfathomable. The lives lost, literally and figuratively. The pasts, the presents and the futures, deeply injured. Unfathomable.

Everyone I know in Beirut has been affected. Everyone I know who is outside of Beirut is affected. Anyone who has met Beirut and seen her charm first-hand has been affected. My peer, Eliana El Khoury (also in Section 2) is hurting. This thick fog of confusion, this feeling of being lost is unfathomable. What other word is there to express the magnitude of the loss created and perpetuated by this explosion?

> *Just a few sad words that I hesitate to utter. That I am afraid to utter, because it will seem all the more real. Not only real in my past, but real in my future. And, I say with a heavy heart, very real for a new generation of tens of thousands of students, young and old, far less fortunate than I ever was.*
>
> *A six-year-old, without a roof over her head, without refuge, only rubble. Insecurity.*
>
> *A mother's fear and anxiety for her children. Loss and trauma dictating her past, guiding her forward blindly.*
>
> SIFE.
>
> *A 12-year-old, coming of age, riddled with confusion. What will happen to her? Her family? So much fear.*

---

4   It is in late August 2020 that I write this epilogue.

A 16-year-old's reckoning with her future, her country's worth. Her own worth. Worthless.

A 17-year-old struggling to belong. To find the place where she will be accepted. Her identity.

Ripped away from her.

An 18-year-old, having opportunity snatched from her hands. What else is there? Future lost.

A 22-year-old with nowhere to work, even while armed with education. Homebase-less.

A 25-year-old. Finally going to leave this fucking place, never to return because how many times can a person go through this shit.

A few seconds of fire, a blast. An irreversible trajectory.

I saw a video of the explosion 20 minutes after it happened: Yasmine, one of my best friends who lives in Oman and who spent a large part of her young adult years in Beirut, frantically emailed our group chat, "Guys, I just heard there was a massive explosion 20 minutes ago. What's going on? The video is fucking insane." When I saw the video of my Beirut blowing up, I reeled physically reeled backwards, right here in New Jersey. I knew this was not a movie. I knew it was real. I thought it was war. I panicked about where my sisters were, where my parents were, where my brothers-in-law were, where my nieces and nephew were, where our family friends, old colleagues and co-workers were. I was paralyzed by the several-second video that showed Beirut going up in smoke and fire and ashes. I watched it again, and then one more time in my efforts to find something about the video that suggested this was fake. But it was real and I knew it. I was just desperate. I ran to my 20-year-old stepdaughter Megan's room, rousing her from her sleep, and just wailing and sobbing. She pulled up Twitter, assured me this was just one explosion and not a war. She then ordered me to calm down and on the fly implemented some strategies to ground me, showing her to be mature beyond her years. I video called my mum, and we wept together, wordlessly, me in NJ, she near Beirut, and my 16-year-old stepson, Tyler, hugging me and comforting me. My 19-year-old stepdaughter, Maddie, texting me.

My husband, John, calling me. I WhatsApp'ed Nadine, my best friend in Beirut—she was covered in blood and bandages, but her pregnancy was miraculously untouched, at least physically. My best friend, Elissar, who also lives in Beirut WhatsApp'ed me—we just looked at each other and cried and cried and cried in a state of utter confusion and loss and pain. My phone kept pinging and beeping and ringing with concern or news from friends and colleagues all over the world. For some reason, I could not bring myself to call my sisters, and I guess they to call me. It took us a couple of days after the explosion to pick up communication again, cautiously at that, and by text at first. I have yet to explore why that was the case.

The moving picture of that explosion is seared in my brain. After seeing it, every blink has become a replay of the explosion; every blink a horrifying memory or feeling or fleeting image from my childhood from before we escaped the war the first time and the second time. From my pre-teen years, our home, bombed by a stray, friendly-fire bomb. From my teenage years, ruins and random bombings. From my young adult years, swiftly executed politically levelled assassinations, among them our former Prime Minister Hariri. From my early 20s, the July 2006 War, which we literally watched and heard and felt. From my late 20s, more bombings, more frequent, frantic phone calls. And now, again and again, the explosion. This time, 5700 miles away. Playing and replaying in front of my open eyes, and behind my closed eyes. Within seconds of seeing the video, a deep-rooted PTSD I did not know of revealed itself. And as well, a powerful surge of identity overwhelmed me. My heart was breaking. My Lebanese heart. Shattered into pieces. A million, never-again-to-be-made-into-a-whole pieces. My broken Lebanese heart, broken for my lost Beirut.

Ô Beyrouth, renaîtras-tu de tes cendres une nouvelle fois? (Merci, Marcos, for the poetic translation). *Shall you rise from the ashes, just once more?* Captivating, charming, loving, warm, majestic, and persistent phoenix, Beirut.

References

Agar, M. (1994). The intercultural frame. *International Journal of Intercultural Relations, 18*(2), 221-237.
Agar, M. (1995). *Language shock: Understanding the culture of conversation.* New York: William Morrow.
Bernat, E. (2008). Towards a pedagogy of empowerment: The case of 'impostor syndrome' among pre-service non-native speaker teachers. *ELTED, 11,* 1-8.
Berry, J. W. (1997). Immigration, acculturation, and adaptation. *Applied Psychology: An International Review, 46,* 1-30Cochran-Smith, M. & Lytle, S.L. (2009). *Inquiry as stance: Practitioner research for the next generation.* New York: Teachers College Press.
Brookfield, S. D. (2015). The skillful teacher: On technique, trust, and responsiveness in the classroom. John Wiley & Sons.
Bochner, S. (2006). Sojourners. In D. L. Sam, & J. W. Berry (Eds.), *Handbook of Acculturation Psychology* (pp. 181-197). Cambridge, UK: Cambridge University Press.
Cook, S. W. (1970). Motives in conceptual analysis of attitude related behavior. In W. J. Arnold, & D. Levine (Eds.), *Proceedings of the Nebraska Symposium on Motivation* (pp. 179-231). Lincoln, NE: University of Nebraska Press.
Decapua, A., & Marshall, H. W. (2010). Serving ELLs with limited or interrupted education: Intervention that works. *TESOL Journal, 1*(1), 49-70.

Dewey, J. (1916). *Democracy and Education*. New York: Macmillan.
Dewey, J. (1993). *How we think* (2nd ed). D.C. Heath.
Freire, P. (1998). *Pedagogy of freedom: Ethics, democracy and civic courage*. Lanham, MD: Rowman Littlefield.
Giles, H., & Coupland, N. (1991). Accommodating language. Language: Contexts and consequences (60-93). Pacific Grove, CA: Brooks.
Gumperz, J. J. (1965). Linguistic repertoires, grammars and second language instruction. *Languages and Linguistics, 18*, 81-90.
Langford, J., & Clance, P. R. (1993). The imposter phenomenon: recent research findings regarding dynamics, personality and family patterns and their implications for treatment. *Psychotherapy: theory, research, practice, training, 30*(3), 495.
Lave, J., & Wenger, E. (1991). *Situated learning: Legitimate peripheral participation*. Cambridge University Press.
Piaget, J., & Cook, M. (1952). *The origins of intelligence in children* (Vol. 8, No. 5, p. 18). New York: International Universities Press.
Macedo, D. (1998). Foreword. Freire, P. *Pedagogy of freedom: Ethics, democracy and civic courage*. (p. xi). Lanham, MD: Rowman Littlefield.
Menard-Warwick, J. (2005). Both a fiction and an existential fact: Theorizing identity in second language acquisition and literacy studies, *Linguistics and Education, 16,* 253-274.
Mori, K. (1997). *Polite Lies: On Being a Woman Caught between Two Cultures*. New York: Henry Holt and Company.
Oberg, K. (1960). Culture shock: Adjustment to new cultural environments. *Practical Anthropology, 7,* 142-146.Piaget, J. (1954). *Construction of reality in the child,* London: Routledge & Kegan Paul.
Rowland, S. (2009). Kindness. *London Review of Education, 7*(3), 207-210.
Sam, D. L. (2006). Acculturation: Conceptual background and core components. In D. L. Sam, & J. W. Berry (Eds.), *Handbook of Acculturation Psychology* (pp. 11-26). Cambridge, UK: Cambridge University Press.
Van Doren, M. (1959). *Liberal education* (No. 86). Boston: Beacon Press
Vélez-Ibáñez, C.G., & Greenberg, J.B. (1992). Formation and transformation of funds of knowledge among U.S. Mexican households. *Anthropology & Education Quarterly, 23*(4), 313-335.

7

Journey Across an Educational Divide

Eliana Elkhoury

A simple email message exemplifies the educational divide I experienced in moving from Lebanon, predominantly a competitive learning environment, to Canada, where collaboration is encouraged, for my doctoral studies. A professor had teamed me up with a classmate to produce three projects together over the semester. My background is one of competition and individual accomplishment. I had never done group or partner work before and had no idea how it was supposed to be done. Besides, I was not interested in collaboration. I wanted desperately to write the papers on my own, convinced I would be more productive. I sent an email to the professor explaining that I was sorry, but I could not do group work and needed to work alone. I remember receiving his reply, telling me I was not allowed to do the assignments on my own and that I had to learn to work with my classmate.

The rest of the semester was a disaster. I remember my classmate sending me messages, trying to collaborate with me, stressed out and upset. I would write something and send it to her one night before the deadline; she would modify and submit it. By the end of the course, we were not speaking to each other. I blamed her for some time, thinking that she was not strong enough to adapt to our different styles. In hindsight, it is easy to see that I was not a respectful collaborator—but I didn't know how to do group work. I realize now that I needed more support to make that experience successful. Probably the professor did not realize my need for support. If I were the professor, I would have directed the student toward group work support and helped them to understand what successful group work entailed.

The following will speak to my early influences within Lebanon, including the pressures of obtaining an education. It will include my undergraduate and master's degrees within Lebanon and my doctoral studies journey in Canada. Throughout the discussion, I introduce experiences and reflect on them by employing the literature. At the end of the chapter, I connect my learning experience to my teaching philosophy and I explain how it impacted my priorities and how I apply it in my classroom. This chapter is not linear. I use my present self to reflect on my past experiences.

Early Influences

I was born and raised in a village of 60 people in Lebanon. Neighbors would greet one another at the village church every Sunday. Lebanon had just come out of the civil war. Happiness, leisure, play, group work, volunteering, and many other Western concepts had no place in our world. Educating one's children was of the utmost importance—and education was expensive. Parents would spend all the money they had on their children's education. The common mentality was that a degree is the gift that parents give their children. This is not an uncommon way of thinking around the world, but in the post-war context—including the trauma, the poverty, the tight social context, and the lack of public education among others—added a level of complexity to the consequences of failing. Competition was therefore key. We were always in a state of competition with the other kids. The focus was to fill our brains with enough knowledge that we would be able to get a degree and consequently have a good life. How the children were ranking in class was the perennial subject of discussion in social gatherings. It was stressful to everyone, us as kids, our parents, and other parents.

Needless to say, I spent most of my school years absorbing information. I went through grade school, believing I wanted to go to medical school, change my social class and bring my family security. After two years of struggling through pre-med, I realized that this path was my parents' dream, not mine. Did I want to go to medical school? No. While I liked making a difference in people's lives, I couldn't imagine all the sadness that doctors witness. At the end of the day, people go to doctors when they are looking for medical support, whereas teachers are bridges to the future and represent hope. I wanted to be a teacher, but in the eyes of my family—of my society—teaching was not a big enough dream.

Abandoning medical school, I tried a couple of majors, including law school, sociology, and English Literature, before I landed on information technology. Technology was booming at the time, and it seemed like the best choice to guarantee a job after graduation. Although I consider the disciplines I tried before sticking with information technology to be a learning experience, it was a process rather than a product; my parents consider this period a failure and a waste of time. They only see the time it took to finish my undergraduate degree, secure a full-time position, and start my life. As such, I did not grow up with the mentality of looking for what I like, enjoying my time, or even taking my time. There was no time. We were always in a hurry: finish high school, finish university, find a job. Given this upbringing and many years later, after coming to university in Canada, I was amazed to listen to students who were taking a gap year or starting with something general while they decide what's really in their heart.

Lately, almost fifteen years after finishing high school, I had a discussion with my husband about how we would react, as two immigrants, if our kids decided to take a year off or change majors in the middle of a degree program. While before, the idea of this may have been unsettling, I am comfortable with it now because I know that learning is a journey. A year off is a learning year, and schooling needs to be enjoyable. Although I can't pinpoint the direct reasons that changed my mind, I am sure the change happened after moving to Canada. I now realize that my best learning experiences have been outside the classroom. All the experiences I had, the people I met, and the failures I went through helped me make better decisions and succeed.

My change in thinking has led me to think about the philosophical underpinnings of education and educational goals in any country. As I deepened my knowledge, I realized educational goals often mirror trends based on greater political, social, and economic events. When I look at the three alternative educational goals explained by Labaree (1997), I am confident that, in Lebanon, parents and students see education as an opportunity for social mobility. The government's goal of the education system still seems unclear to me despite the many reforms that have been introduced to the system. I fail to see a real progress toward citizenry education.

University Schooling in Lebanon

I completed my undergraduate degree in a small Lebanese city with students who came from backgrounds similar to my own. Lessons during these years were mostly teacher-centred. As students, we were mainly required to memorize, repeat, and apply. I recall that computer science and mathematics classes could be divided into two types, each on opposite ends of a continuum: extremely structured, where the teacher had planned every second, and extremely unstructured, where we spent the whole class learning about a formula. I found the first to be too organized and restrictive and the second too boring. In the structured class, I would have preferred a little more room for innovation and creativity. In the unstructured class, I would have preferred for the teacher to be more involved. Neither extreme worked for me, so in both types of classes I would drift away. How I learned anything at all during this era is a wonder.

What I retained was the result of repetition and probably luck. I still remember some instances (for example, how to install an internet cable), and this is likely because I could immediately apply such knowledge in my life.

I often try to look back and analyze the teaching and learning approaches that were used. The organized classroom was influenced by a behaviorist approach. By planning every second of the class time with memorized items and practice items, the instructor guaranteed that we were receiving the necessary information that would allow us to learn. As for the unstructured class, it seemed like an inquiry-based learning model where we needed to explore a question at the beginning and come to answers on our own. The instructor did not consider the multiple inquiries needed to help us as students reach that fourth level of investigation, to develop metacognition to become self-directed learners.

This is because, as an instructor, I acknowledge that students need to be exposed to knowledge, but this must to be coupled with motivating elements and authentic practice as well as timely and constructive feedback. Additionally, I think that inquiry-based learning is a great approach as it allows students to explore knowledge and test their own hypotheses but that it needs to be accompanied with inquiry cycles (Bybee et al., 2006) and awareness of the students' level of inquiry (Banchi, & Bell, 2008). If I were designing an inquiry-based module, I would start by sending a survey to students to assess their prior experiences and knowledge. I would then plan lessons accordingly, with the goal of reaching the fourth level by the end of the semester. I would also help students develop metacognitive skills and empower them to become self-directed learners while still recognizing this is not an overnight process. For some, it could take a full degree.

Although I did an Information Technology (IT) degree and had many opportunities to work in the industry, I chose to work where my heart had always been, at a school, as a computer teacher and teacher trainer. And when the time came to do my master's degree, I chose educational research. Coming from a science background, it was not easy to move to qualitative research, so I added a quantitative element to my approach. Not only was the content of what I studied different from my undergraduate degree, but the context was as well. I did my master's program in the capital city of Beirut. The student body was diverse, culturally, and disciplinarily. In addition, I was involved with the student association and had a full-time job as a technology specialist.

Learning in this era was markedly different than what I had experienced as an undergraduate. Many courses included some type of active learning in the faculty of education, and teachers had charismatic personalities. Moreover, the faculty was smaller; we were all gathered on the seventh floor. The accessible administration offices helped students get to know staff, and the dean's office had an open-door policy. As I reflect, I realize that my learning was influenced dramatically by this social and cultural environment. The relationships I had with the staff, the dean and the student body made me more engaged in the program. So much literature addresses this aspect of learning. As a bigger theory, I can particularly think about sociocultural constructivism. I found that Daniel F. Chambliss and Christopher G. Takacs (2014) explained this point the best in their book, *How College Works*. Chambliss and Takacs describe the people and the connections students make as the most important element of their learning. They state that "emotional connection to others and to a community provide the strongest motivation" (p. 106). In my own experience, having been able to have that emotional connection to my colleagues, listening to their needs, sharing their events, knowing all the staff members personally, and having the dean's office open door policy, motivated me to do more and do better.

Similarly, I was able to apply my learning in my work. While completing my master's degree, I had a full-time position as an educational technology trainer for school teachers. I would meet with teachers daily and support them in implementing learning technology in their lesson design. At first, I was met with resistance and push-back. Teachers were worried that technology would replace them. This reaction led me to think about ways to foster engagement. I realized that I needed the teachers to voice their concerns, so we discussed them together, which led me to research instructional design theories and the importance of talking about prior knowledge. As I deepened my understanding of educational theories, the following points seemed important for every instructor. First, prior knowledge impacts any kind of learning (Vygotsky, 1978). Second, I learned that prior knowledge could be insufficient, inaccurate, or inappropriate (Ambrose, S., Bridges, M., DiPietro, M., Lovett, M, & Norman, M., 2010). I also learned that learners don't usually automatically recall information. Consequently, instructional techniques help them recall this knowledge and examine it to bridge it with the new information (Gagne, R., Wager, W., Golas, K., Keller, J., & Russell, J., 2005).

During one of my one-on-one consultations, I was showing a teacher how to use a specific tool. I kept repeating the same steps, and the teacher kept asking me the same question. I was so upset that I could not teach that person how to use the tool that I went outside and cried. This incident led me to think deeply about adult learning theories, specifically, transformational learning

(Mezirow, 1978), experiential learning (Kolb,1970), and reflection (Boud, D. et al., 1985; Dewey, J.,1933; & Schön, D., 1983).

The following example illustrates how these theories intertwine to build a successful learning experience. I remember when I first started, I had the same lesson plan for everyone. I can say that I was not successful in using the same example for teachers from different disciplines. I soon learned the importance of real-life, hands-on examples. I began asking the teachers to send me their lesson plans for the week, and I would prepare my lessons accordingly. My session's result would be an activity that they could use the following week in their class. Once I connected my examples to their classrooms, I could see the "aha moment" on their faces. Then we would discuss their disorienting dilemma (Mezirow, 1990). I could see the different places my learners were at, and it became clear that their learning happened at their own pace. I offered to sit in these teachers' classes to give them feedback on their learning but also to encourage reflection-on-action and in-action (Schön, 1983). Although it was not the easiest learning journey, I accumulated the most meaningful teaching experiences during this period because of the non-intentional experiential learning involved. I was learning something during my masters' classes, applying it at work, getting feedback from my supervisor, and reflecting on it in my papers.

All of these factors contributed to an enjoyable learning experience. However, the program was based heavily on memorization. There was no space for creativity. In a discussion I had with the dean at the time, she explained that because the student body was multidisciplinary, with students coming from different backgrounds, memorization allowed the leadership to make sure that everyone left the program with the same knowledge. Now that I have deepened my knowledge of learning theories, I would tell her that each learner has a different path, which is the core of learner-centered education. Learner-centered education allows the instructor to facilitate learning based on the learner's needs and abilities, thus leaving some control of the knowledge to the learners. In her book about learner-centered teaching, Weimer (2013) explained the five characteristics of this type of education and recommended stepping away from direct instruction and motivating students by involving them in the learning and the planning. For example, I would suggest allowing students to explore their interests in their courses through an individual project. I would also recommend adding more group work and collaboration in addition to more online learning. I discuss these points in more detail as I turn to my doctoral era.

The Doctoral Era in Canada

As I grew, Lebanon started to feel small. I was looking for more opportunities, new ideas, and more flexibility. I decided to pursue my PhD in Canada. In September 2013, I moved to Calgary, and to a different approach to education altogether. This era represents the educational divide I mentioned earlier. Although I had some exposure to a student-centred approach to teaching, the immersion in an entirely student-centred approach in Canada, coupled with a different definition of authority, the Canadian linguistic and sociocultural diversity, and being an international student summarizes the educational divide that I experienced with my move. Instead of following a path of memorization and one mainstream education, we were encouraged to explore our learning and given the liberty to choose our way. Grades were not final and could be negotiated. Students were in charge of delivering the material and designing the course instead of the instructor lecturing. Much of the learning happened collaboratively and online. The student body was linguistically, religiously, and culturally diverse, with students from all walks of life, but the diversity in Canada was different from Lebanon. In Lebanon, we all spoke the same language, we all belonged to the same racial background, and we shared the same eating and sociocultural habits.

Moving mentally was a harder task than moving physically. I had to transition from a place where I had been told exactly what I needed to do, to a place where I was given total freedom to choose. It took me many years to change my mentality: to accept that the professors were there to guide me and not pour information into me, that the boundaries of authority and respect would be redefined in my relationships with them, and that what I learned in my courses would be only one leg of a lifelong journey of learning. Two main factors helped me make the transition. First, I had a community of practice (Wenger, 1998) consisting of five female academics from the Middle East. With them, I discussed the things I was going through. We provided feedback to one another. I would often ask them about something my supervisor said. They were at different stages of their doctoral career and supplied me with multiple perspectives. The second factor impacting my transition was working on campus. This allowed me to experience the new culture firsthand. I became friends with students who grew up in Canada. Part of my job was to design and deliver training to other students and serve as peer support. I learned a lot from that experience. When asked about recommendations for students coming from abroad, I would recommend working and/or volunteering. Especially volunteering on campus or being part of any kind of service-learning (Sigmon, 1996) available to them.

In Calgary, I had multiple part-time jobs. I was also a sessional instructor. I learned that, at least where I was teaching, it was often considered okay for students to eat in my class or to be late, and that I needed to be flexible. When interviewing an international student to collect data on how students define good teaching, the student mentioned that poor teaching is when students can eat in the class and arrive late, which showed that the teacher had no control over the class. This comment made me reflect on the different perceptions of authority, power, and good teaching. Many scholars studied authority and power in the classroom. Some of the most insightful for me were the four types of authority that occur in a classroom setting were thoroughly studied by Wagner and Herbel-Eisenmann (2009) and the social power explained by Raven (1992). In addition, what one person sees as good teaching, another can view as poor teaching, and that perception can impact the relationship between students and teachers. This is summarized in the different paradigms to education that are mainly socially constructed. As outlined by Brookfield (1995), your previous experience as a learner defines how you would describe good teaching. If you have only experienced teacher-centered instruction, this would be the norm for you. If you have only experienced a certain type of teacher authority, this will impact the way you accept authority. For me, I was used to the "sage on the stage" role of a teacher and the distant authority figure portrayed by most of my professors. You can imagine my dilemma when my supervisor asked me to address her by her first name and when I realized that I did not need to stand up when a higher rank person entered the room.

My seminal group work experience, described in my introduction, occurred during this time. I have since realized not only the importance of group work but also the benefits and joy that come out of the exchange of ideas and multiple points of view. Group work is a skill that needs to be refined. Students need to have a clear idea of group goals and individual accountability (Slavin, 2010). In addition, group work hides a cultural perspective to it that instructors need to be aware of (Flowerdew,1998). I recommend supporting students to hone their group work skills. As a sessional instructor, I incorporate group work, making it a point to be present to support students through rough times. In my experience, I had no support for group work, I never talked with my partner about expectations, and this is something I do regret.

Digital education was another area of growth for me, which has also played a significant role in my teaching and learning journey. In one of my courses, I was asked to write a blog and read other people's blogs. I would generate a quick blog post two hours before the deadline, and I refused to read other people's blogs. Why bother to read their blogs, I reasoned, when I could go to the original articles and read them instead? I remember the professor smiled when I told him that. I am not sure whether he was patiently waiting for me to figure it out on my own. I would have appreciated him telling me that, similar to what sociocultural constructivist theorists advocated for, there are points of view that I might miss on my own, that different people notice different angles, and that so much knowledge can be gained by sharing opinions and conversing (Vygotsky, 1978). But he did not, and I didn't know. My opinion changed when I started teaching, and I saw the remarkable exchange of ideas in a blog assignment among my students. More importantly, I realized that my teaching presence (Garrison, 2007) as an instructor was crucial. For my students to get the most out of their educational blogging experience, they needed to get timely and consistent feedback, to know that someone was reading, and to have prompting questions. If my professor had checked my blog early in the course and encouraged me to stay on schedule, and helped instill a sense of a learning community (Shea, Li, & Pickett, 2006), perhaps I wouldn't have delayed until two hours before the deadline, and maybe I would have enjoyed that experience more.

This leads me to the topic of online courses. I signed up for one as part of my doctoral courses, but I dropped out after two weeks. I couldn't imagine having virtual conversations. I couldn't get comfortable not sitting in a classroom. I was already struggling with group work; the thought of virtual group work made me shudder. I had never taken an online course before. I wish I would have received an introduction to online courses as an international student. Maybe a course about how to learn online or simply a required online course or workshop, anything that would allow me a low-profile learning experience. I would also have appreciated having a mentor who could have addressed these concerns. When I told my supervisor that I was withdrawing because I was not comfortable with the virtual interactions, I wish he had given me some tools and some insight that address my fears of lack of community instead of letting me leave.

In terms of assessment, I was introduced to a number of unfamiliar strategies: peer assessment, self-assessment, and resubmission of assessment were new to me. For context, I provide a definition of the three concepts. Peer assessment is a mutual form of assessment that allows students to grade and give feedback on the submissions of their peers, with feedback being the most important (Topping, 2009). Self-assessment enables the learner to play an active role in their learning through reflecting on their strengths, weaknesses, and needs (Fitzpatrick, 2006). Resubmission of assessment is a form of formative assessment where students resubmit their assignment based on the feedback provided on the first version as described in a study done by Covic and Jones (2008).

Not only did I not know how to do either of the former, I also didn't know the reasoning behind them. When I was asked to do a peer assessment of my colleague's paper, I felt too shy to give any honest feedback, and I returned the paper saying it was great. I would have liked a fuller explanation of the benefits of peer and self-assessment, a rubric to follow, and more direction from the professor. The rubrics and the expectations would have been the most important in learning and accepting these new forms of assessment (Andrade, 2000). It would have provided legitimacy and direction to what I was doing. I would suggest that a rubric be created in the classroom as a collaborative task between the students and the instructor. This would allow students more ownership and create a space for discussion, as shown in a study by Fraile, Panadero, and Pardo (2017). Once, when I got a B+ for one of my assignments, the professor gave me the option to resubmit, providing the necessary modifications in the feedback. Honestly, I had never read feedback before, and not knowing what to do, I declined the offer.

Later, with my students, I began to apply peer-assessment and self-assessment but I make sure that I have a detailed rubric and, when possible, I co-create the rubric with my students. One technique I found useful is to provide prompt feedback the first time my students try these methods to ensure they are on the right track.

Lately, I started giving my students the opportunity to resubmit their assignments. Their engagement with reassessment is often slow. This is similar to the findings by Covic and Jones (2008), where they found that students often engaged with this method if they had failed the course and few use it as a method to improve their learning. My experience with time showed me that I needed to introduce them to this method early on in the course. My solution to their disengagement with reassessment was to inform them, in an introductory email, that I will give them this option after every assignment. I explain to them, using research-based resources, that learning happens when they incorporate the feedback. Last semester, I received an email from my student, who did not take advantage of the reassessment option, explaining that she thought this was a great approach. However, she also said she was too busy to use it, but she would use it with her students. I wish my professors would have done the same with me. I think that faculty members and school leaders who welcome international students, and maybe many of the other students, into their classes need to realize that those students might come from different pedagogical backgrounds and that their relationship with grades is different.

It takes support to change a student's understanding of grades and feedback. Change doesn't happen overnight; discussion, resources, and hands-on experiences would be my go-to support tools. For example, it is crucial to understand where the student stands on this. Based on that, a discussion comes next, coupled with resources, and when possible, an experiential experience that could take any form depending on the context.

The last learning stop I will describe is the exposure to uniqueness. This covers a huge range of topics, starting from accessibility needs, to mental health, to diversity surrounding minority students, international students; in summary, it covers diversity and inclusivity. Uniqueness manifests in many ways. Students are unique with their preconceptions constructed through their previous formal and informal learning and their sociocultural environment. Students are also unique in their knowledge acquisition, which happens at different stages depending on their experiences. Diversity is also the awareness that some learners excel with various assessments and I try to accommodate that. My assessment tools range from rubrics, self-assessments, checklists, presentations, and projects based on community engagement thus allowing students to apply theory into practice. Diversity also refers to the sociocultural and linguistic background of the students. Therefore, I try to implement different points of view and I make sure they are discussed respectfully. And inclusivity refers to exceptional students' specific needs, and for that, I strive to use the Universal Design for Learning guidelines. Building inclusivity into lesson design is one way to try to bridge the gap between the learner and the instructor.

I believe I share responsibility in my own learning and that my sociocultural background played a big role in my learning journey. At the same, I believe that instructors share that responsibility, especially when teaching diverse classrooms. In my personal opinion, it is a lifelong learning journey that starts with a will to help all learners succeed.

As I look back on my own learning, I am surprised by how many things I have forgotten. I wish my teaching and learning had been more involved. I wish we had had more service-learning, more experiential learning, more critical reflection, and—most important—more inclusive learning. I grew up thinking that learning is linear: one needs to study to move from Point A to Point B. Then, one studies a bit more to get to Point C. Now I understand that the journey is never linear. Barriers may appear; divides may need to be crossed. Each journey is iterative and multidimensional, and unique to each learner. Transitioning into my role as an online instructor in a teacher education program and an educational developer in higher education, I realize how much I have learned from my own iterative and multidimensional and unique experiences. These experiences influenced the guiding principles of my teaching philosophy, including professional growth and always seeking innovation in teaching and learning, reflective practice, safe community, diversity, and experiential education.

I frequently wonder how we can create opportunities in teacher education programs and all educational contexts to best support learners, reduce the barriers, and narrow the divides in these journeys. I know it requires effort, time, and commitment, but the outcomes are truly amazing.

References

Ambrose, S. A., Bridges, M. W., DiPietro, M., Lovett, M. C., & Norman, M. K. (2010). *How learning works: Seven research-based principles for smart teaching*. John Wiley & Sons.

Andrade, Heidi Goodrich. "Using rubrics to promote thinking and learning." *Educational leadership* 57.5 (2000): 13-19.

Banchi, H., & Bell, R. (2008). The many levels of inquiry. *Science and children*, 46(2), 26.

Boud, D., Keogh, R., & Walker, D. (1985). Reflection: Turning learning into experience. *Kongan Page, London*.

Brookfield, S. (1995). The getting of wisdom: What critically reflective teaching is and why it's important. *Becoming a critically reflective teacher*, 1-28.

Bybee, R. W., Taylor, J. A., Gardner, A., Van Scotter, P., Powell, J. C., Westbrook, A., & Landes, N. (2006). The BSCS 5E instructional model: Origins and effectiveness. *Colorado Springs, Co: BSCS*, 5, 88-98.

Chambliss, D. F. (2014). *How college works*. Harvard University Press.

Covic, T., & Jones, M. K. (2008). Is the essay resubmission option a formative or a summative assessment and does it matter as long as the grades improve?. *Assessment & Evaluation in Higher Education*, 33(1), 75-85.

Covic, T., & Jones, M. K. (2008). Is the essay resubmission option a formative or a summative assessment and does it matter as long as the grades improve?. *Assessment & Evaluation in Higher Education*, 33(1), 75-85.

Dewey, J. (1933). Philosophy and civilization.

Fitzpatrick, J. (2006). An evaluative case study of the dilemmas experienced in designing a self-assessment strategy for Community Nursing students. *Assessment & Evaluation in Higher Education*, 31(1), 37-53.

Flowerdew, L. (1998). A cultural perspective on group work.

Fraile, J., Panadero, E., & Pardo, R. (2017). Co-creating rubrics: The effects on self-regulated learning, self-efficacy and performance of establishing assessment criteria with students. *Studies in Educational Evaluation*, 53, 69-76.

Gagne, R. M., Wager, W. W., Golas, K. C., Keller, J. M., & Russell, J. D. (2005). Principles of instructional design. *Performance Improvement*, 44(2), 44-46.

Garrison, D. R. (2007). Online community of inquiry review: Social, cognitive, and teaching presence issues. *Journal of Asynchronous Learning Networks*, 11(1), 61-72.

Kolb, H. (1970). Organization of the outer plexiform layer of the primate retina: electron microscopy of Golgi-impregnated cells. *Philosophical Transactions of the Royal Society of London. B, Biological Sciences*, 258(823), 261-283.

Labaree, D. F. (1997). Public goods, private goods: The American struggle over educational goals. *American educational research journal*, 34(1), 39-81.

Mezirow, J. (1978). Perspective transformation. *Adult education*, 28(2), 100-110.

Mezirow, J. (1990). How critical reflection triggers transformative learning. *Fostering critical reflection in adulthood*, 1(20), 1-6.

Raven, Bertram H. "A power/interaction model of interpersonal influence: French and Raven thirty years later." *Journal of Social Behavior & Personality* (1992).

Schön, D. (1983). A.(1983). The reflective practitioner. *Pediatrics*, *116*(6), 1546-52.
Shea, P., Li, C. S., & Pickett, A. (2006). A study of teaching presence and student sense of learning community in fully online and web-enhanced college courses. *The Internet and higher education*, *9*(3), 175-190.
Sigmon, R. L. (1996). *Journey to Service-Learning: Experiences from Independent Liberal Arts Colleges and Universities*. Council of Independent Colleges, One Dupont Circle, Suite 320, Washington, DC 20036-1110.
Slavin, R. E. (1990). Research on cooperative learning: Consensus and controversy. *Educational leadership*, *47*(4), 52-54.
Topping, K. J. (2009). Peer assessment. *Theory into practice*, *48*(1), 20-27.
Vygotsky, L. S. (1978). Socio-cultural theory. *Mind in society*, 52-58.
Wagner, D., & Herbel-Eisenmann, B. (2009). Re-mythologizing mathematics through attention to classroom positioning. *Educational Studies in Mathematics*, *72*(1), 1-15.
Weimer, M. (2013). Teacher-centered, learner-centered, or all of the above. *Faculty Focus*.
Wenger, E. (1998). Communities of practice: Learning as a social system. *Systems thinker*, *9*(5), 2-3.

8

Toward My Educator Identity

Talia Guttin

My Educational Autobiography

Chapter One: Identity

I am the child of immigrants. Specifically, Mexican Jewish immigrants to the United States, and just two generations prior, Eastern European Jewish immigrants to Mexico, fleeing the violence of anti-Semitism. This identity has had profound impacts on my education and growth as an educator. As described by Stets and Serpe (2013), the salience of identity is affected by individual, social, and historical contexts. My identity has depended on where I live, the global historical context, and how others identify me. As I moved through the stages of the student to educator, this identity has driven me to be a lifelong student, to move from a fixed mindset to a growth mindset, to revisit career choices, and ultimately, to become an educator.

Like many immigrant communities, the Jewish population in Mexico self-segregates to maintain their culture and to create a safe space for themselves. The Jewish community in Mexico traces some roots back to Eastern Europe and Russia, driven out of their homelands by anti-Semitism, violence, pogroms, and genocide from the late 1910s to the 1940s. This community maintained a strong cultural identity in their new homeland of Mexico, and it was commonplace for children to attend private Jewish schools. I attended school in Mexico until I was 5, when we moved to the US, and I continued to attend a private Jewish school. Despite the similarity in my educational environment, Judaism felt like my race and ethnicity while living in Mexico, purposefully separate from the archetypal Catholic Mexico. I felt uncomfortably separate from other Mexicans. However, when my family moved to the United States, I suddenly felt very distinctly Mexican, and Judaism became my religion rather than my race or ethnicity.

One pillar of Judaism which was ingrained in me during my K–12 education has infiltrated all my educational experiences: the encouragement of critical analysis. Rabbis and their students debated Jewish law, grappled with it, applied it to their own context, and as students, we were encouraged to do the same. These experiences set me up as a lifelong student and a future scientist, always cynical and always questioning.

My Mexican identity has shifted with time and the context of Mexicans in the United States. When my family first arrived, there were very few Mexicans in Philadelphia. Speaking Spanish was viewed as exotic. The fact that my skin was white and that I was Jewish were not relevant, but as more Mexican, Central, and South American migrant workers moved to the U.S., the category of what it means to be Mexican in America changed. Being Mexican no longer referred to a nationality, but socioeconomic class and race (Hirschman, 2004). Suddenly, I was not a part of this group, not identified as Mexican by other Mexicans or by Americans, despite self-identification as a Mexican immigrant. On college and post-graduate applications, I had to decide what demographics box to check: how I felt or how others saw me. Throughout my life, this is a question that I am still trying to answer.

Chapter Two: A Fixed Mindset
Another aspect of my identity that impacted my education is being the child of immigrants. This inherently comes with hopes, dreams, and expectations. Both of my parents have advanced post-graduate degrees, and it was expected that I would follow a similar path. Educational achievement was expected, and fortunately, it came very naturally to me. I received good grades with minimal effort, barely studying, doing schoolwork at the last minute, and getting top grades. I was praised for my natural intellect. These factors led me to have a fixed mindset (Dweck, 2006). As Dweck describes, a growth mindset is when an individual approaches learning as a continuous path, involving effort and failures, while fixed mindset describes a learner who thinks intelligence is a natural trait, where failure implies a flaw in their identity (Yeager & Dweck, 2012, p. 303). I thrived with praise but did not embrace challenges that required effort and the potential for failure. Instead of working hard at something, like playing the piano, I assumed my natural abilities would get me through. However, this backfired on me during a piano recital. I remember freezing up on the stage, stumbling through the song and stopping halfway. The embarrassment was overwhelming, but even though it was due to an utter lack of effort, this failure felt like an affront to my identity. Instead of trying

harder, I abandoned the piano after that recital. It was easier to not try than to try and fail.

During my college years, I began chiseling away at my fixed mindset. The main driver for this was a love of learning, stemming from my Jewish education and the opportunity provided by being a child of immigrants. My parents never had the opportunity to have an American liberal arts education, so I took this prospect and chose to study the fascinating and challenging topics of cognitive science and religion, instead of what I viewed as the safe path of pre-veterinary coursework that was expected. These years fueled my love of learning for the sake of learning and provided me with my first teaching opportunities.

My first teaching experience as a teaching assistant in an Eastern religion course was transformative, both to my mindset and my future career. I prepared for my first review session for weeks, giddily concocting complex discussion questions that would show how smart I was. The review session began, and with anticipation, I asked my first question. This was followed by an endless silence and blank stares. My teaching partner broke the silence with a short, simple question, "Can anyone define Zen?" I rolled my eyes, but to my surprise, an enthusiastic conversation followed his simple question. I felt like a failure, but a crack developed in my fixed mindset, as I saw room for improvement, and saw this failure as fuel to grow. Over the next few weeks, I realized that proving I was the smartest was not the goal, as I learned from my partner and honed a newfound love of teaching, of creating the environment to enable learning.

Chapter Three: Career Exploration and Re-exploration
After a college experience filled with exploration and inquiry, I was left without a clear career path, but with the seeds of a growth mindset. Through employment, I rediscovered that I wanted to be a veterinarian. While I was not aware of this at the time, finding the language of mindset much later in my career, I remember struggling with how challenging vet school would be. Did I want to go through that challenge? What if I failed? Was the hard work worth the potential failure?

In the end, I dove in, first facing the challenge of fulfilling my pre-requisite science courses, which solidified my newly-discovered growth mindset. In my first physics exam, I failed miserably. I took this failure as fuel, studied harder, practiced more, and received 100% on every subsequent exam. Was I overcompensating? Perhaps. But the sense of accomplishment after an initial failure and hard work motivated me in a way I had never experienced before, which pushed me through the challenge of vet school.

I shifted from student to teacher during my residency in small animal internal medicine, consisting of three years of specialized training after becoming a veterinarian. Residents teach vet students one-on-one through cases, and this was my favorite part of the day. I saw the students grow with each case, as they advanced from content knowledge to true understanding, developing the skills needed to be a successful vet. When I started my first teaching job in the fall of 2017 at St. George's University School of Veterinary Medicine in Grenada, West Indies, I wanted to teach using that methodology. Still, I struggled with translating this into the lecture setting when I felt I had to teach so much content. To face this challenge, I was guided by my identity as a lifelong student. Initially, I enrolled in faculty development pedagogy sessions, which led me to enroll in the Master of Education program. Through these classes, I found myself immersed in pedagogy, wrestling with how to teach for concepts, for true understanding, and less focus on content. As I learned more, I realized that the changes must apply beyond my course alone, but to the entire curriculum.

Around the same time that I was grappling with the issues in veterinary education, I was voted as the chair of the Curriculum Committee. I was concurrently intrigued and intimidated by this challenge. I was new to leadership and felt a fixed mindset sneaking in, telling me not to take this challenge, not sure that I would excel. A parallel exploration of pedagogy and curriculum design in the Masters' program has helped me fight my fixed mindset, embrace the challenge, and strive to improve myself. There is no class I could take, no degree program, for leadership. It was time for me to start applying knowledge, to have confidence that while I may not know everything, I know enough to start trying.

My Educational Philosophy

When I started teaching veterinary medicine in 2017 as a board-certified small animal internal medicine specialist, I was a content expert with no education training, believing and struggling with the notion that my job was to teach a set amount of content. I thought of what worked for me as a student and knew I had to do things differently. I wanted to teach students to first focus on the diagnostic process: the skill of making a problem list, a differential diagnosis list, and a diagnostic plan. As I began to write my first lectures, content and my experience as a student prevailed over this goal. The lectures sounded like a Rolodex, list after list of disease, symptoms, diagnostics, and treatments. My struggle with content versus concepts is common in veterinary education and related medical/allied health fields during the classroom years prior to the clinical rotation year(s). Yet research shows that teaching to content does not help students achieve the outcomes that are required for the job, such as teamwork, leadership, and recognizing limitations (Cake, McArthur, Matthew, & Mansfield, 2017; McTighe & Wiggins, 2012; Rhind, Baillie, Kinnison, Shaw, Bell, Mellanby, Hammond, Hudson, Whittington, & Donnelly, 2011). To successfully teach these skills and build lifelong inquiry, veterinary education can look to constructivism, social learning theory, critical theory, adult learning theory, and growth mindset, and start teaching these skills from the beginning. My current mission is to embrace the challenge of changing the first three years of vet school to make it as transformational as year four, first in my own courses, then ultimately, the entire curriculum.

There are inherent problems with focusing on teaching content that are widely recognized in education. This approach leads to a superficial understanding of the material, does not encourage inquiry, and does not promote transfer (McTighe & Wiggins, 2012). It models for students that knowledge is fixed and finite, which can demotivate adult learners (Knowles, 1980). This can exacerbate the common misconception by educators that just because we teach it, it is understood by the students (McTighe & Wiggins, 2012).

In veterinary education, the literature shows that new graduates are entering the workforce without some of the necessary skills, such as communication, teamwork, decision-making abilities, compassion, integrity, and resilience (Cake, McArthur, Matthew, & Mansfield, 2017; Rhind et al., 2011). These issues are widely recognized, leading the accrediting bodies to add these as professional competencies (Rhind et al., 2011). Worldwide, the veterinary curriculum is changing to reflect these outcomes and ensure that students are achieving them. This requires a change in the teaching approach, away from didactic lectures focused on content, focusing on the acquisition of skills and concepts, via experiential learning, problem-based courses, and collaborative learning to encourage critical thinking.

I am most influenced by Knowles' adult learning theory, which states that adult learners learn differently from children, need to have agency over their learning, and are less dependent on teachers (Knowles, 1980). Knowles states that for adults, "self-directed inquiry will produce the greatest learning" (Knowles, 1980, p. 56). Adult learners bring rich experience and context to their learning and learn best in competency-centered environments (Knowles, 1980). This theory is directly transferable to veterinary education, where our students come into the classroom with high motivation, often extensive experience, and competencies are provided by accrediting bodies. But adult learners need to develop the skills to be self-directed learners, which is where we educators should come in. Our job as veterinary educators is to teach our students to be lifelong learners.

One way of working towards this goal is to use the outcomes outlined by accrediting bodies as the starting point and use a reverse design to reimagine the curriculum (McTighe & Wiggins, 2012). I theorize that with a traditional veterinary curriculum, most of the skills and true understandings are acquired during the final clinical year because that year involves experiential learning. By applying these pedagogical theories to the first three years, students can build and develop these skills through all four years of vet school, leading to deeper inquiry and more prepared veterinarians.

The challenges of integrating this approach are twofold: at the educator level and at the student level. The educators will face the challenge of resistance to change, which can be overcome with leadership, faculty development, and valuation of the effort to make these changes. On the student side, there will be growing pains as students learn to learn in a novel way (Knowles, 1980). I experienced this challenge as a student in faculty development sessions, where I participated in a constructivist classroom predominated by active learning for the first time. I was initially exasperated by the feeling that I wasn't learning enough facts, and I wanted to learn from the experts, not from myself or my colleagues. This frustration eventually yielded with the realization that I was indeed learning at a much deeper level. Recognizing this can help me prepare for my students' transition from the traditional didactic structure to a student-centered, problem-solving, active classroom, and potential resistance.

On a personal level, I started making changes in my own classes. One example of this is in the Clinical Toxicology course, where I incorporated a reciprocal peer teaching exercise (jigsaw) instead of traditional lectures. Students had to look up a toxin to find the symptoms, treatment, and prognosis, then share their research with the class. They acquire the content and the skills of looking up a toxin, extrapolating the necessary information, collaboration, and communication. Throughout my other lectures, incremental changes are being made, incorporating active learning strategies, guided by outcomes, in each lecture session. It is a work in progress, as I continually work on adding elements of collaborative and active learning.

My teaching philosophy starts first with a challenge to change from content-focused to concept-focused education during years one to three. For me, this must begin with a change to my own courses but cannot end there. The traditional lecture-based classroom, while the students are accustomed to learning that way, does not really benefit them, and we have the literature that proves as much. A shift to outcomes-based, problem-posing collaborative learning, combining theories from constructivism to adult learning theory, can help years one to three be as transformational as the clinical rotation year.

My Reflection: Critical Theory in Veterinary Education

Early in my journey as an educator, I had not considered my role as a teacher to be political, partially due to naïveté and partially due to privilege. My identity, educational experiences, first three years as a veterinary educator teaching mainly North American students in a Caribbean country, and as a current student in a Master of Education program, led me to reflect on critical pedagogy and teaching as an inherently political action. I think about my students, who do not shy away from political action. I think of the rabbinical teachings I learned early in my education, stipulating critical thinking and a careful critique of one's place in the world. This is echoed in the foundations of critical theory where the student–teacher relationship is integral to building community, encouraging critical thinking and developing cultural critique (Freire, 1970; Ladson-Billings, 1995). How does this apply to me as a veterinary educator?

Critical theory proposes that an adult learner should question and critically evaluate every fact, tease out hegemony and bias, thus rediscovering what is true (Brookfield, 2005). At face value, critical theory seems irrelevant to veterinary medical education. However, critical pedagogy is necessary for veterinarians to be effective in their field and in society, aiding in societal change and improvement. Veterinarians must explore critical theory to address three significant issues in the field: the underrepresentation of minorities enrolled in veterinary school, to become better scientists, and to better understand the effect of the dominant culture on themselves, their staff, and the pet owners they serve.

First and foremost, veterinary student bodies represent society, and as such, do not adequately represent it. Veterinary school classes in the USA were reported to be comprised of only 2% minorities, compared to 7% minorities in other allied health fields, and far below the general population (Elmore, 2004). Some suggested explanations have included lower rates of pet ownership among minorities, lack of recruitment of minorities, and cost of education relative to expected income (Chubin & Mohamed, 2009; Gilmore, 2004). However, a critical theory perspective would not place the blame for social and educational inequity on people or organizations, but rather posit a societal problem (Brookfield, 2005). In the case of veterinary education, this rings true. To address this, veterinary medicine must critically evaluate this issue not as isolated within the veterinary field, but in the context of society, as we see this trend in many STEM fields. Equity in learning does not just mean equal opportunity to participate, as affirmative action tries to achieve, but also to provide a safe space for participation (Van der Westhuizen, 2012). Therefore, veterinary medicine must not face its lack of minority representation problem alone but face it as a societal problem to form any real solutions.

Second, critical examination of society is also a key component to being and becoming a scientist, one of the key goals of a veterinary education. Veterinary students are adult learners, and critical thinking, critical reflection, and questioning knowledge is key to adult learners (Brookfield, 2005). Critical theory endorses taking every fact one knows, questioning and deconstructing it, identifying whether it is genuinely fact or a false assertion formed by a preconceived notion (Kilgore, 2001). This mirrors the concept of evidence-based veterinary medicine, one of the pillars of veterinary education. Students must learn to rely on evidence from scientific study with proof, rather than relying on personal experience or empiric evidence. Empiric evidence is veterinary medicine's version of hegemony. For example, the dogma of treating kidney disease with high volumes of intravenous fluids was never questioned until recent studies showed this treatment could cause harm. The scientific method demands questioning assumptions just as critical theory demands it for success as veterinarians, who must be lifelong learners.

A third intersection of politics and veterinary practice is in the socioeconomic factors that impact veterinary care. When I was a veterinarian in private practice, the reality of finances guiding medical decisions was an everyday occurrence. This is one of the factors associated with burnout in the veterinary field, and one to look at with a critical theory lens. Rather than placing blame on individuals, this issue must be assessed as a societal construct. On a political level, veterinarians must be aware of how society has perpetuated inequities like socioeconomic factors, race, and gender, explore their contribution to it, and provide solutions. While this is a difficult undertaking, critical theory aims at being transformative, and provides hope for a solution by first identifying the problem (Brookfield, 2005). Critical pedagogy can create veterinarians who are agents of change for societal problems that lead to veterinary issues, like the cost of care. By broadening their view from veterinary medicine to society as a whole, solutions become more attainable.

As a student and teacher who struggles with society's impact on my identity and as an immigrant, I see how inherently political teaching can be, especially in veterinary education. Our students do not shy away from political action, so why should we, their teachers? Instead, we should learn from them, as politics are linked to significant issues in our field and connecting us veterinarians to society as a whole. Thinking politically, thinking critically, and engaging in these conversations in veterinary education can give rise to veterinarians who can become agents of change within and outside of our profession.

References

Brookfield, S.D. (2005). *The power of critical theory for adult learning and teaching*. New York, NY: Open University Press.

Chubin, D.E., & Mohamed, S. (2009). Increasing minorities in veterinary medicine: National trends in science degrees, local programs, and strategies. *Journal of Veterinary Medical Education, 36*(4), 363-369.

Cake, M.A., McArthur, M.M., Matthew, S.M., & Mansfield, C.F. (2017). Finding the balance: uncovering resilience in the veterinary literature. *Journal of Veterinary Medical Education, 44*(1), 95-105.

Dweck, C.S. (2006). *Mindset: The new psychology of success*. New York, NY: Random House.

Elmore, R.G. (2004). Reasons for the lack of racial diversity in veterinary medicine. *Journal of Veterinary Medical Education, 31*(4), 414-416.

Freire, P. (1970). *Pedagogy of the oppressed*. New York, NY: Continuum International.

Hirschman C. (2004). The origin and demise of race. *Population and Development Review 30*(3), 385-415.

Kilgore, D.W. (2001). Critical and postmodern perspectives on adult learning. *New Directions for Adult and Continuing Education, 89*, 53-61.

Knowles, M.S. (1980). *The modern practice of adult education: From pedagogy to andragogy*. Englewood Cliffs, NJ: Cambridge Adult Education.

Ladson-Billings, G. (1995). But that's just good teaching! The case for culturally relevant pedagogy. *Theory Into Practice, 34*(3), 159-165.

McTighe, J., & Wiggins, G. (2012). *Understanding by design framework*. Alexandria, VA: Association for Supervision and Curriculum Development.

Rhind, S.M. Baillie, S., Kinnison, T., Shaw, D.J., Bell, C.E., Mellanby, R.J., Hammond, J., Hudson, N.P.H., Whittington, R.E., & Donnelly, R. (2011). The transition into veterinary practice: Opinions of recent graduates and final year students. *BMC Medical Education, 11*, 64-74.

Schunk, D.H. (2012). *Learning theories: An educational perspective*. 6th Ed. Boston: Pearson.

Stets, J.E., & Serpe, R.T. (2013). Identity theory. In J. DeLameter & A. Ward (Eds.), *Handbook of Social Psychology* (31-60). Dordrecht: Springer Science+Business Media.

Van der Westhuizen, G.J. (2012). Learning equity in a university classroom. *South African Journal of Higher Education, 26*(3), 621-635.

Yeager, D.S., & Dweck, C.S. (2012). Mindsets that promote resilience: When students believe that personal characteristics can be developed. *Educational Psychologist, 47*(4), 302-314.

Zimmerman, B.J. (1989). A social cognitive view of self-regulated academic learning. *Journal of Educational Psychology, 81*(3), 329-339.

Part III

Anti-colonial Ways of Being

9

Awakening Enquiry, Assisting Discovery

My Journey as Learner and Teacher

Antonia MacDonald

"Real education means to aspire people to live more abundantly, to learn to begin with life as [we] find it and make it better." (Woodson, 1933, p. 29)

It Takes a Village to Raise a Child

I teach because of and in response to the experiences that shaped me as a learner. In her poem "Colonial Girls School," the Jamaican writer Olive Senior speaks of a West Indian education that "yoked our minds to declensions in Latin / and the language of Shakespeare" and "told us nothing about ourselves" (Senior, 1985, p.26). My secondary school education in St. Lucia was delivered largely by Irish nuns who believed firmly in their responsibility to school us out of local habits. St. Joseph's Convent, my high school alma mater, was the only high school for girls in the seventies. The tuition was modest and there were government scholarships for those of us who were poor but academically strong, who in local parlance were referred to as "bright children." The curriculum was orthodox—Catholic and colonial. There was nothing Caribbean in the subjects we were studying in preparation to sit the Cambridge Ordinary Level General Certificate of Education. There was no need to be. In our minds and in the dreams of our struggling single parents we were on our way to become "doctors and lawyers"—British trained. Our Convent education would rescue us from the poverty that mired the fate of our less fortunate brothers, sisters, cousins. We, the "bright children," were our families' hope, and every day the rough hands that combed our hair, straightened our uniforms, slapped orange butter into loaves of bread that would serve as our school lunch, reminded us of our responsibility to succeed in school. Each term when we got our report books, our mothers would quietly adjust their expectations—if not a lawyer or a doctor, then maybe a teller in one of the three banks, or a civil servant. Anything better than a shop clerk.

There was always the tendency for me to feel ashamed of my home and my community. I had a grand aunt who was a drunk and there were days when I would pass her in the rum shop near my home, my gaze averted, my head lofty with disdain, wearing my blue convent-girl tunic like a coat of armour should she in a moment of drunken forgetfulness dare to loudly acknowledge that we were kin. And as I grew more accustomed to the pristine environment of the St. Joseph's Convent, I willingly let it rank superior to my home life. I walked differently, spoke like the Irish nuns who taught me, and wore my Catholic faith as an armour that protected me from the teasing and scorn of the young boys who hung around streets that I needed to traverse as I made my way from school to home. High school was my passport to somewhere else. Education would put me out of the reach of all those who threatened to reduce me to ordinariness.

Moving up to higher forms, slowly leaving adolescence behind, the Eurocentric curriculum opened me up to a world far removed, yet familiar. For while I really had no interest in why Hannibal was crossing the Alps or in understanding the function of the subjunctive in Latin grammar, I was at home with the rhythm of that language. For a long time, Latin had been the language of the mass in Catholic St. Lucia. It was the language in which my illiterate grandmother would recite her morning prayers. Now it was the language in which I sang out my conjugations of Latin verbs. In history class, we were taught British history. I was amused by the pettiness of a war over Jenkin's ears. Having been taught to hold in great esteem all things British, I was perversely tickled by the idea of White people behaving so childishly. I read their behaviours to be as infantile as the public squabbles of local Black politicians.

But it was the study of English Literature that allowed me to connect the world of school to the life of my community. Studying the novels of Dickens and Hardy brought me into a landscape that was as loud and raucous, as squalid and gritty, as the one in which I was growing up. I was truly at home in those classes. It was there that I shone—loud and brash. I was unafraid to offer an opinion on characterization, or on themes such as poverty, self-determination. These concepts were ones I was able to filter through my own lived experiences. When giving a local example to illustrate my point I would, in my excitement to explicate, very often descend into St. Lucian Creole English. A fight that happened at the standpipe where we collected water or an unfortunate encounter with the rich landowner whose mango orchard we frequently raided were just as valid as Pip's meeting with the convict in *Great Expectations*, or Tess's accidental murder of the family horse in *Tess of the d'Urbervilles*. While my examples were acceptable, my language of explication had no place in the formality of the classroom. In her essay, "Challenges of the struggle for sovereignty: Changing the world versus writing stories," Merle Hodge captures the ambivalence of Caribbean people to Creole languages: "we speak Creole, we need Creole, we cannot function without Creole, for our deepest thought processes are bound up in the structure of Creole, but we hold Creole in utter contempt" (Hodge, 1990, p.204). My teachers had been educated into a disavowal of our mother tongue and were committed to discrediting Creole English (CE). At the same time, I was part of a Creole community that was loud with language and behaviours that my formal education was taking no notice of. It was this tension between these two states of being that slowly created in me what W.E.B. Du Bois has theorized as a double consciousness.

> It is a peculiar sensation, this double consciousness, this sense of always looking at one's self through the eyes of others, of measuring one's self by the tape of a world that looks on with amused contempt and pity. One feels his twoness, ... two souls, two thoughts, two unreconciled strivings; two warring ideals in one dark body whose dogged strength alone keeps it from being torn asunder (Du Bois, 1903, p.2).

In Caribbean high schools in the early seventies, the curricular path was a narrow one. After five years of secondary education, we would all sit the General Certificate of Education (GCE)-Ordinary Level. The number of subjects we would take depended on the family's finances. Math and English were *de rigueur*, and no student was allowed to take less than five subjects. The bright students and the wealthy ones would take eight or nine. Deemed bright though not at all wealthy, I registered to sit eight GCE subjects. I failed five. The shock and the horror of this dastardly academic performance constitutes one of the major moments in my life. I was bright! Both by my own accounts and by the accounts of my teachers. At that time, I had no explanation for why I had performed so poorly in my GCE exams. Looking back at that experience, I can offer many suppositions. Perhaps it was because these foreign tests were culturally biased that I found myself handicapped by the knowledge that was not translatable in a British colonial context. Or it may be that I had grown used to playing outside the sandbox of a Eurocentric curricula that left no room for experimentation. But these reasons remain mere conjecture.

The nuns graciously readmitted me to repeat Form Five and from that moment onwards, I became a more focused student. Having known the agony of failure, my fifteen-year-old self-vowed that from then on, I would keep my eyes solidly on the academic prize. Mastery in school was all that would matter. I played by the pedagogical rules set by the GCE curricula and was less inclined to seek correspondences between the world of school and that of home. Although I was not overly concerned with being at the top of the class, I wanted to push myself to be my best academic self. Now that my GCE failure had shown me how easily the dream of academic advancement could be destroyed, I quietly set myself the task of excelling at whatever I undertook. The following year I sat and passed all my GCE O-level subjects.

Advanced levels were my next goal—one that the many female teachers at the St. Joseph's convent were quietly supporting. Despite my mother's insistence that I find a job, I enrolled in the newly minted A-level college. My plan was to work on Saturdays and use that money to pay my tuition. Perhaps, the determination that now contoured my actions, persuaded my mother of the futility of deferring me from my goals. Already I had gone further academically than anyone in the family.

My love for literature and my facility with foreign languages led me to choose French, English Literature, and Economics as the subjects I would study at the advanced level. English literature was still my favourite subject and one at which I seemed naturally to excel. Geographic proximity to Martinique made the study of French a practical selection. Economics—a discipline totally new to me—was selected on the basis that it sounded like a subject that would teach me how to make money and maybe get me a job in a bank.

The St. Lucia A-level College was a very different learning space from the St. Joseph convent. Many of the teachers were young radicals who had returned home from university, steeped in Black consciousness, anticolonial fervour, and nationalistic zeal. To these potters, we were clay to be fashioned into change agents. For me, these teachers were examples of what I could be. Promulgators of the ideals of a democratic society. Advocates of a new social order (Counts, 1932). Successful by dint of academic perseverance. Whereas I could not look to my family for academic advice or career guidance, the teachers, keenly aware that many of us were first-generation college students, were happy to provide this much-needed mentoring. While the curriculum they were required to teach was still British-based, they supplemented their praxis with material produced by scholars at the University of the West Indies and from the United States. Every week, we had an hour of class discussion on regional and local issues. Walter Rodney's (1969) book, *The Groundings with My Brothers,* was a seminal work, one which historicized Blackness and gave us a deep understanding of the Black Power movement, which was then dominating the region. Many of our teachers had been part of the Rodney riots in Jamaica. As disciples of Walter Rodney, they were "making knowledge serve the liberation of our communities from the oppressive European histories and epistemologies which seek to contain this knowledge, just as they historically contained our bodies" (Boyce-Davies, 2019, p. xi). Slowly, I was developing a militant Black consciousness. I felt free to negotiate my own future. Afroed and sandaled, dashiki-wearing and vocal, I let my love for literature propel me into avenues of ontology and philosophy that I had once rejected as distractions. I found correspondences everywhere. In my French literature class, the study of the novels of Jean-Paul Sartre brought me to Franz Fanon's *Black Skin, White Masks* (1952) and an appreciation of the excoriating effects of racism and colonialism. Reading *The Tempest* in my English literature class, Shakespeare's Caliban became a model of rebellion against cultural imperialism. At the same time, Gerard Manley Hopkins's *Dark Night of the Soul* was a cautionary reminder of the consequences of straying too far from the religious fealty that I had been so long schooled in. Studying Joyce's *Portrait of an Artist as a Young Man*, I identified with Stephen Dedalus. I too longed to be free of the restrictions of my small island society. Like Stephen, I dreamt of becoming an artist—a St. Lucian woman writer. But that was a very, very secret dream. One that I didn't even dare say aloud. No.

Instead, I gave voice to my other choice—the pragmatic one. I was going to go to university to study business management because that area of study was on the St. Lucian Government's priority list for national development. I applied and was provisionally accepted to the Department of Social Sciences, at the University of the West Indies, St. Augustine campus, in Trinidad. Encouraged by this, I took my teachers' advice to apply for a student loan. I had no collateral to support my loan application—my mother was firmly against the idea of further study. Eight years of secondary schooling was more than enough. But my grandmother, poor and illiterate, believed in my desire for academic advancement and gave me the title of her small plot of land to serve as a guarantee for the loan. She wanted to give me the fullest access to education. As she said to me in *Kwéyòl* [1] that day: "My child, if you tell me that that is what you want, then I will help you. You are a good child. Go and make something of yourself." This unswerving support by a woman who had never gone all the way through primary school is part of what has formed the woman I am today. My grandmother was a market vendor. There were many days that she had sat in the hot, baking sun, hawking vegetables and ground provisions, and had come home empty-handed. But over time, she had squirrelled away enough money to purchase land and build herself a two-roomed house. She is an example of hard work and determination. My mother, similarly hardworking and determined, lacked my grandmother's patience with my dreams. Perhaps she learned that dreams are expensive indulgences because when she was my age (she became a mother at eighteen) she was charged with

---
[1] *Kwéyòl* is the French-based Creole widely spoken in St. Lucia.

the responsibility of a baby daughter. Perhaps too, the sheer daring of my desire to transcend my class and gender expectations frightened my mother. It was bold, it was overreaching, and ultimately it was tempting fate. But while she was loud in her dismissal of my ambition to become a university graduate, she continued to provide me with food and shelter—her form of tacit support. All I was responsible for was succeeding in my A-levels.

The spectre of my failure at the O-levels still haunted me. This time I was leaving nothing to chance. I was so studious that my mother complained that my nose was always in a book and I did not help with any chores. I was steadfast. I needed to pass all my subjects. To that end, I read more than the syllabi required. A newly self-directed learner, I wrote more essays than those assigned and when I didn't receive an A grade, redid the essays until I earned the top mark. My teachers encouraged my diligence with praise. In a small island with such a small population of female students pursuing A-level certification, my teachers were keen to support our academic efforts. But I was careful not to be side-tracked by praise. O-levels had taught me that bitter lesson.

When the A-level results came out, my sterling performance in the Cambridge Advanced-level exam earned me an island scholarship. Every year, based on the performance in the A-level exams, the top male and female performers receive a full scholarship from the government of St. Lucia to pursue studies in any discipline and at any university in the world. Had I ever considered myself an island scholarship contender, I might have applied to universities in the UK, Canada, or the U.S. to read English Literature. But aware of my modest financial resources, I had chosen a regional university and an employable program of study. Now that new options were available, I had the choice to work for a year, during which I could apply to read English at international universities. Instead I chose to stick with the plan: go to Trinidad to study business management. For someone who had never travelled, Trinidad was sufficiently challenging—a brave new world across the ocean that, with its calypso and carnival, was culturally familiar.

My first year at university was wonderful. I lived in a hall of residence where I met students from many other Caribbean islands. Conversations in the hall's dining room would revolve around current political events—the senior students were loud in their advocacy for a social order that validated the working-class Caribbean person. Their revolutionary zeal made me both conscious and proud of the weight of social responsibility that access to university had bestowed on me. My lecturers were experts in their fields and serious about their responsibilities as Caribbean educators. I enjoyed the intellectual rigour of subjects such as sociology and politics which drew so heavily on Caribbean examples to expound classical theories. Through their educational praxis, our lecturers constantly reminded us that access to and the privilege of tertiary education were transforming us into builders of a new Caribbean, architects of independence and sovereignty. And to crown it all, my scholarship stipend was very generous. I had more money than I had ever seen, large portions of which I sent home to my mother and grandmother. It was good to be in a position to make a financial contribution to my family.

But I sorely missed literature.

It was as if there was a hole in my soul that nothing else could fill. And that very, very quiet dream of being a writer was now making its way to the front of my consciousness. Rex Nettleford avers, "if the people of the Caribbean own nothing else, they certainly can own their creative imagination, which viewed in a particular way, is a powerful means of production for much that brings meaning and purpose to human life" (Nettleford, 1979, p. xvii). All around the St. Augustine campus was evidence of this thriving creative imagination—in drama productions, spoken-word poetry competitions, *ex tempo* concerts, calypso shows. I was going to public readings of the poetry of Edward Brathwaite and devouring novels being written by West Indian novelists such as George Lamming, Samuel Selvon and Wilson Harris. Merle Hodge's *Crick, Crack Monkey* (1970) resonated deeply with me. I could identify with the young female protagonist who, growing up under the weight of cultural imperialism, chooses to reject the local in favour of the elsewhere of England. I felt that I too could tell a story similar in voice and *gravitas* to this Trinidadian coming-of-age story. The St. Lucian poet and dramatist, Derek Walcott, worked for a Trinidadian newspaper and was a very frequent visitor to the St. Augustine campus. I yearned to be like him. Maybe I too could earn a living by my pen. Or, less ambitiously, I could become a teacher of literature and encourage other young people to dare to dream of becoming creative writers. At the end of my first year at university I switched from Business Management to English. The lecturers in the Department of English were well-established literary critics who were actively shaping a Caribbean literary aesthetics. Their emphasis on the use of contemporary sources, their training us to develop our research and analytical skills were laudable. Their commitment to expanding Caribbean literary studies was inspirational. I vowed to one day join them in that worthy enterprise.

The road to my career as a university lecturer has been a meandering one—detours including marriage, child-rearing, divorce, migration. Refuelling came in the form of a Fulbright to pursue doctoral studies at Ohio State University;

and a visiting professorship at St. George's University. But, finally, I have settled into my ambition.

She who Learns, Teaches

In the gospel according to Luke, we are told: "To whom much is given, much will be required." (Luke 12:48). This has been my guiding philosophy as a teacher, and as a leader. I am a product of a small, poor, underdeveloped society. My ability to rise beyond the inequalities that poverty produces—limited access to books, poor study spaces, inability to pay for extracurricular artistic activities—was a function of the many teachers who were willing to close the opportunity gap created by my reduced economic status. Not that they made concessions for my poverty, nor were they naïve enough to pontificate that education would be my panacea, the equalizer that would erase the burden of race, class, and gender. But they urged me to look beyond my limitations. I always teach with their voices in my head. Voices that urged me on to what George S. Counts, in *Dare the School Build a New Social Order*, describes as progressive education—an education that has at its core a "compelling and challenging vision of human destiny," one that equips us with the skills to squarely and courageously tackle every social issue, and in the process establishes an organic relationship with the communities (Counts, 1932, p.7). To that end, these teachers encouraged me to make the fullest use of my potential. From them I learnt that education would allow me a life better than my mother's and grandmother's. Education would give me the opportunity to ensure that my children had a better life than mine. Education would allow me to improve my community.

I remain grateful to these teachers. I show that gratitude by taking my responsibility seriously to provide students with a stimulating educational environment in which they can flourish and grow into change agents. I have no formal training in education, but from the day I first stepped foot into a Grade Eight classroom in Jamaica, I was committed to improving my pedagogical skills so I could be a successful teacher of English Language and Literature. My classroom management skills were non-existent, and my learning curve was a steep one. A Jamaican classroom was a far cry from a St. Lucian one. Very often, the students and I had difficulty understanding each other. Jamaican *Patwa* sounded like a foreign language to me. Although I was newly married to a Jamaican engineer, his linguistic milieu had not prepared me for this lexical challenge. Oftentimes I was made rudely aware that my students did not understand my French-inflected accent. In that first year of teaching, there were a lot of tears—mostly mine. But tears notwithstanding, I was resolute in my desire to be as good a teacher as those women who had once taught me.

Wright (2005) purports that the teacher's struggle with classroom management may negatively impact students' motivation and involvement levels. I did not want to lose my learners, and therefore learnt to model my teaching on the successful practice of other senior teachers. I found a way to let authority firm my voice into a "teacher" voice—one that the students would listen to and respect. My speech became slower, more measured. The English curriculum that I was required to teach was modelled on British grammar school education, but fortunately, my grounding in English Literature was thorough. Thus, my enthusiasm for Literature was converted into assurance that with diligence I could get my students to understand and appreciate Literatures written in English. Although I still cried in frustration and self-doubt, I had arrived at the pragmatic wisdom that the students should never see me cry.

So, I faked confidence, and always hoped that my earnest desire to be a good teacher would help me develop the flexibility, responsiveness, and metacognition that Sánchez Solarte (2019) advocates as key components to classroom management. Remembering my excitement as a young student when I could establish correspondence between the text and my own experience, I drew on the increasing body of Caribbean literature to amplify the English curriculum. Moving away from a textbook approach to the English language curriculum, I was able to insert in the margins of these Eurocentric works examples drawn from life in the Caribbean. I encouraged students to make creative use of the Jamaican vernacular in their compositions and to draw on the images around them in their creative writing. I moved our classes outdoors where they could observe nature—Caribbean flowers, Caribbean fruits, Caribbean seasons—and connected these experiences to the works being studied. John Gibson argued that literature "gives substance to the range of values, concerns and experiences that define human reality" (Gibson, 2007, p. 116), but my pedagogical experiment in these classrooms was, through affirmation and validation, allowing Caribbean reality to give substance to British literature. Although I was unaware of it, my praxis was being richly informed by Maxine Greene's philosophy of aesthetic education. I was bringing my students to what Greene describes as "a distinctive mode of literacy, an achieved capacity to break with ordinary ways of seeing and hearing" (Greene, 1980, p. 319). Through my attempts to release my students' imaginations and let them find their voices, my classroom became a microcosmic, federated Caribbean community, rich with the colour, images, and sounds of everyday life in different Caribbean islands.

Eventually, my passion for Literature and my ability to learn through modelling other teachers earned me classroom control and student respect. Berliner

(2004) claims that "expert teachers are more sensitive to task demands and social situations when solving pedagogical problems…more flexible in their teaching…and have fast and accurate pattern-recognition capabilities, whereas novices cannot always make sense of what they experience" (p. 201). While I cannot claim I transitioned from novice to expert during my Jamaica years, I believe I achieved some modicum of effectiveness. There are many young girls I taught in Jamaica who have kept in touch with me. Every Christmas, their cards testify to the impact I had in their lives. I take pleasure from this because embedded in their testimonials is my awareness of the immense payoff from my years of struggle to become a good teacher. That struggle has been formative. It shaped my pedagogy as I went on to teach first at the community college level and then at university. My problem-solving skills, my commitment to motivating students to succeed in challenging learning environments, and my sense of responsibility as an educator who leads by example, are the fortuitous products. My tendency to teach through play is another carryover skill, one to which I would frequently resort to when teaching my daughters or other family members.

"Iron Sharpens Iron" (Proverbs 27:17)

I want to highlight three critical moments that have shaped my beliefs and practices as an educator. These are (1) learning how to be a good single parent; (2) my deep involvement with the Caribbean Examinations Council (CXC); and (3) surviving Hurricane Ivan in 2004.

(1) In 1993, in the space of eight life-changing months, I got divorced, received a Laspau Fulbright scholarship to do doctoral studies, and migrated to Ohio, USA with my two daughters, one eight and the other twelve. In Ohio, I quickly discovered that the authoritarian rules of parenting, which we practiced in the Caribbean—"You do it because I said so!…Children must know their place—to be seen and not heard!"—would not serve me in good stead. Unmoored from the familial support of my mother, grandmother, and aunts, parenting by coercion was counterintuitive. Instead, I had to transition to what Baumrind (1971) has described as authoritative parenting. But superimposed on this was a philosophy of parenting that was feminist in its perspective. I was the product of a female-headed household and was accustomed to practices and ideas that valued women. In Ohio, the matrifocality of my household was extended to my daughters as power-sharers. For example, when they needed something that I could not afford, or permission to go somewhere that I did not approve of, I required them to write me an essay persuading me to the logic of that request. After they had made their case in writing, we would, as a

family, discuss the "petition." They would also have an opportunity to rebut. Although, all this was done with mock formality and barely disguised hilarity, through discussion and negotiation, I was directing my daughters into learning how to defend their position, how to make wise decisions, and how to be socially and, in turn, academically self-reliant. Without fully relinquishing parental control, I had to let them learn these core skills through the process of doing, while at the same time recognizing and affirming what Baumrind postulates as each child's special qualities while setting standards for their future conduct (p. 891). My daughters learned how to take responsibility for decisions made in the process—lessons that would serve them well in the future. Where much of literary feminism focuses on the contested relationship between mother and daughter, I was committed to ensuring that I did not rehearse these antagonisms in my interactions with my daughters. I wanted instead to provide nurturance that, to paraphrase Flax, carried with it a deep concern for the wellbeing of my daughters without demanding that they prove their worthiness of it (Flax, 1978, p. 187).

That does not mean I became permissive in my parenting. I was the adult responsible for them and I took that charge very seriously, even though it meant becoming Janus-faced, when at a moment's notice, I moved from "mother as friend' to "mother as commander-in-chief." I needed to set my daughters' limits. Limits provided structure for the articulation of their freedom and gave me the framework for the judicious exercise of my parental power and authority. But whereas in the Caribbean, parenting tended to be hierarchical where power flows downward from parent to child, I learned that our survival as a family depended on me reshaping that paradigm into a circle of inclusiveness. My children had to help me support them. In this process of shared governance, I had to learn how to be a strong woman in order to teach my children strength. Edith Clarke (1957) talks about Caribbean mothers as fathering. During my three years as a doctoral student in Ohio, my daughters fathered and mothered me even as I mothered and fathered them. The experience of learning by doing, of recalibrating leadership and of participatory governance are what I have carried over into my teaching practice. In my classroom, I provide a framework of critical enquiry and give my students leave to question and uproot hegemonies of dominion. But implicit to this act of dismantling is the responsibility to create new paradigms of equality, justice, and responsible freedom. We are all builders of this brave new world of empowered Caribbean citizenry. My roles as teacher educator, leader mentor, require that I take seriously my role as change facilitator.

(2) In their 1963 essay, "English Literature in the Region…," Carr and Ingledew described Caribbean society as having "not long entered upon the complex and difficult process of finding itself, at arriving at an understanding and generous consciousness of its own identity" (p.63). At the heart of their argument was the emphasis on the Caribbean classroom as a space of knowledge transformation. The increase in nationalist fervor in the region enabled the historic shift from an English-based general certification examination to a Caribbean one where examinations were set and marked by regional educators. The Caribbean Examinations Council (CXC) was established in 1975, and its Caribbean-designed syllabi brought visibility to the region's literature, history, geography and culture. In 1980, I became an examiner with CXC. In that role, I learned first-hand to appreciate the tremendous potential embedded in a curriculum that privileged local and regional sources of knowledge. In time, I became part of the examining team for English literature, first at the secondary level and then at the advanced level as Chief Examiner. Whereas before, I was involved in the marking of the examination, now I was involved in setting the examination. That experience of crafting and testing the examination syllabus for Literatures in English taught me to liberalize the ways in which we assess to privilege different forms of knowledge and, in the process, create more equity. I also developed mindfulness in the selection of the stimulus material chosen for examination. While it was important to ensure that we tested the students' knowledge of other cultures lest we should be accused of training navel-gazers, we needed to be mindful that such cultural experiences were relatable to the average 16-year-old Caribbean student. Moreover, the incorporation of a school-based assessment (SBA) allowed students a range of possible ways of engaging with and representing their experience of studying literary texts. In focusing on learner knowledge in the classroom, these SBAs provided more flexible means of assessing diverse student populations and democratized the study of a subject that had long been deemed esoteric and accordingly not functional. It was this attention to assessments that were cognizant of learning styles that I have been able to incorporate in my university classroom. For example, in a course such as Introduction to Caribbean studies, my students are required to create a portfolio where they imaginatively insert themselves as game-changers in five specific moments of Caribbean history. In bringing together their interest in History, or Politics, or Sociology and Creative Writing, this assignment appeals to students with diverse learning styles and disciplinary training. The breadth and depth of their interventions on Caribbean social transformation also help engender in them a stronger expression of a confident, multifaceted and integrative Caribbean identity.

(3) On September 7, 2004, Category Five Hurricane Ivan destroyed Grenada. St. George's University did not fare as badly as the rest of Grenada. Their roofs held, their phone lines miraculously stood up to the onslaught. But to continue to teach in an island where all other services were now disrupted was not feasible and accordingly, students in the Schools of Medicine and Veterinary Medicine were evacuated to teaching sites in the US. Two weeks later, the School of Arts and Sciences resumed teaching on a campus that was still trying to cope with the infrastructural ravages of the hurricane, in a country where all other services were rapidly deteriorating. Basic needs—food, water, and shelter—remained unmet for a large percentage of Grenadians.

In my capacity as Acting Dean, I had the responsibility of ensuring that our students and faculty, the majority of whom were Grenadians—returned to psychological, physical, and academic wellness. Grace under pressure and calm in the midst of chaos were the core skills I had to manifest in my role as a senior administrator. The resilience, agility, and indomitable optimism I had honed during my Ohio experience now served me as I led my faculty team in delivering quality instruction amidst the chaos of reconstruction and psychic restoration.

Teaching in a time of crisis requires us to lead with care and empathy. While our syllabi had to be retrofitted to meet our pedagogical requirements, we needed, at the same time, to be attentive to the role of the university in the physical and psychic rebuilding of Grenada. The heterogeneity of our student body impelled us to open pathways towards better and more imaginative ways of teaching (Greene, 1995, p.12). Social justice needed to infuse our praxis especially when, at a time of national scarcity, the university was privileged in how many resources it had at its disposal. So together as a faculty, we ideated to construct new connections between the university and the Grenadian community. Core to this was the application of course content to an island community struggling to "build back better." Business, Psychology, Information Technology, Community Health, Marine Rehabilitation were all areas of social need that could infuse our praxis as we worked together to create deep buckets of hope for a wounded Grenada.

At the administrative end, it was crucial that our SAS students and faculty were not overlooked in the larger campus restoration effort. It was my responsibility as the only school Dean (acting) of colour to keep the upper administration always mindful that our reconstruction initiatives needed to be safeguarded against colour-blindness. Return to normalcy could not be predicated on the desires and needs of foreign students who had the financial resources to smooth that process. Given that many of the local students were challenged because their living spaces had been destroyed by the hurricane, and given that many of the campus dormitories were empty because of foreign student evacuation, we initiated an arrangement where local students moved into on-campus accommodation at highly discounted rates. Further, as part of the team coordinating the January 2005 return of all students to the campus, I came to a deeper and richer appreciation of the fullness of the university's commitment to student-centricity, and this knowledge has become a guiding principle in my teaching and administration. Students First. Always. In Spring 2020, when we went under COVID-19 induced lockdown, that principle is what enabled me to guide vulnerable students towards the successful completion of their courses.

Wood already Touched by Fire isn't Hard to Light

Disclosure. Although I may not have always known it or named it, my key beliefs about teaching and leadership are deeply interpellated by Paulo Freire. His *Pedagogy of the Oppressed* (1970) was a landmark text and the essence of ideas therein was being quietly distilled by Caribbean educators: education that is participatory will empower its citizenry, improve our material conditions, and bring about a new social order. My teachers were leaders committed to making optimum use of our human capital. I grew up to become a teacher who leads by example. My key beliefs about teaching and learning contour my professional and personal life. My autobiographical narrative with which this chapter opens is proof of my belief in the transformative power of education.[2] However, I believe education is transformative to *both* teacher and student. The teacher, in always being open to adaptation, grows and changes through the experience of teaching. Moreover, through shared authority for the learning experience, teacher and student discursively enlarge the body of knowledge, each bringing their subjectivity to bear on the material, and in each intervention, they participate in the creation of what Freire has described as good democracy-oriented pedagogy that "forges a school-adventure, a school that marches on, that is not afraid to take risks and that rejects immobility" (Freire, 1998, p. 212). The precise scope of that "school-adventure" is a function of the concatenation of sociocultural, economic, educational, and psychological landscapes. In his infamous *Minute on Indian Education*, Macaulay advocated for educating the colonial subject "to form…a class of person, Indian in blood and colour, but English in taste, in opinion, in morals and in intellect" (Macaulay,1935, p.

---

2 I am aware rereading this narrative that it is a story told by an older self, and that if ten or twenty years ago I was telling the story of myself, that story may be very different in emphases than the one I now tell. That is largely because I am always learning about myself and changing through the process of coming to know. I am always in the process of becoming and the act of storytelling enables that process. What remains unchanged is my enduring belief in the alchemy of education.

729). Speaking to education as a primary colonizing strategy and its purpose in naturalizing one's colonial status, Macaulay's ideology dominated educational practices in the Caribbean for a long time —the examinations offered to the sixteen-year-old English student were exactly the same ones that were sat by colonial students in the outposts of the British empire. Independence dislocated this shared history with England and in the process, the Caribbean educational system has undergone significant improvement over the last fifty years—the liberalization and indigenization of the curricula, access to free secondary education, and the establishment of a regional examination council are privileges that separate one generation from another. These changes in the region's educational landscape bode well for a future defined by equity and access.

Today's Caribbean students are hardly free of challenges. Hegemonies of race and class are still entrenched. Teaching at St. George's University brings me into constant consideration of these hegemonies. Inequality in access remains an ongoing challenge for many students in the School of Arts and Sciences. For students living in poverty, increased access to university does not automatically garner educational success (Gorski, 2017). Although they have access to scholarships, many Grenadian students have difficulty getting to and from the university because of the high cost and unreliability of public transportation. They cannot afford to buy textbooks, nor do they have computers or internet access at home. Additionally, there are hidden costs associated with attending university. As first-generation university students, many lack familial support in their homespaces. Competition for scarce domestic resources, for space, for quiet—that is their reality. How can my praxis recognize and compensate for these educational inequalities? How can I, in my educational practices, be more inclusive? I used to be like them once, but now I am far removed socially and economically, so my critical lens needs to always be calibrated to look at me, looking at them, which means that my capacity for self-reflexivity and self-change must remain finely honed (hooks, 2000). Regenerative. So that I can, in fulfilling my pedagogic responsibilities, remain one who "understand[s] and continue[s] in sympathy with those whom they instruct" (Woodson, 1933, p.28).

While the prominent socioeconomic standing of the university in Grenada automatically invests the students with social perceptions of privilege, that feeling of being special, socially superior even, does not insulate many of my undergraduate students against the consequences of being a racial minority at St. George's University. Many Grenadian students do not believe themselves to be at home here, even while this institution is in their homeland. They belong to a school that is often perceived as a loss leader. Their classroom spaces are often rudimentary: the layout is inflexible, the furniture uncomfortable, and the integration of technology in these spaces is inefficient and ineffective. In the fierce competition for study space, they always lose.

Additionally, the low percentage of Black students on their campus is also for them the daily, visual vocabulary of minority-status. Aware of this challenge, my aim is always to develop in students a critical consciousness (Freire, 2005) that imbues them with the ability to recognize and critique systems of inequality—be they sociocultural, economic, or political, and concomitantly, the commitment to take positive action against these tyrannies. How can we as educators give them the tools to embark on such an enterprise? How can I cultivate in them a critical vocabulary that helps them name and analyse these inequalities? Specifically, how do I, through my lectures and Socratic questioning, enable them to process the long-internalized racism that made them see themselves as objects of a history of oppression and victimization? Perhaps the answer lies in strategic opposition to the pervasive, yet sometimes hidden inequalities perpetrated by race, caste, and class conditions in the Caribbean. In discussing such contentious power dynamics, we are called to be brutally honest about our own complicity in reinforcing these either through silence, ignorance, or fear. My classroom is a safe space where these competing ideas contend.

I believe that education is also passion-filled. This belief is not value-neutral because, as advocates such as hooks and Freire attest, education is political (Freire, 1970, 1973; Horton & Freire, 1990; hooks, 1994, 2000). The curriculum to which I was exposed as a secondary school student is proof of that. So too are the countervailing efforts of my college and university teachers. I am a product of the passion of the latter. In decolonizing my praxis, I hope to enable my students to move beyond a history of lamentation or a litany of blame. Through courses such as Caribbean Popular Culture and Identity, I show them how to better understand the ways in which Caribbean cultural practices have long served as a way of surviving the yoke of enslavement. The dynamism of Caribbean culture is both a reinforcement of our past and a way of emancipating ourselves from the mental slavery (Garvey, 1937). Caribbean popular culture—be it in the spheres of music, festivals, sports, literature, or dance—enables us to be forward-thinking in terms of how our culture can help us to craft a future defined by a strong Caribbean identity. Such formulations empower students to embrace proactivity on a personal, community, and national level. The evolution and movement from understanding to action (Freire, 2005), is key. We must have faith in their ability to be transformative and can facilitate that process by sharing with them stories of transformation—big stories about resistance to marginalization, little stories about coping strategies to remain culturally grounded, Caribbean stories, international stories. To transform, we must be able to story our life. To survive and thrive in stressful situations, we must, following Chinua Achebe, "put away the complexes of the years of denigration and debasement" (Achebe, 1973, p. 3) and instead heed Lamming's (1995) direction in taking an inventory of the traces that comprise the critical elaboration of Caribbean consciousness.

The Short Cut to the Future is Via the Past

In *Where We Stand: Class Matters*, hooks' life story exemplifies a central claim in the book that meaningful solidarity (as opposed to empathy) with poor people is possible only through a willingness both to critically consider where each of us stands within global class hierarchies and to challenge class inequalities through our actions. I am always aware of and critiquing my subject position as a now-privileged, transnational Caribbean scholar. Even while I wish to lead the change that I advocate, it must first be by example if it is to be a successful change. I am aware that students find me a strict taskmaster, but in my interactions with them I hold myself to the same exacting standards—punctuality, accountability, productivity, and commitment. Intent on nurturing my students' curiosity, I share my own ongoing curiosity and interest in education with them —education in its broadest senses and in its widest social and political manifestations.

Another strategy I use in my classrooms is what Clifford Geertz has referred to as "a feeling for immediacies" (Geertz, 1983, p.167). In my deployment of the local and familiar as the starting point of discussions, I am seeking to make connections relatable and relevant. This practice harkens back to my very early years of teaching where I used Indigenous resources to facilitate learning. Extending Wright's edict that the classroom is the true centre of educational experience (Wright, 2005, p.1), I have gone back to my cultural roots where community-based learning happens in informal social spaces and often move my instructional space away from the physical and formal spaces of the classroom to art galleries, dance studios, community centres. In my attempts to encourage my students to actively engage with their society/community and with their instructional material, I am careful to avoid cultural voyeurism. Instead, I offer a guided enquiry that allows for what James Clifford has so beautifully captured as: "insiders studying their own cultures offer[ing] new angle of vision and depth of understanding" (Clifford,1986, p.9) because "…every version of an 'other' wherever found, is also the construction of a self" (Clifford, 1986,

p. 23). Greene advocates that the teacher embrace the adventurousness that is implicit to aesthetic encounters (Greene, 1980, p. 318). That adventurousness is not without its pitfalls. Alongside the deep observation and interrogation of cultural images and artefacts which constitute Caribbean popular culture must exist the realization that as partakers of these images and artefacts we are constantly valorizing and re-inscribing them as part of a dominant discourse. Finally, I incorporate simulations in my teaching because it releases the imagination and makes for what Greene describes as "openings without which our lives narrow and our pathways become cul-de-sacs" (Greene, 1995, p. 17).

I am always learning to adapt. It is only through adaptation I can fulfil my key philosophy that in the creation of a Caribbean knowledge economy, as educators, we need to awaken our students' curiosity, foster their creativity and encourage collaboration that goes beyond geographic boundaries. Teaching at St. George's University is an ongoing adaptation. In Spring 1999, I accepted a position as a visiting professor who travelled from St. Lucia to Grenada every week to teach three literature courses. Every Wednesday morning, I got into a tiny plane and made an hour-long trip to Grenada. Every Thursday evening, heart in mouth, I took another tiny plane back to St. Lucia. In the fall of that year, I became a full-time associate professor in the School of Arts and Sciences. One year later, I was told that the English Literature program in which I had been recruited to teach was going to be terminated because of low enrolment. My intention was to stay here for four semesters to teach out the students in the program.

Those students have long graduated, the program long terminated, but I am still here. Believing I could make a meaningful contribution to the still-fledging School of Arts and Sciences, I was able to repackage my educational expertise as a Caribbeanist to create courses with a liberal focus that were more than literary. Literature now infuses everything I teach, yet for the exception of *Introduction to Literature*, there are no literature courses offered at St. George's University. I have held the administrative positions of Associate Dean and Senior Associate Dean in the School of Arts and Sciences. In 2010, I resigned this administrative position to dedicate more time to my scholarly and creative writing. I have moved offices eight times—eight buildings triangulated across the campus. My office library has suffered dearly with each move, but I continue to persevere. Flexibility and adaptability are my watchwords. The one constant is my belief that St. George's University can play a significant role in the development of Grenada, and that my role is to help in that endeavour. A St. George's University graduate in every household in Grenada—that is the modest future I dream of.

She who does not know one thing, knows another.

I have enjoyed researching and writing this piece, because it allowed me to discover the intersectionality between my discipline and education, not that I was completely unaware of the cross-fertilization of literary and cultural theories with education theories. The work of theorists such as Henry Giroux, Lawrence Grossberg, bell hooks, Peter McLaren, and Raymond Williams reminds us that culture is not free of ideology and is an educational site where power is produced and enacted, and where agency and social change are manifested. Reading educational theory to buttress my argument, I came to understand that very often these theorists were naming a methodology that cultural studies, postcolonial and feminist theories had taught me to deploy in my teaching. Thus, I am reassured that my existing expertise dovetails with these newly discovered educational theories. I have always chosen to valorize and build on what students know—starting with the familiar and moving onto the unknown. Valorization is important because it gives students confidence and self-worth, especially in a Caribbean context where local knowledge was eschewed in favour of the foreign, the colonial, the imperial (Ashcroft et al., 2002). But the need for educational institutions to promote development of self-worth and building of confidence is not peculiar to the Caribbean.

In Ohio, when assisting my daughters with their homework, I was faced with a similar challenge. They were being exposed to an American system of education, which could potentially make my daughters strangers to themselves. Caribbean literature—my touchstone—provides me with rich examples of the alienating effects of some kinds of education (Lamming, 1953; Hodge, 1970; Kincaid, 1985; Senior, 1985; Brodber, 1988). Thus, my training in this field of study allowed me to deploy in my domestic teaching space strategies to mitigate against those dangers.

I also needed to be strategic. The plan was to take 36 months to complete a Ph.D. after which I would return my daughters to a Caribbean educational system. Their reintegration into the Caribbean classroom needed to be smooth and conducive to academic excellence. I realised that many of the concepts they were learning in History, Geography, and Social Studies would not be transferable to the Caribbean when they returned to that education system. I chose, therefore to introduce them to Caribbeanized material—in the form of stories both oral and written—that would meet the learning needs set by their American elementary or junior high school curricula while being useful when they returned to the St. Lucian school system. Education theorists define this technique as the practice of asset pedagogy. I quietly named this cultural exchange and adaptation of different edu-cultural practices, "creolization"

(Brathwaite, 1974; Cohen, 2007). I also needed to help my daughters with background information on American studies that their teachers presupposed they had. In filling those gaps, I taught them to make very heavy use of the community library. Indeed, going to the library became a family occasion. While I studied, my daughters read books or listened to international music they couldn't access in the Caribbean. In a space with such an abundance of resources, I was determined that the Ohio sojourn be as educationally beneficial to my daughters as it was for me—shared transformation of teacher/mother and students/daughters.

In doing the research for this chapter, I have come to an understanding that in my augmenting of my daughters' education, I may have been practicing what education theorists call "universal learning design." But the strategies that I was consciously deploying were ones I had learned from the postcolonial courses that I took during my doctoral studies. Indeed, one such strategy was a reworking of Audre Lorde's famous statement (1984), "the master's tools will never dismantle the master's house." Absorbing as much knowledge about American society as possible, I reasoned that one needed to understand how the master's house was constructed and the tools used to do so, if one were even to attempt to dismantle it. Borrowing such tools, wilfully appropriating them for strategic use, I aligned my teaching philosophy to "subversive agency" as espoused by Judith Butler (1990). My teaching practices of those Ohio years have remained with me—I continue to urge my students to make use of all available resources on campus, to learn from the many cultures that constitute the student population at St. George's University while at the same time, being confident enough to manifest and share their own cultural practices. Moreover, they must meaningfully apply what they are learning at university to the real-life world to which they return daily.

Paris and Alim (2014), in their conceptualization of culturally sustaining pedagogy (CSP) have defended "pedagogies [that] can and should teach students to be linguistically and culturally flexible across multiple language varieties and cultural ways of believing and interacting" (Paris and Alim, 2014, p. 94). I find this concept to be particularly relevant to my praxis. The issue of Caribbean Creole language in an academic setting continues to be a vexed one for many Caribbean students—Grenadian students being no exception (Craig, 1966,1971; Pollard, 2002; Christie, 2003). Socialized into a denigration of Caribbean Creole English (CCE), my students very often develop American accents because they deem it to be more socially acceptable on campus. To counteract this appropriation of American English for identity affiliation, I introduce them to what Brathwaite (1976) famously defined as "nation language", so as validate the contours, rhythm and timbre of a language that reflects our Caribbean heritage. However, integral to this responsibility of teaching them pride in Grenadian Creole is learning how to code switch between Grenadian Creole and Caribbean Standard English because this linguistic agility will serve them well in an age of globalization (Roberts, 1994).

"Put[ting] into practice an education that critically provokes the learner's consciousness" (Freire, 1998).

In this autobiographical staging of myself as learner and teacher, I am often self-conscious about my use of the first-person voice in what is largely a scholarly piece of writing. Moreover, the act of recalling my past without suffusing the telling with emotions that accompanied the experiences is challenging. How do I balance subjectivity with academic enquiry? And in the retelling of the story of myself, how faithfully am I representing memory? Although I have not named names, what is the ethics of this literary storytelling of my family's life? Will the reader be curious about gaps, the things unsaid, the things half-said? Fragmentation, formlessness, and discontinuities characterize women's autobiographies (Jelinek, 1980) and perhaps the same is true of autoethnographies. While I am treading on new theoretical ground, I am curious at the discoveries that I am making. The narrative journey that constituted the creation of this chapter, in affording me a look back, and a look at what I do in the classroom, has been very eye-opening. I had to own how deeply political I am, even when I do not appear to be so, and how didactic I can be in pursuit of social justice and social change. While I may have traded in my dashiki and sandals, the radicalism of my youth is still there—embedded so deep that it is only in telling the story of my "teacherly" self that I have been reacquainted with it. In *Texaco*, the Martiniquan novelist Patrick Chamoiseau advocates for modes of thought that "reveal stories beneath History most essential for understanding us, stories no books speak of" (Chamoiseau, 1997, p. 35). Participating in this storytelling project has brought me to an autoethnographic moment of self-illumination that goes beyond the articulated story. I am now aware of myriad untold, unnarrated stories inhabiting my consciousness, stories that I have yet to, or perhaps dare not, breathe life into. But what of the stories I choose to speak of?

In the story of myself as teacher, I want to foreground my ongoing commitment to a critical pedagogy which, to cite McLaren, provides me with a mechanism for "thinking about, negotiating, and transforming the relationships in classroom teaching, the production of knowledge, the institutional structures of the [university], and the social and material relations of the wider community, society and nation state" (McLaren, 1998, p.15). But I need here to postscript this commitment with the following caveat: It would not serve my students well if my politics transmogrified into brain-washing, or if I imposed on them a coercive way of thinking that is antithetical to sustainable social transformation and development in my zeal to shape them into Caribbean game-changers. I needed to be always mindful not to underestimate what Ian Baptiste describes as coercive power due to educational niceness—niceness in this instance being my desire "to facilitate an intellectually and morally enriching pedagogical environment" (Baptiste, 2008, p. 22).

I remain a strong advocate of social justice. However, in my reading of education theory on social justice in the classroom (Dewey, 1916), I acknowledge that I do not fully subscribe to that philosophy. For example, I am wholly committed to addressing the social issues that confront my students, and while I involve them in the articulation of such, complete democratization does not exist in my classrooms. Accordingly, while students have a voice in matters related to types of assessments, deadlines for assignments, input in course material, and format of exams, the final decision is mine. I haven't decided if there is merit in full democratization. Students need to be trained in that process before coming to university as responsibility for learning implicit to democracy. With so many students coming to St. George's University directly from high school, where no such democratization occurs, to put them into this environment without some familiar footholds means putting them at academic risk. I can, of course, start the process of democratization—but in small steps, baby steps. Hopefully, by the time these students start taking 400-level courses, they will be better prepared to participate in social justice in the classroom and to accept the responsibilities and consequences therein.

Finally, I strongly believe that as Caribbean educators, we need to decide how we adapt the UNESCO pillars of learning to suit our development needs. In envisaging Caribbean society of the future, who we are cannot be seen through the eyes of Hollywood (Batson-Savage, 2010) and the mass media of the global north. While I am always aware that Literature provides my critical lens, these are by no means rose-coloured. In the celebration and valorization of the Caribbean "local," we need to call out regressive practices such as homophobia, ethnocentrism, colourism, sexism, ableism, and heteropatriarchy that are part of our local practices and inflect our ways of being. Increasingly, literary critics such as Mohammed (2012), and Mahabir and Pirbhai (2015) are urging us towards critical approaches that are more inclusive of Indo-Caribbean culture, which is often marginalized especially where the dominant discourse is Afro-Caribbean. Similarly, cultural critics are discursively engaging with Caribbean sexual expressions and identities (Kempadoo, 2009; Nixon, 2015; Gill, 2018). In arguing for the imperative for a more engaged and complicated understanding of sexuality, they are raising issues of sex tourism and transactional sex. These topical issues need to be aired in our classrooms. Ultimately, what is needed is a pedagogy that is sensitive to and respectful of cultural differences. We must be attentive to the injustice perpetrated when different prejudices intersect in our classrooms. The conversation on designing an engaged pedagogy suitable for the creation of the ideal Caribbean citizen must be amplified by diverse voices—each a "personal vocabulary, the individual melody whose metre is one's biography" (Walcott, 1992, p. 57). I am happy to add my voice to this symphony.

References

Achebe, C. (1973). The novelist as teacher. In G.D. Killam (Ed.). *African writers on African writing*. Heinemann.

Ashcroft, B., Griffiths, G., & Tiffin, H. (2002). *The empire writes back: Theory and practice in post-colonial Literatures*. Routledge.

Azikiwe, N. (Ed.) (2016). *Emancipated from Mental Slavery: Selected sayings of Marcus Garvey*. The Mhotep Corporation.

Baptiste, I. (2008). Wages of niceness: The folly and futility of educators who strive to not impose. *New Horizons in Adult Education and Human Resource Development, 22*(2), 6–28.

Batson-Savage, T. (2010). Through the eyes of Hollywood: Reading representations of Jamaicans in American cinema. *Small Axe, 14*(2 (32)), 42–55. https://doi.org/. 10.1215079900537.

Baumrind, D. (1966). Effects of authoritative parental control on child behavior. *Child Development, 37*(4), 887–907. https://doi.org/. 10.2307/1126611.

Berliner, D.C. (2004). Describing the behavior and documenting the accomplishments of expert teachers. *Bulletin of Science, Technology & Society, 24*, 200–212.

Boyce Davies, C. (2019). Introduction. Re-grounding the intellectual-activist model of Walter Rodney. *Groundings with My Brothers*, Verso. pp. xi–xxii.

Brathwaite. K. (1974). *Contradictory omens: Cultural diversity and integration in the Caribbean*. Savacou Publications.

Brathwaite. K. (1983). Caribbean culture: Two paradigms. In Jürgen Martini (Ed.) *Missile and Capsule* (pp. 9–54). Universität Bremen.

Brathwaite. K. (1984). *History of the voice: The development of nation language in Anglophone Caribbean poetry*. New Beacon Books.

Brodber, E. (1988). *Myal*. New Beacon Books.

Butler, J. (1990). *Gender trouble: Feminism and the subversion of identity*. Routledge.

Carr, W. I. & J Ingledew, J. (1963). English Literature in the Caribbean: An analysis based on results of the U.W.I. examinations in English Literature, 1962. *Caribbean Quarterly, 8*(4), 45–63.

Chamoiseau, P. (1997). *Texaco*. Granta.

Christie, P. (2003). *Language in Jamaica*. Arawak Publications.

Clarke, E. (1957). *My mother who fathered me: A study of the families in three selected communities in Jamaica*. University of The West Indies Press.

Clifford, J. (1986). Introduction: Partial Truths. In James Clifford, J. & Marcus G. E. (Eds.) *Writing culture: The poetics and politics of ethnography; A school of American research seminar* (pp. 1–26). University of California Press.

Cohen, R. (2007). Creolization and cultural globalization: The soft sounds of fugitive power. *Globalizations, 4*(3), 369–384.

Counts, G. S. (1932). *Dare the School Build a New Social Order?* Southern Illinois University Press.

Craig, D. (1966). Some developments in language teaching in the West Indies. *Caribbean Quarterly, 12*(1), 25–34.

Craig, D. (1971). Education and Creole English in the West Indies: Some sociological factors. In Dell Hymes, (Ed.). *Pidginization and creolization of languages* (pp. 371–92). Cambridge University Press.

Dewey, J. (1916). *Democracy and Education: An introduction to the philosophy of education.* Macmillan.

Dickens, C., & Mitchell, C. (2003). *Great expectations.* (Original work published 1861)

Du Bois, W. E. B. (1903). *The souls of black folk.* Dover Publications.

Flax, J. (1978). The conflict between nurturance and autonomy in mother-daughter relationships and within feminism. *Feminist Studies, 4*(1), 171–189.

Freire, P. (1970). *Pedagogy of the Oppressed.* Continuum International Publishing Group.

Freire, P. (1998). *Teachers as cultural workers: Letters to those who dare teach.* Westview Press.

Freire, P. (2005). *Education for Critical Consciousness.* Continuum International Publishing Group.

Gibson, J. (2007). *Fiction and the Weave of Life.* Oxford University Press.

Gill. L.K. (2018). *Erotic islands: Art and activism in the queer Caribbean.* Duke University Press.

Greene, M. (1995). *Releasing the imagination: Essays on Education, the Arts, and Social Change.* John Wiley & Sons, Inc.

Greene, M. (1980). Aesthetics and Experience of the Arts: Towards transformation. *The High School Journal, 63*(8), 316–322.

Gorski, P.C. (2017). *Reaching and teaching students in poverty: Strategies for erasing the poverty gap* (2nd ed.). Teachers College Press.

Hardy, T. (2003). *Tess of the D'Urbervilles.* Penguin. (Original work published 1891)

Hodge, M. (1970). *Crick crack monkey.* Andre Deutsch.

Hodge, M. (1990). Challenges of the struggle for sovereignty: Changing the world versus writing stories. In S. R. Cudjoe, (Ed.). *Caribbean women writers: Essays from the first international conference*, (pp. 202–08). Calaloux.

hooks, b. (1994). *Teaching to transgress: Education as the practice of freedom.* Routledge.

hooks, b. (2000). *Where we stand: Class matters.* Routledge.

Horton, M., Bell, B. Gaventa, J., & Peters, J.M. (1990). *We make the road by walking: conversations on education and social change.* Temple University Press.

Jelinek, E. C. (1980). *Women's autobiography: Essays in Criticism.* Indiana University Press.

Joyce, J. & Deane, S. (1992). *A portrait of the artist as a young man.* Penguin. (Original work published 1916)

Kempadoo, K. (2009). Caribbean sexuality: Mapping the field. *Journal of Surinamese and Caribbean Studies*, 27 (1), 28–51.

Kincaid, J. (1985). *Annie John.* Hill & Wang.

Lamming, G. (1953). *In the castle of my skin.* Michael Joseph.

Lamming, G. (1995). *Coming, coming home: Conversations II.* House of Nehesi.

Lorde, A. (1984). *Sister outsider: Essays and Speeches.* Crossing Press.

Macaulay, T. B. M., & G.M. Young. (1935). *Speeches by Lord Macaulay with his Minute on Indian Education.* Oxford University Press.

Mahabir, J., & Pirbhai, M. (Eds.). (2015). *Critical perspectives on Indo- Caribbean women's literature.* Routledge.

McLaren, P. (1995). *Critical pedagogy and predatory culture: Oppositional politics in a postmodern era.* Routledge.

Mohammed, P. (2012). Changing symbols of Indo-Caribbean femininity. *CRGS, 6*, 1–16.

Nettleford, R. (1978). *Caribbean cultural identity: The case of Jamaica. An Essay in Cultural Dynamics.* Institute of Jamaica.

Nixon, A. V. (2015). *Resisting paradise: Tourism, diaspora, and sexuality in Caribbean culture.* University of Mississippi Press.

Paris, D., & Alim, H. S. (2014). What we are seeking to sustain through culturally sustaining pedagogy? A loving critique forward. *Harvard Educational Review, 84*(1), 85–110.

Pollard, V. (2003). *From Jamaican Creole to Standard English A handbook for teachers.* University of the West Indies Press.

Roberts, P.A. (1994). Integrating Creole into Caribbean classrooms. *Journal of Multilingual and Multicultural Development, 15*(1), 47–62.

Rodney, W. (1969). *The groundings with my brothers*. Bogle L'Overture publications.
Sánchez Solarte, A. C. (2019). Classroom management and teaching novice language teachers: Friend or foe? *How, 26*(1), 177–199. https://dx.doi.org/10.1918/how.26.1.463.
Senior, O. (1985). *Talking of trees*. Calabash.
Woodson, C. G. (1933). *The Mis-Education of the Negro*. The Associated Publishers, Inc.
Walcott, D. (1993). *The Antilles: Fragments of epic memory: the Nobel lecture*. Farrar, Straus and Giroux.
Wright, T. (2005). *Classroom management in Language education*. Palgrave, Macmillan.

10

A Piece of Glass

Shaakira Raheem

A Piece of Glass

As the Chicago wind cradles my yellow kite, the peppered scent of jollof rice and grilled chicken delightfully tickle my nose. It is 1995 and time for the annual Nigerian picnic my family customarily attends. My siblings disperse, but I find myself still clinging with one hand to my father and with the other to my kite. His friends laugh, and as they exchange words of wisdom about Islam and Nigerian culture, my father pulls me aside and lovingly whispers that I am his beautiful piece of glass. I wish he were still alive, so I could ask him to clarify his meaning. Although my father often related proverbs that I never quite understood, his enigmatic style always drew me closer to him. The messages my father left with me continue to resonate as I explore the connection between culture, education, and social development.

My experiences inside and outside of the classroom inform my practice and educational ideology. As Don Hamachek (1999) suggests, "Teachers teach not only a curriculum of study, they also become part of it. The subject matter they teach is mixed with the content of their personalities" (p. 208). William Ayers (2001) similarly states "greatness in teaching ... requires a serious encounter with autobiography ... because teachers, whatever else they teach, teach themselves" (p. 122). I will outline some salient educational experiences that gave rise to my educational philosophy. These experiences played a crucial role in my identity development and, consequently, how I view education. Michael Nakkula (2013) found that

> although identity development and self-construction are sometimes viewed as individual endeavors, they are thoroughly interpersonal or inter-relational processes. We do not construct our life stories on our own. We are, rather, in a constant state of co-creating who we are with the people with whom we are in closest connection and within those contexts that hold the most meaning for our day-to-day existence. (p. 6)

When designing a curriculum and a classroom environment, I strive to keep in mind that I co-create with my students. I reflect on the support I wish I had to prepare for the social, emotional, and academic challenges I faced while growing up. I think about the allies, the reminders that we all possess beauty, and the positive reassurances that every soul needs. I think about the reminders that rarely came. I think about how I felt in sixth grade on September 12, 2001 when one of my closest friends said, "It was the Muslims." I think about her ignorance and how her education contributed to that ignorance. I think about the shame and frustration that I felt. I think about my students. The normalization of dead Black bodies on their screens. The sexualization of young girls and boys. The villainization of the Islamic tradition. The dehumanization of Black and Brown folk. The decrowning of their histories and narratives. The consumerist, individualist, and consequently fragile ideals that crowd such young hearts and minds. I think. I reflect. I explore. I want to learn more. I cherish the opportunity to work with youth directly and promote healthy mental, social and emotional development. I strive to always remember that being an educator means that I am a student first. I strive to provide my students with multicultural competence, critical consciousness, relevant curriculum, support and enthusiasm, and most importantly, a sense of belonging.

Support Can Foster a Sense of Belonging and Healthy Academic Identity Development

A sense of belonging builds community. As Perry, Turner and Meyer (2006) state: "Participation and appropriation are key constructs in sociocultural theories of learning and motivation, and people are not merely products of their environments, but, through their participation, create, or co-construct, environments" (p. 333). Students are more likely to actively participate if they have a sense of belonging. Students will also be more comfortable transferring their prior knowledge with a sense of belonging. That is, they will feel that their experience is relevant to what is being taught in class. A sense of belonging can be achieved through a culturally responsive curriculum, pedagogy, and intimate relationships with adults. I encourage a communal space with my students by regularly checking in and participating in mindfulness activities together. As a class, we share our weekly highlights, and sometimes I'll enter class with a theme for the day, for example, "strength" or "gratitude," and students will share something in their life that gives them strength or something for which they are thankful. Usually, these conversations provide insight into the students' personal lives, and they appreciate the opportunity to share a part of their intimate selves with the class. I often give students time to stretch in class, and I also support them academically by scaffolding.

I frequented the assistant principal's office at Abraham Lincoln Elementary School more often than I would have liked. My high marks were overlooked by the red check marks every quarter that indicated that I lacked self-control. I spoke out, held side conversations, and asked too many irrelevant questions. At that time, my teachers and parents did not know that I was simply bored in school. The earliest memory I have of being challenged was in fourth grade when Ms. Ward pulled me aside to offer me deodorant. She also offered me a seat in Ms. Clark's higher-level math class. I had no idea that there was a more rigorous class available. No one had ever mentioned this to me, even though I'd finish my work early enough to make rounds, visit my friends at their desks, get in trouble, defend myself when I got in trouble, and then be seated before the class would go over answers. Ms. Ward was also the first Black teacher I had. Studies show that students of color are more likely to be placed in higher-level courses and excel if they have teachers of color (Kamenetz, 2016). Ms. Ward recognized my behavior and my potential. She invested in me. If I had more teachers like her in school, then I'm positive I would have felt less fragile and insecure when trying to develop my academic identity. In my youth, I was very outspoken and social, yet I could not express my boredom. All students should feel whole and secure in our classrooms. I often check in with students when they seem disengaged and openly ask for feedback. This shows them I am invested in their education and their concerns. I hope to be an advocate for my students. Indeed, Ms. Ward's recommendation and exposure taught me to start insisting and asking more relevant questions.

This skill proved helpful when my family moved to Maryland and, after being placed in remedial classes, I had to personally request to be tested into the "gifted and talented" or G.T. classes. I'm still not sure why the administration assumed a remedial class was the best fit for me. I suppose my race and urban background had something to do with it. I know that without Ms. Ward's exposure I would not have known how to advocate for myself. My parents were immigrants and did not know much about the school system and would not have noticed that I was placed in such classes. As a nine-year-old, I did not like the tracking system because my friends weren't in what they called "White classes." I was the only Black student in the G.T. classes, but was not the only gifted Black child. I'm sure many of the parents did not know that they had to advocate for their children because the tracking system starts at such a young age.

While growing up in Maryland, I lived in three distinctly different counties and had equally distinct experiences. The discrepancies between the public school systems regarding their respective resources upset me. I was surprised when I moved to Prince George's county (predominantly Black), and my middle school had to find a way to bus me to the local high school to take my geometry class. In Howard county (predominantly White), my middle school geometry class was full. The importance of vocalizing my concerns increased, and I realized there were communities that were not aware of these opportunities. I guess, like glass, I learned that transparency in educational opportunities and achievement were important to my understanding of myself as a student. I want to empower my students with critical consciousness so they can recognize and hopefully dismantle the system that perpetuates this inequality. This inequality is not only in access to resources but also in the kind of knowledge that is presented.

Curriculum is Key: Multicultural Competence

The tracking system, rooted in elementary schools, extends throughout life, with branches in the high school system. The International Baccalaureate (I.B.) program was the most challenging curriculum my high school offered. The I.B. history course was a two-year course. The course offered was European and Russian History. I studied European and Russian history for two years while my friends who were "weaker" students took world history. Equating a Eurocentric curriculum with the highest-level courses emphasizes the cultural hegemony that plagues our schools.

This phenomenon reveals the lack of inclusion in our curriculum. The curriculum, designed for students, demonstrates the lack of diversity and cultural relevance for students, and perhaps that the higher-level courses and honors curriculum were not designed for the non-European population in the first place. Geneva Gay argues that the curriculum needs to be culturally responsive if students from diverse backgrounds are expected to excel. (Gay, 2000). I did not enjoy history until college, when I was exposed to more diverse narratives. In high school, the lack of cultural relevance made me feel isolated, insecure and frankly, irrelevant. I learned what was important, what I needed to succeed—and my culture, history, and perspective was not included in that trajectory. Like glass, I had to reflect on what I was learning; however, I could not find an aspect of my identity in the material I was reflecting. I felt isolated without being able to make my own connections and form a healthy understanding. I think it also made my classmates feel like my peoples' history—and consequently my life—was less relevant.

It seems that in many US schools, we are conditioned and taught that White values, White skin, White religion, White politics, White men and women, and White reasoning are superior to all others considered on the periphery. European locations were specified by city, but my classmates referred to Africa as a country. Schools and educators prioritize knowledge, and thus, knowledge becomes political when it shapes our line of thinking and notions of humanity. As long as the curriculum/textbook developers and teachers, are not culturally competent and continue to pursue a euro-centric stance, euro-centric ideals will maintain their status as the knowledge worth knowing. Our formal education primes us to support institutional racism while validating the mistreatment of those we consider to be the "minority."

An example is celebrating Thanksgiving without learning about the atrocities Native Americans faced in this country and the legacy that remains in reservations. Celebrating Christopher Columbus as a great explorer and not critiquing his racist and violent policies. The failure to recognize the relationship between language and power—referring to slaveholders as our "founding fathers" is not inclusive to people of color. The term "founding fathers" implies that there are inheritors, and people of color are perhaps items to be inherited. As an educator, I think the role of school is to encourage and facilitate critical consciousness. Critical thinking promotes citizenship and progresses society. By paying attention to the examples provided above, we teach our students to critically engage in a manner that promotes inclusion, social justice, and freedom for all. Schools are how we condition constituents. If our curriculum and notions of knowledge prioritize White values, so will our society and policy.

At times, I felt like an outsider because of the lack of knowledge my peers displayed concerning my beliefs, background, or line of thinking. Since high school, I have actively sought out experiences that have helped me learn how to relate my perspective to that of my greater community. Teaching and studying in the U.A.E., Palestine, Dominican Republic, Morocco, Tanzania, and Ghana broadened my understanding of knowledge. I hope to convey the vastness and diversity to my students. An international and multiple perspective curriculum is a necessity for students and the community at large. We need to teach humanity of all colors and religions. With informed and empathetic citizens, comes a more informed and empathetic democracy filled with individuals who can question and analyze events around them. A culturally competent and empathetic citizenry will recognize and demonstrate that Black lives matter. If students are not trained to recognize the injustices done to Native Americans after Puritans landed on Plymouth rock, how do we expect them to recognize injustice done in a modern-day context? Education is linked to social justice.

As a teacher, I want to provide space for my students to engage in critical dialogue while exploring their interests. I've attempted to engage students in this manner since my first teaching job in Morocco.

Amideast is a U.S. non-profit organization that strengthens the mutual understanding between Americans and people of the Middle East and North Africa. One class I taught at Amideast, Inspiration 99, was an advanced conversation course for teenagers. During the course, I encouraged my students to express themselves in song. My objective for the course was to expose students to cultures and concepts that broadened their worldview. The excerpt below is a chorus from a rap song my Moroccan students created when asked to write a class theme song. Inspiration 99 proved to be an inspirational class as I realized I had more to offer my students than just the English language.

> If you have grammar problems I feel bad for you son
> I got 99 problems and English aint one...
> I got 99 problems- inspiration aint one
> I'm busy Saturday night, but I still have fun
> *I got 99 problems, and these are just some!*

The students explained the struggles (much fewer than 99) that they faced as teenagers in Rabat. They related them to their academics—thankfully, they did not find the English language as one of the many problems they faced. The activity encouraged them to be creative in the English language and encouraged collaboration as they had to write the lyrics together. The class met every Saturday night from 6–9 p.m., so I faced resistance from the students in the first few sessions. Shortly after, however, the students started filling the classroom with contagious energy before I even entered the classroom. The students grew to love the course as they collaborated in taking ownership of their studies.

Lessons ranged from reading short stories to cooking fajitas. The Tex-Mex cooking the lesson, in particular, exposed the students to the diversity of American culture. My students found themselves debating over what constitutes "Moroccan" or "American" identities. Students were initially surprised to have a Ghanaian Nigerian American Muslim teacher who is fluent in Arabic. As the only Black teacher at Amideast, many students did not believe I was American. It was challenging for me because I could not change the initial responses that my appearances evoked. It was through dialogue, not banking, that the students came to more nuanced understandings about identity. Indeed, education can enable better intercultural communication. I've observed that when learning centers designate spaces for developing such social tools, students have a platform to express themselves and develop an interest in broader issues of social justice. As an educator, I strive to empower communities and learning centers in designing such spaces.

While working in Ghana, I engaged my students in collaborative and introspective practice through reflective warm-ups, journal entries, lectures, book clubs, community service activities, and cross-cultural exercises. These exercises make the learning process personal and individualized. When students can record their thoughts, they can be vulnerable and reflect on their progress. In a pre-reading discussion before starting *The Autobiography of Malcolm X*, a student expressed his disconnect to slavery. It led to a discussion among the students on the relationship Africans have and should have with African Americans and further led them to question how they would be perceived once in the US. In particular, they raised the question, what would it mean to be Black in America? The in-depth dialogue expanded beyond the advising center. These students have developed a strong cohort that continues to support each other. I was blessed with the opportunity to facilitate such growth. I engaged in what Dr. Gay (2010) refers to as culturally responsive teaching, "using the cultural knowledge, prior experiences, frames of reference, and performance styles of ethnically diverse students to make learning encounters more relevant to and effective for them." (p. 31). Working with the Ghanaian students reminded me of my mother, a migrant from Ghana. and the academic culture I never experienced.

Growing up, I had always thought that there was much to learn about my culture. My parents strove to assimilate rather than acculturate, and therefore did not teach me my mother tongue of Yoruba. To an extent, they did not think it was as important as English. A legacy of what Ngugi Wa Thiongo (1981) refers to as metaphysical empires. When expressing feelings of love, frustration, and hope, they chose to communicate with me in English, the imperial language, over Yoruba. The linguistic colonization, coupled with the Eurocentric education to which I was limited, led to a turbulent journey of identity development. The beautiful glass that my father recognized and honored, with all its fragility found strength through diversity and transparency. I strive to support my students through the lens of critical transparency, a sense of belonging and culturally responsive teaching.

Critical Reflection- What I am Learning and What I Envision

Solange's song, "Cranes in the Sky," was on repeat for about two years in my life. The two years while I was in school, getting my Master's, learning to be a mother and learning to be a teacher. There were many cranes in my sky and I was not trying to feel those metal clouds. Some say Solange found her lane with the album, *A Seat at the Table*. I aim to *build* my own table. My long-term goal is to open a wellness center in Ghana. I want people from all over the diaspora to call my center a safe learning space. A home. Vygotsky (1978) explains that "learning results when individuals interact in the social material world, participate in the knowledge practices of a community, and are supported by others in a community that includes individuals more knowledgeable than them" (p. 332). I want to build a learning home, an intellectual living room, a healing space, a sacred space. A place to pause, reflect, and redirect. A place for people to heal, learn about themselves, declutter their minds. A place to write, read, practice yoga, engage in mindfulness, spend time in nature, cook healthy and fresh foods, think, and love.

This is my ideal learning environment. Many Blacks who study, live or work in predominantly White spaces must navigate the White gaze, systemic racism, and implicit bias while existing, expanding and exploring themselves. When discussing effective learning environments, it is important to clarify what effective learning means and what it looks like when a student is learning. There are various cultural conceptions of learning and development (Alexander & Winne, 2006) and it is important for teachers to recognize their perceptions are not universal.

My own experiences teaching in independent schools proves this to be true. I've worked in many places and found the same systemic barriers. In each school, it was the same pattern, and yet I did not recognize it. As a woman of color, speaking up against oppressive structures led to a common cycle that causes low retention rates for faculty of color.

Indeed, this was the cycle in which I found myself. Trying to invest in spaces but leaving soon after facing resistance. Upon further reflection, I find that I have had similar experiences in many schools. By moving from place to place, I did not equip myself with the ability to work on transforming systems or even further developing my practice because I kept changing places of employment. Not only that, but scars from former schools were carried over.

I have walked the hallways of schools with pain, trauma, and distrust. I have been silenced, labeled, and taken advantage of—all while trying to advocate, or hold systems or people accountable. I strive to create my own classrooms where people of color can thrive and now I want to expand my classroom. The work we do as educators is very demanding and the biggest reward comes from the direct work with students. I hope to help create spaces where that work is accessible for all. First, I must create that space for myself. Alexander & Winne, 2006 write: "participation and appropriation are key constructs in sociocultural theories of learning and motivation, and people are not merely products of their environments, but, through their participation, create, or co-construct, environments" (p. 332). Humans are more likely to learn and thrive if they have a strong sense of belonging. I realized that I must carve out spaces of belonging and cultivate them for my students; this takes time and energy.

In writing this piece, I realize that carving out spaces for myself is challenging because I have not necessarily had to do this before. I moved several times in my youth, I attended two different elementary schools (in two states), three middle schools (in two countries) and two high schools (in two counties). While in college, I studied abroad in the United Arab Emirates and Morocco, and after graduating from college, I moved around a lot as well. Although I have been in education for close to ten years, this past year was my first time teaching a course for the second time. After a year or two of settling into a space, I'd move on to the next institution before I could work within said system. Reflecting on my experiences brings to light the fluidity of my experiences. How can I build a strong practice, strong relationships when I am always on the go? When will I find a community of learners and an institution that feels safe enough to settle in? I know that it starts with compassion. Compassion for myself. For my students and colleagues. With compassion, I can learn how to use the tools within schools to rework or advance systems.

These queries are what made me curious to see what it would look like to stay at Sidwell Friends School. Take on a third year (for the first time in my career). What is needed for me to make it? Compassion. It must be channeled when sitting with discomfort. I redesigned my classroom, brought in a couch, materials and artifacts from my home. I tried to create a comfortable learning space for myself and my students.

I have been called divisive for naming divisions and uncollegial for speaking truth that challenges the status quo. Resisting and loving in such spaces is exhausting. My existence in these spaces is radical. However, the only thing radical about me is my ability to love.

I realized that I'm not radical, but just not in a position to be limited. I realize that the table that I want to build may not necessarily fit into the schools that I'm working in. But in the current positions that I have, I learn different ways to eat with people and gather together. My travels around the world have shown me different ways people connect so that when it is time to build that wellness space, I'll muster up my compassion and use the best glass I can. God willing, a sustainable space for growth, reflection and communal prosperity. I'm exploring education from what feels like the most authentic place of mine—my heart.

References

Ayers, W. (2001). *To teach: The journey of a teacher*. New York: Teachers College Press.

Gay, G. (2010). *Culturally responsive teaching: Theory, research, and practice*. New York, NY: Teachers College Press.

Hamachek, D. (1999). Effective teachers: What they do, how they do it, and the importance of self-knowledge. In R. P. Lipka & T. M. Brinthaupt (Eds.), *The role of self in teacher development* (pp. 189–224). Albany: State University of New York Press.

Juvonen, J. (2006). Sense of Belonging, Social Bonds, and School Functioning. In P. A. Alexander & P. H. Winne (Eds.), *Handbook of educational psychology* (p. 655–674). Lawrence Erlbaum Associates Publishers.

Nakkula, M. J., & Toshalis, E. (2006). *Understanding youth: Adolescent development for educators*. Cambridge, MA: Harvard Education Press.

Nancy E. Perry, Julianne C. Turner, Debra K. Meyer. 18 May 2006, Classrooms as Contexts for Motivating Learning from: *Handbook of Educational Psychology*. Routledge. Accessed on: 22 Apr 2016 https://www.routledgehandbooks.com/doi/10.4324/9780203874790.ch15

Kamenetz, Anya (January 20, 2016). To Be Young, 'Gifted And Black, It Helps to Have a Black Teacher. NPR Ed. Retrieved from http://www.npr.org/sections/ed/2016/01/20/463190789/to-be-young-gifted-and-black-it-helps-to- have-a-black-teacher

Thiongo, Ngugi Wa (1981). *Decolonizing the Mind: Politics of Language in African Literature*. Nairobi, Kenya: East African Educational Publishers.

11

A Stranger in My Own Country

Thembelihle Brenda Makhanya

Ellis, Adams, and Bochner (2011) assert storytelling as a tool for professional learning, personal and organisational change, and a process that can help people make sense of their lives, stances, positions, and broader social, cultural, and political worlds. This chapter focuses on my own story based on my experience as a student and a lecturer in higher education (HE). The chapter will narrate my educational encounters and how they have influenced my perception of learning and teaching in HE. The first section explores my educational autobiography. This section presents the narrative of my experiences as a student and a critical reflection of incidents in relation to teaching and learning. The second section presents a reflection on my teaching philosophy. Lastly, the chapter concludes by critically reviewing both educational autobiography and teaching philosophy. The discussion highlights the connections, themes, contradictions, or new understandings that emerged in the writing process. Throughout the discussion of this chapter, the HE experiences are revealed as inextricably and contextually complex.

Educational Autobiography

I am from the rural part of Port Shepstone, located in the Hibiscus Coast local municipality (recently renamed Ray Nkonyeni Municipality), in KwaZulu-Natal Province, South Africa. I come from a society and a family that survived and still survives on informal learning. The learning takes place in diverse events and spaces, such as home environments, izimbizo (traditional community gatherings), istokfela (social clubs), Zulu dance clubs, storytelling, virginity testing, ploughing, herding cattle, and church. African value systems, the culture, the rites of passage, celebrations, oral history and storytelling are the dominant institutions that educate an African child and the society at large (Graham, 1999). In my context, university education was a luxury and, generally, an unattainable dream.

I am among the first generation in my family who enrolled in a higher institution of learning. When I entered university, it became clear that I come from a different cultural background. I was poor and unprepared for this type of education. The journey of my undergraduate degree was uneasy. I experienced difficulties from the first day of orientation and registration, mainly due to language and system barriers. These included obstacles such as restricted access to the university residence, study materials due to financial limitations, and access and use of computers.

The focus of this chapter is informed by my own experiences of the university as a young African[1] student from a rural community. My struggles with language, for instance, contributed immensely to my sense of alienation. The language barrier emulated from that; my first language is isiZulu. IsiZulu is not only isolated to a home environment, but it was a medium of communication also in my high school and the community at large. Unfortunately for me, my university relied on English. Although English was taught throughout my schooling years, English lessons were explained in isiZulu, and the primary medium of communication was isiZulu. This was beneficial to my academic progress since I could easily understand the content. However, the language practices in basic education were very different from those of higher education and the transition was difficult. This supports Coetzee-de Vos's (2019) argument that African students (coming from disadvantaged backgrounds) are poorly prepared for university when it comes to language because of the high use of mother-tongue languages in rural basic education. Clearly, my home and schooling background did not prepare or equip me for institutions of higher learning.

I also think this is a clear indication of how postcolonial universities are not ready to accommodate Indigenous students (Behari-Leak, Chitanand, Padayachee, Masehela, Vorster, Ganas, and Merckel, 2018). The struggle embedded with foreign languages at the university does not mean I came from a weak schooling system. Instead, I came from an Afrocentric community that values the African languages that are deemed irrelevant to the university system. Therefore, I stress the importance of a university system that recognises the background of its students and works toward bridging the gap or building from what the students bring to the university.

I registered during an era when the university was aggressive in addressing equity status and inclusivity, opening its doors to rural African communities in particular. This meant that the university was getting a new breed of students

---

[1] As with Zibane (2017), 'African' in this chapter is not used to refer to any scientific racial categorization but is used as a social construct to classify South Africans of African ancestry. Here I am referring to Black South Africans, who were colonially exploited and dominated because of their racial group (Biko, 1987).

from more diverse backgrounds—students from different socioeconomic statuses and educational backgrounds, and students who are strongly rooted in their Indigenous languages, African culture, and value system. Many elements of my identity did not fit the university environment. I was from a different culture and belief system, spoke a different language, and in the position of another kind of learning. I was a rural girl, 150 kilometers from home, with no funding and no place to stay.

The university is a space that is assumed to promote critical engagement and nurture students' growth and development. Still, my first-year experience as an African student was contrary to this assumption. In my first year of university, I felt lost and a stranger in my own country. I felt as if I was uprooted from all I knew. While I was excited to be a university student, I was very stressed by the fact that I struggled to follow and catch up on the lessons, and I was unable to cope with the assessment requirements. I remember the first assignment, which was to write about yourself. It required that I submit it typed and honour all the obligations of academic writing. My computer illiteracy was a significant stumbling block, let alone the ability to discuss critically the assignment topic in English. My failure to cope with the university's demands made me hate my background and, moreover, undermine my identity as an African woman. To me, addressing equity and promotion of access without addressing the factors that make the university an inequitable and inaccessible institution is a fruitless exercise. In my view, if the university was "truly" committed to equity and was aware of the fact that many African students are from an oral culture, the first assignment about oneself could have been an oral presentation in one's language.

English dominates in all aspects of life in South African universities. In fact, there is a lack of appreciation of Indigenous languages in higher education institutions (HEIs) (wa Thiong'o, 2006). This lack of appreciation emanates from the colonial system and the apartheid regime, which embraced European knowledge systems at the expense of Indigenous knowledge. African languages are often portrayed as barbaric and useless in developing African people (Le Grange, 2014). In a study conducted by Mutasa (2015, p.26), he found that "generally there is scepticism about the effectiveness of teaching content subjects such as history or geography through Indigenous African languages." In many instances, the same academics who preach about the importance of Indigenous African languages at conferences and other platforms do not practice what they preach (Mutasa, 2015). In Mamphiswana and Noyoo's (2016, p.23) view, the dominance of English in South African HEIs as an academic language hinders effective teaching and learning for African students. Hence, in a study conducted by Makhanya and Zibane (2020), African students lamented the need for inclusion and development of mother-tongue languages in South African academia. One of the participants said; "uma usebenzisa ulwimi lwakho ekilasini uthola ukuzizwa nokuzethemba ukubeka umbono uma kuxoxwa" (If you use your home language in class you develop that high self-esteem and confidence even to say something in class engagements.) (Makhanya and Zibane, 2020, p. 11). Thus, multilingualism is the outcry during learning and teaching.

I entered the university unprepared for the new life and academic experiences. My struggle with technology during the first year of study challenges the conclusions made by Brckalorenz et al. (2013), who have asserted that the millennial generation group of students (i.e., born between 1982 and 2002) are highly skilled and innovative in their use of Information Technology (IT). In contradiction, my university experience suggests a significant disparity in the exposure to and use of IT among students due to different schooling backgrounds. Hood and Yoo (as cited in Brckalorenz et al., 2013) also indicate that socioeconomic status and class are factors that influence proficiency in IT use among first-year university students. I thus problematise technological investments that ignore inequalities existing in South Africa, particularly in HE. The country is preparing to enter into the fourth industrial revolution marked by disruptive technologies and trends (World Economic Forum, 2019). This will mean high reliance on blended learning (e.g., combined technological and traditional learning methods and teaching) in HEIs. However, legacies of the past that have left most of the population in disadvantaged positions should equally be addressed. The democratic dispensation still fails to acknowledge the diversity (in the background and experiences) of university students. Although Africans and disadvantaged students from poor backgrounds are accepted at the university (unlike during apartheid), the university still fails to address such underprivileged groups (Biko, 1987; Ndlovu-Gatsheni, 2018). This suggests a need for decolonial university education to ensure that African students (in the African context) and their experiences are placed at the centre of the curriculum (Seepe, 2004).

It is important to note that despite the difficulties and others not mentioned in this chapter, I managed to complete my Bachelor of Social Work degree through some survival strategies. Some of this involved funding support by the Student Representative Council (SRC) and the Hibiscus Coast Municipality. The municipality provided first-year registration fees and the SRC supported my second-year registration at the university. I also received support from other students. Student mentors, classmates, and tutors guided me on the computer and clarified academic content (in most cases using my mother-tongue language). These were support services that contributed to my academic success and development at the university. Indeed, Scott (2016) perceives support services at the university as the fundamental structure that enhances academic performance and the holistic wellbeing of a student. It is also vital to mention that I was present during the 2015 and 2016 Fees Must Fall students' movement in South African universities, of which some of the demands were the call for decolonised free higher education and accessible and safe students' accommodation. This movement is relevant to mention because it tackled some of the concerns presented as hindrances for my progress at the university.

After I graduated, I did not wish for any student to share my experience. I thus registered as a postgraduate student and participated in the tutoring and mentorship programs for first-year students. In all my class discussions with students, I used a bilingual approach—explaining the content in isiZulu and English. My own experiences of alienation influenced this approach. Coetzee-de Vos (2019) argues that all South African languages are not developed in academia, except English (a colonial import), and Afrikaans (imposed during apartheid), hence speakers of the other nine languages experience difficulties in the absence of multilingual practices in HE. South African universities have thus been struggling to shake off the vestiges of the colonial legacy (Mutasa 2015, p. 52).

English as a colonial language is the language of power in post-apartheid South Africa. South Africa has eleven (11) official languages, namely: English; Afrikaans; Zulu; Xhosa; isiNdebele; Sepedi; Sesotho; Siswati; Xitsonga; Setswana; and Tshivenda. But English is the only normalised academic language in South Africa (Coetzee-de Vos, 2019). This reveals how the new democratic dispensation of HE has continued to privilege the colonial master at the expense of Indigenous people. There is thus a need for a teaching strategy that validates the intellectuality of African languages in academia.

In my experience of tutoring and mentoring undergraduate students, I witnessed that the vast majority of students at risk of being academically and financially excluded from the university are Africans. During our individual and group sessions, such students cited their disadvantaged background as preventing them from adapting to the demands of a university learning environment. Indeed, in 2020 the University of KwaZulu-Natal (UKZN) attempted to academically exclude 2000 students who could not pay 15% toward their historical debts (Bhengu, 2020). This followed protests against the financial exclusion of poor students. This suggests the exclusion of students coming from a disadvantaged background as conspicuous in South African higher education.

While the university was actively recruiting such students, it failed to meet their needs and make education easily accessible to them. My story is not unique for a student of higher learning in post-apartheid South Africa. This is evidenced by a range of studies, articles, and commentaries published on the topic (see, for example, Abdi, 2006; Bozalek, 2011; Clows, 2013; Le Grange, 2014; Ndlovu-Gatsheni, 2015; Mamphiswana and Noyoo, 2016; Mbembe, 2016). In particular, I consider Ngugi's comments about "cultural bomb" as relevant to my experience. Although I adopted the university culture, structure, and system to complete my degree, it came at the cost of considering my traditional background and culture as a stumbling block to success. Assimilation into dominant White cultures (Bazana and Mogotsi, 2017) became the only option of survival. Thus, Ngugi wa Thiong'o (2006) would have called my university experience a "cultural bomb." This implies the wiping out of Indigenous identity for colonial domination (wa Thiong'o, 2006).

As in wa Thiong'o's quote, I identified my background history "a wasteland," which made me desire to distance myself from it. I wanted to be removed from my background to identify with modernised students, such as trying by all means to adopt a dominant foreign language and culture. This sense of a wasteland was influenced by the fact that while issues of English as the sole language of learning were not addressed, my technological ignorance and limitation to Western literature capped the alienating experiences of my learning at the university and posed a threat to my academic progress.

The above discussion suggests that Social work education and training in South Africa have been deeply affected by colonialism and apartheid. Dumbrill and Green in early 2008 also posited that, despite the commitment to inclusion and diversity, social work continues to be taught in Eurocentric philosophies that colonize the Indigenous knowledge system. Mkhize, Mathe, and Buthelezi (2014) particularly highlight that the social work code of ethics continues to be dominated by the epistemological paradigms of the Western colonial conquerors. This suggests a need for the development of an Indigenous knowledge system in education. Asante (2014) also asserts that development and advancement within the African perspective are rooted and are explained in terms of people's culture, beliefs, structures, language, and traditions.

My educational experience has been saturated by the pain of being in an environment that ignores my culture, language, and tradition. This discussion indicates how colonial legacies became evident in my experience as an African student and exposes the extent to which South African university training roots or uproots the African students within their experiences, value systems, epistemologies, and philosophies. The chapter raises such questions particularly as part of the call for the decolonisation of South African universities and curriculum.

The above discussion highlights that the struggles of previously disadvantaged students at the university are linked to the hidden agendas of coloniality. Building from Bozalek and Boughey's (2012) assertions, the point that must be explicitly brought to the fore is the continuation of African students' alienation, which indicates the extent of embeddedness of colonial effects on the educational structures and system. Thus, it is of fundamental importance for universities in South Africa to focus on social transformation, not only in terms of access but also in providing an African-centred curriculum. This also calls for social work education transformation and restructuring to renew the discipline of human service (Mkhize et al., 2014; Mamphiswana and Noyoo, 2016). These authors call for the transformation of social work education because the same old, less responsive, and disempowering social work education still exists in some South African universities (Mamphiswana and Noyoo, 2016). In collaboration with such voices, a decolonisation exercise is necessary to attain anti-oppressive practices, social inclusion, and culturally relevant education.

A relevant curriculum can only be obtained from the diversified and active deconstruction of education philosophies and the inclusion of African narratives. It is also crucial for academics to be at the forefront of these changes. Vandeyar (2019) argues that the decolonial curriculum should be enforced through inclusive pedagogies. Thus, there is a need in this post-1994 democratic dispensation for the university to construct teaching and learning methods that are sensitive to African ideas, interests, and needs. Concerns of irrelevant practice due to colonial hegemony in academia will drop away through anti-colonial and African-centred teaching and learning. My social positioning as an African woman from a disadvantaged background resembles these observations.

Teaching Philosophy

Articulation

Chism (1998) describes teaching philosophy as a stimulating reflection on practice. It is the vision of teaching and desired learning for students that informs the design, implementation, and evaluation of teaching, learning, and assessment (Spiller, 2012). My experience as a university student, my professional background and work experience influenced my teaching philosophy to a certain extent. Indeed, Vandeyar (2019) asserts that teachers' beliefs in classrooms are influenced by their diverse experiences, such as schooling, classroom practices, family, and community backgrounds. For instance, I previously worked for a non-profit organisation as a Social Worker. I also worked at the university as a practice coordinator, a mentor, and a tutor. These are some of the essential experiences that taught me about students' holistic needs at the university.

As a lecturer at UKZN in the discipline of social work, I believe that social work is a unique profession that promotes human, community and family wellbeing, and social justice (IFSW and IASSW, 2014). Therefore, social workers are guided by a personal and environmental construct, a global perspective, respect for human diversity, and scientific-based knowledge and skills. Thus, my teaching philosophy is influenced by several diverse beliefs rather than a fixed, unidirectional idea. For instance, my teaching goal is to build a good relationship with students through respect; this is to allow a sense of community in the classroom. While setting appropriate limits, I believe in students' freedom of expression and room to grow. I am aware that such teaching and learning should come from a welcoming environment by celebrating student diversity and their equity access to learning. My teaching belief is thus centred on students.

Although several theories exist to explain teaching beliefs, my philosophy of teaching fits well with the approaches stipulated by Pratt (1988). Pratt's approaches are not only comprehensive but also acknowledge empowerment and praxis teaching, which speaks to the values, ethics, and skills of social work education and practice. Therefore, my teaching strategy is influenced by five perspectives, namely, transmission, apprenticeship, developmental, nurturing, and social reform (Pratt, 1988). Although my fluid strategy adopts some or all of these perspectives based on the context, stage of understanding, and multiple intelligences existing among students, my beliefs are mainly influenced by developmental, nurturing, and social reform perspectives.

A developmental perspective is a learner-centred teaching philosophy (Pratt, 1988; Spiller, 2012). My own belief and values in teaching and learning are student-centred, meaning that as a teacher and a learner, we are all involved in our education, and we learn from each other. It is about engaging students with what they already know and expands their knowledge. Thus, my teaching recognises students as bearing rich data for teaching and learning. For instance, I adopted an approach to have data (such as locations, background knowledge, age) about my students in each module to help understand them and build on what they know. My responsibility as a teacher is to build bridges between learners' present knowledge and further knowledge within the discipline (Spiller, 2012).

I believe in adult education principles (developmental, nurturing, and social reform perspectives), which acknowledge that students are self-directed, want to exercise choice, and only learn when they are motivated and enthusiastic (Pratt, 1988). I have also recognised that students become excited about learning if I also show excitement about teaching and eagerness in testing new approaches. The fundamental aspect is acknowledging that students learn best when they enjoy the learning process, learning material, and learning methods. For example, I have learned to call students by names or pick names randomly from the register, making students feel valued during engagements. Furthermore, my teaching assumes that students have accumulated a foundation of life experiences, knowledge, skills, and values that they want to be acknowledged, respected, and incorporated into their learning experience. This means that effective teaching needs to be founded on the understanding of how students learn. Thus, teaching activities need to bring about learning based on insight and knowledge about students' needs. This suggests learning as not a single event/thing but exploring different ideas, methods, and approaches (Fry, Ketteridge and Marshall, 2009) that encourage students to learn.

Implementation

During class discussions, I invest in modern developments in the fields through research, and by that, I can arrest my students' attention and encourage them to learn new things and gain more knowledge. Scholars such as Vandeyar (2019) report how knowledge can vary based on additional information and expectations. This suggests a need for research to be part of one's teaching strategy, encouraging both the teacher and the student to open their minds. I also enforce this open-mindedness by using mainstream media topics of interest to engage students and provide real-world examples.

My class management system also draws on the multiple intelligences existing among students. Due to students' increasing cultural diversity, Vandeyar argues for the need for teachers who can communicate with students coming from different backgrounds and accommodate their different learning methods. Thus, my teaching uses different methods of knowledge, dissemination, and assessment. Different teaching styles, methods, and assessments are adopted to ensure the equal learning of all students. For instance, I ensure that I am approachable to my students (by encouraging consultations and active use of the Moodle discussion forum), and I make use of technology such as emails, e-learning sites for information sharing and discussion and PowerPoint presentations.

I assess the effectiveness of my teaching philosophy by providing both formative and summative assessments. Vandeyar (2019, p. 8) also argues that teaching in South African universities should allow for a multiplicity of voices. Thus, assessment is developed in a way to ensure that all students learn. For instance, the formative assessment consists of individual or group presentations, individual or group assignments, tests with a different set of questions, based on Bloom's taxonomy and role-plays. The summative assessments are based on the final examination consisting of a different set of questions, also revised against recent Bloom's taxonomy, placement in social service agencies for students to practise what they have learned, and a portfolio of evidence. Encouraging students' engagement with communities extends learning outside the classroom, promoting experiential learning through the delivery of services.

My teaching philosophy is therefore, value-driven by excellence, accountability, integrity, human dignity and respect, innovation and criticality, ownership, and leadership. For example, I learned the importance of accountability when assessing students. Students need to know what they will be evaluated on. I include criteria for such assessment and evaluate only what students have learned. All assessments are based on what was discussed, taught, and learned in class. It is also essential to provide feedback after assessments and focus on the individual approach of each student. This assists students in learning not only for academic progress but also for understanding.

The University of KwaZulu-Natal (UKZN) language policy now promotes bilingual practice through the inclusion of isiZulu for academic engagement (UKZN language policy, 2014). The practical concern about this policy is that its implementation is not compulsory to be adopted by all academics during teaching and assessments. Hence, English-only still dominates. In my teachings, I practise this policy to ensure the academic progress of all students, because Zulu-speaking students dominate the social work degree program at UKZN. I use language as a cognitive tool that allows students to communicate and engage in high order thinking freely.

The involvement of support structures available at UKZN has enhanced my teaching approach and learning of students. For instance, the availability of Academic Development officers (ADOs) (for academic counselling), tutors, and mentors (for content clarification and guidance on assessments) have made learning and teaching to be enjoyable. This is because these structures tackle the aspects that influence students' learning. This has also allowed extra classes, online discussions, and integration of technology to be possible. University support services have thus improved students' performance, eliminated failure, and decreased dropout rates (Van Heerden, 2009).

I believe that collaboration creates meaningful teaching ideas—I value peer evaluation and co-teaching. I also use internal and external moderation of assessments to get feedback on the relevance, transformative nature, and applicability of the content taught in class. Vandeyar (2019) argues that a decolonial curriculum calls for academics to be open to critical analysis for their teaching philosophy and to be willing to relearn and unlearn. To allow for such analysis, I keep a teaching portfolio for assessing my teaching beliefs and its developmental contribution to students' growth. This suggests that my teaching philosophy is explicit and open to both students and colleagues.

Reflection

Writing this chapter made me realise that my experience as an African student in a previously White university and my teaching philosophy focuses on the need for teaching strategies that are influenced by students' context. Otherwise, HE will continue to be a provocative reminder of the colonial and apartheid legacies in the new democratic dispensations of the South African university. Mbembe (2016) also acknowledges the anti-African curriculum and structures of the universities in the postcolonial regime as perpetuating the un-healing of the past wounds. This means that the structural design and education of the university still serves to colonise Indigenous people. This suggests a need for learning and teaching to address structural injustices and alienating Eurocentric norms and cultures that sideline previously disadvantaged students. Hence, South African higher education institutions were gripped in 2015 and 2016 by the Nationwide #FeesMustFall university students' movement. These protests have been towards free and decolonised higher education in South African universities. Moreover, students have called for contextually relevant curricula free from the colonial influences (Membe, 2016).

Bozalek and Boughey (2012) highlight that there is a limited link between policies that aim to increase inclusiveness and the experiences of students and staff in South African HE. Mamphiswana and Noyoo (2016) argue that the shortcomings are exacerbated by the reluctance of some South African universities, including social work faculties, to address known discriminatory norms and practices in the curriculum (which further alienate and misrecognise the voices of African students and staff in higher education). Therefore, restructuring is necessary since training was originally developed to maintain colonial and apartheid systems and professionals were not equipped with the skills to work with the disempowered African population (Mamphiswana and Noyoo, 2016).

I articulate the need for the university curriculum to be based on learners' inclusive needs and interests and the selected content of the curriculum to be based on the life experiences of students for contextual relevance. My own experiences as an African student and African academic emphasise the importance of including Indigenous knowledge systems in education. Gray, Kreitzer, and Mupedziswa (2014) also express the need for Indigenisation of social work education, inclusionary practices, and context-based solutions. This requires the curriculum, its epistemology, and pedagogies to rely on students' experiences for contextual relevance. In addition, although universities have increased access for Africans, lack of an inclusive and context-based curriculum leads to injustice and exclusion of African students in South African higher education, resulting in the alienation of the voices and experiences of African students. These are the same principles that governed the colonial and apartheid regimes—this is a clear call for decolonisation in African HE.

Several studies have been conducted to address decolonisation in HE. For example, Abdi (2006) in Canada has examined the Eurocentric discourses and African philosophies and epistemologies of education. Nwanosike and Onyije (2011) in Nigeria have also focused on education and colonialism. In South Africa (North West province), Tamburro (2013) has also conducted a study focusing on the inclusion of decolonisation in social work education and practice. Similarly, Smith (2014) in Johannesburg examined the historiography of South African social work, challenging the dominant discourse. Le Grange (2014) in Cape Town has also examined the Africanisation of the university curriculum. Thus, decolonisation concern has received much attention in South African universities. As a result, the 2017 Social Work International Conference held in Johannesburg was on the decolonisation of social work education. The battle of decolonisation is, however, still at an infant stage in South Africa and in KwaZulu-Natal HE.

The use of colonial language within social work education has placed unfair limitations on African students in terms of epistemological and pedagogical access. This limitation leads to irrelevant practice in social work. For instance, social workers are expected to analyse individuals within their environment, using the clients' languages and cultures for the proper gathering of information (Schenk, Mbedzi, Qalinge, Schultz, Sekudu, and Sesoko, 2015). As such, how are social work graduates expected to master such skills if social work education at the university fails to incorporate and value the Indigenous languages of clients and students in academic discussions? This demonstrates how practice in settings dominated by Indigenous languages remains a challenge for social work graduates trained using the English language only. A lack of developing Indigenous languages in social work education hinders effective practice for Social Workers working in Indigenous/African communities.

Another limitation is the lack of expertise in information technology (IT). Social workers need to use IT in diverse fields such as health care, child care, family care, youth, addiction, and substance abuse, trauma, and bereavement counselling (Schenk et al., 2015). In compliance with the requirements of these fields, social workers are expected to conduct administrative tasks, type and produce reports, gather and present information, conduct research, and keep records, etc. This work is not possible if social work education at the university ignores the importance of IT training among students. This suggests that education at the university needs to ensure that students are technologically equipped and advanced not only for academic success but for proper service delivery during practice.

The South African university must be sensitive and acknowledge the country's historical context and its still-existing injustices and inequalities, which mostly affect poor students. There is a need for the curriculum to adopt a humanising pedagogy (Zembylas, 2018). Thus, the fundamental question is what will be the nature of inclusive and decolonial teaching and learning in the new democratic dispensation of the African university—and how to answer this question based on the voices and lived experiences of students and academics themselves, rather than from the academic papers produced by Western writers or from the African author consumed by Eurocentric ideas.

This chapter's argument embraces a need for the "decolonial turn" (Maldonado-Torres, 2011) in HE. Indeed, scholars such as Biko (1987), Vorster and Quinn (2017), Ndlovu-Gatsheni (2018) and Twikirize and Spitzer (2019) similarly acknowledge the necessity of a decolonial turn in HE that involves contextually relevant transformative activities for equal access. Thus, Tshepo Madlingozi (2019) perceives the decolonial turn in South African higher education as a needed transformative process, which must be influenced by time, space, and context for relevance. This implies that decolonial transformation in a profession such as social work can be obtained from the context-specific voices of the people it ought to serve.

This calls for a "culturally relevant pedagogy" (Vandeyar, 2019, p. 9) in teaching and learning. This pedagogy aims to address past injustices by moving away from a "deficit approach" (Vandeyar, 2019). A deficit approach perceives marginalised African students as bankrupt of any knowledge, culture, and intellectual language in education and society. It then normalises the Eurocentric or Western domination in the academia of the world. This chapter's argument suggests the need to abandon such an approach since it hinders diversity and inclusion in HE. Thus, there is a need to adopt an asset-based approach (Vandeyar, 2019) that values diverse cultures and backgrounds in the university community. This also suggests a need for teaching in South African universities to validate "home-based knowledge" (Vandeyar, 2019) of the students and their experiences to understand the knowledge and its construction.

Conclusion

The educational autobiography, the teaching philosophy, and the reflections of this chapter highlight the importance of acknowledging that diverse student bodies shape higher education globally. This diversity is influenced by different social positioning of students such as location, language, class, and race. Such different positions make for uneven access and success of students at the university. The disadvantaged and poor students remain neglected and marginalised in subtle and hidden entities, yet ignored by the new dispensations of democracy (Maringe, 2015). This chapter problematises this exclusion and argues how it causes students coming from disadvantaged backgrounds to be oppressed and deprived at the postcolonial university.

Although teaching and learning in HE is inevitably influenced by the fast-changing and globalising education and workplace, the new dispensations of democracy in South African higher education need to be sensitive and acknowledge the historical context of the country, and its injustices and inequalities that mostly affect poor students. The discussions of this chapter have shown some of the realities of colonial legacies in education and how the university responds—or has failed to respond—to the call for decolonisation of South African HE.

This chapter calls for researchers' urgent attention, workshops, and programs that address inequalities based on power, class, and race in HE. Although South African universities are on the mission of transformation, neglect of such issues (power, race, and class) will result in the danger of separating decolonial and transformed universities from the country's social contexts and its citizens. The focus should be on the systems, structures, and cultures that govern the university. These inadequacies should be exposed and become the focus of the university community.

References

Abdi, A. A. (2006). *Eurocentric discourses and African philosophies and epistemologies of education: Counter-hegemonic analyses and responses*. Edmonton, Canada: University of Alberta.

Asante, M. K. (2014). *Context and theory: Molefi Kete Asante and the Afrocentric idea*. Albany, NY: University of New York Press.

Bazana, S. and Mogotsi, O. P. (2017). Social identities and racial integration in historically white universities: A literature review of the experiences of black students. *Transformation in Higher education in Higher Education, 2*(0),1-13.

Behari-Leak, K., Chitanand, N., Padayachee, K., Masehela, L., Vorster, J.E., Ganas, R., Merckel, V. (2018). How to be or not to be? A critical dialogue on the limitations and opportunities of academic development in the current higher education context. *South African Journal of Higher Education, 32*(6), 401-421.

Bhengu, L. (2020 March 12). UKZN removes 2000 professional students who've taken eight years to do a three-year course. *Sowetan Live. Retrieved from* https://www.facebook.com/sowetanlive/posts/ukzn-removes-2000-professional-students-whove-taken-eight-years-to-do-a-three-ye/4010517172322256/.

Biko, S. (1987). *I write what I like.* Oxford: ProQuest LLC.

Bozalek, V. & Boughey, C. (2012). (Mis)framing higher education in South Africa. *Social Policy and Administration, 46*(6), 688-703.

Bozalek, V. (2011). Acknowledging privilege through encounters with difference: Participatory learning and action techniques for decolonising methodologies in Southern contexts, *International Journal of Social Research Methodology, 14*(6), 469-484.

BrckaLorenz, A., Haeger, H., Nailos, J. & Rabourn, K. (2013, May). Student perspectives on the importance and use of technology in learning. Paper presented at the Annual Forum of the Association for Institutional Research, Long Beach, California.

Chism, N. V. N. (1998). Developing a philosophy of teaching statement. *Essays on Teaching Excellence, 9*(3), 1-2.

Clowes, L. (2013). Teacher as learner: A personal reflection on a short course for South African university educators, *Teaching in Higher Education, 18*(7),709-720.

Coetzee-de Vos, G. (2019). Reflections on language transformation at Nelson Mandela University, *Language Matters.* doi: 10.1080/10228195.2018.1524923..

Dumbrill, G. C. & Green, J. (2008). Indigenous knowledge in the social work Academy. *Social Work Education, 27*(5), 489-503.

Ellis, C., Adams, T. A &Bochner, A.P. (2011). Autoethnography: An overview. *Forum: Qualitative Social Research, 12*(1), 345-357.

Fry, H., Ketteridge S. &Marshall, S. (2009). *A handbook for teaching and learning in higher education: Enhancing academic practice.* New York: Taylor and Francis.

Gray, M, Kreitzer, L. &Mupedziswa, R. (2014). The enduring relevance of indigenisation in African social work: A Critical Reflection on ASWEA's Legacy. *Ethics and Social Welfare,* 8(2),101–116.

Graham, M.J. (1999). The African-centred worldview: Toward a paradigm for social work. *Journal of Black Studies, 30*(1),103-122.

International Federation of Social Workers general meeting and the IASSW General Assembly. (2014 July). Global definition of Social Worker. Retrieved https://www.ifsw.org/what-is-social-work/global-definition-of-social-work/.

Le Grange, L. (2014). Currere's active force and the Africanisation of the university curriculum. *SAJHE, 28*(4), 1283-1294.

Madlingozi, T. (2019). Social movements and the 'decolonial turn' in constitutional theory. *The Seminar Series called "Ukutshintshwa kweendlela/[Re] Directions". Organized* by the Chair for Critical Studies in Higher Education Transformation (CriSHET) at the Nelson Mandela University. Retrieved https://www.youtube.com/watch?v=u_2m1dyrKuE&t=506s.

Maldonado-Torres, N. (2011). Enrique Dussel's Liberation Thought in the Decolonial Turn. Transmodernity: *Journal of Peripheral Cultural Production of the Luso-Hispanic World.* Retrieved https://escholarship.org/uc/item/5hg8t7cj.

Makhanya, T.B. &Zibane, S.Z. (2020). Students' voices on how Indigenous languages are disfavoured in South African higher education. *Journal of Language Matters.* doi: 10.1080/10228195.2020.1711533.

Mamphiswana, D. & Noyoo, N. (2016). Social work education in a changing socio-political and economic dispensation: Perspectives from South Africa. *International Social Work, 43*(1),21-32.

Mbembe, A.J. (2016). Decolonizing the university: New directions. *Arts and Humanities in Higher Education, 15*(1), 29-45.

McPhee, P. (2009). Forward. In; Becher, T and Trowler, P. (Eds). *Academics Tribes and Territories,:Society for Research in Higher Education*. Buckingham: Open University Press.

Mkhize, N., Mathe, S. & Buthelezi, N. (2014). Ethical decision-making in cultural context: Implications for professional practice. *Mediterranean Journal of Social Sciences, 5*(23), 2413-2419.

Mutasa, D. (2015). Language policy implementation in South African universities vis-à-vis the speakers of Indigenous African languages. *Perception: A Journal of Language Learning, 31*(1), 46-59.

Ndlovu-Gatsheni, S. J. (2018). *Epistemic freedom in Africa: Deprovincialization and decolonization*. New York: Routledge.

Ndlovu-Gatsheni, S.J. (2015). Decoloniality as the Future of Africa. *History Compass, 13*(10), 485-496.

Nwanosike, O. F. & Onyije, L.E. (2011). Colonialism and education. Proceedings of the 2011 International Conference on Teaching, Learning and Change. Retrieved http://hrmars.com/admin/pics/170.pdf.

Pratt, D.D. (1998). Five perspectives on teaching in adult and higher education. Retrievehttps://eric.ed.gov/?id=ED461013.

Schenk, R., Mbedzi, P., Qalinge, L., Schultz, P., Sekudu, J., & Sesoko, M. (2015). *Introduction to social work in the South African context*. Cape Town: Oxford University Press.

Scott, I. (2016, October). Academic development and student support: Significance, challenges and costs of expansion. Presentation to the Fees Commission.

Seepe, S. (2004). Editorial notes. *S. Afr. J. Higher Educ, 18*(3), 9-16

Smith, L. (2014). Historiography of South African Social Work: Challenging Dominant Discourses. *Social Work/Maatskaplike Werk, 50*(3), 305-331.

Spiller, D. (2012). *Tertiary teaching: Exploring our beliefs, teaching development*. Hamilton, New Zealand: Wāhanga Whakapakari Ako.

Tamburro, A. (2013). Including decolonization in social work education and practice. *Journal of Indigenous Social Development, 2*(1),1-16.

Twikiriza, J.M & Spitzer, H. (2019). *Social Work Practice in Africa: Indigenous and Innovative Approaches*. Kampala: Fountain Publishers

University of KwaZulu-Natal. (2014). Language policy. Uhlelo lolimi olubukeziwe. Retrieved http://registrar.ukzn.ac.za/Libraries/policies/Language_Policy__CO02010906.sflb.ashx.

Vandeyar, S. (2019). Why decolonising the South African university curriculum will fail? Teaching in higher education. Retrieved https://www.tandfonline.com/loi/cthe20.

van Heerden, M.S. (2009). *Providing and Managing Student Development and Support in Higher Education in A Developing Country* (Unpublised Ph.D thesis)., University of Pretoria, Pretoria.

Vorster, J & Quinn, L. (2017). The 'decolonial turn': What does it mean for academic staff development? *Unisa Press Journal, 21*(1),1-25.

wa Thiong'o, N. (2006). *Decolonizing the mind: The politics of language in African literature*. Nairobi: East African Educational Publishers.

World Economic Forum 2019. The Fourth Industrial Revolution: what it means, how to respond. Retrievedhttps://www.weforum.org/agenda/2016/01/the-fourth-industrial-revolution-what-it-means-and-how-to-respond/.

Zembylas, M. (2018). Decolonial possibilities in South African higher education: Reconfiguring humanizing pedagogies as/with decolonizing pedagogies. *South African Journal of Education, 38*(4), 1-11.

Zibane, S. Z. (2017). Negotiating sexuality: Informal sexual cultures amongst young people at a township high school in KwaZulu-Natal. (Unpublished Ph.D. thesis). University of KwaZulu-Natal, Durban.

12

Beyond the Shadows of My Educational Experiences

Bridging the Gap Through Reflexivity

Debbie Devonish

Introduction to a Journey

As I attempt to recollect and reconnect with the avenues of my past and present journey, I wonder if my narrative will read familiar with someone else's or enlighten someone to the cultural, social and sociopolitical conditions that differently frame our educational journeys. My name is Debbie Devonish. I am the elder of two daughters borne of Shelley and Patricia Whittle in 1978. My parents are retired teachers, my mother an English teacher and librarian, my father a mathematician and Economics Lecturer. I tell you of humble educational beginnings in the land of wood and water, Jamaica.

In Jamaica, national education is a mixture of government, private, and parochial schools. Schooling in my formative years was within parochial institutions. My formal education started in a basic school operated by the Quakers in the rural parish of Portland, in a district called Hectors River. The Quakers were among the earliest colonial settlers in Jamaica, having come to the island after the English conquest in 1655. The Catholic church maintained the most significant hold on schooling in Jamaica, upholding the notion that moral development and education are inseparable. We can still see the remnants of this today, as church-owned schools are a post-colonial feature that continues to shape the educational landscape in Jamaica, and more broadly in the post-colonial world (O'Donoghue, 2009).

Growing up, I lived with my parents in a teacher's cottage on the compound of the Happy Grove High School. I grew up in an environment of educational practitioners: my whole family, cousins, uncles, and aunts were all educators. Those who were not headmasters or headmistresses were teachers, and those who were not teachers were married to teachers. From a very early age, educational excellence was the primary expectation in my family. My mother thought teaching to be the noblest of professions, and from a tender age, I had to do well at school, guided by her tutelage. All around me in my childhood environment, there were examples of reverence for educational success. My parents were young professionals fresh out of Mico Teachers' College. Presently, Mico University College is the oldest and only teacher training institution established in the British colonies within the Western Hemisphere that still exists (Whyte, 1983). As a child, the perception was that Mico was the premier institution of choice in Jamaica.

Our small family of three would often leave our little cottage during school breaks to visit relatives. All my family would congregate at my grandparent's home in Bath, Saint Thomas, and all school-aged children had to take report cards for Uncle and Aunty to see. The adults would congregate in the yard and update each other on the family's educational progress, among other things, and it was at these events that the children would present themselves for praise or hide away to escape scolding. Eventually, we children would sneak away for a fun time at the river, while the adults took their time to catch up.

Today, I am an associate professor at the University of Technology (UTech), Jamaica. I have been the head of the biology department for the last six years, and my major responsibility is overseeing the teaching of biology modules, including biological electives that fall in different courses of study. I also train science teachers in the rudiments of science pedagogy. As I reflect on critical incidents in my experience as a student, I would like to share four themes that shaped my journey and how I perceive my own educational practice.

Motivation and Interest in School

In Jamaica, school children three to six years old attend the infant school, and children six to eleven years old go to primary school. After leaving the Parish of Portland, my parents got teaching posts at Jonathon Grant High School in Spanish Town. This was in the parish of Saint Catherine, and I went to Spanish Town infant school and onward to the 'feeder' school, Spanish Town Primary. As old as you are, you likely still recall your teachers from your early school life because you remember them for how they made you feel as a student in their class. My preschool teacher, Mrs. Jones, and my grade-five teacher, Mrs. Lewis, both made me feel special. These two teachers always gave me additional class responsibilities, such as class monitoring, counting off the lunch money to balance the class canteen accounts, delivering messages to other teachers, or being the team lead during grouping activities in lessons. This boosted my confidence as a student, and I enjoyed going to school then. I also recall having lots of playtime before and after school because my primary school was a 'shift' school.

The shift system was introduced into the Jamaican school system in 1774, to maximize the usage of school-building space. One group of students attends school in the morning, and a completely different group attends school in the afternoon. This arrangement has lasted well over two centuries, though it was never intended to be a permanent fixture of Jamaican schools (Bray, 1990). I particularly enjoyed being on evening shift because I could play longer before school between the morning and evening shifts. The Jamaican government embarked on removing the shift system from the nation's schools in 2017 and proposed a three-year projection to remove the shift system.

Grade one at primary school is forever etched in my mind as a tumultuous time in my young student life. I did not like school and I did not like my teacher. Another student in my class also bullied me. She was tall and big; she pinched me hard and constantly referred to me as "Red-Red." I was not a *dundus*—otherwise known as a Jamaican albino, but I surmise I was teased because of my very light brown complexion, which was not as 'socially fashionable' then as it is now, with the more recent cultural obsession with skin bleaching. Jamaica has a complex history: slavery, Spanish rule, British colonization, indentured servants, and uninhibited immigration. We are now a little island with English as the dominant language, a multiplicity of ethnic backgrounds, religious persuasions (though mainly Christians), with over four hundred denominations and people of varied skin tones. My maternal grandmother's pictures were of a skinny brown woman with long flowing hair. I am told that my family was either Scottish or Irish and the names of my grandparents, *Newland* and *Whittle* originate from parishes of England, thus my inherited features.

I did not seek any assistance from my teacher about being bullied because I did not have the confidence to intervene in the matter, and I also felt that she disliked me. She never allowed us to play or do fun things in class during lessons and she always asked me if I was "deaf" for ignoring her, and she always said I was talkative. There were many other instances throughout primary school that made me feel and remember that it was unpleasant in transitioning to primary school. I felt bored, I received corporal punishment because it was not yet discouraged in the Jamaican school system, I was called a chatterbox, and eventually I grew afraid to participate in class, especially after the response I got, ("Are you an idiot?" "You must be the biggest idiot.") when I told the teacher one day that the sea was salty because of Lot's wife (I now find my response rather hilarious). That primary school lesson episode is quite memorable, but the nine-year-old child who had read this incredulous story of a woman turning into a pillar of salt perhaps was bored and wanted an opportunity to discuss the scientific possibilities. Only an experienced and efficacious teacher could have turned the situation into a teachable moment (*The composition of Life...*) to make the connection between ions, decomposition, weathering and running off into the sea. Children have to learn fantasy–reality distinctions; it is a natural part of development (Shtulman, 2009), socializing between life episodes of fiction and fact. According to Holyoak, Junn & Billman (1984), analogical transfer can apply relevant information or concepts from one context to a relationally similar context. Children must be engaged by the very nature of science to understand the interconnectedness of life, scientific principles and life support systems, a narrowly comprehended concept that I bemoan even today, where lesson exploration for science is minimal and disparaged in the Jamaican primary school lessons.

On another note, I remember the point in my school journey that I departed from Physics. It was just one concept, but I thought my teacher could *not make me understand,* and I remember how during the lesson, I literally gave up when someone verbalized, "If you cannot understand, then you are foolish." That was when I was done with the formal training in Physics. This was in grade twelve in high school. I recall this incident, and as a teacher, I am very careful of what I say and prioritize creating a safe learning atmosphere for my students. I am mindful that my words to the learner must always be of encouragement and the learner's personal feelings must be respected. Humanism is a paradigm emerging in the 1960s, focused on developing self-actualized and efficacious individuals, individuals who thrive via personalized learning with a teacher who encourages and facilitates learning according to the affective and cognitive needs of the learner. This requires a supportive context of teaching and learning (Chatelier, 2017). An education grounded in humanism must include a teacher with a positive attitude towards students. As a teacher, I must be socially responsive and attentive, willing to adapt instruction to the needs of each student and attend to their wellbeing.

The 'Unspoken' Challenges of the Jamaican Education System

Reflecting on my early school life, 1989–1996, I did not consider myself excellent, just a persevering student. I recall that I would excel when I waged a 'self-challenge'. I read or heard something intriguing; it would often be the catalyst to make me silently move into an *I-can-do-that mode.* For example, I recall that I did not have a consistent mathematics teacher for the seven to ninth grades. Those were the days when we had no form room, and the class spent some sessions under the big old rubber tree by the basketball court. Unfortunately, even today in 2020, some schools go through the school year without students having a consistent mathematics or science teacher for the entire school term/terms. Nonetheless, I yearned to do well. I wondered if I could excel at mathematics and that was my self-challenge. I went to extra classes with my father and worked diligently at school.

Until now, whenever I have decided to do something, there are always three steps to my approach. Firstly, I need to know everything because knowledge is the key to unlocking the unknown; secondly, I need to know why, because understanding is irreversible and empowering; and finally, I need to know what else, as in what else is there to change my position, and how will it affect my perspective? I think I adapted these three steps because of my experience at home. My father was the head of the household. His word was law and we all obeyed. His motto was 'prepared for action'—*Ad Agendum Semper Parati*—and in later years, he would constantly remind me of the study of "Decision Science." There was seldom anything of importance asked of my father that was not answered with, "I will think about it." There was never an opinion that my father shared that was not considered a favorable decision.

In contrast, my mother was impulsive and acted emotionally, but having both parents in my life provided the delicate balance I needed. I grew to understand the value of thinking about a situation before responding, the complexity of finalizing decisions, and the virtue of gracious empathy.

There could be no shortcuts to my three-step process because I could act decisively if I followed it. I was to be a lifelong learner, there was to be no time for repetition or lost goals. This was how I felt, so even at school, I could stand independently by my decision or set tasks to be achieved and get them done solo. I always felt that if I could do something once, then I could prove myself repeatedly. Therefore, I became a consistent planner; my steps had to be ordered. I found that as a teacher, after assessing my students' prior knowledge, and my own lesson goals and outcomes, I also diligently planned for our success through the use of timelines.

I recall, during high school, of all the subject disciplines, the Science and Mathematics teacher shortage was very apparent, and my school administration had to implement strategies for addressing such. The insufficiencies of the Mathematics and Science subjects, and the lack of resources in terms of science equipment have been a disastrous impediment, and I dare say it was not unique to my school (Polis, 1990). I remember classes getting substitute teachers who were newly graduated students I recognized from upper school. I also recall Cuban, Indian and Nigerian science teachers being employed for brief periods to teach us in upper school, grades ten to thirteen.

As a former British colony, Jamaica also adapted British examinations, so we followed the General Certificate of Education (GCE) Ordinary (O-level) and Advanced Level (A-level) examinations. This was a subject-based terminal examination for grade twelve and thirteen secondary school offered by institutions in the United Kingdom and the educational authorities of British Crown dependencies to students completing secondary or pre-university education. Jamaica eventually replaced the General Certificate Education awards with Caribbean Secondary Education Certificate (CSEC) and Caribbean Advanced Proficiency Examination (CAPE). Both exams are offered by the Caribbean Examinations Council (CXC), which was established in 1972 under agreement by the participating Caribbean governments. In Jamaica, there are many exams available to high school students, and the exam you are prepared for depends on the 'type' of high school and their offerings. As schools were developed in Jamaica, there were the church-run traditional high schools, and then there were the other schools that became upgraded high schools, such as the Junior Secondary, Technical High, and All Age Schools. The traditional high schools did the mainstream examinations, GCE and then CSEC and CAPE for traditional subjects, while in the other schools' programs, students were prepared for the Jamaica School Certificate (JSC) for students exiting school at grade nine (all age school) and the Secondary School Certificate (SSC) on exiting grade eleven. Students could also pursue the Union of Lancashire and Cheshire Institute (ULCI) examinations, but in these schools, the emphasis was on vocational subject areas. In Jamaica, every child has equal access to secondary education, and all are encouraged to go to school and prepare for any exam of their choice.

Of course, some schools thrive and others struggle. For example, my dad explained that when he went to school at Happy Grove High in the 1960s, the school and its science labs were well-resourced by the support of the Quakers, and he indicated that the mixed cadre of teachers there included qualified men and women from England. What I now understand is that it is between the inequity of individual and community support within the schools, and failing government policies, lasting social change has been a challenge. As a result, children from more affluent homes are more likely to go to traditional schools, and the social complexity that exists is a pervasive remnant of the British system (Sherington, Peterson & Brice, 1987).

My school was a typical traditional Catholic school, but was hampered by a lack of science equipment and teacher support, and I was disheartened. In the A-level exam, six years into high school, was the first time I touched a microscope. I didn't even know the school had any, but I was expected to use one with expertise under exam conditions. This is not a unique experience to some students in Jamaica, even now. The exam names may have changed but when they get to tertiary institutions, they are ill-prepared for science. Even now, in an era where research-driven policies should transcend the complexities of the issues at hand and comprehensively acknowledge the importance of Science, Technology, Engineering, and Mathematics (STEM education) and its impact on national development, we are still found wanting.

In Jamaica, the highest recorded budget expenditure on education was 6.4 percent of gross domestic product (GDP) in 2010 (*World Fact Book*, p. 353). It would seem that though we have taken over our national affairs, the issue of education financing is still a major challenge. On top of addressing how much money is spent, we also must address how that money is spent. Educational development requires change in the access, equity, efficiency, and quality (Welsh, 2012). There are so many areas within the education system in need of monetary attention. However, I am a firm believer in developing and investing in a foundation of science.

My student experience, then, has made me most appreciative of Educational Technology and the support systems available online. Even if lab space or equipment is not available, students can still be engaged in simulation exercises, virtual labs, videos for 'vicarious' learning, and inquiry-based teaching, which can be utilized to meet the deficiencies that may exist. These approaches are even more possible for 20th-century teachers and learners alike, with the prevalence of online teacher–learner resources. As a student, there were limited phone booths on the streets, no home landline phones, internet, or smart android phones existed, so we were limited with using technology to support teaching and learning. Now, as an educator in 2020, I maintain a high level of interaction within social networks for sharing with other educators and students.

Looking back, I can see that my commitment to perseverance, persistence and precision was instilled from an early age. The seed of awareness for the value in education was sown; the yearning for success by the application of knowledge was empowering and transforming. As a high school student, I earned awards for my overall Caribbean Secondary Examinations performance and received top subject prizes. Upon leaving high school, after a much less glorious sixth form performance, I moved on to tertiary education at the University of the West Indies (Mona).

Tertiary Training in Jamaica, Endless Possibilities

I pursued a Bachelor of Science degree, majoring in Zoology and Botany, from September 1996 to 2000. During my first degree, there was one significant thing I noted about my experience that influenced how I teach. To do well in a subject area, one has to have a good foundation on which to build. I recall for my chemistry courses, the tests were all multiple-choice questions, but if you did not attempt a question, you lost more points than if you had an incorrect answer. These grading conditions made me fearful. There were students who went into the finals with a negative grade and there were those who had severe test anxiety. I remember how the grades were ranked and posted on the wall. I usually started looking for my student identification number from the bottom of the list.

I despised the thought of being fearful about achieving an acceptable grade. To overcome the fear of such a testing regime, I knew I had to be confident about my content and skills. I eventually converted the situation into eustress. Eustress is positive stress "that challenges us to grow, adapt and find creative solutions in our lives" (Hales, 2000, p. 17). It challenged me to start from the beginning, right back to chemistry basics. In so doing, I could get through the courses to level two with confidence. In my practice now as an educator, I am very empathetic when students are not able to perform at the expected standard, especially when they express how hard they have tried. I understand how they feel and find that guiding them through foundational content to address conceptual gaps is very rewarding. Also, I consider it a privilege if students seek assistance because it signals their willingness to be guided and a confidence to do better, a path towards self-directed learning.

After my first degree, I got a departmental award and enrolled to study Entomology. The process of doing research taught me patience and the virtue of managing time for research work and writing. After completing the Master's in 2004, I went on to do a postgraduate diploma in science teaching, then a doctorate. I will speak of my postgraduate experience to show how I developed a passion for science education.

Shaping My Mission in Science Education Training

In September 2007, I decided to pursue my doctorate. I had just undergone tragedy in my motherhood life, and I was advised to occupy my mind by pursuing a new goal. I walked into the colorful garden campus of Northern Caribbean University (NCU), North Campus; the university is operated by the Jamaica Union Conference and the Atlantic Caribbean Union Mission of Seventh-Day Adventists. It is situated in the cool hills of Mandeville, Manchester, where the raindrops pelted the soil and unearthed the rich earthy smell. The outskirts of the land were draped with large tall palm trees, flowers, and fruit trees. There were three glass-enclosed gazebos for our students' convenience, and a large country house converted into what was to be my postgraduate administrative schoolhouse for nine *long* years.

My graduate school life before was mainly in a natural sciences faculty, which, as it turned out, was entirely different from this new university culture. For example, they prayed before every class; this was new to me, coming from an environment where religion was not mentioned at all. Individualism had been the way through my graduate studies thus far. You went out into the field alone, you were in the lab alone, you analyzed your data, you prepared, presented, and defended as in combat. But now I was in a new environment, with a different culture of learning.

It was during my doctoral journey I concluded that I wanted to research science education. I had become more aware of the influence of teachers on the changing landscape of education (Clandinin, Downey & Huber, 2009). Teacher efficacy is the most consistent variable for overall academic success (Costa & Garmston, 2002; Fullan, 2007). During my research, I learned that effective professional development for science teachers can transform student academic performance (Devonish, 2016). I became a student of Cognitive Coaching (Costa & Garmston, 1994), which I focused on as a science teacher professional development model.

I began to notice how my thought process towards teaching changed. I became more flexible, more empathetic, and more understanding of my role to serve (Greenleaf, 1991). Now, I utilize and incorporate into my practice what I was learning for more effective science lessons. These included cooperative structures such as random call (by the use of random call cards), the continuum (a criterion arrangement of persons in a series), praise the deed (a best practice for acknowledging participation during lessons), and the ranking exercises (Green & Henriques-Green, 2008). There were the more formal cooperative strategies (Kagan, 1985) such as Jigsaw; along with theoretical perspectives of collaborative teaching and learning (Panitz, 1999), student-led reciprocal teaching (Palinscar & Brown, 1984; McLymont, 2000), and cognitive coaching tools (Costa and Garmston, 2000). While I was in my course of study and learning about these pedagogical strategies, I was able to apply them immediately to my practice. I was navigating and operationalizing the theories, and I was formally documenting my experience for action research as a classroom teacher.

The action research created professional knowledge that drew on theory (in this case, cognitive coaching theory) and practice (eclectic teaching of my lessons). It brought continuity between my teaching, the students' coursework, and my own educational studies (Ulvik, Riess & Roness 2018). I ensured that

I executed proper protocols for cooperative learning if I wanted more than just grouped activities. I spent time assessing learners and acknowledging theories that explained their learning differences—namely different learning styles (Kolb, 1985) and multiple intelligences (Gardner, 1993), to assess activities and tailor my instruction for their lessons and documented the same.

Finally, in my doctoral journey, my misunderstanding of the qualitative tradition was corrected. There was a place for qualitative studies, the methodology had to be 'robust' and trustworthy, and its application offered flexibilities in research I had not considered. My paradigm shifted and I embraced Mixed Methods; I set out as an enhanced researcher, navigating two 'research worlds' beyond a science laboratory. For me, research is no longer a lonely, singular endeavor. The scientist, student, and educator can collaborate in research to tell the whole story from varied informed perspectives. I now have a mission to ensure that natural science research is translated in a way that educators can understand and appreciate it. I aim to increase scientific literacy, to bridge the gap between what are considered "complex or technical" scientific issues and the realities of our daily lives.

I am deeply committed to science teacher education because I want to be the conduit that ensures that every science teacher in their professional development knows the science standards but also knows how to teach science in engaging ways *(I am currently a panel member for the national science standards committee)*. Not one student should leave the science classroom unenthused. The nature of science should positively impact students; it is the most important role of any science educator to ensure that our students develop scientific literacy.

Teaching and Leadership Philosophy

I seek to be a catalyst for change. In the classroom, I aim to develop self-directed learners. Students should identify assistance and resources, apply critical thinking skills, problem-solve, and work toward achieving their goals. I currently teach at the tertiary level. I am the head of the Biological Sciences Division. The division's central role is to provide service modules to other faculties and students within my science faculty. The division caters to students of a mixed population. I am aware they enroll to do a biology-based subject because they require fundamental biological concepts and skills for their courses of studies and their ultimate choices of career. I therefore owe it to my students, the nurses, medical technologists, sports science majors, environmental health officers, medical information officers, the science teachers and all students who require a biology elective within their course of study to provide robust content, effective communication, and a robust contextual framework that will be meaningful for their career path. I chose to major in biology because I was inspired by a teacher. I enjoyed the study of biology, I enjoyed the secondary school science curricula, and I thought the subjects were very practical and relevant to understanding life. I came from a family of educators, and I had often thought that, as a teacher, I could provide a better learning experience for my students than I had. I wanted others to appreciate the science subjects; I wanted to infuse a higher level of enthusiasm and importance to its study. I studied education at the post-graduate level because I wanted to be a leader in the field of science education (Sergiovanni & Starratt, 2002). I wanted to be better able to inform best practices in my science teaching and learning.

Self-efficacy (Bandura, 1994) means a lot to me; I need to be effective, and I concentrate on being efficacious in content, skillset and communication, because I want to be impactful for my audience. Therefore, I believe that a good teacher is also a good learner. I translate this to my students by telling them that in the lessons, we are going to learn and share in the teaching and learning experiences. I usually tell them I look forward to the lessons they will teach me, to which they usually giggle in disbelief. Still, it's a strategy that gives me the opportunity to invite students' participation and set the tone for a social constructivist environment with much interdependence. I acknowledge that in order to be impactful, theory has to be operationalized or, in other words, I have to utilize all that I know and believe in executing pedagogical approaches, and students have to understand and assimilate cognitively to change their behaviour as well. I also take the time to explain my mode of action whenever I need to infuse pedagogical intervention or make changes to their learning schedule, because I want them to feel a part of the teaching and learning process.

To be a teacher is a most honorable profession. As an educator, my greatest joy is to see in my students' exploration, perseverance, and achievement. I am happy when I see that my students are not focused on their grade, but they are willing to explore an educational journey that will enrich their skill set for not just a job but for life. When I see my students persevering despite the challenges, in order to achieve mastery, I know I have carried out my role as a teacher.

For the students to whom I teach biology, especially for the biology teachers in training, my main aim for teaching in this field is to encourage them to become knowledgeable of biological content, them to become critical thinkers and to challenge common thought. I want them to become teacher leaders to impact other teachers positively and collaboratively develop the science teacher stock (Sergiovanni & Starratt, 2002). Most of all, I want them to impart the science knowledge, skills, and attitudes they learned through their learning experience to better influence others, while I work to improve my craft at teaching.

Critical Reflection

I wrote a story of an educational journey spanning over 34 years. The story will continue because the journey has not stopped. However, this unending story reveals the reasons that a little brown Jamaican girl became a science teacher, and what she hoped to achieve. The story illustrates that, through her reflection, she hoped to be a catalyst for change, to help improve science education, filling in whatever measures possible to address inefficiencies in the science education system in Jamaica. She realizes that it is a tall order, a heroic feat, but has embarked on such a task by starting with her own professional practice.

The story reminisced, starting from preschool, through to post-graduate terminal studies. The stories were nostalgic, exposing, informative, and revealing. Nostalgia is a pleasurable emotion and, as I remembered and wrote of specific incidences in my educational journey, I was reminded of good times. I remembered being a child playing about in the country with my cousins, playing at primary school, role-playing teacher and student in a typical dolly-schoolhouse setting. I remembered the innumerable cohorts of students I taught over the years at different institutions. Even now, as I pen the final words for this book chapter, I recall how daunting it felt, how exposed I would become for those who do me the honor to read my story to the end. I wondered if I would be able to tell the undiluted story, to speak the truth about my feelings, even when I felt it should be hidden behind literary devices. Ultimately, I found that things sometimes became jumbled, lengthy, and the worded expressions became void of clarity in telling the story. In those instances, I had to concentrate and write clearly to express my thoughts so the readers could understand my life experiences, for justification of the end result. I was writing an autobiography, not a thesis on scientific principles and conjectures, but the task was just as awesome, with similar intentions for fruitful informative, educational dissemination.

I was informed by the process of writing this story of my educational background. There were points within the story where I sought to interject facts about the lived Jamaican context. I note there are colonial remnants found within our education system still influencing how policies are enacted in the school system even now. Therefore, the historical rendezvous, trying to recollect the theorists and using the theories to critique my own practice was entirely informative. Highlighted were unspoken challenges in the education system that I faced, that my students continue to face, and that we all face nationally. In writing this story, there were instances where I had to consider that my audience may not be Jamaican, or Caribbean, and thus the context and explanation for some terms became necessary. Though I could have spoken endlessly on societal self-image issues or bullying in schools, I just briefly mentioned skin bleaching and my unfortunate bully encounter and acknowledge there is only so much that can be told.

What a revelation! I would encourage all professionals, students, everyone to tell their story. A story of where you were, or where you are, and why you are there can only be told by the individual. It is now a record documented in the pages of history, and history will allow those who read to make sense of their current reality. Professional development is a process, it is a journey, and more often than not, the story is told after the journey has reached a point where the narrator has pinnacled at success. However, now that I have told a portion of my story, I know my school experiences and familial influences led me to become an educator. I love the old adage, "Experience teacheth wisdom," and I, through this process, have been a student in a constructivist classroom. I know there is so much more that can be done to improve my practice and I am sure that those who have read my story can give pointers for doing better.

References

Ball, R. (2002). Boring science? Blame the curriculum not the teachers. *Electronics Weekly, 2067*, 18.

Bandura, A. (1994). Self-efficacy. In V. S. Ramachaudran (Ed.), *Encyclopedia of human behavior* (Vol. 4, pp. 71-81). New York: Academic Press. (Reprinted in H. Friedman [Ed.], *Encyclopedia of mental health*. San Diego, CA: Academic Press, 1998).

Chatelier, S. (2017). Beyond the Humanism/Posthumanism Debate: The Educational Implications of Said's Critical, Humane Praxis. *Educational Theory, 67*(6), 657–672.

Clandinin, J. D., Downey, C. A., & Huber, J. (2009). Attending to changing landscapes: shaping the interwoven identities of teachers and teacher educators. *Asia-Pacific Journal of Teacher Education, 37*(2), 141-154.

Costa, A. L., & Garmston, R. J. (1994). *Cognitive coaching: A foundation for Renaissance Schools*. Norwood, MA: Christopher-Gordon.

Costa, A. L., & Garmston, R. J. (2002). *Cognitive coaching: A foundation for Renaissance Schools* (2nd Ed.). Norwood, MA: Christopher-Gordon Publishers.

Designing the future of Jamaica's students through experimenting science. (2020, February 20). UNESCO Newsletter. https://en.unesco.org/news/designing-future-jamaicas-students-through-experimenting-science

Devonish, D. D. (2016a). The cognitive coaching approach: A professional Development model for science educators and for students' academic achievement. (Unpublished doctoral dissertation). Northern Caribbean University, Manchester.

Devonish, D. (2016b). Games in science teaching: The trainee teacher and perceptions of their classroom experience. In C. Onyefulu, (Ed.), *Advancing education in the Caribbean and Africa* (pp. 19–43). Akure: Nigeria: Science & Education Development Institute.

Devonish D. D. (2017, February). *A teaching approach enhancing science pedagogy to improve environmental awareness in Jamaica.* Northern Caribbean University Research Week 2017–Education Symposium and William M. Smith Lecture Series -February 6-9, 2017. Northern Caribbean University, Manchester.

Devonish, D., Lawrence, P. & Zamore, C. (2018). Voices of Pre-service Teachers on Science Pedagogy: A Case Study on the Challenges of Implementing Diverse Instructional Strategies into the Science lesson post University. *Journal of Arts Science & Technology, 11*(1), 55–71.

Fullan, M. (2007). *The new meaning of educational change.* New York, NY: Routledge.

Gardner, H. (1993). *Frames of mind: The theory of multiple intelligences.* New York, NY: Basic Books.

Green, W. H., & Henriquez-Green, R. (2008). *Basic moves of teaching: Building on cooperative learning.* Victoria, BC: Trafford Publishing.

Greenleaf, R. K. (1991). *Servant leadership: A journey into the nature of legitimate power and greatness.* New York, NY: Paulis Press.

Holyoak, K. J., Junn, E. N., & Billman, D. O. (1984). Development of analogical problem-solving skill. *Child Development, 55*(6), 2042–2055. doi:10.2307/1129778

Kagan, S. (1985). *Cooperative learning resources for teachers.* Riverside, CA: University of California at Riverside.

Kidman, G. (2008). Asking Students: What Key Ideas Would Make Classroom Biology Interesting? *Teaching Science, 54*(2), 34–38.

Kolb, D. (1985), LSI learning style inventory: Self-scoring inventory and interpretation booklet. Boston: McBer.

Lyons, T. (2006). The Puzzle of Falling Enrolments in Physics and Chemistry Courses: Putting Some Pieces Together. *Research in Science Education, 36*(3), 285–311.

Mayhew-Smith, A. (2002). Is science boring? *Electronics Weekly, 2061,* 13.

Peters, E. 2005. "Reforming Cookbook Labs." *Science Scope 29*(3): 16–21. http://search.ebscohost.com.ezproxy.utech.edu.jm/login.aspx?direct=true&db=eric&AN=EJ722115&site=ehost-live.

McLymont, E. F. (2000). *Mediated learning through the coaching approach facilitated by cognitive coaching* (Doctoral dissertation). Retrieved from ProQuest Dissertations & Theses Global. (Order No. NQ59634).

McLymont, E. F., & da Costa, J. L. (1998). *Cognitive Coaching the Vehicle for Professional Development and Teacher Collaboration.*

Ministry of Education Youth and Information (2019, October). Microscience Training gets a boost. The Gleaner. Retrieved from http://jamaica-gleaner.com/article/art-leisure/20191006/microscience-training-gets-boost

O'Donoghue, T. (2009). Colonialism, Education and Social Change in the British Empire: The Cases of Australia, Papua New Guinea and Ireland. *Paedagogica Historica: International Journal of the History of Education, 45*(6), 787-800.

Palinscar, A., & Brown, A. L. (1984). Reciprocal teaching of comprehension-fostering and comprehension-monitoring activities. *Cognition & Instruction, 1*(2), 117.

Panitz, T. (1999). *Collaborative versus cooperative learning: A comparison of the two concepts which will help us understand the underlying nature of interactive learning.* Retrieved from http://home.capecod.net/~tpanitz/tedsarticles/coopdefinition.htm or http://files.eric.ed.gov/fulltext/ED448443.pdf

Polis, A. R. (1990). Where have all the math teachers gone? *Vital Speeches of the Day, 56*(22), 687.

Sergiovanni, T. J. & Starratt, R. J. (2002). *Supervision: A redefinition* (7th ed.). Boston, MA: McGraw-Hill.

Sherington, G. Petersen, R.C. and Brice, I. (1987). *Learning to lead: A history of girls' and boys' corporate secondary schools in Australia.* Sydney: Allen and Unwin.

Shtulman, A. (2009). The development of possibility judgment within and across domains. Cognitive Development, 24(3), 293–309. doi:10.1016/j.cogdev.2008.12.006

Stafford, G. (April 26, 2009). The truth about school based assessment. Retrieved at http://mobile.jamaicagleaner.com/20090426/focus/focus4.php

UNESCO, International Bureau of Education. (2010). Jamaica World data on education, 7th edition 2010/2011. Retrieved from http://www.ibe.unesco.org.

Ulvik, M., Riese, H., & Roness, D. (2018). Action research--connecting practice and theory. *Educational Action Research, 26*(2), 273–287.

Welsh, R. O. (2012). Overcoming Smallness through Education Development: A Comparative Analysis of Jamaica and Singapore. *Current Issues in Comparative Education, 15*(1), 114–131.

Williams-McBean, C. (2018). Issues in School-based Assessment: The Reliability-Validity Paradox. *Caribbean Journal of Education. CJE, 40* (1&2) p. 110-138.

Whyte, M. (1983). *A short history of education in Jamaica (2nd ed.).* London: Hodder & Stoughton Ltd.

World Fact book. US Central Intelligence Agency. Washington, D.C.: Printing and Photography Group.

Part IV

Social Class, Politics and Education

13

"Education is something that can never be taken away from you!"

Theresa Conefrey

Before I was a teacher, I was a learner. My narrative begins with a series of chronological, place-bound, pivotal moments in my learning journey, which shaped the teaching philosophy that follows. My account concludes with connections and contradictions in my experiences as a teacher and learner and a call to readers to reflect on how their teaching practices are intertwined with their educational autobiographies.

My Educational Autobiography

Secondary Education Moment

"Look! See that building! When you get off the first bus, you have to head towards it. You turn left; then, keep walking past the bus stops until you see the number 17. Do you see it? That's the second bus you take." It is a sunny Saturday morning in downtown Birmingham, England. My 10-year-old twin sister and I are jostling and giggling, excited to be by ourselves on an excursion with our father, but he is not smiling. He is becoming exasperated. Our father wants to make sure we memorize the route from our home to school because we have not taken busses by ourselves before and worried we might get lost. After taking the standardized test that British children sat during the last year of elementary school, we had qualified for grammar school. Known as the 11-plus exam, this test streamed children according to academic ability into three different types of schools: grammar, secondary modern and technical schools. However, the British education system was in a period of flux, with many local grammar schools, including ours, transitioning into non-selective admittance comprehensive schools for all academic levels. My mother, who along with my father, had emigrated from rural Ireland to England in search of more opportunities, was a firm believer in the power of education to open doors. Concerned that such schools might not be as rigorous during the transition period, she had found our places at a grammar school in a distant suburb.

Undeterred that this school might be a stretch, she encouraged us to believe that we could succeed in whatever we put our minds to. Common exhortations of my childhood were: "Reach for the stars!" "Don't give up!" "Education is something that can never be taken away from you!" My father's concern was more pragmatic: that my twin sister and I could get to school and back safely.

Undergraduate Moment
I've swapped busses for trains. Soon after my 18th birthday, I'm waving goodbye to my family and setting off, suitcase in hand from tree-less, inner-city Birmingham to the Norfolk countryside, the first person in my family to attend colleges. My father's construction job at a local quarry has kept us all clothed and fed, but would not have stretched to cover a college education for his seven children. Fortunately for us, the *Education Act* of 1962 mandated that local authorities pay tuition fees for all who qualified for university (and living expenses in cases of demonstrated need) and my siblings and I were all able to complete college degrees. However, at that time, only about 10% percent of the population could take advantage of the government's largesse because most schools did not offer all the advanced (A) level subject tests required to satisfy the university entrance requirements. Had it not been for those long bus rides to that grammar school, I probably would not have had that opportunity.

Teacher-Training Moment
I am playing "nun splitting" in Paris after having taken the Metro to Saint Lazare. The rules are simple: When you spot a group of nuns walking together, your goal is to approach them in a way that forces them to separate from each other to let you pass. I'm taking a break from being a tour guide for a group of Master of Education students from the university where I am completing a Postgraduate Certificate of Education (PGCE), which is the required qualification for teaching in public schools in the UK and in some other European countries. Although my bachelor's degree and TEFL (Teaching English as a Foreign Language) certificate had led to teaching positions in Finland and Japan, I'm aware that this higher-level teaching qualification would lead to even more opportunities. Furthermore, tuition and living expenses are covered for all who are admitted to the course. One day, our instructor asked if anyone was available to lead a study-abroad trip to Paris for students in the Master of Education program. As none of those studying how to teach French volunteered, I raised my hand; a free trip to Paris was too hard to refuse. Even though German was my subject area, I had confidence that I'd be able to revive my high-school French. This trip was consequential because visiting international organizations such as the World Bank, listening to lectures by

French education ministers, and interacting with the international group of master's students seeded the possibility of furthering my education.

Graduate Studies Moment

"Excuse me, but which way is it to the Greyhound Station?," I ask a local police officer. "Go two blocks east and one block north; you'll see it on the south-west corner," he obliges. I wonder which direction is east, unsure how to translate his directions into the more familiar left and right that I am used to. I've just flown from Heathrow to Chicago O'Hare Airport to begin a master's degree in the Teaching of English (MATESL) program. Although the PGCE had opened up positions in Denmark and Spain, I soon realized that despite the thrill of these new opportunities, I missed the "aha" moments of intense intellectual focus and began strategizing about returning to university life. Unfortunately, my luck with public funding in the UK had run out as grants were mostly limited to STEM fields. Undeterred, I considered other options and became a frequent visitor to the Danish-American Fulbright Commission in Copenhagen, realizing that furthering my studies in the U.S. might be a possibility. After a year of teaching and dodging Basque separatist attacks while living in Bilbao, I'd saved enough money, completed the application process, and was heading to the vast cornfields of the Midwest. My father called me "work-shy" when I told him about my plans; he wanted me to "settle down and get a real job." I assured him that I'll be home for good after my master's degree, not realizing that like my parents, I too was emigrating.

Bewilderment with the Chicago police officer's directions should have tipped me off to other potential differences in our "two nations divided by a common language." Higher education in the U.S. was a cultural shock because of the differences in pedagogical practices. No longer could I follow my own intellectual interests during term time as long as I crammed sufficiently in the weeks before finals. I could easily take additional courses in the UK if I was concerned about my GPA because the lowest scores would be dropped. However, in the U.S., all weekly homework assignments and pop-quizzes counted toward the course grade and all courses counted toward my GPA. For the first time in my educational journey, I faced pressure to play it safe by enrolling in classes with familiar content rather than seeking new learning adventures that might compromise my GPA.

College Teaching Moment

As a new assistant professor, I am watching the annual parade of students in their traditional dress at the University of Hawaii, Hilo (UHH). Marching behind the Indigenous Hawaiians wearing leis and hula skirts are the native

Alaskans sweating in fur hats and coats under the tropical heat. Unlike them, my adaptation has been smoother. Once I had adjusted to the U.S. education system, I decided to continue my studies after completing my master's degree. When choosing among doctoral programs, I decided on the one that had the fewest specific requirements so that I could follow my multidisciplinary interests by taking classes in the English, Anthropology, and Sociology Departments. Taking such a diverse body of classes enabled me to make connections across concepts, integrate ideas from one field to another, and experience those epiphanic moments that drove my learning (Denzin & Lincoln, 1994). For my doctoral research, I was able to weave together diverse concepts into an ethnographic study of a life sciences laboratory, using conversation analysis to focus on issues of gender, language, and power.

What I'd neglected to consider during my graduate career were which courses to take or teach to support job applications once I'd finished the doctoral degree. Unfortunately, I had little contact with my advisor and few opportunities for mentoring during my program. Years later, I realized that peers who had parents or other family members in academia were much better prepared. I had no real concept of what lay beyond graduate school and little time to stop and reflect during my studies. As a result, despite my GPA, my multidisciplinary background had rendered me a less desirable candidate for more traditional programs, and securing an interview proved challenging. Fortunately, I was well-suited to UHH's more progressive ethos. Within a few years, I had established enough cordial relations campus-wide that I was able to gain support from the curriculum committee to create a Writing Studies track as an alternative to the more traditional literature-focused English major.

Gap Year Moment
My toddler is chasing squirrels on a well-manicured lawn at Santa Clara University (SCU), while I am awkwardly toddling after him, squeezing his four-month-old brother close to me in a baby sling and wondering if my formal teaching and learning journey has come to an end. As my spouse had not been able to find an appropriate position in Hawaii, I had taken a leave of absence just before my first son's birth to accept a short-term research position at the Institute for Research on Women and Gender (IRWG) at Stanford University, assuming I'd be able to resume my career. However, soon after my second son's birth, I gave up the adjunct position at SCU that followed after and became part of the "leaky pipeline," the metaphor used to describe women (particularly in STEM fields), who leave academia before reaching senior position. Ironically, this was the phenomenon that I had been researching

as a graduate student (Conefrey, 1997); however, it was not until my family situation led me to reluctantly give up my own tenure-track position that I fully understood the complexity of women's lives and the difficult choices they make, often as caretakers of both children and elderly relatives.

Fortunately, I still retained an evening course in SCU's Graduate Engineering Management Program, but it was a confusing time for me. Was I a housewife with a part-time job? Had I "let the side down" by giving up what other women had fought hard to gain? Had feminism failed me or had I failed it? But time to ponder was limited as my days were filled with chasing after two young boys and answering their slew of questions: "How far is it to the moon?" "Why do wolves eat chickens?" "How does a fire extinguisher work?" Walking, cooking, and other everyday experiences were chock full of teachable moments.

Return to Academe Moment
My co-presenter and I are skimming our slides and checking that the projector is working. We are in Washington, D.C. for the 2020 AAC&U ePortfolio Forum, preparing to begin our presentation on the use of ePortfolios to engage and retain STEM majors. My sons are now teenagers and I have resumed my full-time career at SCU. Five years earlier, some technical writing faculty resigned suddenly upon receiving a better offer from a neighboring university, and colleagues who knew me from my work in the graduate program had approached me about covering some of their classes. Although the prospect of teaching undergraduate engineering majors was outside my previous experience, I was sure that I would be able to figure it out and hopeful that the position might lead to other opportunities, which it did. A year later, a year-long lecturer position opened up and, after that, the renewable-term Lecturer position that I currently hold. Much to my relief, I was able to resume teaching, research, and committee work quite seamlessly. And after a few more years, I could barely remember what it had felt like not to be a full-time faculty member.

My Teaching Philosophy

As a result of my educational autobiography, it is not surprising that my teaching philosophy foregrounds a growth mindset coupled with a passion for learning. My goal is to motivate students to continue their education after they graduate to better themselves and their communities. I view life-long learning like fire. In the same way that heat, fuel, and oxygen interact with one another to sustain a fire, self-efficacy, metacognitive awareness, and self-direction are required for life-long learning. According to Bandura (1977; 1999; 2001), who has spent his career researching what leads people to become efficacious, self-efficacy is malleable and can be specific. For example, students who have scored well in standardized math tests may believe they are good at math, but if they have received low grades in English classes, they may decide that they are poor at language arts. Students need to believe in their ability to be engaged and interested in deepening their learning. Without self-efficacy, they are unlikely to persist in the face of inevitable obstacles and occasional failures (Zimmerman, Bandura, & Martinez-Pons, 1992).

When I teach writing, I scaffold my assignments in such a way as to progress gradually from lower order to higher-order skills (Bloom, 1956). I focus on transparency in assignment design and adequate scaffolding, which is beneficial for all students and, in particular, those who are typically underrepresented in college classrooms (Winkelmes, 2013). I solicit anonymous midterm feedback from students and invite colleagues to sit in on my classes to offer their perspective on my teaching. I encourage former students to serve as Peer Educators to address questions and concerns about assignments that students might not feel comfortable bringing to me and to provide feedback about student learning challenges. I offer opportunities for students to discuss exemplary essays with their peers, have students work with writing tutors, and provide a step-by-step plan for completing longer assignments so that they do not feel overwhelmed. When my pedagogical techniques are successful, students reappraise their efficacy beliefs about writing and come to realize that with effort their writing can improve. In other words, they move from what Carol Dweck (2006) has labeled a "fixed mindset" to a "growth mindset". A significant body of research suggests that even modest "mindset interventions" can be powerful in changing students' perceptions about their abilities (Falco & Summers, 2017; Paunesku et al., 2015).

Self-efficacy and growth mindset interventions are most consequential during a student's first year at college because this is when the risk of attrition is highest. Based on my own research and that of others, I know that successfully completing the first year of college is generally the best predictor of successful college completion (Cataldi, Bennett, & Chen, 2018; Conefrey, 2018). As core undergraduate courses set the foundation for students to gain confidence in their abilities, I try to make the transition from high school to college writing as smooth as possible. Students who have scored well in high school English classes are often convinced that they have learned all they need to about writing and can be reluctant to let go of familiar writing formulas that have served them well. Other students are less confident about their skills but believe that good writing is less important since they are majoring in STEM fields. Equally, some students feel at a disadvantage because other languages are spoken at home, or because their school did not offer Advanced Placement courses APs (college equivalent courses) and they have not had much practice in writing essays. Regardless of their prior experiences, the transition from the wide-funneled, five-paragraph, broad-focused essays of high-school that are written the night before to the longer, research-based, thesis-driven, more narrowly focused essays of college is challenging for many students. To accommodate the different experiences that students bring with them into the classroom, I pay particular attention to ensuring that these differences and prior academic opportunities are acknowledged so that all students feel welcome and supported.

The second component of my teaching philosophy of life-long learning relates to metacognitive awareness. I help students understand how learning works and what study skills and learning experiences are most effective. The tool for developing this metacognitive awareness is reflection. Dewey (1933), reminds us: "We do not learn from experience, we learn from reflecting on experience" (p. 78). Connections in learning experiences can be explored in and across courses, for example, students can connect content taught in their intermediate-level biology course to concepts that were built from formulas learned in an early math course and then, try to imagine how their current course will be relevant when they carry out their independent senior capstone research.

Reflection is central to attaining higher-order skills, to being able to progress from remembering, to understanding and eventually creating (Bloom, 1956). Metacognition refers not only to thinking about thinking but also reflecting on learning. As they progress in their academic careers and the intellectual demands increase, students need to acquire effective study skills and make connections across their courses to apply foundational skills in novel situations. While the external validation of a satisfactory GPA, a supportive learning environment, role models and encouragement from the instructor are all influential in promoting self-efficacy, metacognitive awareness and self-regulation are necessary for students to begin taking more responsibility for their educational journeys and to start applying and synthesizing their learning. While reflection does not necessarily lead to integrated and intentional learning, it is a necessary component of it as it enables a more agentic and holistic experience of one's education.

Reflection can be developed in many different ways. For example, I ask students in my first-year writing course to fill out surveys about their goals for the class, and midterm feedback on what is and is not working for them. Alternatively, the activity of reflection can also be more focused such as when

I ask students to write a "Reflection Essay" at the end of the first-year composition course discussing and providing evidence of progress they have made. To complete the assignment, students must reflect on their awareness of their own thinking (metacognition), their study skills (self-regulation and learning heuristics), and their beliefs about their learning abilities (self-efficacy and mindset). First-year students usually realize that unlike high-school, they cannot complete college assignments effectively while socializing with friends or waiting until the last moment they are due.

Learning how to learn is a big part of becoming self-directed because students cannot make decisions about what to learn unless they have gained a deeper understanding of themselves as learners. Once students have developed this metacognitive awareness, the final step is motivating them to take charge of their own learning journeys. When students have increased their self-efficacy and self-regulation, they are ready to make an effective transition from the tightly-structured, prescribed learning environment of high-school to the open-ended, self-directed learning required to succeed in college and in ever-changing, uncertain future careers. While this transition is difficult for all young adults, it is especially challenging for those who are extrinsically rather than intrinsically motivated and those who are used to parents and teachers making learning decisions for them rather than exercising their own agency. Progress for me is moving students away from questions such as, "Are you the kind of teacher who likes short sentences or long sentences?" or "Will I get penalized if I have additional sources?" and towards, "Is it okay to do my own study instead of using only library sources?" or "Can I choose a different topic that relates to what I'm passionate about?"

I welcome the use of technology in college classrooms and view it as a way to promote self-directed learning as well as make college courses more inclusive and engaging. Technology makes more knowledge available to us than was ever imaginable before the internet age and unlike libraries with their set opening hours, this information is available all day every day. Textbooks can be supplemented with engaging videos, multi-modal projects can be assigned as alternatives to text-based essays, lectures can be recorded and reviewed, and work can be assessed and completed online individually and collaboratively.

Learning management systems can provide students with time management tools to help them schedule when and where they will complete coursework. Digital devices such as phones greatly expand the possibilities for how, when, and where learners can engage with their courses and submit assignments. With the newer cloud-based technologies, the possibilities of technology for enhancing learning and fostering life-long learning are limitless.

After experimenting with a variety of different technologies in my courses over the years, I have discovered that my favorite educational technology is the ePortfolio, the digital successor of the portfolio, because of its potential to promote reflection and integrated learning. ePortfolios are student-owned websites that can be used in individual courses and across courses for curating and showcasing student learning and also for assessing it. ePortfolios encourage students to take more responsibility for their education, for building an academic identity and for improving their social media skills. In my upper-division, applied technical writing course for engineers, I assign career ePortfolios. The use of ePortfolios can ameliorate curricular fragmentation by helping students connect concepts and content inside and outside their major to foster linkages with co-curricular and extra-curricular learning. Showcasing their signature work helps students develop digital communication skills and create an intentional online identity so that they can demonstrate to employers that they possess the most sought-after workplace competencies such as critical thinking, problem solving, teamwork, professionalism and effective communication.

In addition, ePortfolios, which were recently named a high-impact practice (HIP), combine well with other HIPs such as experiential learning, capstone projects, and writing-intensive courses and are particularly advantageous for first-generation, low-income, minority, and other traditionally underrepresented student populations (Kuh, 2008; Watson, Kuh, Rhodes, Light, & Chen, 2016). Curating content, composing for different audiences, paying attention to the presentation of one's digital self, and the telling and retelling their stories helps students figure out who they are, and what they value. The skills they learn in building and managing their ePortfolios also help prepare them for intelligent, responsible and creative citizenship in careers that may not yet exist. With these skills, they can become life-long learners, contributing to their communities by synthesizing what they learn from all forms of experience, weeding out "fake news," and by making informed connections between theory and practice to make effective decisions about the increasingly complex issues we face.

How my Learning has Shaped my Teaching

This writing process has helped me to understand the origins of my beliefs about teaching and to realize how much my teaching philosophy is informed by my own learning experiences. While my educational autoethnography includes many transformative experiences, the earliest were the most consequential. My mother's faith in education is central to who I am. Then as now, I recognize the conviction in my first-generation students that education is the surest route to social mobility and equality. My focus on self-efficacy and self-directed learning also lies in my childhood. Although my parents did not have the opportunity for further education, they could figure out anything they set their minds to and they instilled in us a growth mindset that has led all their children to earn multiple degrees and experience various careers and career changes. It continues to spur us on to keep challenging ourselves with new learning. As my personal learning journey continues, I reflect and grow and my classroom practices change and evolve. These practices also inform and are informed by the scholarship of teaching and learning research (SoTL), that is, published scholarly inquiry into student learning to promote effective pedagogical practices.

My faith in technology also developed at an early age. As a high schooler, I remember my physics teacher telling us repeatedly at my all-girls school that women with tools were the equal of men, that with the power of machines, women were no longer the "weaker sex." Later, as a graduate student at the University of Illinois UIUC, watching Marc Andreessen demonstrate hyperlinks in Mosaic, I realized that technology could make knowledge more accessible and more readily available to everyone than ever before. Educational technologies such as the ePortfolio embody self-directed learning because they place the student in the role of creator rather than consumer of knowledge and they permit learning anywhere on any device.

My teaching philosophy is also rooted in my Catholic primary and secondary education, which inculcated the values of social justice, service, and civic engagement. Teaching at a Catholic, Jesuit university, where Ignatian values are part of our mission statement, continually reinforces them and guides my teaching and research. St. Ignatius, the founder of the Jesuit education system, frequently ended his letters with the phrase, "Ite inflammate omnia," which has been loosely translated as "go set the world on fire." I want my students to be agents for social change, to make the world a better place, to form people "for others" in keeping with the Jesuit philosophy of education.

This writing process has also illuminated where my learning journey has not necessarily benefited my teaching. Reflecting on my own personal learning journey has helped me realize that attempting to inculcate in my students a passion for life-long learning might not lead to the best learning experience for all students. For example, urging first-year students to take responsibility for their own learning might make for a difficult adjustment for those recent high school graduates who have experienced little choice in their prior education and who have had few opportunities or incentives to think for themselves. Students who were used to writing research papers where they were given a topic and told to take a stance before locating a specific number of sources to support that stance struggle when I require them to choose their own topic and identify the range of current opinions on it before adopting their own position. Likewise, those who have had little practice in comparing and contrasting ideas find it challenging to synthesize differing opinions because they have not yet developed those higher-order thinking skills (Bloom, 1956).

Similarly, while I initially believed that my upper-division engineering majors would be relieved that my assignments had minimum constraints, I discovered that those with a low tolerance for ambiguity found it extremely frustrating to not be told exactly how many sources to include. Some also complained that they were not able to start writing their reports because they were confused about whether the references should be included in the page count or whether they were part of the appendices and not counted. From my frame of reference, they should still have been able to create an outline, read their sources and complete some of the other tasks involved in composing the report but from theirs, they needed the exact "specs" before starting.

I also remember some furrowed brows when I responded to a question about whether they would be penalized for essays that did not match the length requirements by replying I was more concerned with the ideas than the exact page count, noting that this could vary depending on how many graphics were included. It took me a while before I realized that we were viewing the assignment from very different perspectives: I saw my assignment as offering students an opportunity to research a topic that was relevant to them to come to some new and exciting understanding, whereas some saw it as unnecessarily ambiguous and the page limit necessary to know when to stop writing. Others said they would prefer to be told what to write about because they resented the extra time it took to choose a topic for a general education class that they viewed as a distraction from their engineering courses.

With more experience, I have learned that I need to ascertain where students are on their own educational journeys before selling them my vision of life-long learning. I need to introduce more cautiously the idea of self-directed learning, evaluate students' self-efficacy and plan growth mindset interventions where necessary. I need to accommodate those students who believe that their steep tuition fees pay for them to "receive knowledge from experts" and do not yet understand the value of active learning or working in groups to discover the information for themselves. I need to be as transparent as possible with those who crave assurance that they have the "correct" answer, to gently nudge them from binary to more complex thinking. Rather than asking students to reflect on how their learning in my class will be of use to them in their other classes, and to see patterns and connections across subjects, I need to first check that they have developed their reflection skills. As their higher order thinking skills deepen, they will gradually begin to view the curriculum as less fragmented and begin to integrate their learning across different disciplines. Most rewarding are those epiphanic moments when students make a connection between a classroom exercise and a real-world problem or discover more about their values and who they want to become.

Reflecting on my teaching and learning experiences has helped me understand how my teaching is ineffably intertwined with my personal learning journey. I recognize that life-long learning is foundational to how I view myself as a teaching-scholar and, like the two sides of a continually flipping coin, it is challenging for me to think about teaching without simultaneously thinking of learning. I believe that I have succeeded as a teacher if students leave my class confident that their knowledge and skills have grown, that they have the tools to keep honing their abilities, and if they are driven to continue their learning long after they graduate. If students have increased their self-efficacy and begun to take more responsibility for their own learning, then I have ignited the fire of life-long learning.

References

Bandura, A. (1977). Self-efficacy: Toward a unifying theory of behavioral change. *Psychological Review Psychological Review, 84*(2), 191-215.

Bandura, A. (1999). Social cognitive theory: An agentic perspective. *Asian Journal of Social Psychology, 2*(1), 21.

Bandura, A. (2001). Social cognitive theory: An agentic perspective. *Annual Review of Psychology, 52*, 1-26. doi://doi.org/10.1146/annurev.psych.52.1.1

Bloom, B. S. (1956). *Taxonomy of educational objectives / the classification of educational goals*. New York, N.Y.: McKay.

Cataldi, E. F., Bennett, C. T., & Chen, X. (2018). *First-generation students: College access, persistence, and post bachelor's outcomes (NCES 2018-4210)*. Washington, DC: National Center for Education Statistics. Retrieved from https://nces.ed.gov/pubs2018/2018421.pdf

Conefrey, T. (1997). Gender, culture and authority in a university life sciences laboratory. *Discourse and Society, 8*(3), 313-340.

Conefrey, T. (2016). Technology in the college classroom: Crisis and opportunity *Educational Technology, 56*(4), 37-40.

Conefrey, T. (2018). Supporting first-generation students' adjustment to college with high-impact practices. *Journal of College Student Retention: Research, Theory & Practice*. https://doi.org/10.1177/1521025118807402

Denzin, N. K., & Lincoln, Y. S. (1994). *Handbook of qualitative research* (three-volume paperback ed. ed.). Thousand Oaks, CA: Sage.

Dewey, J. (1933). *How we think : A restatement of the relation of reflective thinking to the educative process*. Buffalo, N.Y.: Prometheus Books.

Dweck, C. S. (2006). *Mindset: The new psychology of success*. New York, NY: Random House.

Falco, L. D., & Summers, J. J. (2017). Improving career decision self-efficacy and STEM self-efficacy in high school girls. *Journal of Career Development,46*(1), 62-76. doi:10.1177/0894845317721651

Kuh, G. D. (2008). *High-impact educational practices: What they are, who has access to them, and why they matter.* Washington, DC: Association of American Colleges & Universities. Retrieved from http://ueeval.ucr.edu/teaching_practices_inventory/Kuh_2008.pdf

Paunesku, D., Walton, G. M., Romero, C., Smith, E. N., Yeager, D. S., & Dweck, C. S. (2015). Mindset interventions are a scalable treatment for academic underachievement. *Psychological Science, 26*(6), 784-793. doi:10.1177/0956797615571017

Watson, C. E., Kuh, G. D., Rhodes, T., Light, T. P., & Chen, H. L. (2016). Editorial: ePortfolios - the eleventh high impact practice. *International Journal of ePortfolio, 6*(2), 65-69.

Winkelmes, M. (2013). Transparency in teaching: Faculty share data and improve students' learning. *Liberal Education, 99*(2), 48.

Zimmerman, B. J., Bandura, A., & Martinez-Pons, M. (1992). Self-motivation for academic attainment: The role of self-efficacy beliefs and personal goal setting. *American Educational Research Journal American Educational Research Journal, 29*(3), 663-676.

14

They Named Me Candy

An Unlikely Academic Success

Candyce Reynolds

I am an unlikely academic success. As a tenured full professor at a sizeable doctoral-intensive university, I have reached the pinnacle of my profession. I have had the privilege of teaching thousands of students, delighting in their discoveries and successes. I have the luxury of engaging in lifelong learning through my study and scholarship. Unbelievably, I am paid to read, think, teach, and write about ideas that spark my interests and passions. Looking back, I often shake my head in disbelief.

As the child of urban, working-class parents in middle America, who dealt with transient poverty, this trajectory would be virtually impossible today. The beginning of my academic journey occurred during a brief period in U.S. history when our society's policies supported education. The "War on Poverty," declared by President Lyndon Johnson in 1965, spurred programs to eliminate poverty and provide opportunities for individual and societal advancement (Bailey & Danziger, 2013). Programs and policies, such as food stamps, TRIO, Pell grant programs, and an influx of idealist recent education graduates who flooded the impoverished city schools I attended, fueled my ability to consider that I might even be able to achieve the American Dream.

As a woman, my success as an academic was also unpredictable. Born in the late 1950s, my mother's dream for my future was to marry a man who had a good job and income and live happily ever after as a loving mother. My parents named me Candy, a name for a wife and mother, not the name of a woman with an advanced degree. My mother wanted nothing more than to stay home and raise her kids, but she didn't have the luxury of not working. She was part of a dual-income family before the term was even invented. And here I was, wanting the glamorous life I thought she had—riding the bus into downtown, dressing in high heels, and carrying important stacks of file folders down the hall. Little did she know that her success in the workplace was a model for me—I could not imagine being a stay-at-home mom. Coontz

(2011) discusses women's roles during the 1950s and 1960s, concluding that our ideals for women's roles in the family—housewife, mother—did not match many families' economic realities. In turn, this reality actually changed how we perceived women's roles in our society. This was certainly the case in my family.

During this period, birth control and the sexual revolution also changed expectations about a woman's place in society. "Women's lib" became a cultural phenomenon shepherding the idea that women were capable of doing the work of men. I got my first job while in high school from a column in the "help wanted" section labelled "jobs for women." My choices were office work, waitressing, or cleaning. I knew though that I wanted the jobs listed in the "jobs for men" column, and I hoped that could happen in time.

My educational journey is one of beating the odds. As a working-class young woman, I was an unlikely candidate for a Ph.D. and an academic career. If my extended family had been betting people, they would never have placed a wager on my trajectory. The shifting tides of American society made a different path possible. My journey would have looked very different ten years earlier or today. In the 1960s, there would have been few opportunities, supports, or models for me; in the 1980s, the concept of first-generation students was well-established. By the beginning of the 1980s, women had begun to surpass men's enrollment in college (Borzelleca, 2012). From my current perspective, I understand that our cultural context makes the odds. My journey into the world at this certain time made all the difference. I want to ground this educational autobiography in the cultural and historical context to help me and my readers understand that our individual experiences must always be seen through this lens.

I have always been considered bright. But I know that this wasn't the only thing that allowed me to be successful in school. My parents struggled to keep our family safe and solvent. The next utility bill and minor illnesses requiring a doctor's visit or a missed day at work were constant tensions in our lives. We moved frequently. I know now that sometimes this happened because we were evicted, but, at the time, I had no idea that our moves were anything but an adventure. My mom would tout our new apartment's virtues across town and the joys of meeting new friends at daycare or school. I learned about resilience and so much more—but my mom called it the *next step*, as in, "Well, our next step will be this….!" This phrase has been my go-to in challenging personal and academic situations and one I use to help my students navigate difficult times in their lives as well as in completing an assignment. The message is that with any problem, we just need to figure out the next step (and that there *is* a next step).

I realize now that I was lucky to have parents that fought against the odds and modelled this for me. "The next step" philosophy aligns well with the recent research on the concept of Grit. Angela Duckworth describes five characteristics of grit: 1) courage, 2) conscientiousness, 3) perseverance, 4) resilience, and 5) passion (Duckworth, 2018). My parents, relatives, and community modelled these behaviors daily. From watching my parents continually struggle with their circumstances—weekly meal and grocery planning, going to work in blinding snowstorms, relishing in finding a new board game at a thrift store—I learned the concept of grit without having a word for it. There is much debate in the literature if grit can be taught or how it can be taught, but I believe my parents and community taught me this.

Part of the definition of grit that stands out for me most is perseverance. I learned early that if I didn't know how to do something or about something, that I could learn. I never saw myself as a smart person. However, I was a person who understood that hard work and persistence meant that I could learn what I needed and wanted to. I'm fortunate that I recognized this early on in my life. In Dweck's (2007) terms, I had (have) a growth mindset—a belief that time and effort makes me smarter, versus a fixed mindset, a belief that my intelligence is a fixed trait that can't be changed.

I had many champions as I traversed primary and secondary public schools that recognized my "next step" attitude. Teachers, community members, neighbors, and friends of the family made small and big gestures to help me along the way. Yosso (2005) posits that communities of color provide their own cultural capital to cope with oppression, may apply in my case, even though I am White. Her framework names several types of capital: aspirational capital, familial capital, social capital, navigational capital, resistant capital, and linguistic capital as forms of capital vital to the health and wellbeing of communities of color. Many of these types of capital are relevant for me. Garriott (2019) has applied this model to low-income, first-generation students and argues that a critical lens must be used in working with low-income, first-generation students. My community taught me success strategies I brought with me in my early adult life. An elderly neighbor served as my pretend "kindergarten teacher" when my parents couldn't afford it, welcoming me for tea and reading lessons every weekday afternoon. My second-grade teacher lobbied to have me skip third grade. An after-school caretaker exposed me to libraries and museums. The circle of adults in my early life allowed me to see beyond the boundaries of my family and neighborhood and understand that life could look different.

This circle of caring and encouraging adults continued in high school and propelled my next steps. My family had moved to southern California by this time. I was fortunate to encounter teachers who had recently graduated from college and were eager to be positive influences on youth.

An early reader of this paper commented that many of my positive experiences had to do with extracurricular activities. On reflection, I find this is true. My formal education was limited—large classrooms, limited resources, and little opportunity to learn beyond a very basic curriculum. Luckily, my English teacher encouraged me to participate in extracurricular activities, and I became involved in theater productions, the school newspaper, student politics and the marching band drill team. My journalism teacher had just graduated from UC Berkeley and pushed me to see that I was college material and to consider Berkeley instead of the local community college. All of these activities, especially serving as the editor of my high school newspaper, taught me about the power of community. There was a synergy that occurred in putting a newspaper together. All of us had to work individually and together as we created a new whole.

While I had aspirational capital from my community and at school for pursuing academics further by attending college, my parents thought it was a bad idea. They wanted the best for me, and, as a woman, a secure marriage was a more direct path. They wanted me to marry my boyfriend, who had a union job—well-paid, well-respected, and secure. While they wanted me to lead a successful life, they did not and could not support me financially or emotionally in my choice to go to college.

As a first-generation college student, Berkeley was an eye-opener. Having always been one of the best students in schools, I found myself at the wrong end of the grading curve many times. As a first-generation college student, I did not have the cultural capital to understand how the university works and what I needed to do to be successful. Fortunately, the Educational Opportunity Program (a newly-funded federal program for poor and first-generation college students) and my friends in the dorm helped me learn the culture of higher education and taught me academic and time management skills that I had not needed or been exposed to in high school. I figured out what needed to be done and was often called streetwise or scrappy by my peers in college. Using Yosso's (2005) concept of social and navigational capital and the resilience modelled for me in childhood, I figured out what needed to be done.

However, despite my ability to look and do okay, I often felt like an imposter, waiting for someone to recognize that I didn't belong and escort me off the campus. Many working-class scholars experience "imposter syndrome," a condition in which high achieving individuals cannot internalize their accomplishments and consistently feel as though they will be discovered to be a fraud (Clance & Imes, 1978). I found, though, that my professors and colleagues found my working-class perspective refreshing and compelling. In my sophomore year, an anthropology professor found my participant observation project on racial boundary-crossers in my dorm to be interesting enough that he invited me to submit my paper to a journal he edited. I was merely trying to understand what I was experiencing. It was at this moment that I understood I might have a place in academia. I hadn't even known that was an option.

As I moved through college, the need to focus on a career became more urgent. I had a hard time figuring out what I should major in. Fortunately, I couldn't choose a major until junior year. The time and exposure to a variety of disciplines and possible careers was important. I started out wanting to be a journalist or a teacher, both professions I had seen up close. College was about advancing myself and my family in the future. This was a crucial decision. Almost every course I took led me to my next aspiring career, though—anthropologist, environmental scientist, and finally, psychologist.

I had little opportunity to know what careers were out there for college-educated women. Psychology seemed the most practical major of the courses I enjoyed. The ethos of Berkeley was that school was about education for itself. While I believed that to a certain extent, I also knew that my education needed to fund my future.

Graduate school became an option because my work-study eligibility landed me a job working as an office assistant for a psychology researcher who quickly saw something in me that I didn't see myself. Again, another adult reached out and insisted that I further my education. I worked for a year after graduation and then entered a Ph.D. program in Counseling Psychology. There, I again faced the imposter syndrome—I was one out of 10 in my cohort. There were only three women in the cohort and only one female faculty member. I had never been in that small of a classroom setting. There was nowhere to hide, and I doubted that I could keep up with my peers. Luckily, we all worked together to learn together, challenging and supporting each other along the way. As part of my program, I received a fellowship that required that I teach, participate in research projects, or lead a service/student affairs program. I had the opportunity to do all three, and I learned that while I might doubt myself, I was indeed capable of doing what was asked of me. My next step philosophy helped once again. I just needed to commit to learning and it worked out.

I made a conscious choice to legally change my first name from Candy to Candyce when I received my doctorate. On the threshold of becoming a young psychologist, I wanted to take a name that portrayed more seriousness than the cute name of Candy. Plus, I wondered if anyone would trust a psychologist named Dr. Candy. Making this change from Candy to Candyce set me up to take myself more seriously, too.

I took a circuitous route to my work in the Academy. In a Counseling Psychology program, one is trained for multiple possibilities—a therapist or faculty member or both. I purposely applied for jobs where I could be both an academic and a clinician. After stints in tenure-track positions at several universities, I chose to take a position as a clinician/administrator at Portland State University, giving up a tenure-track position. Tenure-related positions were stressful for me—I found the work environment to be competitive and isolating. To be successful meant that I would not be able to work with students and colleagues in the way I wanted. The environment did not fit my background.

Ultimately, I ended up back in a tenure-track position, figuring that I was older and wiser. I was offered a tenure-related position in a new general education program, and I decided to take a risk. In fact, in returning to academia, I valued my perspective and saw what I brought as a working-class scholar as an asset rather than a deficit. I felt I had an opportunity to perhaps change the environment for future scholars. While receiving tenure in my 40s was not easy; I entered the endeavor with a sense that I had something to offer—my teaching and scholarship reflected my experiences. When I started this position, I promised myself I would work at not being intimidated by my colleagues (and sometimes my students). I also decided to model for students and colleagues friendly and supportive collegiality, allowing myself to be collaborative and encouraging, rather than stodgy and competitive. I was determined to mentor my students as I had been throughout my schooling and career. I would teach and write about things that mattered and made a difference, and I would collaborate with others. If I didn't get tenure, so be it.

Fast forward to today. I did get tenure and am now a full professor. I look back and marvel at my trajectory. My background and experiences have influenced my changing goals and decisions along my educational and career path. As one will see in the teaching and leadership philosophy that comes next, I favor a collaborative and supportive learning environment.

Teaching and Leadership Philosophy

In the program I teach in, we ask our Master's students who are preparing to work with adults in a variety of settings to craft a Guiding Principles statement rather than a Teaching Philosophy. As it is an adult education program and our graduates are often not directly in the classroom, this seems a more appropriate statement. Because of this, I have created my own Guiding Principles statement instead of a formal Teaching Philosophy as a model for this practice but also because it represents my philosophy and practice as an educator. This statement appears in my ePotfolio[1] to which all of my students have access. The ePortfolio is a way for me to explore my own development as an educator and share it with my students.

My Guiding Principles
I tend to wear many hats: teacher, administrator, facilitator, listener, problem solver, dishwasher. Whatever hat I happen to be wearing, these principles guide my work. *Relationships are Key.* Inherently, learning is social (e.g., Bandura, 1986). To learn, one must interact with ideas and knowledge and others who can encourage, challenge, and contextualize those ideas. Learning does not happen in a vacuum. I need others to react to my ideas to understand and refine them and vice versa. More ideas from diverse groups of people make for a better outcome. In my work, I strive to create environments where people can come together to make something bigger and better than they could on their own.

The most meaningful and impassioned moments in my career have occurred when I have deeply engaged with those I'm working with...

- Following the line of questioning a student raises even if it isn't on my lesson plan,
- Listening to a student's ideas for their future and making a connection with a person who is doing that work,
- Helping a student understand that she does have the ability to be successful,
- Brainstorming ideas with a colleague for a research project.

It is in relationships that things happen, and I thrive.

New Stories. I am trained as a psychologist. Once a psychologist, always a psychologist. I love people's stories. Stories teach us and lead us to discoveries. My grandma was a great storyteller. As the wife of a coal miner in rural Illinois during the Depression, she saw hardship and experienced resilience. I believe her resilience came from her ability to understand that life's experiences have a beginning, middle, and end and that we always can influence our stories.

---
1 https://pebblepad.com/spa/#/public/GctzZ7smh66wznxRmpnwpthtwM

Narrative therapy theorists (Denborough, 2014) tell us that our lives and paths are not fixed in stone but shaped in our telling and understanding of our story. I would cry to her about some mishap or vexing problem, and she would always ask, "So, how does this story end, little girl?" She helped me understand that while I may not control everything in my world, I have the power to influence the outcome of almost anything. Did I have to marry my boyfriend from high school? No—my future was mine, not his. Could I go to college? Yes—if I acted like I was college material. I enjoy working as an educator because I have the opportunity to help my students develop their own beginnings, middles, and ends. Do not be surprised if I ask you how you see your story ending. You'll see this storytelling in my teaching through my use of many reflection activities—reflection provides us a way to understand what has happened and determine where we want to go (Alterio & McDrury, 2003).

Imagine More, Be More. As an undergraduate, I worked for Norma Haan at the Institute of Human Development at UC Berkeley. I started as a work-study student coding data for her studies and ultimately became her lead research assistant when I graduated. Norma taught me that I could learn whatever I set my mind to. I achieved things that I never thought possible—managing a complex longitudinal database, organizing an international symposium funded by a major foundation, and supervising a team of research assistants that were older and more experienced. Norma saw more in me than I saw in myself. I have carried this forward. Believing in others and encouraging them makes a difference and I offer this to others as much as I can. In my teaching, you will see this in my truly curious questions to my students about our readings—what do you think? How does this apply to the problems you face? You'll see it in my comments on my students' paper—pushing them to go to the next level—to think harder than they think they can. You'll see it in my steady encouragement and my nudging my students to improve their skills. Vygotsky (1978) argued that we learn when we work collaboratively to push ourselves a little bit further. Small steps make big progress.

Trust the Process. I spent many years working hard to be the best teacher, adviser, therapist, etc. I have not given up striving for excellence but I have learned that trying to control everything can often interfere with the magic that can happen when you recognize that learning has its own pace and methods. In my practice, this looks like…

- Focusing on the broader learning outcomes of a course and reminding myself that my actions need to follow those (e.g., Wiggins & McTighe, 2005).

- Not being afraid when I have not "covered" what I said I would cover when the class has had a deep and enriching conversation.

- Trusting that students are drivers of their learning. If they turn in assignments late, I trust that they are managing their lives as best as they can. Their learning will happen whether I impose deadlines or not.

- Appreciating that our cultural heritage, upbringing, and experience influence our learning and trusting that my students and colleagues bring their unique and valuable perspectives to all of our learning (e.g., Yosso, 2005).

Final Reflection

I did not look at my Guiding Principles before I started writing the first part of this chapter, and truth to be told, I'm surprised how well these principles seem to reflect what I have said about my educational experiences.

Throughout my own educational experiences, relationships have been key to learning. My family members, teachers, peers, and community members all supported and guided me through my educational journey. I couldn't have learned as much or become who I am without their presence and influence. My Guiding Principles reflect this. In my Guiding Principles, I note the activities that illustrate this principle. These are the things that others did for me in encouraging and supporting my learning—listening carefully, making connections, fostering a growth mindset.

In my educational autobiography, I shared the story of my mother's favorite catchphrase, "The next step," which has helped me persevere even in times of great struggle. In my Guiding Principles, I share my grandmother's notion that every story has a beginning, middle, and end and that we have control over much of our own stories. I am laughing now that my mother obviously got her "next step" attitude from my grandmother. Their influence has carried forward in my work with students. I am always ready to help a student see themselves in a different light and help them create the future they desire. Related to this is the theme of championing my students' effort and work. Believing in others helps them believe in themselves and promotes their own learning and success. There are so many that believed in me, which helped me become successful.

In my Guiding Principles, I discuss trusting the process. This principle is the outcome of all of my experiences. As I was writing my story, I relived some of the anxiety and fear that I experienced through my own education. Despite my insecurities and fear, I pushed through them and learned through my experience that I could trust myself and the process of learning in my work. However, it is only with experience that my students and I can get to this point. This principle also acknowledges the serendipity that happens in the learning process. A student's discussion post may lead to a related thread that helps others understand a concept more deeply or the topic turns from the discussion of theory to a discussion of how one studies.

I am reminded too of the serendipity of when we are born and how the cultural and historical context influences our educational trajectory. I grew up in a time that had both challenges and advantages. I had caring and inspiring adults in my life who were committed to a life of service based on their ideals. I attained my undergraduate and graduate degrees with no debt—paying through my own work, grants, and scholarships. However, I struggled as a first-generation college student when that construct was not even named. There were virtually no models of success I could follow. As a woman, I also had few role models and endured micro- and macro-aggressions throughout my schooling and career.

Ultimately, my commitment as an educator is to provide the inspiration and support I received to weather the new challenges faced by our students. While more students from diverse backgrounds have access to higher education, the cost and debt associated with attendance has thwarted then haunted many. Besides, diverse students often don't feel comfortable in the Academy, which calls for more equitable educational practices. My commitment is also to use my position in the Academy and encourage others to fundamentally change our institutions to address the challenges our students face. We can change if we have the will. There is a "next step."

References

Alterio, M. & McDrury, J. (2003) *Learning through storytelling in higher education*. Routlege.

Bandura, A. (1986). *Social foundations of thought and action: A social cognitive theory*. Prentice-Hall, Inc.

Borzelleca, Daniel (Feb 16, 2012). "The Male-Female Ratio in College." *Forbes*. https://www.forbes.com/sites/ccap/2012/02/16/the-male-female-ratio-in-college/#2fcdc8cefa52

Clance, P.R. & Imes, S.A. (1978). The imposter phenomenon in high achieving women: dynamics and therapeutic intervention. *Psychotherapy: Theory, Research and Practice*, 15(3): 241–247.

Coontz, S. (2011). *A Strange Stirring: The Feminine Mystique and American Women at the Dawn of the 1960s*. New York: Basic Books.

Denborough, D. (2014) *Retelling the stories of our lives: Everyday narrative therapy to draw inspiration and transform experience*. Norton.

Dweck, C.S. (2007) *Mindset: The new psychology of success*. New York: Ballantine Books.

Duckworth, A. (2018) *Grit: The power of passion and perseverance*. New York: Scribner.

Garriott, P. O. (2019). A critical cultural wealth model of first-generation and economically marginalized college students' academic and career development. *Journal of Career Development, 47*(1), 80-95.

Vygotsky, L. S. (1978). *Mind in society: the development of higher psychological processes.* Cambridge, MA: Harvard University Press.

Yosso, T. J. (2005) Whose culture has capital? A critical race theory discussion of community cultural wealth. *Race Ethnicity and Education, 8*(1), 69-91.

15

A Political Education in Community Wealth and Transformative Learning

Sonja Taylor

What It Means to Learn

My educational experiences have been shaped most forcefully by growing up poor, being a woman, and having unconventional and anti-establishment parents. When I was younger, my family background made me feel uncomfortable because my peers thought I was too intense about politics. Since I grew up in a small town with low diversity and a high degree of conservatism, my left-leaning tendencies made me stick out like a sore thumb. My hometown is located on the Central Oregon Coast. My mother had imagined the tranquility and beauty of raising me in a small coastal community, and her circle of friends was almost exclusively restricted to artists and musicians who had probably come to the Oregon Coast for the same reasons. Her friends did not have many children my age and my own circle of peers was decidedly more stereotypically rural. The children in my grade had parents who had grown up in our small town, and most of them seemed to be people who regularly attended church and voted Republican.

I clearly remember coming home before winter break during first grade with a "weekly reader" (a news magazine geared toward children) with a photo of Ronald Reagan on the cover. It was 1980, and he had just been elected and was getting ready to take office. My parents had never been married and had split up when I was two, but my dad happened to be there because it was winter break and he was coming to visit. I told them about how wonderful Reagan was and all the great things I had learned about him in school that day. My parents both turned around and said, "No!" in unison and then proceeded to give me a lecture about the problems with Reagan and how they had preferred Jimmy Carter. Thus, I began my political education, tied directly to the public school system I had just entered. This was my first introduction to the concept of being in conflict with "the system," and this is a theme that still resonates in both my work and family life. The conversations I have with my sons often center on dismantling systemic racism and inequality based on gender and social class. Like my parents, I interrogate their schoolwork but unlike me in my formative years, my sons have generally encountered a curriculum that supports social justice views.

As far back as I can remember, politics and education have been intimately tied in my lived experience. When I entered first grade, my mother started working more because of a change in the welfare policy. Previously it had been possible to draw partial benefits and work part-time, which allowed her to spend more time with me and less on childcare. However, a change around the time I started school made it, so people (women) had to refrain from drawing cash benefits. My mother wanted to work, so she learned to live on a shoestring budget. We still had housing support from the government and food stamps, and my healthcare was paid for by the government, but those supplements did not cover all of our expenses. My mother worked in a local restaurant attached to a bookstore, and I would go there after school and read—usually eating her shift meal for dinner.

Growing up with a bookstore as a babysitter was a massive benefit to my learning journey. I have always loved to read, and it was like having my private library with all the latest bestsellers. I read everything, including books that scared me and were maybe not the most appropriate for my age and emotional maturity level. For example, I read some of Stephen King's books—to this day, I am not a huge fan of clowns. An additional supplement to my education came from being placed in a program called "Talented and Gifted" (TAG) when I entered first grade. TAG is a federally funded program that identifies students from low income and historically marginalized groups who demonstrate outstanding ability or potential. Academic potential could be determined either generally or in a specific subject area by scoring in the 97th percentile on a nationally standardized test. Records are created for students who are identified to track their progress.

As an educator who is interested in equity-based learning practices, I find it troubling that my placement in TAG was determined by an emphasis on my performance in standardized tests, but I also notice a sense of pride attached to the idea that I scored so highly on those tests. I think this demonstrates the success of social conditioning around grades and evaluations. I recently looked up the criteria for TAG and didn't know that there was an emphasis on including children from minority groups and economically disadvantaged children. I wonder how the language around criteria might have changed over the years or if it is frozen in time like so many of our practices in education. In looking up the program, I learned that detailed records were created to track students who were labeled as "talented and gifted." I am curious about the record they created in my name, and I wonder if I could get access to that record and see what people wrote about me.

When I was growing up, our school's TAG program was well-funded, but eventually, that would go away—another connection between politics, policy, and education. In elementary school, TAG meant being pulled out of regular classes on a semi-regular basis to learn things like making our cameras and developing film, making our paper, learning about recycling, and, most importantly, it meant Junior Great Books. Junior Great Books was a reading program based on critical inquiry, and this was my first exposure to problem-posing education as opposed to the banking model of education—although I did not learn this terminology until I encountered Paulo Freire's work in college. Freire's *Pedagogy of the Oppressed* focuses on a "problem-posing" approach to teaching and learning where students and teachers explore topics together. The problem-posing approach is offered by Freire (1970) as an antidote to the traditional "banking" form of education, where students are seen as objects to be filled with knowledge by the teachers who are (of course) the experts when it comes to valuable knowledge.

Later, during my time in the University Studies general education program at Portland State University, I would be introduced to Freire, in addition to the perspectives of Black feminist scholars like bell hooks (1994), who saw education as a path to liberation, and eventually to historians like William Cronon (1998), who emphasized the importance of connection in reaching the goals of liberal education. Freire, hooks and Cronon would form the theoretical basis for me to grow my own philosophy of teaching and learning as they resonated with what made learning meaningful for me growing up—the social responsibility and consciousness of my parents, the social mobility and freedom found in education, and the importance of connection and relationship throughout. Later, in my own scholarship, I would build on this foundation with the concept of "funds of knowledge" (Rios-Aguilar et al. 2011)—a concept which illuminated the important social and cultural capital my parents gave me by modeling engaged and informed citizenship, which requires one to be practiced at learning.

As an elementary school student, I was one of two "TAG kids" for my grade level. I think there were two from each grade. When we went to middle school, TAG transformed into reading for all students who performed at advanced levels. This increased the number of students from each grade and made TAG a daily experience, focusing on reading and discussion—more inquiry-based learning. When I think of middle school, I think of TAG as the place I learned, the place where my brain was encouraged to think. Unfortunately, TAG was not available when I entered high school and, while I was eligible to enter the advanced level communications class, I elected to join mainstream communications because being smart as a girl was decidedly uncool. Later I would learn more about misogyny and gendered performance and how girls socialize themselves away from being a "nerd" so that they can be "normal" (Nielsen & Davies, 2017; Scholes, 2019).

When I think of social identities that inform my experience, poverty clouds everything— but gender began to emerge more explicitly with adolescence. During my freshman year of high school, I was troubled by a math teacher who kept putting his hands on my shoulders and breathing in my ear. Although I complained about his behavior, I was told that he didn't mean anything by it and made something out of nothing. However, they eventually moved me into a different class. My grade in the original math class had been very bad—maybe a D or an F. It had been impossible for me to focus on what the teacher said because I just wanted him to leave me alone. After moving into the different class, I got A's in math and improved my overall performance in school. During my sophomore year, I decided I wanted to get involved in student government and began the process, but the vice-principal took me aside and said I was not qualified to run because of my first semester grades, despite the fact that I had improved my GPA by more than two whole points for the second semester. I was discouraged. When I reflect on this now, I am struck by the rigid and retributive nature of this barrier to my participation in the social norms of school. There was no celebration or encouragement for my progress, and, more importantly, I see now that there was no trust.

Jenney & Exner-Cortens (2018) describe the challenges of shaping self-esteem within the context of toxic masculinity and the failure of institutions to offer adequate support when they discuss the "failure of adult systems to adequately respond to youth" (p. 411). When I was not allowed to run for student government, I felt like all of the work I had put in to raise my grades had been meaningless. I shut down. Halfway through my sophomore year of high school, I dropped out. I got in trouble. I drank. I got my GED. I got pregnant. I got an abortion. I felt like my life was over before it began. Sometimes I wanted it to be over. I missed the joy of learning and I felt ashamed. All my life, people had told me how smart I was, how much I could accomplish, how much I had to offer. I felt ashamed that I had not lived up to people's expectations.

One day, I had a conversation with a woman whose children I babysat. I told her how discouraged I was and that I felt like I had failed, that I wasn't ready to be out on my own. Even though I had many negative experiences at school, I missed my friends. My friend's mom said, "why not see if you can go back to school?" I decided I would try, and the administrators allowed me to re-enroll. I had done so many advanced courses and summer school to try to get finished as quickly as possible, I was able to graduate a year early—even with taking the second half of my sophomore year off (which might suggest a bit about the rigor of high school in my town, but that is a story for another time). As soon as I graduated, I moved to Eugene and enrolled at Lane Community College (LCC). This move placed me in a community where the politics felt much more aligned with my own and where my father was in close proximity. I mainly focused on journalism and became the youngest editor-in-chief of their weekly newspaper and then became editor of their art & literary magazine. I spent most of my time in the newspaper office and not enough time studying for classes.

I always think of my time at LCC as a failure academically. Still, recently I went over all of my transcripts, including those I transferred to Portland State when I decided to finish my Bachelor's degree in Portland. I actually had fairly decent grades, with the exception of one. My one and only college F is in the course "Interpersonal Communication." I laughed when I saw that because interpersonal communication is everything I do and having strong skills in that area is crucial for my job. That mark on my transcript is proof to me that grades do not measure aptitude or intelligence, they only measure performance in a specific context. This knowledge I have carried for a long time, and it informs my approach to students who are part of Senior Inquiry at Portland State University (PSU). I have absolute faith in each of my students' abilities, even if they are not performing at expected or hoped-for capacity when they are in my presence.

My main struggles as a student were related to my insecurity and sense of self, exacerbated by barriers that came from being poor and the toxic masculinity I encountered in high school. Research has emphasized the lack of serious interrogation directed at the causal mechanisms surrounding identity formation and self-esteem for girls—suggesting that we have tended to focus our attention on negative outcomes (Jenney & Exner-Cortens, 2018). This focus creates an opportunity for victim-blaming, and it also hinders a young woman's ability to look outside of herself and understand the structures that might be influencing her ability to develop a strong and empowered sense of self. I thought that any problems I encountered in school were personal failures and that if I had only been more like the "ideal" girl in school, then things would have been different.

Luckily I always had a strong support network of friends, even though I did not access it as much as I could or should have. In terms of strategies, I have a hard time giving up. Even if I need to take a break, if I have not finished something, I tend to come back to it—I am tenacious. I think tenacity is one of the most valuable qualities I possess.

When I look back on my time as a student, I am most proud of my willingness to keep going and learn from failure. I think that part of my relationship with failure as a mechanism for learning comes from my grandmother. I lived with her during college and again after my divorce, and she became not just my grandmother, but my life partner, mentor and friend. She lived to be 97, and even though she never went through any formal education after high school, she was curious and a lifelong learner. She had a tough life and she somehow found the strength to keep going and (more importantly) to value herself in the process. Because of our relationship, I was fortunate enough to have the opportunity to tell her often that the way she modeled self-esteem saved my life.

I am most surprised that I actually completed a doctoral degree. My first attempt at college was not very successful, and when I returned to finish my undergraduate degree at PSU, I wasn't really sure that I would be able to get into a doctoral program. Being an undergraduate mentor had shown me that I loved teaching, but I doubted my ability to become an academic. My first and second attempts to enter a doctoral program were rejected. My first attempt was after I finished my Bachelor's and my second attempt was after I already had one Master's degree. When I was rejected the second time, it came with an offer to enter the master's program for Sociology. I decided to accept the offer and by the end of my second Master's, I knew that I needed a Ph.D. to be able to teach full-time in a university (I had been teaching as an adjunct for eight years by then). I applied again for the doctoral program and this time I was accepted. Sometimes I tell my dad, "If anyone wants to know if they can get a Ph.D., they should try banging their head against a wall for two years and if that doesn't destroy them, then there is a good chance they can make it."

I am most concerned that my students today might not believe in the opportunities that are waiting. I think the level of inequality currently in our society makes it difficult to believe in opportunity, and this brings me back to the connection between politics and education. I believe whole-heartedly with bell hooks (1994) that education is liberation, but how can we be truly free when disparity reigns supreme? Education has been a source of liberation for me, and I continue to see the effects of that as I advance in my career. When I was growing up, the income disparity was not as steep as it is today, but the odds were definitely not in my favor—despite the odds, I continue to believe in education as a means of liberation.

There are too many formative moments in my journey to detail here, but I began with a moment in first grade that stands out and I would like to offer an additional moment that occurred during my second year of teaching in the dual-credit program I now run. I wanted to help my students develop skills for peer editing, and I thought a good way to start would be to have them mark up an old paper of mine that I had submitted as an undergrad. I told them to be brutal and, as an added exercise, I told them that I would rewrite my paper based on their feedback and would try to track down my old professor to look at the revisions and give me updated feedback. I wasn't sure if I could find the professor, but I tracked him down at his current location as a book publisher in Seattle. He responded to my email and agreed to read over my revisions and give me feedback—I think he thought it would be fun.

I got a great deal of constructive criticism from my students and I used it to rewrite my paper and sent off both papers to my former professor for feedback. His response showed that we were both changed by this seemingly small thought experiment in profound ways. The following is taken from the letter he sent me:

> Today, my comments on your first paper seem kind of harsh to me. I'm surprised that I was pushing you so hard to give me answers to problems that I was struggling with at the time (and still do). On the other hand, maybe it's good that I did that. I mean, your revisiting of this issue makes it clear that you DO have good ideas for how these openings can lead to new solutions and new practices and new ways of thinking about things.
>
> I understand that this is all an exercise for your current students and I know that feedback and constructive criticism is what your class is focusing on, but I couldn't bring myself to "mark up" your rewrite on a line-by-line basis. I'm not quite sure why (I edit and rewrite for writers every day for my job), but it just didn't feel appropriate or needed. After all, you have given me the gift of a new history/memory experience and you have opened some good questions for me.
>
> I'm struck by the possibility that the Sonja of today was already in the words of your paper of 20 years ago, as potential, as an abundance of meaning that had yet to articulate itself. And a new abundance of meaning is packed into this new paper. I'm sure the Sonja of 20 years in the future is in there! Very interesting. From my perspective, it gives me a new way to think about student papers, and what it is that we should be demanding of them.
>
> When you are breaking new ground, conceptually, you will always be frustrated with yourself to some extent. But that frustration can lead to some pretty amazing thinking. As long as a professor or critical reader doesn't do something to drive you away from the thought process forever. I suppose that's one of the most difficult things about giving comments/edits/feedback. Maybe the goal should be to push the writer forward, not to get an A or to have answered all of the questions, or to be satisfied with your answers...

Even reading his words today as I paste them into this document brings tears to the back of my eyes because the authenticity and power of the connection made between us and our shifting roles as student and teacher is so clear. His words remind me to have faith in the possibility contained inside students and teachers of all ages and backgrounds—but they also remind me of how important it has been on my journey to have mentors who believed in me and who continue to encourage me.

What It Means to Mentor (Teach) Students

For a long time, I imagined being a teacher meant that I was on a learning journey along with my students— that we were following a map and I happened to be further along on the path and could therefore point out barriers and pitfalls to them. When I had conversations about learning journeys with my colleagues, we often discussed this analogy and the importance of "meeting students where they are at," sounding a little as if we needed to bend down to reach them and lift them up. At the same time, I also felt that it was my job to help students figure out how to participate in their own learning process, taking seriously the words of Paulo Freire (1970) and rejecting the tired banking model of education where students are expected to remake their minds over into the image of their instructors.

Eventually, I realized that no one is on the same learning journey, nor are we using the same map. My notion of somehow being ahead on a shared journey has stopped making sense. Further, I noticed that I started feeling resistance to the phrase "meeting students where they are at" because of the implication that teachers somehow bend in a downward direction in order to do this. I am not sure that educators who talk about meeting their students understand that we are also asking the students to meet us where we are, and sometimes that means they have to bend. This shared bending seems key to the idea of collaborative learning.

In other words, students also need to meet teachers where they are. I have found this particularly relevant in the digital age, as many students understand technology's capabilities much more deeply than many of their teachers. When I visualize a learning space, I see teachers bending forward to meet their students—yet, I also see students bending forward to meet their teachers. So, when I say shared bending in connection with collaborative learning, I recognize that students and teachers contribute knowledge to what we learn together. In theoretical terms, we all come to our learning spaces with different forms of human capital.

In my scholarly life, most of my research is connected to understanding different forms of capital that can be activated and exchanged for agency in different institutions. The concept of cultural capital, in particular, resonates with me. Prior research on cultural capital has observed that "educationally thriving groups are assumed to possess (adequate quantities and types of) social and cultural capital, by virtue of their success; those groups not as triumphant are assumed to lack forms of capital, and would do better if they acquired more of them" (Rios-Aguilar et al 2011, 170). In response to this "deficit" understanding of capital, a "funds of knowledge" theoretical approach has been developed to examine the forms of capital not privileged by the dominant group (Rios-Aguilar et al., 2011, p.171). They argue that we all possess specific skills and knowledge, and those may be directly related to what we are learning about. If someone helps us make a connection, we can use our own knowledge as a resource to help us succeed.

Moll, Amanti, Neff & Gonzalez (1992) discuss a mechanism for building connections between students and teachers into a relationship based on mutual trust, in which knowledge is shared, and skills are developed. The mechanism offered is the establishment of reciprocal practices between people who experience each other through thick "multi-stranded" connections that allow each person in the relationship to experience each other as whole people. Moll et al. (1992) recognize that the typical classroom provides an isolated or "thin" experience because the teacher only sees the student through the lens of the classroom setting and, in that environment, they are likely to struggle with understanding the perspectives of all of the students. One consequence of a traditional classroom with a thin connection between student and teacher is that certain types of knowledge are more valued than others and students from backgrounds different than that of the teacher are marginalized; historically, this most often occurs with students of color (Yosso, 2005). In contrast, recognizing students as whole beings who bring expertise allows them to access "the potential of community cultural wealth to transform the process of schooling" (Yosso, 2005, p. 70).

I started to think of my classroom as a place where I look for common intellectual ground with my students so we can all bring our expertise in and expand the circle of common learning—common learning, not necessarily common knowledge. Knowledge is far more intimate and personal than we express in our culture. We may sit in the same room and hear the same people speaking, but how we understand what we hear is entirely different based on our history, our personalities, and even our mood in the moment. There may be common vocabulary and even shared reactions that we discuss, but the only person who really "knows" our worldview is ourselves. Maybe that is why learning together is a form of community-building. When we discuss ideas with our peers, we are sharing and learning from each other, but the learning looks different depending on who we are. When we learn together in a truly open and accepting way, we create an environment that embodies intimacy.

What it Means to Teach and Learn Together

Last year I experienced an extended period of merging both teaching and learning across the realms of my personal, professional and scholarly spaces. My grandmother transitioned through her last year of life, and I was her primary caregiver and became her personal representative when she passed. During the last year of her life, I was also finishing my doctoral degree and navigating my first year as the Director of Senior Inquiry at PSU. Senior Inquiry is a dual-credit program that embeds college professors in high school classrooms to deliver a first-year seminar college experience. The faculty work in teams of three, with two teachers from the high school for each section of our course. We have classes in six schools across four different districts—it is extremely complicated. I had been part of a very competitive regional search the previous year, and my first year officially inhabiting the role of director was challenging and full of powerful lessons. My dissertation committee was filled with extremely smart and exacting professors who did not always agree and pushed me in ways I often felt ill-prepared to comprehend. I knew my grandmother was in the final year of her life. My children were going through their lessons in navigating family and school—I knew that how I worked through my challenges during that year would inform the progress of my children in ways I did not fully comprehend.

While working on revisions for this chapter, I am also trying to settle the affairs of my grandmother's estate. While searching through some of my paperwork, I came across my personal statement for my first Master's degree in Conflict Resolution that began with a quote I took from a book my grandmother had just purchased. The second paragraph begins with what I learned from my parents about social responsibility. My third paragraph is about the University Studies Program at PSU, the program for which I now work. My fourth paragraph describes how I fell in love with teaching. I wrote that paper twenty years ago.

In the twenty years since I wrote that statement, teaching and learning have woven themselves into my identity. Now, they infuse and inform everything I do—from social media, to hanging out with friends for happy hours. When I look now at my autobiography and my teaching philosophy, it is clear to me how one informs the other and how both inform my scholarly interests. I have learned the academic language for discussing problem-posing and banking education and concepts like "funds of knowledge" that validate the lived experience of those of us who come to a scholarship from unconventional spaces. Marginalization matters to me because I felt marginalized, and I take that value with me into the classroom.

It is deeply ironic that I now run a dual-credit program and teach mainly in a high school context—given that high school had to be the source of my most painful experiences of growing up. On the other hand, how could I do anything else? I am motivated by the idea that education liberates. Not just because it broadens our horizons and increases our pool of social capital, but because it gives us our political voice and entrance to civic engagement. I was almost lost in the transitional space between high school and college, so it seems only fitting that now I stand ready to help others across that bridge.

When I look back, it is clear that the moment with my parents in first grade was a pivotal moment to me—I think this is because it is the first example I can think of where there was a clash between the institutions of school and family in my life. The relationship between family and school has become a nexus for my own research, and I wonder if the seed for that was planted in this experience with my parents. I also believe that my love of reading was a saving grace because I developed a way to travel (metaphorically) early on and consider other perspectives and points of view. Importantly, I found mentors who helped me along and who encouraged me to believe in myself. Coming to Portland State and learning about University Studies was transformative because I finally felt like learning had a purpose that aligned with my core values as a human being. I keep thinking about how lucky I am that all my choices brought me to the place I am now. PSU is a place where I continue to learn. My lived experience helps me develop the empathy and humility required for teaching and learning in a society where the need to harness our collective capabilities has never been more needed.

Just now, as I am getting ready to send in this chapter for review, we are in the midst of a global pandemic due to the coronavirus COVID-19. Everyone working in education is scrambling to figure out ways to teach and learn remotely and stay connected socially when we must avoid physically gathering together. It is a moment of significant change, chaos and uncertainty, and yet there are incredible opportunities and learning experiences on the horizon. Some are already manifesting as we learn to let go of the things and activities we don't need. For me, it is true now more than ever that "more than anything else, being an educated person means being able to see connections that allow one to make sense of the world and act within it in creative ways" (Cronon, 1998, p. 5).

References

Cronon, W. (1998). " Only Connect..." The Goals of a Liberal Education. *The American Scholar*, *67*(4), 73-80.

Freire, P. (1970). *Pedagogy of the Oppressed* (Myra Bergman Ramos, Trans.). New York: Herder.

hooks, b. (1994). *Teaching to Transgress Education as the Practice of Freedom*. New York: Routledge.

Jenney, A., & Exner-Cortens, D. (2018). Toxic masculinity and mental health in young women: An analysis of 13 Reasons Why. *Affilia*, *33*(3), 410-417.

Moll, L. C., Amanti, C., Neff, D., & Gonzalez, N. (1992). Funds of knowledge for teaching: Using a qualitative approach to connect homes and classrooms. *Theory into practice*, *31*(2), 132-141.

Nielsen, H. B., & Davies, B. (2017). Formation of gendered identities in the classroom. *Discourse and education*, 135-146.

Rios-Aguilar, C., Kiyama, J. M., Gravitt, M., & Moll, L. C. (2011). Funds of knowledge for the poor and forms of capital for the rich? A capital approach to examining funds of knowledge. *Theory and Research in Education*, *9*(2), 163-184.

Scholes, L. (2019). Popular girls aren't into reading: reading as a site for working-class girls' gender and class identity work. *Critical Studies in Education*, 1-16.

Yosso, T. J. (2005). Whose culture has capital? A critical race theory discussion of community cultural wealth. *Race ethnicity and education*, *8*(1), 69-91.

16

The Many Layers of My Life

How My Relationships Shaped Me

David B. Ross

My First Layer: My Family

My educational story started in a small Massachusetts town during the 1950s to 1970s. My parents, Henry and Toby, understood they had to work very hard to put food on the table and have the necessities of life, as my grandparents, who immigrated in the early 1900s from Russia and Eastern Europe, were uneducated and poor. Although my mother completed high school, my father decided to withdraw from high school in the eleventh grade to enlist in The United States Navy during World War II. Nevertheless, they continued to instill the importance of education combined with a strong work ethic to succeed in all possibilities. Even though my father did not complete his educational career, he was a self-made business leader who successfully created his own business.

After World War II, my father started a vending company in the Boston area, where he later retired at 42. He illustrated that with hard work and determination and a strong educational background, anything was possible for his son and daughter. He stated this many times to my sister Linda and me because he missed out on that part of life and did not want his children to miss out on that opportunity that could positively affect their future. I could be educated because my father made sacrifices to better the lives of my sister and me. A loving parent wants their children to succeed and not follow in their footsteps, especially if there are any trials and tribulations they do not have to encounter.

Although I was born in the Baby Boomer era, my parents' philosophical views were instilled in me based upon their Silent Generation characteristics. The Silent Generation characteristics encompass values that are loyal and astute, where relationships are personal and sacrificial. They cared deeply about religion, which is why they wanted me to go to a religious school during high school, as I rounded my beliefs in learning and practicing from the Old and New Testament. Most importantly, education was a dream within this era.

That said, my parents valued education, especially as they did not have the opportunity to complete high school. My mother and father taught me many life expectations that stood out for being an educated leader; these characteristics were to read, learn, treat people for who they are, and know that it takes a team to reach high accomplishments. When I was growing up, my father taught me that no one starts at the top, but instead, you have to work from the bottom up. This was brought to light when I worked for my father in his company's factory. It made me realize that if I pushed myself hard enough through his guidance, I could be just as successful as he could. When I teach my students and provide them with assignments that entail critical thinking, I am applying the same philosophy that my father instilled in me by making my students work hard in hopes that they realize that they could become successful in the future.

My Second Layer: My High School Education

At that time in the 1960s, my father felt that formal education was required to gain knowledge and understanding in order to apply it during our adolescence to adulthood. I am sure every generation has barriers to education, as my parents faced their societal changes and responsibilities as young adults to take care of their parents from the 1920s to 1940s. So yes, these times were different from my era regarding educational achievements and world events, but as long as we knew how to move forward with making meaning and sense of issues, we would triumph.

I was very fortunate that my parents wanted me to not only attend college but also be prepared for college and life; therefore, they enrolled me in an elite boarding and religious high school, Kent School for Boys, which was located in Kent, Connecticut. In addition, there was the Kent School for Girls located five miles away. In 1971, entering as a freshman student, socially and academically, I felt that I fit in because this school ranged from grades 9 to 12; therefore, we all started together at the same time. We lived in the dorms and developed a relationship that one could compare to a family's bond. We dined together, we learned together and even went to church together. I felt like I had older brothers in this extended family because I felt like the older boys mentored me. This was an experience that money could not buy and shaped me to be the independent man I grew up to be.

My first mentor in education was William H. Armstrong, who taught ancient history and general studies. Mr. Armstrong authored a book in 1969 titled *Peoples of the Ancient World* and a 1956 book titled *Study is Hard Work*. To me, he was a teacher, author, and mentor who taught us about life, personal reward, compassion, and how to organize and balance life. He felt the classroom was a place to obtain knowledge and understanding, make mistakes, learn from the mistakes, and then test them in the external environment. One day he asked me to stand, as he did with all the students, which we did out of respect while learning the essence of formal communication and tell my peers about Mesopotamia, which today is known as the Middle East. Since I was able to give a response that was acceptable by Mr. Armstrong, I knew that my dedication to homework, reading, and being proactive, as well as time management, definitely paid off. This was mirrored regarding how my parents taught me, which was based on their cultural background. Learning from my parents and Mr. Armstrong gave me insight into who I wanted to be as an individual. Now that I reflect on my relationship at Kent with Mr. Armstrong and my peers, we were able to learn and grow from one another, which is critical. These lessons help me share interactions with my students and colleagues and be prepared and proactive. We learned that if you studied and were prepared for class, he would reward you and acknowledge your triumphs by taking the rest of the class off to enjoy the outside or the library; he actually used the word *triumph*.

The following is an illustration of how Mr. Armstrong taught us about learning and reward. My roommate Seth Fairhurst and I would always notice these small birds (i.e., chickadees) outside of our dormitory window and throughout campus that never stopped singing. One day, there was a chickadee at the window of our class; Mr. Armstrong called on me and asked, "Mr. Ross, could you tell me the bird that is singing at our window? If so, you may take the day off and again, enjoy the wonderful day outside." When I stated the type of bird, he rewarded me the day off; you could imagine how Seth felt like only days prior, he told me the type of bird. Seth was not annoyed by this; rather, we laughed about it. This taught me the importance of listening to others who have valuable information to share. It was so memorable that at our 25th reunion, Seth reminded me of that small gesture by Mr. Armstrong as we reminisced about our mentor, who passed away a year before our reunion. During those wonderful days of class, he continued to challenge our understanding of ancient history, but also about life and nature, preparation and time management, and character education. To this date, I still have his book *Study is Hard Work* as well as a daily planner book he asked us to create to stay focused for school and personal time. Keep in mind this was 1971, before any Day Runner or Outlook. Mr. Armstrong also authored *Through Troubled Waters* in 1957 after his wife passed away, which was based on how to understand and deal with grief after losing a loved one. In 1969, he also authored *Sounder*, which became a major motion picture in 1972; he was awarded the John Newbery Medal and the Lewis Carroll Shelf Award in 1970 for *Sounder*.

I was so fortunate that my parents decided to send me to Kent School, a great learning experience academically, personally, and spiritually. The beauty of Kent School was how diverse the student body was. I was fortunate to be surrounded by individuals who came from all continents of the world, including the female population from the Kent School for Girls, which opened my horizons to all nationalities and gave me a learning experience like no other. My three closest friends were from Guatemala, Nicaragua, and Chile. From a young age, I learned about the many customs and traditions from Central and South America, which made me very well rounded and knowledgeable. These relationships prepared me for today's student body who are enrolled in universities where I teach. It is critical to have this background knowledge on the various cultures and identities to adequately teach and create assignments that they can relate to and implement in their diverse workforce. All of my students that I am currently teaching come from all lifestyles and from all over the world; I have had the opportunity to teach different social classes, gender, and race. If it was not for attending Kent School, I might not have had the experience that allowed me today to create these relationships with my diverse student body, whom I had the privilege to teach face-to-face in the Caribbean and Central America, in addition to the students whom I regularly teach globally online.

My Third Layer: My College Education

My educational path was unpredictable as the Vietnam War was taking place. I found myself to be rather hesitant, which way I was to go. Was I to take the same path of my father, go to war, or take a different path and continue with my education? But, a month after I turned 18, the Vietnam War ended, and I enrolled in the local community college, Broward Community College, where I eventually received an Associate of Arts in Business. This continuation of education was a smooth transition to my undergraduate years at Florida Atlantic University and then at Northern Illinois University. I was part of a professional business fraternity, Delta Sigma Pi, which was for both men and women, where I made treasured friendships and connections both academically and socially. Several years later, I became one of the Board of Directors of the fraternity, in charge of Southern Province, consisting of 40 business chapters within nine states. All of these chapters were diverse based on social identity, race, and gender. During my tenure as a Board member, I was part of the team that was responsible for creating the risk management policy and the understanding of having a strong diversity plan that was placed in the pledge manual.

After receiving my Bachelor's degree at Northern Illinois University, I furthered my graduate work at the University of Alabama and Florida Atlantic University. During these years, which also led to my doctorate degree, I had to work full time while attending college. It was at this point that my relationships were solely based on professional networking. During my graduate and post-graduate years, these experiences helped me realize that the higher education field was going to be where I would be able to share my established philosophical views with my potential future students. All of my previous and current education had led me to transfer knowledge that is relevant for my present students. While pursuing my doctorate, I had two significant mentors who shaped my higher education perspective, which led me to assist and mentor my students. Dr. Valerie Bryan, my dissertation chair, helped me understand research, publishing, mentoring, and helping others become successful. She always told her other students and me that once you graduate, you need to find a better position and a better job while mentoring others. This was an important component of a faculty-to-student relationship. As time went on, I have copied or mirrored the same philosophy with my dissertation students. A majority of my dissertation students also went on to better jobs and promotions, in addition to further co-authoring with eight of them.

My first doctorate course, a leadership course, started in the evening at Florida Atlantic University. Dr. Donald MacKenzie started the leadership course by stating, "welcome to our course." I felt comfortable and influenced by the first moment as he continued to demonstrate that all students are welcomed and have the freedom to share their experiences and expertise. This created an environment of collaboration and trust as we all had common characteristics as doctorate students pursuing many goals to educate ourselves. He also showed us a sign on the door that stated, *Test in Progress*. I found this very interesting as the sign was posted on the *inside* of the classroom door, rather than the typical location outside the classroom door. After he explained his reasoning, it was clear why he asked all of us to *pool our wisdom and thoughts*. He felt that when a group collaborates and communicates effectively they can begin to find solutions and take risks as leaders. At the same time, in a protected environment such as a classroom, we would be well prepared to face our real-world challenges outside of the classroom. This is where the true *test in progress* would be for us. Now, a scholarship bears his name within the Department of Educational Leadership at Florida Atlantic University, which is set up to award students who are in good standing, preparing to assume leadership positions in schools. Based on the philosophy by Dr. MacKenzie, I continue to use this in my teachings by telling my students that our classrooms are for collaborating, decision making, and problem-solving, as well as taking risks; all characteristics of a strong leadership way of thinking.

My Fourth Layer: Professorial Years

I would say that primarily because of my relationships with my parents, mentors, educators, and my two best friends Rick Bodine and Mel Urban, most of my learned experiences in life have to lead me to become a competent adult educator, leader, and trusted person. I have learned how to strive for a goal and to be sensitive to other people's needs as well. For instance, when I meet with my dissertation students for the first time, I ask them to explain their potential research topics. I want them to tell me what they want to research and not direct them toward a research topic that might not benefit them in the future. This builds a relationship of respect and a strong foundation to complete one's dissertation. Whether a family member, friend, colleague, student, employee/employer, and/or community member, I treat everyone with fairness, honesty, courtesy, and respect. I have learned to promote an atmosphere that fosters open communication and collaboration, to listen carefully, and to understand through open two-way communication. I deeply value a supportive environment to coach and participate with others, which brings out people's energies and talents. Throughout the years, I have been a dissertation chair to an array of students, whom I have strived to aid both academically and professionally. Below are acknowledgments collected from some of my students' dissertations:

Dr. Carswell wrote,

> I was privileged to have you as my instructor. Whether in class or with regard to my dissertation, you have always encouraged me to produce only the highest quality work, and you held me accountable when it was not. Your expertise and confidence throughout my research and dissertation writing was always comforting, yet the continual prodding to move forward kept me just a little outside my comfort zone…. you were always there to provide guidance, advice, feedback, and cajoling to keep productive. I will always be indebted to you, and I will always admire you for your authentic approach, wisdom, and kindness.

Dr. DeWitt wrote,

> I have appreciated his down to earth approach and genuine concern for me as a student and person. I am honored to call him my chair and look forward to our life long connection. I enjoy our conversations and am indebted to his insight and perspectives. I look forward to future writings together.

Dr. Eleno Orama wrote,

You are a model educator that is devoted to your students and their success and without your support, this study would not have been possible. Your knowledge, patience, attention, and confidence in me sustained the commitment and motivation needed to complete this dissertation process. Thank you for the endless support through this journey.

Dr. Sasso wrote,

You inspired me and helped me grow in a plethora of venues. I have never crossed paths with an educator such as yourself who is so committed and loyal to their students and ensures that your students not only succeed but surpass one's expectations. You truly are the epitome of what all educators should be, a gem amongst stones, and someone I am thankful for and will cherish eternally. God broke the mold when he made you.

Dr. Vazquez wrote,

As my professor, mentor, and chair, I will always be indebted to him for sharing so much of his knowledge with me. As an award-winning professor and a dedicated human being to the education profession, he has earned my lifelong respect for his attention to detail, commitment, and mastery in his craft. I am privileged to have been his student and mentee.

Positive and supportive environments align with leadership participation and coaching, which possibly could lead to increased job satisfaction and positive organizational outcomes and behaviors to commitment and performance (Fallatah & Laschinger, 2016; Glavelia, Karassavidoua, & Zafiropoulos, 2013; Mechbach & Larsson, 2011). To me, this is where innovation, leadership, education and training, and recognition are considered essential. This has been a positive model based on my students' success rates regarding graduating in a timely manner and publications, which has led to notoriety in their perspective fields.

Educational Philosophy

Looking back on my years of teaching, I have observed that the purpose of education has many avenues. Before I explore this area, I have a philosophy of my own: I feel that all teachers can teach, but I do not feel they all have the capacity to facilitate learning. I once read a comic strip that illustrated how teachers can either teach or facilitate learning. In the first frame, two boys and a dog were standing near one another when the first boy asked, "What are you doing with your dog?" and the other boy answered, "I am teaching my dog how to whistle." The first boy put his ear to the dog's mouth and said, "I do not hear anything." The boy replied, "I said I taught him, I didn't say he learned it."

What I perceived from the basis of this satire was very simple; not everyone can facilitate learning. Dr. K. Patricia Cross, whom I studied in my doctoral-level adult education courses had stated that "learning can occur without teaching, and often does, but teaching cannot occur without learning; teaching without learning is just talking." Cross (as cited in Plank, Enerson, Milner, & Johnson, 1997) quoted that, "while learning has many ends, teaching has only one: To enable or cause learning" (p. 11).

I think that for teachers who can facilitate learning, it is the teacher's position to mold the minds of students so they can function in our global society. When educators transfer knowledge in the forms of expectations and theories while making them significant and relevant, students would be able to perform in any situation and can learn something from the curriculum components. In the past, as a high school teacher, since I did not feel that everyone was college-bound, I was an advocate for preparing my students, not only for post-secondary schooling, but for the real world.

I have learned that having an educational philosophical statement can be beneficial in helping to understand myself as an educator and the needs of my students. A philosophy statement in education can contain many issues such as meanings, aims, and objectives, curricula, the roles of teachers, students, administrators, and society. As a faculty member, I believe that faculty and teachers should examine their philosophy periodically as it has a positive impact on the curriculum and instruction; our philosophies can be researched and updated many times as a person progresses through life experiences and then reflects on their understanding of their field as well as personal strengths.

Thus, I always strive for informed, responsible, and collaborative decision-making at all levels, drawing upon the wisdom and knowledge found throughout the organization or educational setting. The value of *pooled wisdom* (e.g., group intelligence, group dynamics, shared solutions) cannot be overemphasized. Howe (2009) defined a crowd as "a group of people united by a common characteristic" (p. 143). Within a group of people, lies diversity with individual perspectives, the influence of averaging, and resolving issues in a collaborative process (Herzog & Hertwig, 2009; Howe, 2009; Surowiecki, 2004). This process is conducted at all times within my courses, as I want to hear the many perspectives from my students. I consider my students as experts in their fields who can add so much to a discussion, whether in a face-to-face course or a blended online format.

I consider myself to have more than one philosophical view in regard to learning. For instance, while researching additional information on constructivism, I found the Constructivist Learning Environment Survey that was initially designed for science teachers can be used for other disciplines with some changes. The Constructivist Learning Environment Survey has several sections: learning about the world, learning about science, learning to speak out, learning to learn, and learning to communicate. While reviewing this survey, I realized that many of these questions pertain to my style of teaching. In my classrooms, I encourage students to ask questions about the content and the process, and I welcome them to give their opinion. The students and I take a collaborative approach to decide on what they will learn, what projects will be used, and how much time will be spent on the projects. I also allow my students to communicate freely with other students to obtain other perspectives pertaining to class topics.

The Constructivist Learning Environment Survey has four scales: Personal Relevance, Student Negotiation, Shared Control, and Critical Voice. These scales help students make use of their everyday experiences to help develop their scientific knowledge. The students are able to explain and justify to other classmates about their newly developing ideas, to listen and reflect on one another's ideas, as well as their own. The students also exercise a degree of control over their learning, promoting an interest in student empowerment. There is a need to show how a constructivist perspective can help plan and deliver instruction and how technologies can significantly support effective and theoretically sound teaching to increase student achievement. The challenge is to understand how to promote deeper, substantive learning. There are three principles needed to understand this process: the product of actively relating new and prior experiences, a function of learning facts and core principles of a discipline, and a consequence of using and managing intellectual abilities.

I researched another reform model, First Things First (K–12), which also conforms to my constructivist philosophy pertaining to what is most important for students to learn. I feel that a curriculum should include higher-level thinking to help the students in the classroom and when they are taking a standardized test. This reform helps engage all students, prepares them for high-stakes assessments, and helps encourage students to think at a higher-level using classification, application, analysis, and creativity (Connell & Klem, 2006). By using these higher levels of thinking, it will help raise the academic performance of all students to do well in school and prepare them not only for life skills but also for many levels of education. This reform and the constructivist philosophy also agree with having a strong relationship between teachers and other students. I am certain that the role of the teacher in the relationship of the curriculum should be to provide the best possible learning environment for their students.

Additionally, I agree with the quantum-learning reform model as the curriculum has teachers capture students' attention by making the school environment more relevant, engaging, and dynamic as well as designed to initiate change, enhance teacher capacity, and increase student achievement. Students should be engaged in their learning by being involved, rather than just taking a back seat as a spectator in their education. I strongly believe the purpose of education is to help students build on their experiences and needs, their life skills, and basic skills. The quantum-learning model has components that focus on leadership, involvement from all stakeholders in the students' achievement, and learning life skills that align with my philosophy. Both my philosophy and the quantum-learning model align with one another to establish a meaningful curriculum relevant to their future and understand that all students cannot only learn but learn differently, as long as the curriculum is engaging and challenging.

As educators, we are challenged to identify, invent, adopt, and use classroom practices that are consistent with our constructivist philosophy. Consistency between theoretical conceptions of learning and teaching practice has been shown to support effective applications of technologies to increase achievement. Learning conducted in classrooms should be designed to be learner-centered, thought-provoking, relevant, provided time to learn and provided with opportunities to elicit frequent and facilitative feedback and support. When educators exhibit these qualities, it will be more effective with all learners. Of course, to have this philosophy become successful, there is a need for a collaborative effort of the entire schools' staff, including the approval of the leaders.

Leadership Philosophy in Education

My philosophy of leadership requires that an organization must determine the success of its products and services. When an organization fails to meet the changes in economics, society, and technology, then strategies, products, and services become outdated, even dilapidated. "There is pressure on organizations and workforces to deliver continuous improvement in products, systems, and processes" (Bassett-Jones & Lloyd, 2004, p. 929). Many organizations fail because of their refusal to keep up with changing times and conditions, especially with the rapid change in technologies and diverse/generational workforce. In addition, failure occurs when human capital is ignored, building no relationships. Based on Herzberg's *Two-Factor Theory*, recognition, achievement, and growth (Riley, 2005), reward and performance management are important motivators within an organizational structure (Bassett-Jones & Lloyd, 2004; Fischer, Malycha, & Schafmann, 2019). Leaders, administrators, and management teams and staff must be growth-oriented to embrace realistic expansion plans, which facilitate dynamic change. Organizations that want to encourage change are using advanced technologies to manage and evaluate their employees by examining the relationship between how people behave and how they perform (Meyer, 2015). A stable leadership in top administration and the *rank-and-file* is necessary. When leadership changes frequently, the internal structure is fragmented, and productivity, quality, and creativity then suffer. I believe effective leadership builds organizations with enough stability to ensure loyalty among employees through the constructive principles of cognitive reasoning, understanding, confidence, openness, growth, and knowledge.

There are many areas of philosophy that, when understood, lead to the attainment of *wisdom*, which, in turn, can lead to breakthroughs. One philosophy is metaphysics, which has to do with the essential nature of life's events. It offers a view of human existence and how one perceives life. I believe ethics and social responsibility are essential to governing one's life and guiding one's decisions in the pursuit of goals. One's own ethics should be an instinctive compass to keep one on the right path. I believe that my moral values guide my behavior. I also believe that people should be free to be creative and not controlled or coerced into following another individual's thoughts or beliefs.

In the field of education, an effective administrator, as it relates to the curriculum, should spend time with the community and employees at all levels, in both informal and formal settings. This practice helps the administrators learn what is going on throughout the community and organization and allows them to take a more active part in what is being taught in our schools. By communicating commitment and caring, truthful interaction can be fostered in a school environment; it simply takes the belief and initiative of the school administrators to help reach this goal. I strongly feel that by communicating a vision by being idealistic and authentic, an atmosphere is created in which people will naturally adopt the goals and mission of the school. I believe an educational leader builds relationships with most stakeholders if they walk around frequently and consistently, contacting everyone within the community and school setting, asking for their input to improve student achievement. As a member of the School Advisory Council for a local school, we work as a team to create policies to promote student success and build relationships with parents and the community.

Several school reform models can drive the curriculum. When designing a curriculum, curriculum leaders need to take into account several issues: pedagogical and andragogical methods, classroom arrangements, and students' learning outcomes. Curriculum leaders must be growth-oriented to embrace realistic expansion plans, which facilitate dynamic change; a stable leadership format is necessary. When leadership changes frequently, the internal structure is fragmented, which in turn causes productivity, quality, and creativity to suffer. Education should be related to a student's life, with the end goal of education being to prepare the student not only for the classroom and all types of assessments but for real-world applications. Students need to engage in realistic exploratory learning situations because they will encounter them outside of the classroom. The curriculum should be relevant, not just busywork. The curricula in my courses are designed to allow students to think critically without wasting time with irrelevant content. As a leader, I give my students all the tools and materials they need to be successful. Therefore, my course platform only contains pertinent information for them to succeed in the real world.

A curriculum leader should utilize instructional time to focus on students' needs. The classroom environment should be very relaxed, allowing students to reflect and discuss their views on each topic, reflecting the constructivist philosophy. As a curriculum leader, I emphasize students' creativity to empower them when facing the real world. A good administrator will find options to keep all the disciplines in the curriculum. The curriculum leader should also encourage students to network with other students, family, friends, teachers, administrators, and utilize many resources such as books, computers, libraries, and field visits. This form of relationship building will help them gain the knowledge, skills, abilities, and other characteristics to be successful and compete in today's global market.

As an educational leader, I take great pride in my communication skills. My goals are to show more responsiveness and establish better communication, so I recognize my students' frame of mind to reinforce their learning. While setting the mood for learning through instigation, stimulation, and relevance, I continued to link the curriculum through research and awareness of the literature. Today's adult learners face many obstacles, which will keep them from furthering their studies, their dreams, and their goals; thus, the reason I have developed new course procedures continually. I condition my students that the environment is open for dialogue to discuss any concerns or issues they might have regarding their course work. However, students need one key aspect, which is to review every document and correspondence in detail. Communication is not only sending a message but also having effective listening and practice reading skills.

I believe in a structured format regarding the due dates of all assignments and weekly discussion topics. The reason is to have equity in the course and one crucial aspect: So that I can remain consistent in my work ethic of returning assignments within the same due date week. I strongly believe in immediate yet positive feedback so that the students can learn and produce future assignments and discussion topics at a higher level of achievement. If students were allowed to submit work at any time, there would be a lack of structure to help students learn from submission to submission. I feel an academic paper needs to sound great (i.e., content), but look great (i.e., format). This will help students in all of their studies, especially their dissertation and other future writings and publications.

In summary, I continuously revisit my evaluations to make sure I can improve my skills as a professor and deliver a great lecture through the transfer of knowledge that is relevant to my students' needs. One other point that I pride myself in is to keep all courses current and show the relevance of how it aligns with today's local and global issues. I continuously send new topics to my students through online announcements, which keeps the student and myself updated on new worldly events.

Reflection

They say that every action causes a reaction, yet the positive actions that I have experienced from my family, mentors, friends, educators, and students, have caused me to be more proactive. My proactive approach stemmed from my parents instilling the importance of hard work and dedication towards education, my mentors' ability to guide me in the right direction and broaden my horizons both educationally and professionally, as well as my students' tenacity and belief in me to guide them to success. These experiences are what shaped me to be the person I am today. Relationships have played a role in strengthening these experiences.

There was one prominent theme that stood throughout, which can be found in my story regarding relationships. This theme pertaining to relationships are personal and can demonstrate a family bond process among my parents, childhood friends, my high school roommates, college friends, work, and the community. These relationships made me a very competent individual so that I was able to mentor others. This was based on my mentors' philosophies of a pay-it-forward approach and the relationship I had with them. All of my educators/mentors, including my parents, collectively showed me that you could connect people through education. Because of the strong relationship I had with my parents and mentors, a bond was developed that I was able to learn from, and it made me the educator and mentor I am today toward others. My lifetime experiences shaped me and allowed me to shape others professionally and through publications and presentations.

As I reflect on these relationships, my philosophy of teaching is to allow the student to become involved in their education, just as I have. This has been my educational belief from teaching high school, community college, state university's undergraduate and graduate levels to doctoral level in a private university to include dissertations. My students became involved in their education, as I provided them the freedom to select their topic when it came time for them to write their dissertation or project. No student will complete their dissertation or project if they do not feel passionate about their research. This perspective has proven beneficial as various students succeeded in life, work, and education, especially winning dissertation awards due to my leadership and philosophical styles of facilitating knowledge. As a professor, I should teach a student theory and, most importantly, promote the use of critical thinking and integrating real-life situations, no matter the educational level and other demographics. In today's classroom of higher education, which is constantly changing, I rely on many philosophies of adult education; this approach allows me the flexibility for future change: technology, student diversity, goals, and plans. I encourage my students to be forward thinkers, futurists, and game-changers.

As a professor, I continue to make modifications based on my students' learning abilities and barriers, so they have an equal chance to learn in our classroom regardless of their difficulties. My curriculum is structured to facilitate learning relevant to a student's personal and professional life. The end goal of education is to prepare my students for real-life applications outside of the classroom. As a professor, my philosophy is to facilitate learning from many directions: faculty to student, student to student, and student to faculty. Since every student has expertise in several areas, I use many techniques to involve them through instigation, stimulation, and evaluation of the learning process. This philosophy is based on andragogy's progressive style as I communicate culture and societal structure to encourage social change. This gives my students practical knowledge and problem-solving skills to reform society.

Additionally, I use the radical style of andragogy to bring about fundamental, social, political, and economic changes in society through education. This philosophy also places the student equal with the teacher in the learning process, as my students have had prior experiences and expertise. By sharing best practices and experiences, we build upon our relationships to discuss our similarities and differences. The students feel part of their learning experience and learn more than one perspective of the lessons and topics. Although I have always brought information to the classroom to show the students the relevance of their learning, my courses have made me look deeper into real-life situations to show them the link between theory and practice.

Reflecting as a lifelong learner and facilitator of knowledge, I will continue to stay focused on my students' needs. When teaching either a face-to-face class or logging into an online classroom, I will be accessible to my students and create an organizational structure that will benefit today's adult learners. I will promote student-faculty interaction and student-to-student collaboration as students, not only faculty, bring expertise and experience from their personal and professional lives to the classroom. I am aware that the students are from different generations, learning styles, and communication styles. While trying to meet these various styles, I will challenge them independently to create learning situations best used by these students.

References

Bassett-Jones, N., & Lloyd, G. C. (2004). Does Herzberg's motivation theory have staying power? *Journal of Management Development, 24*(10), 929-943.

Connell, J. P., & Klem, A. M. (2006). First things first: A framework for successful secondary school reform. *New Directions for Youth Development, 111*, 53-66. doi:10.1002/yd.182

Fallatah, F., & Laschinger, H. K. S. (2016). The influence of authentic leadership and supportive professional practice environments on new graduate nurses' job satisfaction. *Journal of Research in Nursing, 21*(2), 125-136.

Fischer, C., Malycha, C. P., & Schafmann, E. (2019). The influence of intrinsic motivation and synergistic extrinsic motivators on creativity and innovation. *Frontiers in Psychology.* https://doi.org/10.3389/fpsyg.2019.00137

Glavelia, N., Karassavidoua, E., & Zafiropoulos, K. (2013). Relationships among three facets of family-supportive work environments, work-family conflict, and job satisfaction: A research in Greece. *The International Journal of Human Resource Management, 24*(20), 3757-3771.

Herzog, S. M., & Hertwig, R. (2009). The wisdom of many in one mind: Improving individual judgments with dialectical bootstrapping. *Psychological Science, 20*(2), 231-237.

Howe, J. (2009). *Crowdsourcing: Why the power of the crowd is driving the future of business.* New York, NY: Three Rivers Press.

Mechbach, J., & Larsson, L. (2011). Young coaches and supportive environments. *Sports Science Review, 20*(5-6), 25-56.

Meyer, P. (2015). Fostering change. HR Magazine. *Society for Human Resource Management.* Retrieved from http://web.a.ebscohost.com.ezproxylocal.library.nova.edu/ehost /pdfviewer/pdfviewer?vid=20&sid=8f256ae5-26c2-465e-8f71-7ce435cc2f7 %40sessionmgr4006&hid=4112

Plank, K. M., Enerson, D. M., Milner, S., & Johnson, R. N. (1997). Learning to teach, teach to learn. https://digitalcommons.otterbein.edu/fac_ctl/1

Riley, S. (2005). *Herzberg's two-factor theory of motivation applied to the motivational techniques within financial institutions.* Senior Honors Theses. Paper 119.

Surowiecki, J. (2004). *The wisdom of crowds.* New York, NY: Doubleday.

Part V

Changing Pedagogical Practices

17

Finding Your People

Co-storying Higher Education Teaching and Learning in Lockdown

Kathryn Coleman, Clare McNally & Brian Martin

This chapter is written at a time when we are connected but physically far apart. Teaching our students remotely and connecting to our colleagues via Zoom. This chapter is called "Finding Your People," and the three of us have become a supportive group of innovators, people who have found each other because we have likeminded ideas around learning, shared pedagogies and practices, and a keen interest in ensuring that higher education is an inclusive, creative learning community. As a group of colleagues who don't work with each other day-to-day, co-writing and co-designing a co-story was enabled by our digital connections as a professional learning community (PLC). As Morrissey (2000) asserts, a professional learning community provides an infrastructure to create the "supportive cultures and conditions necessary for achieving significant gains in teaching and learning."

Over time we have iteratively reflected, discussed, and talked in Zoom about how we found each other; why finding each other matters to our teaching, learning, and research; and how a shared story as a PLC with a shared inquiry model might be of support to others. As a result, this co-storied chapter is co-written to explore the complexities of digital learning, teaching, assessment, and research cultures in higher education from our sites as practitioners. As a PLC, we have felt the impact of collaboration and the agency that this relationship has on our practice. This co-story is part of a community infrastructure that highlights how important it is to have colleagues you trust, respect, and can grow with professionally.

We invite you into our shared story and ask that you reflect with us. We have found that "participation in learning communities impacts teaching practice as teachers become more student-centered. In addition, teaching culture is improved because the learning communities increase collaboration, a focus on student learning, teacher authority or empowerment, and continuous

The month we all went home. An image of us exhausted early in the pivot to online teaching, March 2020 (top: Brian and Kate; bottom: Clare)

learning; …when teachers participate in a learning community, students benefit as well…" (Vescio, Ross & Adams, 2008, pp. 87–88).

Who Are We?

Kate: For many years, I have lived and worked in rhizomic digital spaces, exploring the potential of portfolio pedagogy for reflection, metacognitive growth, and identity exploration. I am a senior lecturer in education, specifically in art and design secondary education. My doctoral a/r/tographic research (Coleman, 2017) explored the relational and agential openings for rhizomatic portfolio pedagogy in art education through digital portfolios and narratives of Australian and international artists. This philosophy underpins my teaching (Wright & Coleman, 2019) and is informed by socio-material, cultural, and technological practices. I am a feminist, artist, researcher, and teacher. My work focuses on integrating digital pedagogies and digital portfolios for sustained creative practice and assessment. The digital is an inherent aspect of my pedagogical practice, my researcher persona, artmaker self, art educator, personal life, and embodied praxis. This praxis proposes that digital portfolios are creative art encounters that contain purposeful, artful, cyclical, and iterative reflection moments and provide a space for transformative learning through an ongoing dialogue with the self as maker and viewer. It was portfolios as authentic learning spaces that connected us and developed this PLC.

Clare: My path to becoming the teacher I am today has been long and varied. As a dental hygienist, I started my professional life, a role that is inherently about education but mostly one-on-one in a dental clinical setting. During my hygiene program, I was inspired by Professor Marc Tennant, my anatomy and local anesthesia lecturer who had a Ph.D., was a researcher and scientist and a captivating teacher. This resonated on all levels, I wanted to be what he was—a highly qualified academic who thrived in the classroom. It took me almost twenty years to get there. Still, I completed my clinically-based Ph.D. (Medicine) in 2019 and am now focused on reforming dental education by adopting a digital pedagogy to improve the student experience. I have established a reflexive approach to my teaching (Sting, 2012), seeking regular feedback from students; I see them as my partners in the classroom. This approach empowers the students to drive their learning (Jacobs, 2015).

Brian: I am a *reformed* management consultant currently forging a professional career in higher education in the third space (Whit church, 2008), supporting university executive and academic staff through operational and strategic advice on the affordances of technology-enhanced learning. My emerging teaching philosophies are centred on creative use of constructivist (Schunk, 2008) spatially and temporary agnostic pedagogies, media, and storytelling to develop novel solutions to challenges such as linking curriculum to the development of situated interpersonal skills, and social belonging in an impersonal temporary and spatially constrained education system. My leadership philosophy aligns with my teaching ethos, which is strengths-based rather than focusing on managing perceived deficits. When leading others, I rarely use authority to reach outcomes, preferring to reach consensus through a more thoughtful and relationship-focused process of influence (Sinclair, 2007).

Collectively we are digital thought leaders, pushing perceived boundaries of what can be understood as evidence of learning and how we can epistemically shift ideological and philosophical notions of authentic and agentic assessment design. This co-storied chapter is written as a collective of three colleagues who practice in different fields and parts of the university who have found each other to support pedagogical shifts and turns in digital learning, teaching, and assessment spaces as a PLC. Our co-design has occurred as do many shifts in practice, when we found that collectively, even though in different schools and sites of the institution, we shared pedagogies in the relation between the digital and physical, reflection and evidence inquiry-driven learning-centered curriculum design. Together, we have found ways to open opportunities for re-thinking and re-positioning digital learning, teaching, assessment in our programs and communities of practice/s. We each hold very different stories that overlap and entangle, intertwine and relate, and when woven together, have offered new sites and sights. This critical autoethnographic co-storied chapter is designed to perform the connections we have felt as an effect through a curated and co-designed collection of threads.

Being digital connects the stories woven here and is a thread we have drawn from our textural sites of practice to co-reflect, co-write, and co-inquire as co-laborers. The paper is storied through a patchwork of narratives that are curated to invite you into the place/s we currently work. We thread our stories through a textural overlapping of ideas that seek to provoke new ways of assessing higher education through exploring the digital demands of learning and teaching within a digital visual culture that calls for action, activism, creativity, and critical engagement with disciplinary and interdisciplinary knowledges.

As a co-story, we embody and perform this story-ing and invite you to weave your way through each telling. Each telling is an autoethnography: a layered and intertextual theory and story. We have done this "because theory and story exist in a mutually influential relationship; theory is not an add-on to story. We cannot write our stories and then begin the search for a theory to 'fit' them outside of cultures and politics and contexts. Instead, theory is a language for thinking with and through, asking questions about, and acting on—the experiences and happenings in our stories" (Holman Jones, 2016, p.229).

Patch #1: Teaching and Leadership

What makes a leader in education; what is educational leadership? We have troubled these concepts together and, through developmental mentoring (DeVries, 2018), come to see the relationship as reciprocity that provides agency to us in our individual spaces to be empowered to develop new epistemic cultures. Through collaboration with multidisciplinary peers, we take ownership of our own professional development and career trajectories supported by the trust of the PLC to support, model, question through a shared belief in learning, innovation, and curious learning environments. This chapter is co-storied because of our shared beliefs in collaborative practice. However, we each hold differing leadership roles and serve as leaders in our communities of practice very differently. John Hattie's research is focused in schools, but our higher education ecology is similar and suggests that:

> [W]e must stop allowing teachers to work alone, behind closed doors and in isolation in the staffrooms and instead shift to a professional ethic that emphasizes collaboration. We need communities within and across schools that work collaboratively to diagnose what teachers need to do, plan programs and teaching interventions and evaluate the success of the interventions (Hattie, 2015, p. 23).

Sharing our beliefs about teaching and leadership has allowed us to share our philosophies and beliefs, and through trust and respect mentor each other to develop further our beliefs and values during this time of crisis.

Brian: My beliefs about teaching, and what makes great teachers, are linked to the idea that creative, passionate raconteurs are able to transcend theoretical and applied concepts to provide learning opportunities that make meaning within disciplinary contexts. These teachers can use a wide range of pedagogies, media, and technologies to scaffold and assess learning outcomes. Leadership in the third space is extremely complex, with the need to balance institutional drivers concerned with quality and scalability, on the one hand, with academic freedom, on the other. Leading experts in technology-enhanced learning, educational content, and learning design are academically-minded, but have different drivers and motivations that can place them in conflict with their faculty colleagues and require skillful navigation to reach positive outcomes. These quasi academic roles, which can span central authority, enabling teaching and learning support functions, and faculty-ed collaborative academic development projects, are sources of opportunity for new meanings and relationships to be made. Nonetheless, the forays of professional staff into the faculty domain do not come without challenge and potential for conflict (Whitechurch, 2008). In this sometimes-fraught context, as a leader, I hold myself and others accountable for creating safe places for team members and colleagues to work and create; moreover, I feel a strong sense of responsibility to encourage, help, and explore with team members "where they are at" in their unique personal and professional learning journey and do whatever is within my influence to help them become what they want to be.

As a Master of Education student in 2019, I wrote about the stickiness of the grammar of tertiary education (Tyack & Tobin, 1994) and its intractability in terms of the physical and temporal constraints of traditional modes of on-campus delivery and timetabled learning events. This led to a call for more spatially and temporally agnostic pedagogies such as the community of inquiry (Swan, Garrison, & Richardson, 2009) to come to the fore. Ironically, we are now in the COVID-19 world, where spatial and temporal constraints have been removed instantly. This PLC now provides me, as a centrally positioned third-space professional, with an opportunity to grow my knowledge of the hybrid pedagogies that have long been part of Kate's practice. Perhaps now *is* the time when new professional and academic staff relationships and communities—such as those Kate, Clare, and I have developed—forge new understandings and more effective working partnerships?

Clare: My key belief about teaching is inclusivity. Giving students an opportunity to learn in a variety of ways allows them the chance to be individuals and excel. Students also need to earn an income and to have time to experience life outside of the Institution. As teachers, we should help facilitate this wherever possible by adapting our programs to enable students to have independence, food, and financial security (Broton & Goldrick-Rab, 2018). Dentistry and oral health degrees are preparation for practice, the outcome for each student at graduation is that they can register with the appropriate dental or health authority. Traditionally, dental programs are very hands-on, practical, and rely on the face-to-face style of education. This requires a time commitment from students that means they often sacrifice many of the things I described earlier, in particular employment, which has a follow-on effect on the other aspects of their life: food security, socialisation, and independence. Moving dental education into a digital space, embracing a blended learning approach that provides students with the flexibility to learn in their own time, provides students with the opportunity to do other things. The search for how to best take dental education online is how I first connected with Kate and Brian.

Kate: Teaching and leadership are entangled and often not separated. As a Feminist scholar and researcher, I am committed to de-colonising the academy to remove sexist, racist, and bullying practices and build an intercultural and inclusive community of practitioners. I am committed to improving student learning through critical pedagogies and practices, interdisciplinary teaching and research, and designing sustainable accessible digital outcomes across the education landscape. My teaching and leadership contributions in secondary schools and universities stem from a passion for relevant real-world learning and teaching, more pronounced now as I begin to work with teachers for the *new* normal.

Patch #2: The Underpinning that Support Our Beliefs

As a PLC, this co-storied chapter has allowed us to further collaborate, mentor, and support each other as we learn through inquiry-based practice to ultimately improve student learning. This co-storying has specifically offered us space to learn by *doing, being, thinking, knowing* together through practice within a shared inquiry model that includes purposeful and creative, collaborative practice-based learning interventions through meaningful sharing and discussion about learning and teaching in digital spaces.

Clare: Recently, I have started to draw on the work of Harriet Schwartz who uses Relational Cultural Theory (RCT) to inform Connected Learning, which is the title of her recently published book (Schwartz, 2019). This theory considers how the teacher–student connection drives both teaching and learning and empowers the student to succeed. This seems more relevant than ever in the COVID-19 classroom. Maintaining a connection with students in a traditional on-campus class is easy; you can share emotions, you can move around in the space together, or, particularly in dentistry, you can work with a patient together. None of this is possible currently, but to have our students continue to progress through their courses we need to maintain a connection that ensures ongoing learning so that they are ready to jump straight back into clinical practice whenever it is possible again.

An Urgency of Teachers: The Work of the Critical Digital Pedagogy by Sean Michael Morris and Jesse Stommel is a collection of works published in the authors' blog and other online sites (Morris & Stommel, 2018). In this collection of works, they focus on achieving clarity in your teaching. They focus their work on the student and creating the best experience possible. The most valuable component of this work for me so far is the process of ungrading. As competition for marks disappears and students can have some more flexibility in the activities. This ties in nicely with what brought all of us together in the first place: the plan to develop self-regulated work in an ePortfolio program.

Twelve months ago, I recognised that, while teaching came naturally to me, I lacked the theoretical underpinning and confidence as I had no formal teaching qualification. I set about becoming a "completist," listening to all of the episodes of the *Teaching in Higher Education* podcast: "Faculty Development for Professors" (Stachowiak, 2019). The host, Dr. Bonni Stachowiak from Vanguard University in California, USA, interviews a different higher education academic weekly. Since discovering this podcast, I have listened to, read, and researched education to shape my teaching almost to the exception of everything else. The people who have had the biggest impact in shaping this new approach and shift in thinking include: Professor Ken Bain author of *What the Best College Teachers Do* (Bain, 2004). This book is a compilation of interviews and observations of a wide variety of higher education teachers that tie the teaching activities demonstrated to improve students' learning. Dr. James

Lang, author of *Small Teaching: Everyday Lessons from the Science of Learning* (Lang, 2016) and curator of the Teaching and Learning in Higher Education Series at West Virginia University Press (Lang, 2019). Dr. Stephen Brookfield recognises the need for higher education students to be considered as adults, and I have adapted his Critical Incident Questionnaire (CIQ) to obtain feedback from my students that shapes my teaching weekly (Brookfield, 2015).

Brian: In many ways, my journey is like Clare's, while working in various academic support and professional roles, mostly with an educational technology focus, I discovered—almost by accident that teaching and learning came naturally to me. I think this was mostly due to the analytical and methodical parts of my brain that were well-honed in my consulting career, finally being allowed to combine with the more creative sides of myself—where I have interests in creative writing and performing. Combined, these two attributes work well in the educational context, where the ability to creatively yet constructively aligned (Biggs, 2003) learning resources, activities and assessments seemed a logical, but creative challenge. That being said, like Clare, I also felt keenly the need to put my work into a theoretical and recognised qualification framework. Therefore, I undertook the Graduate Certificate (Education), Tertiary Teaching between 2016 and 2018 while leading a team of learning technologists, educational media designers, and academic skills advisors at Federation University Australia. During this time, I was influenced by Biggs' work and that of Garrison around the community of Inquiry.

My current role at the University of Melbourne and my continued studies as a Master of Education student is exposing me to the broader historical framework of educational theory, and I have made some epistemic progress towards understanding education within a broader interdisciplinary context. One example of this is a deeper appreciation of space and its critical role in social constructivism (Tanner and Lackney, 2006). Working alongside more erudite colleagues such as Kate and Clare, consistently challenges me to lift my game to a higher level. I am also interested in similar hybrid pedagogies (Buchan, 2017) as cited by Kate and Clare, as they afford numerous opportunities to transcend and disrupt our typical mode of delivering higher education. I am further intrigued by the intersection of virtual and physical spaces to design more opportunities for creativity, serendipitous encounters, and social connections (de Rond, 2014; Meusburger, Funke, & Wunder, 2009) through more flexible and inclusive place-making. Other encounters with scholars in literature and the humanities have forced me to reconsider some of my knowing, leading to several interesting and novel counter-narratives, e.g., balancing the benefits of learning analytics against notions of power and resistance by students and teachers in the online context (Foucault, 1982) and questioning the role of the disempowered teacher in commodified online education (Biesta, 2012).

Kate: I am connected as both a Connectivist (Siemens, 2005) and hybrid digital pedagogue (Stommel, 2014), an interventionist a/r/tographer (Coleman, 2017) and relational art practitioner (O' Donoghue & Irwin, 2012) always excited by the potential of disruptive (Oblinger & Grajek, 2013) and creative technologies (Allen, Caple, Coleman & Nguyen, 2012). As an educator, my scholarly communities drive how I intervene, teach, facilitate, and democratise practices that underpin the relationship between learning and wellbeing through a socially-just education. I am always living and working within a critical pedagogy framework (Friere, 2000), as a practitioner who sees practice as recurring and situated actions informed by shared meanings (Schatzki, Knorr-Cetina & Savigny, 2001) and designing for ways of collecting and curating learning as da[r]ta and thinking with these as digital archives or da[r]tafacts. I add the [r] into data to re-imagine how data is visual, digital, and practice generated in a shared space between practitioners—such as the storying of place in this chapter. Scholarship offers me a site to open and respond to new sights and cites through storying-place as a border pedagogy (Alexander, 2001).

Patch #3: The Strategies that We Draw that Align with Our Key Beliefs

Through collaborative research, a PLC thus functions as a site of action research whereby participants from a range of disciplines and backgrounds are linked by a common creative inquiry into their own epistemic beliefs and practices. We are from different spaces, disciplines, faculties, and methodological places within the university. Without our common digital pedagogies, we might not have met and even established this PLC as a site of practice. A focus on practice emphasises the relational and enacted nature of epistemic beliefs. That is, epistemologies are understood in terms of how they are done rather than something an individual has—making them dynamic, contingent, and relational. Core tenants of a PLC are collaboration and shared collective responsibility. These partnerships allow all participants in a PLC to work on a singular idea focused on practice in a supportive, creative, personalised, reflective, and mentored ecology. This design and conceptual framing supports risk-taking, play, and creative ideation through curiosity and *"what if"* practices in inter- and cross-disciplinary teams, important cross-cutting skills that teachers seek to develop in their students often without experience or skills. This chapter was developed in that cyclic process, where we co-storied, individually responded, co-storied sought feedback and then, now, re-frame our research as a chapter. Through this cycle of learning as a PLC, we can explore the alignment of our teaching philosophy and beliefs here.

Kate: As a contiguous site of artistry, research, and teaching, I learned new ways of doing, knowing, and being through the digital turn (Westera, 2015) in portfolio pedagogy. This turn was epistemological, ontological, conceptual, and material and has led me to reconsider the possibilities for digital learning, teaching, and assessment as wayfinding spaces in education. As a digital and visual autoethnography, I try to "make personal experience meaningful and cultural experience engaging, but also, by producing accessible texts"…I am "able to reach wider and more diverse mass audiences that traditional research usually disregards" (Ellis, Adams and Bochner, 2010, npn).

Clare: Since inclusivity is a significant aspect of my teaching, I engage in a lot of group work and reflection. Students use a variety of methods: weekly video feedback in first year and weekly written blogs in the second year. The final year students do a combination of both. These activities have allowed me to appreciate each student's experiences, but the biggest benefit has been how the students have integrated across the year levels. This has helped me realise that a whole program approach to curriculum that encourages more peer learning is a positive and beneficial thing to nurture. I plan to evolve these individual artifacts into ePortfolio programs to create a self-regulated approach to assessment that encourages students to map their work to the competencies of the graduating dental clinician; this is a crucial component of any preparation for a practice degree. Kate inspired me to think about integrating all these aspects of my teaching into a portfolio program to benefit the students. Brian has offered the practical support and novel ways of how I might achieve this.

Brian: As a student of education, I am challenging myself to study formally new or intersecting disciplines such as leadership, architecture, philosophy, policy, literature, and equity and diversity. The broadening of my understanding of education within a richer ontology is a deliberate and rewarding strategy to increase my ability to undertake meaningful discourse with more learned colleagues and lead to new and novel pathways of inquiry—some of which may inform future publications and research. In addition to developing more reflective and relational approaches to leadership (Sinclair, 2007), I have recently challenged myself to be more assertive in professional and interpersonal contexts. In these in-between roles where power dynamics are driven by position, authority, and intellectual hierarchies, it is important to be mindful of the impact on your wellbeing of adopting non-assertive behaviour. As such, I have begun to consider assertiveness as a particular and vital form of self-care (Bolton, 1986). Working closely with Clare and Kate has also made me more mindful of the power dynamics and influences they are subjected to in their roles within the academy. Finally, building and sustaining PLCs such as this is a key strategy for me because my current role is situated within a non-academic and non-teaching specialist context, but is expected to contribute substantially to high-level teaching learning plans and strategies. Doing so without a strong support community of knowledgeable educators has been particularly challenging, and at times demoralising, in this time of isolation.

Patch #4: What Shaped Our Beliefs and Practices?

Practice is the common thread that holds the multiple dimensions of this chapter, as a research project, together. Here we define practice as recurring, situated actions informed by shared meanings (Schatzki, Knorr-Cetina & Savigny, 2001). Practice is critical in our daily roles and responsibilities in the university; we teach and learn with practitioners to develop knowing through doing.

Kate: My practice invites a personalised digital storied understanding of learning for both artist and audience in the pattern of a loop that action of reflection for/as learning provokes. This action of reflection creates an artist and audience loop where you can at once be making and doing as an artist, and then seeing as digital curator and audience in the action of presenting the digital portfolio online for audiences to participate in your practice. Over time, through the actions of design, develop, build, the artist "learns to learn" and the audience "learns to see" cyclically through reflection (Coleman, 2018). This digital pedagogical approach loops practice-based and practice-led methods through ongoing critical and creative reflection that continue to weave through my teaching, learning, and assessment.

Clare: In 2019, three weeks before the semester was due to start, our first-year cohort essentially doubled in size from an expected 36 students to 64. I learned during this time that I am very good at organising a timetable at short notice. However, my initial five-week introduction to dentistry program suffered due to a lack of planning and preparation. This process helped me realize that I can cope with significant change but that I need to focus on planning my content not to allow the teaching to suffer. What was most beneficial was the use of the CIQ. Each week, I used an online polling program to ask the students when they felt most engaged and most distant in their learning. I have collated a year's worth of feedback that allowed me to change my teaching in real time and influence how I shape the same subject in 2020.

Since entering isolation and rapidly shifting our teaching to an online space there has been lots of advice on what to do to make your teaching student-centred and inclusive. In 2019, long before COVID-19 was a thing, one of our Muslim students only ever recorded her reflective videos with a black screen. I criticised her and said how much I wanted to see her face to understand her emotions. She said that she takes off her scarf when she gets home and she didn't want to put it back on just for the videos. She thought her voice would be enough. And, of course it was. This specific incident and the COVID-19 crisis have helped to consolidate this sense of inclusivity and have changed my thinking around participation and engagement.

Brian: My practice in third space leadership (Whitechurch, 2008) within higher education has been heavily influenced by a series of negative and positive encounters and experiences. I reflect often on how these events have shaped my current and future aspirations to lead in this sector. How will I curate relationships and circumstances where highly qualified, experienced educational technologists will not be dismissed as "tech-support"? How will I ensure those within my sphere of influence are encouraged to apply their skills and knowledge in areas they are strong and enjoy? How will I foster relationships where the joy of co-creating with academic staff in curriculum and pedagogical reforms can be valued by all? How will I mentor and support others to believe in their potential, as I have been fortunate to experience from my mentor? My leadership practice has coalesced around accepting these experiences and undertaking to model behaviours I know to be congruent with my own wellbeing, as well as the psychological safety and intellectual growth of others. My practice and growth as an educator is currently somewhat lumpy as I move between personas of student, colleague, and employee. Each role affords different opportunities to apply, learn, and grow—naturally the roles of student and colleague lend themselves to more intellectual freedom and support creativity and taking risks. Writing this chapter is one such risk, which in its taking is providing new opportunities to connect and make meaning of my career in higher education to-date through this collaborative enterprise with Clare and Kate.

Patch #5: Where Did We Come From?

Feldman & Orlikowski (2011) identify three different dimensions that practice theory enables in a study of practice:

1. Empirical – how participants in an organisation such as a PLC act and how PLC is organised through routine and in-the-moment activities.

2. Theoretical – how the relations between participants' actions, the activities of the PLC, and workplace practices are understood, and how the dynamics of these change over time.

3. Philosophical – how practices are constitutive of the lived reality of the PLC and individual experiences of engaging in it.

As practitioners who learn with and from each other, this chapter is the beginning of these different dimensions outlined by Feldman and Orlikowski. Evidence of these three dimensions can be seen in our reflections below.

Clare: I was a mediocre student in secondary school, with a passion for learning, but I had an ambivalent attitude and the teachers couldn't see my potential either. I didn't get appropriate guidance for the subjects I should select, but I truly enjoyed my high school experience. I completed a traineeship as a dental assistant after finishing my secondary education. This program started me on the path of reform. I joined the Royal Australian Navy (RAN) as a Maritime Warfare Officer, navigating ships ranging from submarine support vessels, to tankers and a guided missile frigate. This short-lived experience changed my attitude about myself. I gained confidence and maturity and, forevermore, when everything seems like it is too hard, I can say to myself, "as a 19- year-old, I drove a warship; there's nothing I can't do."

The Navy life wasn't a long-term thing for me. So, I returned to study dental hygiene and as I described earlier, the significant influence of Prof. Marc Tennant would shape the next 20 years of my career. I didn't have a Bachelor's degree. At the time, dental hygiene was a two-year Associate Degree. So, I started on the long path of a Graduate Certificate Health Promotion (2006), a Master of Philosophy (Dentistry), (2012), and finally a Ph.D. (Medicine) (2019). These were all completed part-time while I had various clinical dental hygiene and sessional teaching roles. What stands out from all of this time is that I loved teaching, whether it was my patients about how to clean their teeth or students about how to look after their patients.

I never felt drawn to teaching. My paternal grandmother, who I adored, was a teacher of German, French, and music and would always take time to teach me bits and pieces, nothing formal. Many of my relatives, including a sister and brother, are teachers. But I never had a vocation or calling to be a teacher. Now, it is all I want to do. I have found my calling and hope to continue to grow and learn from my co-authors and colleagues to influence others in the same way I have been.

Kate: As a child, I grew up surrounded by art, books, and music. It is a lovely memory that I have of growing up in a world surrounded by knowledge, and art played a big role in that. I was the recipient of many art gifts growing up and I was lucky enough to have both creative and travel-loving parents who took us as a family to many cities and countries and always to each museum and gallery in those spaces. I also grew up knowing what artists did, and I knew that art teachers played a big role in developing, shaping, and supporting a young artist through their formative years. My mum and her art teacher friends were great mentors and impacted on their students' lives, and I knew all about each of my mum's students, their practice, and their struggles through my mum's stories of school. I have nice memories of winning an art prize when I was young and a moment in year seven that marked moments when I knew I could do art. I was a stereotypical art student in school, a challenging student and a pain for many of my teachers, including my art teacher, from whom I craved attention to direct and shape my practice. I wanted a knowledge of art and the art world, and I needed to know more about the stories. The lives artists led, where they lived, who they were friends with and what they learned. My mum was the mentor in this space and loved to tell the stories of the artmakers. She knew so many of the life stories and anecdotes of artmakers that she told through great stories.

My mum pushed me to make, remake, and often start over with my artworks, and, alongside the historical and theoretical discussions about art, she shaped the way that I later taught art. It wasn't until I was at art school becoming an art teacher myself that I realized that my mum had been such a catalyst for my career. She had, earlier, at the same institution, her visual arts knowledge directed by Eisner's (1968) domains of studio practice, criticism, history, and aesthetics. "Just wait until you get to art school" was a quip that my mum used to get me through the drudgery of high school that I loathed. My mum had been right, and when I got to art school in Sydney it was what I had been waiting for. I met people who loved art. Lived art. Were artmakers, art storytellers. I was able to experiment, play, make, create, and learn in this disciplinary art world in which I would later teach to my own students.

I was a high school art teacher for just over a decade before I embarked on a new educational journey in higher education. I loved teaching art and I loved high school art teaching and artful encounters with my artist-students. I was a hardworking, successful teacher and had the joy of working with tremendously talented young people in Australia and America. Looking back at that time is always filled with joy. I felt lucky to play a role in developing a love of art in my students and privileged to develop and extend their creativity and develop a sense of self as they learnt about history, culture, society, themselves, and the world through art. My art education journey began solidly. I only applied for art education courses when I finished high school. My first option was a Bachelor of Art Education degree at the City Art Institute in Paddington, New South Wales. I was lucky enough to be accepted into this four-year Bachelor of Art Education program at the City Art Institute in 1991, later to become The College of Fine Arts, University of New South Wales and be taught by the leaders, movers, and shakers of art education in Australia. As a product of the time, I was taught to question, challenge, and take nothing for granted as a postmodern artist, researcher, and future teacher at a time when curriculum change was rupturing the "known" in modernist classrooms, and my lecturers were those responsible for the development of a new syllabus in New South Wales. I learnt to make art, teach, and research amongst some of the best Australian painters, theorists, sculptors, writers, critics, and art educationalists.

Brian: I am the child of two secondary school teachers, so it is perhaps surprising that I have arrived in education as a third or fourth career. Reading was a very formative activity for me during childhood, and I think that gave me a good head start in primary school. Still, I recall being a bored, restless, and slightly resentful student at having to suffer the constraints of the uncomfortable classroom and the expectations of appropriate behaviors. The secondary system was something of a fight for survival. The narrow curriculum offered in a country secondary school perhaps didn't allow me to explore and identify areas of strength and interest. My resulting pathway through years eleven and twelve was shaped by a lack of competency in STEM, against the choice of studies in economics, accounting, and the then-emerging discipline of information technology, which were made through the influence of older siblings' pathways and perceived economic benefits associated with a future career in commerce. I don't recall a truly active consideration and outlet for my relatively powerful capacity for imagining and creating worlds—I couldn't paint or draw. Still, I did enjoy working with my hands using wood, clay, and metal. The perhaps obvious missed opportunity was a more humanities-based pathway, but for one reason or another, I and others didn't identify this as an option worth exploring.

I took double Bachelor's degrees in business and information technology, doing well in subjects with human, analytical, and logic elements, and less well in pure accounting and programming. I secured graduate employment with consulting giant KPMG, and it took me the next six years to figure out that I really didn't enjoy the working culture and the work itself. I allowed myself time to explore different interests, including fitness and acting. A year in a part-time acting school led to several revelations and discoveries, the most important of which was increased confidence to express myself and a prompt to begin creative writing for theatre. A number of years later, when I serendipitously secured employment at Federation University Australia, this creative experience helped drive a curriculum innovation where scaffolded digital video narratives were created and mapped to learning outcomes across the key undergraduate programs of nursing, business, and information technology. This idea has stayed with me and is the likely research pathway I will take at the conclusion of my Master of Education.

Patch #6: Defining Moments You as a Learner

PLCs tend to be mistaken for Communities of Practice (CoPs) (Lave & Wenger, 1991), yet there is an important distinction between these two communities and how they work. Professional learning communities are more formalised than CoPs, which grow organically around common interests and membership of a community. Critically, PLCs are held together through a common line of inquiry, with educators working purposefully to create and sustain the learning culture. This, in turn, relies on the contributions of all members of the community who work together towards a common learning goal with a view to improving student learning outcomes. This co-storying has opened space for us to see the common threads in our learner stories and why our PLC is so generative, reciprocal, and deeply connected to our practice.

Clare: The education in the dental assistant traineeship and the RAN was very structured. There was little flexibility; you learned a task you studied, passed a test, then moved on. In the Navy, I learned that I had an exceptional memory. Once a colleague told me how she studied, and I copied her; I was able to memorise anything. But I didn't always understand. I had a hard time passing the ship driving licence test. You needed to achieve 100% and as I didn't understand what ship navigation and driving was all about, having never done it before, I kept failing. Once I got to sea and was able to learn how these things all related to the actual job of ship-driving, I became the first woman in my class to get her Alpha (Warship) Ocean Navigation Certificate. This provides me with an important lesson: not all students learn in the same way, and memorising content does not equal content mastery. Reinforcement and application are required.

Kate: I think that our stories are who we are (Ellis & Bochner, 2000). The stories I carry of being and becoming a learner are threaded throughout my teaching, research, and assessment, and they guide my educational design. I am a storyteller and placemaker of stories and I learn through these placestories, always craving more knowledge and more know-how in relation to the sites and cites I am practicing within. They have shaped a person hungry for collaboration, social justice, and equity.

Brian: I think my defining moments as a learner have come in three waves. Firstly, the missed opportunity to channel my strengths and creative mind through primary and secondary school, and some particularly discouraging feedback from an English teacher, combined with my own economic motivators, probably led me into the tertiary system in disciplines I was ill-suited to. The second wave of learning occurred undertaking the Graduate Certificate Education (Tertiary Teaching), where I found myself excelling even compared to more highly qualified and experienced teachers. This was a strong signal to me to pursue this area of strength that allowed me to channel creativity and analytical logic toward very interesting and artistic outcomes. My current, and third wave of learning is occurring as I work with colleagues from different disciplines and begin to see the threads of intersection between education and other disciplines such as philosophy, architecture, sociology, psychology, and literature studies. The latter is a strong source of interest to pursue as an interdisciplinary research study to sustain my motivation to work towards completing a Ph.D.

Patch #7: Arcs and Themes in Our Experiences

Ways of knowing (epistemologies) are created, shared, organised, revised, and passed through communities of practice (Wenger, 1998) and PLCs alike. The limitation of this is that disciplinary practitioners can be constrained to discipline-specific epistemic beliefs, making it difficult to be aware of what these epistemic beliefs are and what effects they have on teaching and learning (Clarence, 2016). The link between epistemic beliefs and teacher practice can be explained through Bourdieu's (1984) concept of "habitus." Habitus (not to be confused with habit) is created through social and relational contexts, situated in norms and cultures. Habitus is not a fixed state of practice but underpins our everyday practices and helps to account for how individuals and communities become caught up in specific patterns of practice—without necessarily intending to do so and without necessarily being able to identify the consequences of doing so. Habitus helps researchers to understand the complex, multi-dimensionality of practice and why shifts in unhelpful patterns of practice can be so difficult to make and sustain. Arguably, developing teachers' critical awareness of epistemic beliefs and their work is a crucial point of intervention for sustained improvements in teaching practice. This co-storied chapter has created the conditions for us to challenge our epistemic beliefs and practices through the formalising of our interdisciplinary professional learning community.

When practitioners from a range of disciplines come together, they bring a range of epistemological beliefs and practices that stem from the disciplinary cultures within which they practice (McNair, Davitt & Batten, 2015). Professional collaborations that cut across disciplinary boundaries foreground the existence of different epistemic beliefs and bring into view how these impact teaching and learning for the future. We know that learning and teaching leadership required for a new higher education space requires cross-cutting capabilities to allow for disciplinary knowledge that is transformative across disciplinary boundaries (McWilliam, Hearn & Haseman, 2008).

Brian: The common arc in my experience to date is one of discovering where my strengths lie through a process of taking risks, i.e., leaving unsatisfying jobs and careers and moving towards those that fulfil me creatively and align more closely with my values. My journey in higher education has been mixed, as depending on context, my strengths and skills as an educator have not always been welcomed; so, to some extent, escaping the box that others sought to put me in has been important for me and necessitated a move to a new role and institution. I continue to see and feel that I am on a growth journey within the third space in academia while learning to navigate the professional and academic staff divide. A key part of this journey is finding and aligning myself to colleagues that value my different perspective and experience, such as Kate and Clare. This is also helping me overcome occasional feelings of illegitimacy and a lack of sense of belonging within a sector that I have now been part of for more than six years.

Kate: For me, it's all about people, persistence, determination, creativity, and strength. My doctoral research offered me space to reify these arcs and write those stories. It also gave me time to see the narrative threads and draw them together to create a new story for other changemakers and leaders in education who lead, but not from the front, but from within. This is why finding my people has become such an important aspect of and for learning for me. Just as my mum suggested, "Just wait 'til you get to art school," she was telling me to wait until I found the people who would support and strengthen my learning opportunities.

Clare: Evolution and change. Higher education provides educators with this unique opportunity to evolve curricula, assessment, and delivery each time a course is delivered. Things that don't work this year can be adapted and tried again. In cohort-style degrees, where the students spend the whole three years together, they can evolve with you and influence change; this is powerful. And as Kate says, finding your people helps you drive this change as well. Without Brian and Kate, I could not have evolved my teaching in such a meaningful way, in such a short time.

Patch #8: What Roles Have Our Various Social Identities Played in Shaping Our Educational Experience?

"Place and identity are inextricably bound to one another. The two are co-produced as people come to identify with where they live, shape it, however modestly, and are in turn shaped by their environments, creating distinctive environmental autobiographies, the narratives we hold from the memories of those spaces and places that shaped us" (Gieseking & Mangold, 2014, p.73). We know each because of our work, but we know how each other works because of our practices.

Clare: I have spent 20 years progressing through different levels of education from the TAFE sector through to finally reaching the end goal of a Ph.D. I have completed four higher education programs at four different universities. I have grown throughout these programs gaining more independence at each different level. I feel this diversity in my own education allows me to understand the students and how they feel when they start their program. The Graduate Certificate of University Teaching (GCUT) I recently completed has probably been the most enlightening. It allowed me to see how different educators approach tasks and how much detail and support students need.

Brian: I have learned from being a consultant, an IT professional, a leader, an educator, and being a student, firstly in the Graduate Certificate Education, and now in the Master of Education. Because of my willingness to take risks and move between employers, change industries, and embrace previously unexplored areas of my education, I've found I am attached to a specific professional identity. In some ways this is helpful, as it allows me to be more authentic in my interactions with others, and to be able to admit where I do not have existing knowledge or experience. Socially, this means I've moved through circles of very different kinds of people that perhaps struggled to get a read on exactly where I was coming from, and where I was going to. I probably enjoy my identity as a student most of all, as there are limited or no expectations of what you should know—this gives me a great deal of freedom to safely explore a range of new knowledge and assimilate it into my professional and personal identities, which continue to evolve.

Kate: I have spent a lifetime in education. I left high school for university and have been a high school teacher, art educator, and academic, so my identities are all tangled and intertwined. I am a learner, teacher, mother, partner, sister, daughter, friend, and other things in between, all at once. My identity is woven. As an active researcher in my communities of practice, I am privileged to have the opportunity to speak and ask questions of the leaders, innovators, and disruptors in education in person, or through social media. I feel very honoured that these seminal thinkers share so much with me. I live in several professional learning communities as a researcher and practitioner, in the digital educational technology space, in the art space, and as an educational researcher. I love this global learning community of practice that allows me to live in the spaces between art, research, and education, "locating researchers in a contiguous dynamic of collaborative practice" (Fendler, 2013, p.789). This ongoing discourse with the self, changemakers, and innovative educationalists is a powerful part of who I am and how I approach education.

Patch #9: The Contexts that Shape Our Learning Experiences

"Exploring the relationship between place and identity deepens our understandings of identity formation and the role of place in social and psychological development. The bonds between place and identity can influence social formations, cultural practices, and political actions" (Gieseking, Mangold,

Katz, Low & Saegert, 2014, p.73). They also help us to see how we are affected by those learning experiences and can affect the learning experiences of others.

Brian: Being able to shift my context frequently through different professions and careers has freed me from previous self and situationally imposed constraints on my thinking. A purposeful move twelve months ago to escape a context that was constraining my intellectual and career growth into a new work and study context has accelerated my development. The new working and social connections this move has facilitated are providing frequent opportunities to learn from colleagues, new friends, and my student peer group. Acceptance of my academic mindset in these new contexts and social roles has also been validating, confidence building, and has ultimately affirmed my decision to change my context to continue to learn and grow. Our current state of isolation is particularly challenging for me. Having made these new connections, I now find myself physically separated from these new people, places, and the support they provide. Shared projects such as this provide a welcome chance to recharge my intellectual batteries and have highlighted the importance to me of social connections built and maintained around shared academic interests.

Clare: I completed my Graduate Certificate of Health Promotion as a distance learning program. I found this challenging at the time. In 2006, I realize that online learning was not what it is now with smartphones and tablets. I was unsure about teaching in the online space. However, after listening to the amazing online educators in the Teaching in Higher Education podcast and completing my Graduate Certificate of University Teaching, I realise how valuable it is to give students an opportunity to learn and study in their own time. Dental programs are very full-time, and any opportunity to allow students space from the clinic and time away from university should be embraced.

Kate: Site is an important aspect of my work, as a life-wide learner, as an artist, as a researcher, and as a teacher. The contextual nature of learning is site-specific; the site shapes the learning experience, and I have always felt the impact of site on my practice. In 2016, I had a solo show for my doctoral artworks in Blackheath in the New South Wales, Blue Mountains. This site holds a special place in my heart and the show was held here because it's a place that has shaped my learning experience. Blackheath is a town that I have found myself returning to since childhood for family, work, study, relaxation, and writing. For a week over Easter 2016, I curated my first solo show at Virgin Walls, a small gallery near my family mountain home. I worked on this exhibition for over a year with work developed over the last three to four years. This show was held to create a space for critical reflection in a physical site of cultural importance, a turn to open and present the turn to praxis. My work intertwined and, woven from the digital, pedagogical, and theoretical, is hidden, often invisible.

Blackheath is the top of the Blue Mountains, the highest point on the topographical map, and has its own weather pattern. You can drive to the towns on either side of Blackheath and encounter very different temperatures and climates. It is a beautiful place, a town that many artists have come to flourish in, and has a history of artisans and writers living in the community. I had gone to Blackheath every Easter since I can remember, give or take a few years as an adult when I lived overseas or now, in a pandemic, when there are state-based travel bans. It is a beautiful town where my great-grandfather lived with his family; my grandfather was born there, as well. We still have this home in our family and my parents live here. The gallery where my Ph.D. research was curated is located a street away.

Patch #10: The Social/Cultural/Political Sphere that Shapes Our Educational Experiences

"Places do not have intrinsic meanings and essences; they simply have meanings that are more conventional and "appropriate." ...[The] meanings of place are created through practice." (Creswell, 1996, p.17) and enabled by the educational experiences that give us the power to utilise our agency in them.

Clare: I have always felt that I shaped my own experiences independent of society. However, I realise now how naïve this is. I come from a middle-class white background and inherently have the privilege associated with that. I teach a wide variety of cultures, new Australians and International students, and high-achieving local students. I am very aware of ensuring that I teach with inclusivity and try to ensure that all students are safe with an understanding of their support.

Kate: I am a White, well-educated cisgendered woman, a product of a post-modern school education, post-structural university education, and I chose to practice within a bundle of methods, to teach, learn, and research in the liminal spaces and not be bordered and bound by methodologies and methods that have only served a few. I am intrigued by human and non-human relations, drawn to the digital humanities and social science research that interrogates the spaces between the self and selves. My research has always been interested in the digital and visual as a socio-cultural political site, and how humans design, develop and curate their identities. I research in the space of identity and creativity, particularly how fluid and multiple identities can be understood through the digital humanities, arts, and social sciences, with a focus on art education. Using autoethnography here personalised the research and enables a connection between sites. This has been shaped by knowing I am an artist. I have always drawn, and I am the child of an artist, educator, and storyteller, and an entrepreneur, accountant, and computer buff. Together they created a home that was artful, innovative, creative, supportive, and hard-working. Living the life created between parents like this, my sisters and I were treated to a life of books, travel, art galleries, computer games, imaginative and artistic play, and stories. I was an art kid and always drew, coloured, and wrote poems and songs—this shaped the way I experienced education, often not by me but by those around me.

Brian: I have certainly experienced many awakenings in recent years concerning understanding the advantages of being a white, middle-class male child of educators with tertiary qualifications. Working at Federation University Australia (FedUni) provided numerous opportunities to empathise with its cohort of largely regional, low socioeconomic, and disproportionately first-in-family students and understand the particular challenges these groups face in terms of accessing and engaging with what must seem a very alien environment—one where the inhabitants of that environment speak and write an almost entirely different language. The process of providing staff and student support for learning technology was continually referencing the impact of teaching and learning practice on students, their wellbeing, and their potential for success. This immersion combined with very strong leadership and mentoring around the literally life-changing benefits of education has allowed me to fully understand the many things I have taken for granted. I feel I have brought this empathy for the student with me to a university far more at ease with privilege, but also going through its own strategic awakening that cares for students, their wellbeing, and belonging is equally as important as academic achievement. Ironically, the mission of the FedUni learning and teaching strategy was to utilise blended, flexible, and online modes of delivery as a means to provide access to education that might otherwise be not possible to its cohort—something that is now very front of mind for all of us in this new COVID-19 world.

Patch #11: Learner Struggles

Woven through our success stories and love of education, are stories of challenge and confrontation as learners. Just as we connected over our digital leadership, we also have interwoven stories of a love of learning, a joy of knowing, and a passion to know more across our learner journeys. Like many colleagues in higher education, we have learned for many years, gathering and gaining new ways of knowing, doing, and being across credentials. We have had many discussions about our learner struggles, but we've chosen to leave this patch unfinished, still to be neatly stitched in place.

Brian: I did feel a sense of illegitimacy completing a tertiary teaching qualification as a non-teacher. One aspect that was a struggle, and continues to challenge at times, is the positing of applied knowledge and creative ideas in the context of a broader and evidence-based theoretical framework—in essence, developing a more scholarly approach to complement a lot of creative ideas and intuition. For example, I am currently working on a university-level strategic paper to help position ePortfolio practice to align with actual teaching and learning strategies and our institution's academic culture. Intuitively this makes perfect sense to me, and on a practice level, I have observed, designed, and been a participant as a learner within successfully executed ePortfolio pedagogy. However, the challenge of aligning the theoretical canon of ePortfolio literature to create the conditions for ePortfolio praxis with the stated strategic aims of a prestigious university as developed by leading education scholars has been daunting. Being able to turn to Kate for advice on approaching this challenge is reassuring and will ensure that the product of my labour hits the target instead of a possible near-miss of working on my own. At times I struggle with the methodical nature of academic writing, but more recently I have begun to get a better handle on how to write both creatively while sustaining a novel argument supported by the literature. One recent example was to use George Orwell's *1984* to sustain an inquiry into student resistance to surveillant learning environments.

Clare: Throughout my secondary education, I had no idea that I could be a good student, that I had a fantastic memory, and that I just needed the right teacher to identify my strengths. The past few months of struggles throughout the COVID-19 classroom have highlighted how our traditionally face-to-face dental program has essentially drip-fed the information to students sequentially throughout the semester. Our students had to adapt very quickly to a new way of learning, so many struggled. I was able to empathise with all of them. I took a long time to learn how to learn. My students were thrown into the deep end and had to adjust in a matter of days. This experience will feed into how I design my teaching from now on, ensuring I consider how hard it is to learn new things and how good teachers focus on making their teaching accessible to all.

Kate: I find this idea of struggle interesting, as we are obviously very successful learners. We have very different educational backgrounds and disciplinary spaces that we inhabit. This patch is less connected than others because what connects us is our leadership, values, and beliefs about education that need further exploration. As learners. I am one of those annoying talkers. So, my struggles as a learner are lifelong. Needing to know, with a desire to know, but often annoying others around me and the teacher, of whom I asked many questions. I am always on the edge of wanting to know and do more, yearning for ways of being and understanding more about the worlds around me but thinking I should be quiet, or being asked to be quiet.

I think what you can see from our story here is that, like many successful learners, we are self-regulated learners. We have the self-efficacy to persevere, despite challenges and frustrations.

Patch #12: The Resources, Supports, People and Strategies that Help Us Overcome Struggles

As a group of colleagues who don't work with each other day-to-day, co-writing and codesigning a co-story was enabled by our digital connections as a PLC. Our stories of the communities we have connected to are common across our learner and learning stories. We have common communities of practice in our institution, and digital networks and nodes play a role here. "Having one's social identity as a group member activates a sense of belongingness and raises one's self-worth" (Burke & Stets, 2009, p.121) and finding your people aids in feeling like you matter and what you have to share matters. It is in communities of practice and professional learning spaces that we have learned to thrive.

Brian: I do find my level of faith in myself to overcome struggles does fluctuate with some of the professional tasks I undertake in this nebulous third space. Due to the professional and organisational positioning of my role within the university, there is quite a limited immediate support network of educators in my orbit. The irony is there is a wealth of knowledge and expertise in this place; so the formation of PLCs such as this one, where I can informally connect and collaborate with colleagues, is increasingly important to sustain the sense that I do belong to a community of educators within the University of Melbourne. I've been fortunate to have an exceptionally supportive mentor for the past six years who, while I was within her portfolio, was an empowering leader and excellent role model—sustaining that relationship is important to me in helping to orient my career and maintain a sense of purpose in the tertiary sector.

Clare: Being empowered by experience in the Navy that, regardless of your intellectual ability, hard work and determination do pay off and enable you to reach your greatest potential. So, like Brian, I rely a lot on myself to find a way through difficult situations and challenging circumstances. I am always busy; I achieve a lot in my day, and, like Kate, I am also still wanting to learn and understand more, asking so many questions. Being a part of this PLC and other PLCs like Academic Twitter has made me feel included, accepted, and offer an alternative resource for "bumping" ideas off and collaborating. This has been crucial for me, this opportunity to network and collaborate has helped me shape my teaching and reassured me that I am on the right path. I have been successful in meeting my goals of transforming the dental hygiene curriculum in our school. I could never have achieved this without the support of my PLCs.

Kate: We have explored our different worlds across this story, and mine is driven by my practice and identity as an artist that continues to provide me with a sense of possibility, to be resourceful, and to feel supported by people around me. Through my practice as an artist, I have found my people, and our shared practices become the resources, supports, people, and strategies that help me overcome struggles.

During the pandemic, we have established ways of connecting to support us as we lead, teach, learn, and research away from the university. While Clare and Kate have been designing learning and teaching on the ground for our students in new spaces, Brian has been leading digital change and transformation differently. When we catch up, it is the telling of this story that has kept us close, as we share our personal digital stories; laughing, questioning, and recognising our struggles and achievements. We cross paths in our digital networks on Twitter and have created a shared space in Microsoft Teams that has provided us a site to strengthen our partnership through collaboration, the mutual sharing of ideas, and belonging. To build and develop the capabilities of belonging is an important factor in our PLC; belonging is built on trust and respect and has empowered us to contribute to and connect to networks and learning spaces within the wider university ecosystem.

Patch #13: Looking Back, We are Most Proud as a Student when...

Writing autoethnography is personal, performative, reflective, and embodied. We live within our stories; they are our experiences, always tangled in the histories of others, but ours to recollect and choose to share. Looking back together has allowed us to see why we found each other in our careers that may not have crossed.

Brian: I am proud of my ability to quickly apply theoretical concepts to applied practice and to engage with the process of reflection in a way that leads to meaning-making and intellectual growth. More recently, I've been proud of assessment tasks I've completed where I have been able to take risks and find new and interesting ways to intersect creative endeavors and discipline knowledge in the educational context—these have been rewarded for their novel, creative, and scholarly merit. In a personal reflective essay, I was able to ground a long-standing interpersonal workplace conflict within the scholarly literature of leadership while invoking Sylvia Plath's Fig Tree as a metaphor for the personal costs of a lack of assertiveness and use a Derek Walcott poem to illustrate notions of assertiveness with self-care. I was also able to use the creative writerly part of my brain to develop digital performance poetry that captured the suffocating aesthetic of being a teacher and being a student within surveillant learning environments.

Clare: …I was able to submit a finished Ph.D. thesis that I was proud of. I had more obstacles than anyone would have liked during this degree: a torn ankle, two unexpected pregnancies (and two gorgeous boys), and then I simultaneously fractured both arms. Finally, I started my full-time role at the University of Melbourne, still needing to complete the write-up. It highlighted that I am resilient, and I can do anything I set my mind to. As an undergraduate student, I am still most proud that I nearly achieved a perfect score for the subject taught by Prof. Tennant, the inspiration behind my academic career planning.

Kate: I am proud of my resilience to design and then follow my own path as a learner. My earliest memories of learning are framed by questions, questioning, and a desire to seek out people who knew or might know more. During my senior years of high school art, I called Australian artist Brett Whiteley on the phone to ask questions about his practice as part of my research. I still do this today and contact many scholars, artists, and leaders in their fields to talk about their work and to hear from the inside what the stories are. I am known to connect with colleagues worldwide via Twitter and then track them down to ask questions and develop a connection. I have always known that knowledge and education are political; it is both a power and a privilege to have this access and be empowered to harness it.

Patch #14: What We are Surprised or Concerned About

> A precondition for doing anything to strengthen our practice and improve a school is the existence of a collegial culture in which professionals talk about practice, share their craft knowledge, and observe and root for the success of one another. Without these in place, no meaningful improvement—no staff or curriculum development, no teacher leadership, no student appraisal, no team teaching, no parent involvement, and no sustained change—is possible. (Barth, 2006, p. 13)

Through this co-storied work, we come to know practice and see how colleagues support us to grow as practitioners.

Brian: I am most surprised by how close a fit education was to my existing attributes of creativity, interest in people, and analytical approaches to problems. I am continually surprised when I encounter resistance to student-centred teaching practices; and, like Kate, I find troubling the slow adoption of hybrid pedagogies to facilitate more innovative, flexible, and accessible education. Undoubtedly, the current crisis we find ourselves in will be something of a turning point, with the new normal being a significant step-change. I am excited and worried about this opportunity: excited by the possibilities and worried that those best positioned to lead and influence change may not have a strong and participatory voice.

Clare: I am surprised that until recently, our program had no online options whatsoever. The learning management system was used as a content repository rather than a teaching opportunity. My one experiment with an online learning module in 2019 was so successful, and our students have been asking for us to modernise for so long. I am concerned that if we don't heed the lessons of the 2020 pandemic and rapidly adapt our teaching, we will be left behind. Academics used to teaching long lectures face-to-face are not prepared to make this change to blended or online learning design. With Brian and Kate's support and advice, I have been making changes over the past two years to take my teaching online. I identified the need to bring our curriculum forward into the online space, so many colleagues have reached that realisation yet.

Kate: I am concerned by the slow nature of change in a world that needs changemakers and leaders in innovation, and this began for me in high school. Learning for me is political and now in this space of isolation I am more concerned about digital teaching and its openings, but also many closures to innovation and imagination. Now as an educator, the decolonisation of the curriculum, schools, and education is an important facet of my teaching and I am concerned this is not more widespread. I am concerned by the state of the climate, xenophobia, political unrest, inequality and racism—this drives me every day.

Patch #15: If We Met Our Teachers from Across Our Lives Now, We Would Tell Them How to Better Support Us as Learners.

Clare: That not every student learns in the same way. Take time to get to know your students individually and find out what makes them respond well and thrive. It is worth the effort because they will reward you over and over with their results.

Kate: That "knowledge is relational, dependent on contexts and philosophy, and cannot be separated from an understanding of the self and its multiple embedded identities" (Suominen Guyas, 2008, p. 25) and that sharing, telling, and re-telling stories is learning and teaching.

Brian: Encourage strengths toward creative expression in writing and performance, encourage wider/broader educational context, and keep criticism to a minimum as it stays with you.

Research has steadily converged on the importance of strong teacher learning communities for teacher growth and commitment, suggesting their potential contribution to favorable student outcomes. . . Effective professional development might thus be judged by its capacity for building (and building on) the structures and values, as well as the intellectual and leadership resources, of professional community (Little, 2006, p. 2).

Kate: Co-storying and co-laboring are important pedagogical effects in higher education. Just asking Clare and Brian to have this digital autoethnographic conversation with me was a pedagogical and political act. "Becoming pedagogical is an active, living inquiry whereby teachers are in a continuous process of inquiry, engagement, and learning as pedagogues" (Irwin & Leggo, 2013, p.4). In this *becoming pedagogical* space, we had time and space to look inwards and then outwards at ourselves and see why finding your people is such an affective position to take in higher education. We are now informed by each other's stories, insights and cites and can see and notice the common threads in our practices.

Brian: I have noticed that I am continuing to develop my understanding of the academic role even after more than six years in the sector. Third space[r]s may be highly innovative and effective educators, but lack the time and scholarly training to publish and research their practice. I can see the attributes and job responsibilities needed to be effective third space leadership inherently conflict with some aspects of developing an academic profile and persona. This constrains the growth, and potential acceptance, of third spacers by their academic colleagues. For me, co-writing this paper is laying the foundation for ongoing partnerships with Kate and Clare and providing me with a practice model to continue expanding my scholarly learning at the intersection of educational theory with other disciplines. Importantly, this experience has provided me with further context and empathy for the various struggles, power dynamics, and pressures associated with the academic role that is the lived daily experience of Clare and Kate.

Clare: I was recently awarded a Learning and Teaching Initiative Grant. Just being able to put this application together with my colleagues has been affirming. We are all from very different backgrounds and have quite different roles in the university but have collaborated closely to apply for funding to implement our ePortfolio program and also to complete this work. This process and this co-story have also highlighted how far I have come in just two years of full-time academia. A large part of this growth and affirmation is thanks to the people whom I am collaborating with on this application and paper. They have confirmed for me that change is crucial, being able to adapt and to work towards your goals will pay off, even in the face of opposition.

Stitching the Patches Together and Looking Forward to Future Practice

Kate: As Holman Jones, Adams, and Ellis (2013) tell us, autoethnographic characteristics are "(1) purposefully commenting on/critiquing of culture and cultural practices, (2) making contributions to existing research, (3) embracing vulnerability with purpose, and (4) creating a reciprocal relationship with audiences in order to compel a response" (p. 22). Doing a co-storied autoethnography with colleagues is a new opportunity to co-locate your pedagogies, principles, politics, and practices. Now told as a cluster of performed stories we can see how we connect and relate to each other within our institution.

Brian: I am continually reflecting on the development of leadership strategies and attributes for the third space specific to leading and influencing academic colleagues while educating educators about the value of third space professionals. I'm also selfishly looking forward to sustaining this PLC (and developing others) as an important personal and professional support as I navigate the complexities and challenges of developing a more senior and impactful career in this quasi-academic third space. I also see the PLC as an integral model to thrive and survive the next phase of my educational journey as a higher degree research student.

Clare: Brian thinks it is selfish to look forward to our PLC continuing to grow, but I see it as necessary and exciting. I feel as though we have just started on this journey and there is such a long way to go; there is just so much potential. As Kate says, we have nurtured this small cross discipline PLC and we now need to increase our network to share and inspire innovative teaching and learning across our institution.

We have co-written a performative and embodied place story as *pedagogical becoming* to explore the complexities of digital learning, teaching, assessment, and research in higher education. We are a trio of colleagues not unlike others who find themselves in professional learning communities after being told they should meet each other. We did follow up on these meetings, and now collectively, as digital thought leaders, we have looked inwards, outwards, back and forth to see why and how we collaborate. Together, we have found ways to open opportunities for re-thinking and re-positioning digital learning, teaching, assessment in our programs and communities of practice/s as a professional learning community. As Louis, Leithwood, Wahlstrom, & Anderson (2010) state,

> Professional community amounts to more than just support; it also includes shared values, a common focus on student learning, collaboration in the development of curriculum and instruction, and the purposeful sharing of practices …. the presence of a professional community appears to foster collective learning of new practices—where there is principal leadership (p. 42).

In our co-storied dialogue, you can see that we each hold very different values, beliefs, memories and stories that overlap and entangle, intertwine, and relate, and when woven together have offered new sites and sights of educational leadership. We have as the editors citing Bateson (1989) noted felt the effect of storytelling that "is fundamental to the human search for meaning" (p. 34). This critical autoethnographic co-storied paper is curated to perform the connections we have felt as affect through a co-designed collection of threads within our enacted PLC. *Being digital* connects the stories woven here and is a thread we have drawn together like a patchwork from our textural sites of practice to co-reflect, co-write and co-inquire as co-laborers.

References

Alexander, R. (2001). Border Crossings: Towards a comparative pedagogy. *Comparative Education.* 37. 507-523. 10.1080/03050060120091292.

Allen, B., Caple, H., Coleman, K. & Nguyen, T. (2012). Creativity in practice: Social media in higher education. Paper presented at *ASCILITE: Future Challenges-Sustainable Futures Conference*, Wellington, New Zealand.

Bain, K. (2004). *What the best college teacher's do.* Cambridge Mass: Harvard University Press.

Barth, R. (2006). Improving relationships inside the schoolhouse. *Educational Leadership*, *63*(6), 8–13.

Biggs, J. (2003). Aligning teaching for constructing learning. *Higher Education Academy, 1*(4). Retreived from:https://www.researchgate.net/profile/John_Biggs3/publication/255583992_Aligning_Teaching_for_Constructing_Learning/links/5406ffe70cf2bba34c1e8153.pdf

Bolton, R. (1986). People skills. Simon and Schuster

Brookfield, S. (2015). *The skillful teacher: on technique, trust and responsiveness in the classroom.* New York. Harvard University Press.

Broton, K. M., & Goldrick-Rab, S. (2018). Going Without: An Exploration of Food and Housing Insecurity among Undergraduates. *Educational Researcher, 47*(2), 121–133. Accessed: 21 December 2019. Retrieved from https://search-ebscohost-com.ezp.lib.unimelb.edu.au/login.aspx?direct=true&db=eric&AN=EJ1171368&site=eds-live&scope=site

Buchan, J. (2017). Learning without boundaries: Reconceptualising the curriculum in Innovative Learning Environments. In Imms, W., Mahat, M. (Eds.), *Transitions Australasia: What is needed to help teachers better utilize space as one of their pedagogic tools?*, (47-55). http://hdl.handle.net/11343/198087

Coleman, K.S. (2017). An a/r/tist in wonderland: Exploring identity, creativity and digital portfolios as a/r/tographer, Ph.D. dissertation, Melbourne Graduate School of Education, University of Melbourne, Australia, 2017. Retrieved from http://www.artographicexplorations.com

Coleman, K. (2018). Mapping the nomadic journey of becoming in digital portfolios: Digital way finding in art education [online]. *Australian Art Education, 39*(1): 91-106. ISSN: 1032-1942.

de Rond, M. (2014). The structure of serendipity. *Culture and Organization*, 20(5), 342-358.

Eisner, E. (1968). Curriculum Making for the Wee Folk: Stanford University's Kettering Project, *Studies in Art Education, 9*(3): 45-56.

Ellis, C., Adams, T. E. & Bochner, A.P. (2010). Autoethnography: An Overview [40 paragraphs]. *Forum Qualitative Sozialforschung / Forum: Qualitative Social Research, 12*(1), Art. 10, http://nbn-resolving.de/urn:nbn:de:0114-fqs1101108.

Ellis, C. & Bochner, A. (2000). Autoethnography, personal narrative, reflexivity: Researcher as subject. In Denzin, N.K. & Lincoln, Y.S. (Eds*.), Handbook of Qualitative Research* (2nd ed., pp.733-768). Thousand Oaks, Ca: Sage.

Fendler, Rachel. (2013). Becoming-Learner. Coordinates for Mapping the Space and Subject of Nomadic Pedagogy. *Qualitative Inquiry, 19.* 786-793. 10.1177/1077800413503797.

Foucault, M. (1982). The Subject and Power. Critical Inquiry, *8*(4), 777-795.

Freire, P. (2000). *Pedagogy of the Oppressed.* New York: Continuum.

Hattie, J. (2015, June). What works best in education: The politics of collaborative expertise.

Holman Jones, S. (2016). Living Bodies of Thought, The "Critical" in Critical Autoethnography, *Qualitative Inquiry, 22*(4): 228–237.

Jacobs, MA. (2015). By Their Pupils They'll Be Taught: Using Critical Incident Questionnaire as Feedback. *Journal of Invitational Theory and Practice, 21,* 9-22.

Jones, S., Harvey, M., & Lefoe, G. (2014). A conceptual approach for blended leadership for tertiary education institutions. *Journal of Higher Education Policy and Management, 36*(4), 418-429.

Laing, J. (2019). *Teaching and learning in higher education.* West Virginia University Press. Available at: https://wvupressonline.com/series/teaching_learning_higher_education

Laing, J. (2016). *Small teaching: everyday lessons from the science of learning.* San Francisco, CA: Jossey-Bass.

Little, J. W. (2006). Professional community and professional development in the learning-centered school. Washington, DC: National Education Association. Retrieved from www.nea.org/assets/docs/HE/mf_pdreport.pdf

Louis, K. S., Leithwood, K, Wahlstrom, K. L., & Anderson, S. E. (2010). Learning from leadership project: Investigating the links to improved student learning. Final report of research findings. Retrieved from www.wallacefoundation.org/knowledge-center/schoolleadership/key-research/Documents/Investigating-the-Links-to-Improved-Student-Learning.pdf

Meusburger, P., Funke, J., & Wunder, E. (2009). Introduction: The spatiality of creativity. In *Milieus of Creativity* (pp. 1-10). Springer, Dordrecht.

Morris, SM. & Stommel, J. (2018). *An Urgency of Teachers: the work of the critical digital pedagogy*. Hybrid Pedagogy. Available at: https://urgencyofteachers.com/

Morrissey, M. S. (2000). Professional learning communities: An ongoing exploration. Accessed at www.sedl.org/pubs/catalog/cha45.html on November 3, 2015.

Oblinger, D.G. & Grajek, S. (2013). From Disruption to Design: How Technology Can Help Transform Higher Education, *TIAA-CREF Institute white paper*. Retrieved from https://www.tiaa-crefinstitute.org/public/pdf/from-disruption-to-design.pdf

Schatzki, Theodore R & Knorr-Cetina, K. (Karin) & Savigny, Eike von (2001). *The practice turn in contemporary theory.* Routledge, London; New York.

Schunk, D. H. (2008). Constructivist theory. Learning Theories: An Educational Perspective. Upper Saddle River, New Jersey: Pearson Merrill Prentice Hall.

Siemens, G. (2005). Connectivism: A learning theory for the digital age. *International Journal of Instructional Technology and Distance Learning*, 2(1), 3-10.

Sinclair, A. (2007). Leadership for the disillusioned: moving beyond myths and heroes to leading that liberates. Allen & Unwin.

Stachowiak, B. (2019). *Teaching in Higher Ed* podcast. Available at https://teachinginhighered.com/episodes/

Stîngu, M. (2012). Reflexive practice in teacher education: facts and trends. *Procedia – Social and Behavioural Sciences*. Vol 33, Pp 617-621.

Stommel, J. (2014) 'Critical Digital Pedagogy: A Definition'., *Hybrid Pedagogy*. Retrieved from http://web.archive.org/web/20150325002121/http://www.hybridpedagogy.com/journal/critical-digital-pedagogy-definition/

Swan, K., Garrison, D. R. & Richardson, J. C. (2009). A constructivist approach to online learning: the Community of Inquiry framework. In Payne, C. R. (Ed.), *Information Technology and Constructivism in Higher Education: Progressive Learning Frameworks*. Hershey, PA: IGI Global, 43-57.

Tanner, C. K., & Lackney, J. A. (2006). History of Educational Architecture (Chapter 1). In Tanner & Lackney, Educational Facilities Planning: Leadership, Architecture, and Management. Pearson Allyn and Bacon.

Tyack, D., & Tobin, W. (1994). The" Grammar" of Schooling: Why Has It Been So Hard to Change?. *American Educational Research Journal*, 453-479.

Vescio, V., Ross, D., & Adams, A. (2008). A review of research on the impact of professional learning communities on teaching practice and student learning. *Teaching and Teacher Education*, 24, 80–91.

Weiss, A. (2007). Creating the Ubiquitous Classroom: Integrating Physical and Virtual Learning Spaces. *International Journal of Learning*, 14(3), 77–84.

Whitchurch, C. (2008). Shifting identities and blurring boundaries: The emergence of third space professionals in UK higher education. *Higher Education Quarterly*, 62(4), 377-396.

Whitchurch, C. (2009). The rise of the blended professional in higher education: a comparison between the United Kingdom, Australia and the United States. *Higher Education*, 58(3), 407-418.

Wright, S. & Coleman, K. (2019). studioFive—A Site for Teaching, Research and Engagement in Australian Arts Education. In Chee-Hoo Lum and Ernst Wagner (Eds.), *Arts Education and Cultural Diversity*. Singapore: Springer.

18

A Vet's Journey Out of the Cave

Plato's Allegory of the Cave in *The Republic*

Rohini Roopnarine

> *"It is the task of the enlightened not only to ascend to learning and to see the good but to be willing to descend again to those prisoners and to share their troubles and their honors."*

Autobiographical Perspective

Plato, in his famous allegory of the cave in *The Republic*, reminds us of the struggle to think critically to question our beliefs about reality. Personal beliefs, assumptions, values, and social and cultural influences impact one's approach to teaching and learning (Brown & Parker, 2007). Learning about and engaging in the process of reflective practice has led me to consider the impact of my experiences on my current teaching approach (Alvine, 2001). Through my reflections, I have realized that social and cultural context played a significant role in my learning processes, commencing with primary school education and culminating in my most recent doctoral pursuits in higher education. This realization happened in our doctoral modules, through the learning logs—though I felt frustrated at the time to have to complete those reflections, the process helped me truly understand my learning process. Alvine advocates that in reflecting upon their own childhood teaching experiences, educators can identify what tools used by their favourite teachers precipitated their own interest in learning, such as teaching projects, art displays, and memorable books. Alvine expands on this, explaining that by drawing on our lived experiences as learners, we as educators can more meaningfully embed theoretical frameworks in our teaching practice. Alvine equally mentions the negative impact that an ineffective or ill-guided teacher can have on the learning process. Reflections on what did not work for us as students can be equally as powerful.

Through my dissertation research, I was forced to engage in metacognitive reflexivity (Archer, 2003). This process led me to consider how my values align or differ with organizational values with implications for informing change. Reflective practice has enabled me to remain mindful of my biases as an educator and how that influences my assumptions about institutional issues and the findings that have emerged from my research. I began to evaluate my values, cultural and educational background influenced my perspectives on teaching and leadership. Additionally, the peer learning that occurred markedly increased my learning power, as colleagues shared perspectives on group discussions that led me to learn from their own experiences. Here, I share my educational autobiography and teaching philosophy as I reflect on how my experiences as a learner shape who I am as an educator.

Rote learning was a feature of my primary school education rooted in a historical British colonial educational structure. The post-colonialist era left remnants of a stringent exam-focused and recall-based approach to learning. As a 10-year-old in the West Indies, the Common Entrance Examination decided your fate for the next seven years, ultimately leading to tertiary level opportunities. The high stakes of that exam caused extreme stress because it was focused on passing an exam to obtain a placement at a public "prestige" school rather than fostering a curiosity for learning. The society in which I was brought up undoubtedly influenced my social identity with my assumptions of academic trajectory, influenced by the expectations of my family and societal context. Education was always associated with social mobility and prestige and thus the path to higher-level education was assumed to be the one I would take.

I continued on the academic trajectory focused on one important block of examinations after the other. The learning experiences varied across the disciplines. I became increasingly aware of the impact teachers' attitudes towards their subject and students had on me. If I did not perceive the teacher as approachable or interested in their subject matter, I was completely turned off the class. These experiences profoundly influenced my teaching approach and philosophy as a senior academic today. Brookfield (2015) reminds us that learning is an emotional experience for the student and that a supportive learning environment that builds on peer support and positive feedback from teachers is crucial to their learning experience.

The experience of learning in a classroom where teachers reflected their passion about their subject area led to my own developing interest in English and Greek literature, where the dramatic portrayal of the historical relevance of literary events created a depth of emotion that fueled an interest in learning more. These classes promoted peer discussions and led to enhanced learning as we drew on Vygotskian principles of social learning, constructing the experiences of historical characters such as Macbeth and Odysseus. In other classes, the experience was a feeling of social disconnect with the learning environment, created by teachers that used rote didactic methods. These teachers imparted no sense of interest in their subject matter nor had any awareness of the boredom that permeated the classroom. Others simply taught their content and were completely unconcerned if most of the class grasped the concept.

Then there was the social experience of peer bullying. As a quiet and shy individual in primary school who experienced the early loss of my father, I retreated into an inner world. It was these experiences of peer bullying by classmates and the lack of support by teachers that profoundly influenced my later philosophy as a teacher educator, to be different in my approach.

From ages 10 to 18, the years of secondary school led to similar varied teaching experiences, like primary school but with an exam-focused directive aimed at successful entry into University. Veterinary school in the UK followed with an extended focus on examination-driven learning, very similar to the context in which I am now an academic, where students are driven by the requirements of their qualifying examinations in the professional programs.

At university, there was an expectation of the need to attend lectures and simply prepare for the examinations without questioning or challenging the faculty approach. A very different experience to the very positive later experience I had at veterinary school in Scotland. What had felt like a dictatorial approach to teaching and learning in 1990 at the Liverpool University veterinary school transformed into a heavily student-focused teaching and learning experience at the University of Glasgow in 1997. At Glasgow, the students were given a voice, and as a clinician, I became aware of the importance of respecting student opinion as it was an expectation of faculty members, and one the institutional administration promoted!

It was 2015 when I was debating what I should do next to assist my career advancement, boards in Veterinary Public Health seemed the natural career progression. I am a veterinarian and lecture in the area of Veterinary Public Health. The veterinary program provides a strong scientific background and prepares its graduates for a career that is focused on health and medicine, treatment and diagnosis. As with medicine, veterinary study exposes students to research methods focused on quantitative approaches such as surveys and questionnaires and the classical statistical approach to analysis based on data collected using standard methods. My partner, an MD but also a psychologist, encouraged me to join an online educational listserv, as he was aware of my interest in educational technology. I was reluctant to do any further veterinary medicine programs as I began to feel I needed to broaden my knowledge. The veterinary field is small and almost insular, and I was beginning to feel I was missing out on an entire area in education I knew nothing about. In reading through the listserv emails, I began to develop an interest in the discussions on curriculum, technology, and research on student perceptions. I began to consider how I could merge my background in veterinary medicine with education and technology. One member encouraged me to join an Ed.D. program he was currently pursuing, and I began to explore. The exposure with the online classroom, coupled with my involvement as a participant in a Teaching with Technology workshop at my institution culminating in an award for Teaching with Technology excellence, promoted an interest in fusing technology with pedagogy.

To date, the journey of the Ed.D. has led me through nine modules that completely transformed my view on educational research, theory, and leadership. The modules began with a challenging entrance into epistemologies and ontologies, terms new to someone such as me without any background in formal education studies. Tutors exposed us to literature on learning theories that led to discussions on forums that involved meetings and critical reflection with colleagues in education from around the world and from various academic backgrounds. Our learning teams brought together colleagues from Japan, Canada, Australia, Africa, Barbados, Chile, and the US. Some colleagues were teaching English in Japan while others were involved in language education or special needs education.

Modules on educational research methods opened my world view of research from a different and key perspective, that of the research participant, commonly neglected in scientific-based research. In scientific-based approaches to research, the focus is on research of a quantitative nature without regard for the participant's lived experiences. Herein lies the benefits of the qualitative approach that can add a depth of understanding to statistical findings by providing a lens into the participant experience that may explain numeric findings.

One fascinating experience was the requirement to conduct my first interview—albeit on our past Provost. Not only did I learn much about the history of my organization and its values, but I obtained insight into the leadership attributes and strategies that had led to institutional sustainability and success. The clear camaraderie that had developed among the founders had led to a real commitment by senior leaders to foster a culture of supportive relationships between the institution and the people of its geographical context. Importantly, my interviewee clearly thoroughly enjoyed the experience of recounting his own time at the institution from its founding days as he proudly described the institutional accomplishments. What better way to learn about our context and to cultivate our institutional social capital than by obtaining a deeper insight into the minds of our leaders. A survey could not have achieved this insight. The experience of analyzing my first interview having connected with the participant also made me feel connected with the data in a manner a survey could never have done. This led me to reflect on my own views about the organization and what I could learn from my interviewee going forward. It also made me feel far more connected with my institution as I learned from the personal experiences of one of its founders on its development through a 30-year period in a nutshell.

Specifically, coupling the use of qualitative with quantitative methods in a Mixed Methods Research approach in my thesis research led me to explain the respondents' survey scores, based upon their lived experiences within their programs. I learned about qualitative methods that enable the researcher to give voice to the research participant and focus groups that enable discussion in group forums. I realized these methods enabled a view into different perspectives and rationales and led me to understand how little I knew in my role as an Institutional Research Board (IRB) member, when I was invited to become one.

Never before had I been aware that IRBs are not prepared to deal with ethical conflicts that arise from educational research! How do you ensure that minority groups in ethnographic studies are protected by research involving an investigation into their cultures and habits? How does the practitioner-researcher with an incumbent responsibility to protect the respondent participating in organizational research, balance their acquisition of sensitive knowledge about the organization with protecting organizational participants? Action research was another fascinating methodology that I had never been aware of. I began to consider my institutional relevance and how I could involve colleagues across the organization, fostering institutional social capital with implications for driving institutional change.

The learning that occurred on the Ed.D. forums were akin to my research into Interprofessional Education (IPE). After all, we were all students, mid-career professionals from diverse educational positions seeking to improve our practice and ascend in our respective career orientations. I began to think about what theories and values occurred in the program that could be used to develop IPE initiatives? Large class sizes, scheduling, siloes that exist across disciplines of medicine and veterinary medicine obstruct the collaborations in practice that can advance global healthcare. In our own Ed.D. discussion forums, I often felt different as a veterinarian because everyone else was a social scientist. Colleagues were kind and gradually, as we got to know each other and understand our academic areas of expertise through these discussion forums, we all began to see a similarity. The ascendency from novice to expert we all discussed in our own fields revealed shared experiences and challenges. Modular discussions and assignments on personal and professional values and organizational values led to interesting comparisons across institutional experiences that brought in shared personal autobiographical experiences about our own learning.

One colleague shared her terrible experiences in the math class in primary school that led to her losing her confidence, which she later found in recognizing her strengths in the English class. I also reflected on my own experiences in higher education where, if you did badly on a quiz or assignment, the tutor did not even recognize you or make an effort to reach out and discuss how they could assist your learning. The latter trend was common to my own and the experiences of many in this program. As I reflected on this, I realized the impact my own experiences have contributed to my own teaching philosophy, that even the weakest students can be the best. It would be worthwhile to conduct interviews with students to ascertain how they perceive their own learning in different courses and the challenges they face, including those that may involve obstructions to learning because of the instructor expectations and attitudes. I would not have thought of researching this or an alternative method to surveys before conducting this program.

Enter the Mixed Methods Approach. The window widened into the fascinating world of combining the conventional scientific quantitative methods with qualitative ones and the comprehensive picture that could be obtained in researching issues challenging our learners and those of our colleagues and the organization. The program provided a window into alternative leadership patterns akin to negotiating capitalist versus socialist governments. Distributed leadership and transformative leadership approaches provided thought into how one could utilize the shared expertise of colleagues for driving small organizational changes in the absence of administrative support.

Importantly, the program has created friendships and the thesis stage WhatsApp group has led to sharing of experiences on how we can support each other through this stage. Regardless of whether we are veterinarians, pastors, engineers, or language teachers, the discussions focused on approaches to learning we could all share. If IPE could draw on this, what would this look like? As I bring my learned reflective skills to the fore, could it be that peer learning by medical, veterinary, and public health students could develop into relationships directed ultimately at how patient care could be optimized? These methods that incorporate social approaches to problems are focused on an end goal, our learners or our patients, untarnished by the disciplinary cultures of professional programs in medicine and veterinary medicine, which bring with them hierarchical assumptions about roles, power structures and a culture that fosters exclusivity of other groups and the roles they may have in improving our own job satisfaction.

The theoretical framework of Lave and Wenger's communities of practice (CoP) have greatly influenced my approach both as a teacher and a practitioner educator. The CoP's formed as learning teams within the Ed.D. promoted shared learning as we all drew on the same goal of improving practice, but within a social context that also promoted a sharing and appreciation of the personal and professional experiences that impacted us all as educators. Discussion groups to address infectious disease cases akin to our Ed.D. discussion forums would promulgate each disciplinary group to offer an insight into their roles, fostering discussions that may emerge from newfound appreciation about how collaborative practice may better the overall care of our patient. Widening diagnostic considerations, treatment, and prevention alternatives can emerge from a broader understanding of how the environmentalist perceives the impacts of climate change on health; the public health professional perceives the role of preventive methods targeting socio-behavioral and environmental causes of poor health. Poor mental and physical health emerge from a range of factors that are not limited to disease origins.

Importantly, these discussions led to the development of bonds simply through the types of communication that emerged on the forums. After all, learning forums dictate a level of respect in response that fosters learning and trust and community in having to assist one another to complete the assignments successfully.

The doctoral program ended in the defence of my thesis on IPE in a *viva voce* in the UK. As I navigated the defence in discussion with the examiners, I was prompted to reflect even more deeply on the overall experience of the doctoral program and the thesis stage. The defence promoted a critical reflection of the skills learned regarding how the program had promoted by development as a practitioner educator. I realized at this point that embarking on the thesis stage had revealed how the relationships developed with colleagues over the years had resulted in the ability to engage them in collective and critical reflection on institutional issues within focus group interviews. This enabled collective reflection and approaches to how issues could be addressed to inform organizational change, leading to a positive impact on students and the institution (Roopnarine, 2020). The latter, coupled with the palette of research approaches I had now developed, will hopefully provide me with the confidence required for the next stage in my development as an educator.

The Role of Reflection in my Teaching Philosophy

My own development as an educator impacted my teaching philosophy. I now recognize that each student is an individual in their own right and realize the importance of enabling learners to engage in their peers' learning process. As a teacher, I try to remain mindful of my own past challenges as a learner that the process of the Ed.D. has enabled. The role of the student and faculty has been hard to negotiate but at the same time enabled me to view how the student perceives the tutor that appears out of reach. Encouraging interactions with students through peer learning activities, small group discussion that can be facilitated through virtual spaces leave opportunities for students to construct their knowledge under the distant yet gentle guidance of the facilitating faculty.

Five principles provide the fundamental structure for me as an educator, through which I shape my teaching approach: creation of a learning environment that is non-threatening to the student; using positive feedback in response to answers they provide to questions posed; remaining mindful of the emotional and social factors that impact learning; provoking a curiosity and motivation for learning; and to promote a growth mindset as opposed to a fixed one (Dweck, 2015). My teaching style is influenced by my own experiences as a learner as well as an educator. As a visual learner, I am aware that students have their own learning preferences and not all learners can process information using the same route. I am also aware that students must feel interested and not fearful of learning and thus I try to create an inclusive environment in the classroom, moving around the class to capture the student responses.

My teaching style draws on Knowles' theoretical framework of andragogy, approaching students as adults who need to construct their learning, applying their knowledge by augmenting didactic methods with problem-solving approaches to deliver course content. The motivation for learning is often self-driven, but, as an instructor, I realize my responsibility to provoke the student's curiosity for learning outside of an exam-focused goal. Thus, I draw on factors that provoke my own learning about these topics in public health that I am passionate about. As an example, I draw on current global events pertaining to public health, such as the COVID 19 pandemic, as I discuss their responsibilities as future veterinarians. Epidemiology can be a fairly dry topic for students and so I aim to expose students to current news and relevant websites that enable them to see the relevance of the principles learned in the course to their role as future veterinarians in mitigating the effects of many of these emerging diseases.

An Overarching Reflection That Considers the Ways That Writing the First Two Pieces Uncovered Who You Are as a Learner and Teacher

In reflecting upon my autobiographical influences and my teaching philosophy, I have begun to unpack who I am as a teacher and learner. As a practitioner educator, I have come to understand the two roles are fused. My experiences as a learner have influenced the commitment I have to position my teaching approach as one that incorporates respect for each student. I am committed to remaining interested in my subject and attempting to bring its relevance to students to provoke their curiosity. I aim to model for my veterinary students my attitudes toward learning and teaching to hopefully encourage them to respect their teachers and appreciate their responsibility as professionals in protecting their clientele.

As a teacher, I have also recognized the influence that Ernest Boyer (1990) has had on me through the paradigm he proposes on the Scholarship of Teaching and Learning (SoTL) that acknowledges that scholarly teaching involves making connections between teaching practice, educational research, and the student experience – in other words, it promotes the reflective and intentional inquiry of the educator into their teaching, learning and assessment practices. So now I move forward with an emphasis on engaging in further educational research that seeks to improve my practice as an educator through SOTL research, engaging my students where possible in the process, with the ultimate aim of enhancing their learning experiences.

References

Alvine, L. (2001). Shaping the Teaching Self through Autobiographical Narrative. *The High School Journal, 84*(3), 5-12. Retrieved from https://www.jstor.org/stable/40364393

Boyer, E. L. (1990). *Scholarship reconsidered: Priorities of the professoriate.* Princeton University Press.

Brookfield, S. D. (2015). *The skillful teacher: On technique, trust, and responsiveness in the classroom.* John Wiley & Sons.

Brown, H., & Parker, D.C. (2007). (Eds.). *Foundational methods: Understanding teaching and learning.* Toronto: Pearson Education.

Dewar, Brandy A., Jennifer E. Servos, Sandra L. Bosacki, and Robert Coplan. (2013). "Early childhood educators' reflections on teaching practices: The role of gender and culture." *Reflective practice, 14*(3), 381-391.

Dweck, C. (2015). Carol Dweck revisits the growth mindset. *Education Week, 35*(5), 20-24.

Lave J. & Wenger, E. (1991) *Situated learning. Legitimate peripheral participation.* Cambridge: Cambridge University Press.

Lundgren-Resenterra, M., & Kahn, P. E. (2019). The organisational impact of undertaking a professional doctorate: Forming critical leaders. *British Educational Research Journal, 45*(2), 407-424.

Plato, Halliwell, S., Plato, & Halliwell, S. (1988). *Republic 10.* Warminster, UK: Aris & Phillips.

Roopnarine, R. (2020). *Factors That Influence the Development of Interprofessional Education and One Health for Medical, Veterinary and Dual Degree Public Health Students at an Offshore Medical School.* [Doctor of Education thesis], University of Liverpool. http://livrepository.liverpool.ac.uk/id/eprint/3073226 [Accessed March 11, 2020). doi 10.17638/03073226

Seldin, P., Miller, J. E., & Miller, J. E. (2009). *The academic portfolio: A practical guide to documenting teaching, research, and service*. San Francisco, CA: Jossey-Bass.

19

From Boredom to Discovery

Storytelling as a Tool for Teaching and Learning Science

Andrew Sobering

Part 1: Educational Autobiography

Finding Confidence

Growing up in a small town in rural New York, I feel fortunate to have had many teachers in grammar school who genuinely cared for my education and development. I have a clear memory of an exercise in first grade where the students were assigned math problems to work on individually. Afterwards, we were encouraged to discuss the problems with our classmates and could change our answers. In one of these sessions, I felt correct, but a classmate easily convinced me that I was wrong. Lacking confidence and changing my correct answer according to his suggestion, I later lost marks for being wrong. Upon telling the teacher I had the correct answer but changed it at the urging of a classmate, the sage advice given to me was that I should learn to trust my own work.

That first-grade experience was a beginning of recognizing my internal thought process and analytical ability—a process I now understand as metacognition (Shea, 2018). I recognized my lack of confidence and could not understand how a self-assured (yet incorrect), classmate could change my mind. Where was my confidence? Years later, as a medical genetics and biochemistry teacher, it became clear to me that similar situations continuously arise in all of us (Andrews, 2010). Such scenarios play out in different ways. How do we know when to trust our conclusions and when to recognize a need for help? So many years ago, this small event contributed to my development as a student, an adult learner, and a teacher. I am reminded of this memory when counseling students. I see it written about in different ways—from Galileo and his early use of the telescope to the most cutting-edge research: we must learn to trust ourselves and maintain confidence in our reasoning ability (Kloosterman, 1988).

Recognizing That Applying Oneself Is Important

Like many other young kids, I wanted to explore, play, and laugh. Although I always loved to read, I did not want to write. I recall my third-grade teacher, Mr. Case. He would ask me why I would not work just a little bit harder, stating that I was clearly smart, but just coasting. Mr. Case decided to introduce me to a new classmate named Joe and explained that Joe consistently worked hard to finish assignments and that maybe we could become friends.

Joe kept a seagull feather on his desk next to his pencil, and he told me that the feather reminded him of how hard seagulls work to get through each day. Joe used the feather as a tool to inspire his motivation (Siegle & McCoach, 2005). Still a little kid, I only recall being suitably impressed by this new friend who possessed both focus and the ability to use words such as "assiduous." No matter how interesting (if not a little weird) the seagull feather was, I remained unmotivated, unfocused, and quite the opposite of assiduous. I was not interested in school—I might not ever know exactly why, but I suspect that it was dawning on me that my parents were going to separate. Or maybe the lure of camping, fishing, wasting time, and getting into general mischief was too strong to compete with a seagull feather of motivation. For whatever reason, I just was not interested in school.

A few years later, Joe and I indeed became best friends. And yes, I found out more about that feather he kept on his desk. How a third-grader discovered *Jonathon Livingston Seagull: A Story* (Bach, 1970), read it, and applied the literal aspect of the book to his own life, I don't know, but Joe and I stay in contact to this day. Although it took me many more years to find my own motivation, his sense of drive helped me learn how to learn. But first, I floundered: low-to-mediocre grades, a cross-country move in high school, and lack of money made college prospects dim. In my senior year, the realization that studying and learning could be joyful, finally and permanently, seized me. Unfortunately, college would have to wait as I'd already committed to the US Air Force.

Learning I was Smart

Reading has always been a joy for me; I was the kid who often had his nose in a book. However, the books in which I had my nose were books of my choice. I balked at assigned readings. I simply would not read about a subject if I deemed it uninteresting, choosing instead to face the music of not turning in an assignment rather than read something boring. Developing the ability to attend to tasks lacking my immediate interest took the development of focus, an understanding of how I learn best, and metacognition. Equally important, however, was the recognition that one can have a certain level of understanding of a topic but that full comprehension is impossible without the appropriate foundational knowledge. Learning to be an active reader served as my key to developing breadth and depth of knowledge on a subject. Taking the time to learn this skill is, in my opinion, a critical step in academic advancement.

Teaching Others
When in grammar school, some of my classmates struggled with reading and math; it was clear when they could not read aloud smoothly, or count by fives, or orders of magnitude. When I was able to perform these tasks, I felt proud of myself. A spark ignited, and with it, a deep-seated belief that I was smart. From one year to the next, it began to grow, despite my grades. The spark grew still brighter when I mastered unit conversion within the metric system, spurring the desire to memorize the definitions of the basic units (centi- is one hundredth, kilo is one thousand, etc.), and to order in multiples of ten logically. As an 11-year-old child, I knew that some of my teenage brother's friends had difficulty with this very subject! And then, just like a scene from a television sitcom, there I was: the socially awkward, nerdy prepubescent boy teaching science lessons to the cool teenage girl. I clearly remember hearing her exclaim to my older sibling, "Your little brother is so smart!" I was then surprised to find myself realizing that she could have been spending her time better: here she was drinking and smoking on a Sunday afternoon, and she had an exam the next day! This was another step toward realizing my inner learner and the point when I realized that I truly understood the metric system. Memorization, followed by application, and finally interrelation to other concepts. The metric system is a perfect example of this learning paradigm and is important at all levels of society and science (Craig, 2012).

Even with these early positive experiences, I never felt as if I was as smart as the others in my grade. Occasionally over the years, with reflection on my early schooling, I glean insight into exactly why I did not feel capable as a youngster—I was just unsure of myself. Later, when at the top of the class in college-level science courses, I came to realize that confidence is key: it provides the fuel to excel. By earning 'A' grades in college-level classes, I felt like a snowball rolling down a hill, getting bigger and stronger, and generating increased momentum with each rotation. In a sense, this confidence can be thought of as the nidus of the development of my mindset for learning (Yeager, et al., 2016). Confidence must start somewhere, and my early experience with the metric system helped get me rolling. Now, as an advisor, I try to help my students recognize their achievements in the hope that they can walk out of my office with increased confidence and fuel to excel in all their courses.

Stability is Essential

Smart does not guarantee success. One year, I performed poorly in algebra and had to remediate the course in summer school. While my friends were at the beach, I was in math class with the others who had failed the class. Without completing the course, I could not graduate with my peers. We had just moved, and my new friends were proud of not doing well in school—a poor performance on a test was considered a mark of defiance. Why did I underperform in this high school math class the first time around? Where was my motivation? Why did I not care? Why did I choose to spend my time with a group of friends who were likely to drop out of high school?

It would be difficult to point a finger at a single cause. However, the stability of my family life was certainly a contributing factor. My parents had split, and we had moved more than a thousand miles away, where I was attending a new school in a new state. Maybe for these reasons and others, I was not motivated, and math lessons were the furthest thing from my mind. In the end, my summer school experience was positive, as I learned to overcome personal hardship and persevere. I recall my math teacher—his calm southern accent and the patience he would demonstrate as he attempted yet another way of explaining an approach to solving algebra problems. The demeanor of my summer school math teacher occasionally comes into my mind when I find myself repeatedly describing an application of the Hardy-Weinberg equilibrium to the same student. I have come full circle as an educator, and now I get to enjoy witnessing the flash of understanding that happens to a student who finally understands a difficult concept.

That summer school math class impacted how I interact with my genetics and biochemistry students. Sometimes, a struggling student benefits when an academic counseling session shifts to discussing potential underlying factors. Occasionally, just giving a student time to voice frustration provides the necessary motivation to succeed. Interestingly, students seem to appreciate hearing that a respected professor also had academic problems in the past and that there is a path forward! Students appreciate honesty, and honesty helps develop a sense of mutual respect. Mutual respect between students and professor hopefully creates a class dynamic whereas students are more likely to spend time with, and learn, the material.

Insights Into Science Can Come From Unexpected Places

As preteens, my younger brother and I amassed quite a large chemistry set of the type no longer available in our current societal climate. In contrast to today's sets, which contain little more than sodium bicarbonate, table salt, vinegar, and litmus paper (Zielinski, 2012), we garnered a diverse collection of interesting and potentially dangerous compounds. Our father was always bringing us new glassware, including condenser coils, flasks, test tubes, and measuring devices. We had alcohol burners, a triple-beam balance, every salt you can imagine, and a diverse assortment of purified molecules. The joy of experimenting with flame tests was linked to our love for fireworks and the identification of various metals by their colored emissions, even more so when we secured the use of a plumber's propane torch (we knew our limits and stayed clear of the kitchen stove). My enjoyment of the home chemistry set was an exercise in self-exploration. My younger brother and I developed our interest. We did what we wanted, we set our own boundaries, exams were not involved, and we learned because we wanted to learn.

Whether the removal of various chemicals from children's chemistry sets was a consequence of cost or of safety and litigation (Hudson, 2012), all I know is this: by having so many reagents and learning their names, my brother and I demonstrated to each other a comprehensive range of the solubility laws. We became intuitively familiar with the names of a multitude of salts and their chemical formulae. As preteenagers, we learned how ionic compounds came together and the fundamental rules of stoichiometry. I recall my college-level general chemistry course: many of my friends had trouble recognizing the theory being taught because they were lost in the vast array of new vocabulary. Because I was already familiar with so many of the names, I could focus on the underlying chemical/physical concepts and principles. When counseling students, I sometimes reflect on this aspect of learning. In biochemistry and genetics, there is a tremendous amount of new vocabulary and jargon. The student who actively enjoys exploring the subject is likely to discover and incorporate more of this vocabulary, and therefore attain a higher level of intuitive understanding of the topic.

My younger brother and I were not limited to colored flames and colored water. We dabbled in pyrotechnics, smoke bombs, and stink bombs. One day, after amassing a rather large amount of a highly energetic compound (we were going to make a rocket), one of my older brother's friends visited our lab (the laundry room). He was smoking a cigarette and we advised him that it was not a good idea to smoke in our lab because we were preparing 'dangerous' rocket fuel. Of course, regarding us as ridiculous kids, and after taking a deep, Humphrey Bogart-style drag on his Marlboro, he jabbed the burning red ember into our precious fuel. Whoosh! The burnt hand teaches best, and we earned the respect of the teenagers that day. Unfortunately, we also scorched the ceiling, and a three-day-stench of sulfur permeated the house. Luckily the damage was not severe, my brother's friend did not get blisters on his face, and the house did not burn down.

Compared to such experiences, I was often bored in primary school science classes because I had the impression that I already knew the material. The problem was that I did not know what I did not know; I did not realize how much more there was towards deeper understanding of the concepts. I did not recognize that there was always something else to learn, nor did I understand the value embedded in an organized and structured teaching curriculum. I was unable to communicate that, for my age, I had relatively advanced skills in the sciences, nor how to articulate my desire to learn more. Worse, I did not understand how important it was to have language and writing skills for communication in the sciences until I found myself working towards my Ph.D. Writing is key for success in all endeavors, including the sciences. When I was in grade school, I recall being "told" that writing is a practice, and with practice it will get better, but I failed to 'hear' it.

Importance of Self-Improvement

In the eleventh grade (junior year of high school), my chemistry teacher (Mr. Harshman) gave me a "solid" B in the course even though I had the highest test scores in the class. When I protested, he replied that my lab notebook was a mess and that I should have been in the honors chemistry class. I vaguely remember Mr. Harshman telling me, "You choose an easy way out by taking this course, so you should be able to live with an easy B grade." Wow. At the time, I was as angry as a teenager can get. Now, I reflect on this as an important learning experience: thank you, Mr. Harshman.

I did not consider myself a good student until the end of my senior year (twelfth grade) of high school. By then, it was too late to apply for college, as I had already joined the Air Force. For some reason, during this last year of high school, I found myself in an honors anatomy and physiology course; this was my first "A" and the venue where I sat next to the girl with whom I slowly fell in love—she who would eventually become my wife. Before we graduated, our teacher (Mr. Harmon) signed my yearbook. He wrote, "You will be a good science student, *if you want to be.*" It took me years to recognize what he meant by saying that I had to "want" it. To be a good science student, one needs to want it in a very real way. Wanting to be a good science student also means nurturing a love for the material; this is more than just being willing to put in the effort. A desire to embrace learning was glowing brighter for me, and once it began, it would grow.

Mr. Harshman and Mr. Harmon were very real and very important people in my development as a learner who would one day become an educator. To honor them properly, their names have *not* been changed. I thank them both in this essay. Working hard to prepare is *not* the same as "wanting" to work hard to prepare. Some people say they "want" to work hard, but never do. However, in most cases, the desire to work hard usually comes before the hard work is done. What makes a person "want" to work hard? Where does motivation originate? How many people work hard at something but do not know why they are doing it, or worse, hate their work? For me, motivation starts with an interest in the topic, followed by a desire to learn more about it, and then realizing that the more I learn about it, the more fun I have with it. I strive to pass on to my students a love of science that breeds motivation to learn science.

Military Service
Coming out of high school, I recognized that I was not academically prepared for college. This was compounded by a lack of confidence and, most importantly, insufficient funding for tuition (thank goodness, it would have been a waste). For some reason, I am not sure why, I joined the military and served in the US Air Force as a jet mechanic, an experience that was my first step towards becoming an adult learner (Pew, 2007). To learn how to fix airplanes, one must go to school. In this case, a technical school. For some reason, many of the instructors discussed educational theory with the class. I now surmise this is because these instructors were recently exposed to educational theory seminars received during their training to become teachers.

One example of education theory I learned about came when a teacher told us, "*The successful instructor will lead the students from what they know into what they don't know,*" meaning that we must always be able to touch the basics and develop critical reflection before moving to the next step. Another example was a discussion about why outcome objectives are important in team-taught classes. This was the first time I had heard about "objective-based" instruction. I wondered if my previous primary school educators set objectives, and if so, was I just not paying attention, or did they not share them with us? A different instructor claimed that, in his opinion, there are two types of underachievers. The first are those who will not start and hence never get anything done. The second is illustrated by those who take on more than they can handle. When it does not get done, they have a built-in excuse: it was not attainable anyway. Having a formal set of objectives helps a student to recognize and track individual progress. Having clear objectives set each day in aircraft maintenance technical school demonstrated how on each day, progress can be made. I was elated when I graduated from this technical school at the top of my class, with honors.

Recognizing How I Learn Best

While earning my B.Sc. in biochemistry at SUNY Stony Brook, I was an excellent science student. However, as with most of us, there would be academic stumbles. One example was a poor performance on a cell biology exam. I understood the concept of the central dogma of cellular biology and could give examples. For instance, I could explain the various steps of mRNA processing and give diverse examples of protein modifications. Still, I had not bothered to learn how to describe these complex events in terms of their most basic definitions. Which is to say, I did not understand the most basic aspects of the central dogma of cellular biology. In the end, I earned a "C" grade on this focused topic because I did not commit to memory the most basic aspects of the language (jargon) that was used to describe nuances of the material. The result on my essay exam contained actual (and factual) points, but it was a disjointed, incoherent mess. In retrospect, I am grateful that the exam was based on essays so I could get the low grade I deserved. If the exam was based on multiple-choice questions, I believe I would have earned a much higher score and missed an opportunity to realize what I did not understand.

In the end, my low score meant that I had to go back to learn the jargon and put the pieces together. Remembering this lesson, I endeavor to show students how the relatively simple and defining organizational systems in biology are essential to know to learn the complexities to follow in advanced studies. Because of this low score, I found myself creating concept maps without knowing the term. Exploring and developing these maps using multicolored pens helped me to excel in upper-level college science courses. The creation of concept maps and linking out to lists and tables that had to be reproduced from memory allowed me to demonstrate to myself that I had mastered the material (Novak, 1990).

My experiences as a student were invaluable in defining an approach for teaching in both the premedical sciences and in medical school, for human genetics and biochemistry. I am often reminded how to place complex material into basic concept maps, and to maintain empathy when students appear to have "all the facts" but not know where these facts belong in the bigger picture. Past difficulties in science classes also helped me to realize the importance of "brute force" memorization. Sometimes the best way to approach a subject is to first retain a list of all items in that section, so that later they can be placed into appropriate categories and linked together.

Reflecting on these seminal moments in my development as a student, a learner, a teacher, a leader, and finally an academician has made writing this essay a joyful experience. An overall arc throughout my life has been to embrace writing. Earning a Ph.D. in biochemistry and molecular biology, and post-doctoral research in genetics and cellular biology required continuous effort at the lab bench. However, the real payoff comes when one describes one's work by oral communication, or the written word. To write well, one needs to love to write, and I did not begin to love to write until I fell in love. A few years after our tenth-year high school reunion, I found myself writing letters with the woman who I sat next to in that long-ago honors science class during our final year of high school. Eschewing email and telephones, we spent many years writing letters. It was this love that fostered my desire to learn how to express myself with the written word. Learning, without love for the subject, is just tedium. Of course, one never stops learning, but it is important to not stop paying attention to ourselves, to the ones we love, to our writing, and to our students.

Part II: Teaching Philosophy

Fostering Inspiration and Motivation

As a teacher of human genetics, cell biology, molecular biology, and biochemistry, I aim to help medical students develop conceptual intuition in the biological sciences. My goal is to foster medical students as they develop into life-long learners and to support their application of fundamental aspects of biology to medicine. When the underlying concepts in the sciences are understood by the medical student, at an intuitive level, aspects of complex pathophysiology and pharmacology are more accessible. Attaining an intuitive understanding in biochemistry and genetics requires scaffolding of concepts. For instructors to build these layers of thought, we must be able to penetrate the perception filter of our students (White, 2012).

Over the past 12 years, I have developed a love for teaching in the basic sciences for medical school and premedical coursework. Within this experience, I find that many medical students have a fear of upper-level integrative biology subjects such as biochemistry, molecular biology, cell biology, and genetics. This fear is often engendered by the overwhelming aspect of the material itself, along with negative experiences from previous encounters. In response, I strive to project excitement for the material and to communicate parameters of what is being taught. Students require clear boundaries for what they will be required to know for their next exam. Failure to establish this communication engenders frustration among students, potentially leading them to leave the course with less knowledge of the material than they possessed when they started the class. Of course, well-developed learning outcome objectives are essential, but for many, the objectives can become daunting themselves. A significant contribution of the teacher, therefore, becomes helping students to interpret the learning outcomes as they are often purposefully written in a broad fashion.

Generate Interest Among Students
Leading students on a path of learning and discovery in the biological sciences is more than just presenting facts and clearly articulating what must be memorized. Successful teaching also relates new material to topics that students should have already attained. Motivation and hunger for more knowledge amongst students might sometimes occur when the new material becomes the centerpiece of an interesting personal or historical example. For instance, one of the most difficult topics in a typical medical genetics course deals with probabilities, population genetics, and using the Hardy-Weinberg equilibrium. I remind students about some simplifying assumptions that can be applied to these problems by quoting Albert Einstein, who reportedly said, "Everything that can be counted doesn't always count, and everything that counts can't always be counted."

Another example I have used relates splitting water into hydrogen and oxygen by electrolysis. My general chemistry students delighted in my story of how my father created a hydrogen gas generator with dilute sulfuric acid from an old car battery and zinc filings. Combined with soapy water, what seemed like endless entertainment ensued for my three brothers and me. This being the 1970s, we chased the floating hydrogen bubbles with cigarette lighters to cause mini explosions in the kitchen. I have used this brief tale to illustrate concepts of energetics, density, stoichiometry, kinetic reaction theory, and thermodynamics to my students. For whatever reason, the image of four boys chasing around hydrogen gas bubbles with butane lighters always seems to energize the class.

A third example comes from bananas, which are relatively high in the radioactive isotope potassium-40. As part of a human genetics course (DNA damage), I explain to students about exposure to ionizing radiation which includes the background radiation we receive from Earth. After explaining how a person would have to eat approximately 100 bananas to simply double our natural daily exposure (the so-called banana equivalent dose, or BED). I then tell a story about how I once attempted to do just this but had to stop at 46 bananas. Have you ever tried to eat 46 bananas? See if you feel good after 40…

Shared laughter picks up the class, gets everyone excited, and allows me to continue the class with enthusiasm and energy. Learning is best when we maintain our humor, stay energized, and yet remember that education is serious.

Students appreciate these "stories" and leave them with a lasting impression of how the subject fits into a bigger picture. Conveying memories of personal experiences that directly relate to course content creates personal connections with students by fostering shared interest and increasing how students care about the material in a positive way. The student who is interested will learn more. Many students find science conceptually difficult, overly detailed, and obtuse. If students can be "sold" on the idea that the topic is interesting, in addition to being important and attainable, they will be more likely to enjoy themselves as they internalize the content into their own. In this light, I see myself as a bit of a "salesperson," and the product being sold is interest in the subject being taught. My salesmanship often comes in the form of being a light-hearted, but serious instructor. Importantly, I ensure that students know that I care for them and their learning, and that I am seriously vested in their education, but I do it with a smile.

Incorporation of Technology

Technology is changing the landscape of education, and I employ it in various ways; using clickers (audience response devices) to facilitate an interactive classroom experience is an example. At the very least, clickers can be an enticement for students to interact with the material in real time. A useful side-effect of using clicker questions in lectures is that it helps to refocus student attention back to the subject being taught (Kay, 2009). However, the clicker device is not the only tool available to a teacher (MacGeorge et al., 2008), and it is not universally agreed that all students appreciate the technology, especially when used to track attendance. Clickers can also be used to structure a large group discussion session. Importantly, this type of session can be facilitated by a single instructor, which eases faculty demands. I developed this concept into a research study and published my findings in a peer reviewed medical education journal (Hassumani, Cancellieri, Boudakov, Uphadhya, & Sobering, 2015).

Pre-recorded video is another useful technology tool that I use to enhance my teaching. I use video in three different ways. One use is to assign video for student viewing before the assigned classroom meeting. A few days later, instead of having a lecture, the students attend a session in which students must reflect on the videos by answering clicker questions. In this way, class time becomes a discussion and analysis session instead of a content delivery session; this is the flipped classroom (Ramnanan & Pound, 2017). Clicker devices are a natural tool to facilitate this interaction, and they allow a single instructor (content expert) to interact with a large group of students. In this way, my role as a teacher becomes one of active facilitation instead of passively speaking (Bordes, Walker, Modica, Buckland, & Sobering, 2021).

Professional Organizations and Research

Human and medical genetics is a rapidly changing field. Each day, it seems that a new disruptive technology is developed, or a guideline for the first tier "best" test is updated. It is easy to get lost in the minutia. A variety of approaches help keep the focus of my teaching current while ensuring that the important background and historical aspects are not lost. I maintain membership in the Association of Professors of Human and Medical Genetics (APHMG), serving as a council member for three years to help plan and organize workshops. Once yearly, we meet and discuss educational aspects of our teaching, discuss how to update and improve our core educational objectives, refine and develop new testing methods, and consider implementing new teaching tools. These meetings are invaluable to my continuous development as an educator, as the broad range of experiences, opinions, and attitudes of educators from diverse institutions come together to share and work toward the same goal: improvement.

In a sense, researching and publishing in a field means that one participates in a global conversation about where that field is going. With hard work, and maybe a bit of luck, I created a medical genetics consultation outreach program with board-certified medical geneticists, within underserved communities. When appropriate, we obtain consent for parents to allow us to tell their story, enabling me to write and publish in peer-reviewed journals. Of course, my teaching is also affected by this activity. Now, the phrase "they are doing this" becomes "we are doing this," and as a result, my teaching feels more authentic, and I learn better ways to convey complex aspects of clinical genetics to my students.

Part III: Critical Reflection

Good Teachers Motivate Their Students to Learn

Starting with my earliest recollections of grammar school and reflecting through high school experiences, military training, university, and finally graduate studies, I have gained an increased appreciation for the importance of the human connection in the learning process. The teachers that had the most impact on me as a student were those who inspired me. Working on this project has helped me to recognize these relationships and enabled my growth as a teacher.

Students look to their teachers for more than transfer of knowledge regarding a specific topic. Teaching also involves being a leader, and a good leader helps others to attain. An important aspect of this is the creation and maintenance of a culture of mutual respect. Most students want to be challenged in a fair and respectful way. Often, students will reflect on what we tell them and may come back with new questions, comments, or deeply personal experiences that must be handled with professionalism and tact. If handled incorrectly, a student can be thrown off course and be lost from the subject. When discussing specific disorders in human and medical genetics, I often have students relate personal stories about a loved one in their family who has the same disorder. Students who have these personal experiences can be lost if appropriate language is not used during the teaching session, emphasizing how mutual respect is part of the foundation of professional behavior.

I first thought about the concept of leadership as a developed skill and a learned behavior when in a high school Junior ROTC class. Here we would discuss basic aspects of leadership theory such as modeling behaviors, following chain of command, and the importance of mutual respect (Funk, 2002). These early discussions on leadership theory helped me to recognize the role that leadership plays in the classroom. When we model appropriate professional behavior in the classroom, students are more likely to respond in kind with professional behavior of their own, and internalize their motivation for the learning process. While engaging in this writing process, I became reconnected to the central role of leadership in the classroom and have found new ways to implement it. It is generally accepted that most medical students matriculate as thoughtful and compassionate people (Wear & Zarconi, 2007), and one of the roles of the faculty is to help students further develop into the profession. In today's multicultural educational environment, educators must empower their students to express themselves, and it is our responsibility to help them develop the tools to do so (Cook-Sather, 2002).

Students Who Connect to the Material Become Inspired

I have discovered that, when the "information" in the course content is crossed with some amount of entertainment "infotainment," knowledge is transmitted in a fun and engaging way, and students leave the course with a sense that something was attained. There is no dictum which states that our students must be miserable or bored by their instructors or the material we teach. Over the years, from elementary school through graduate school and to professional seminars, I have found that my best learning and inspiration comes from speakers who are knowledgeable about their material and engaging, personable, and know how to incorporate humor when telling a story. In this way, education becomes more than just learning, it becomes fun, it becomes entertainment. When our coursework is fun, we not only meet our objectives and enjoy watching students pass our exams, we get the satisfaction of knowing that we have also inspired our students and set them on a path to life-long learning.

My favorite comments in student evaluations are often from students who claim to have struggled in past genetics or biochemistry courses; these students report that my light-hearted but serious approach to the subject comes across in a straight-forward, accessible, and engaging manner that is more positive than their previous experiences. Like all sciences, genetics and biochemistry require a substantial amount of memorization. If a student is having fun with these subjects, it becomes easier to convince them to work towards this crucial step: once they get the language, understanding is more likely to follow. My enjoyment in writing this essay has helped me to understand the central role that storytelling has in my development as a teacher.

Helping Students Understand Depth Required for the Course

In a sense, the extent of content within genetics and biochemistry approaches infinity, and if too much is assigned at one time, or too much detail is being presented, students will quickly get lost—the confusion of being lost leads to frustration, and possibly abandonment of the material. Once lost, it is difficult to get students back. I recall being in the "lost club," and it is not a good feeling. Although we might not want to remember it, all of us in the sciences have likely been there at one point. It pays to remember that when we admit our past frustrations to our students, we can help them get back on track. We should acknowledge to our students that we might have had trouble at some point. They must see that we once had the same difficulties that they are experiencing. In addition to letting them know that they are not alone, it also gives us a natural segue to offering additional explanations and suggestions for improvement, a way forward, a new approach, or supplementary material. Crafting stories to our students then becomes a useful tool for helping those who struggle to stay on track.

Memory is finite, and in the age of instant access to information, we need to rethink what we ask students to memorize. Requirements for memorization should become more focused on what is needed for the student to appropriately search for and interpret information. To incorporate this into our courses, it has become ever more essential that we clearly communicate to our students what we expect them to memorize for them to progress.

An example of this change in memorization requirement is the Metabolic Map project. I am a proponent of this project for medical school basic sciences and its inclusion on Step 1 USMLE exam (Spicer, Thompson, Tong, Cowan, & Fulton, 2019). If eventually adopted by NBME (National Board of Medical Examiners), this resource will likely be included on most medical school exams, since almost all medical school subjects have some underlying biochemistry aspect. This slow change in the landscape of medical biochemistry education reflects how current technology can be used to bridge the ever-increasing gap in the body of *what is known*, to *what is searchable*, and finally to *interpretation of the results of the search*. A key aspect of our curriculum then becomes teaching what students need to know so they may understand the information they find.

Students Appreciate Personal Stories
From participating in this project, I found that storytelling is a central theme that defines my teaching. Without realizing it, I have developed into a teacher who helps students discover an interest in the subject that I teach and telling stories helps accomplish this goal. For some of my students, interest develops naturally, for others, it is a more arduous effort. A common theme in my teaching with stories is related to the power that comes from a personal connection. For instance, one of the early editions of Stryer's textbook of biochemistry relates a story of how, in the 1970s, carbon monoxide (CO) poisoned some children who swam around houseboats. The culprit was a small hollow under the hull of the boat where exhaust from the generator motor vented. Naturally curious children would discover this space and, if the generator was on, were at risk of CO poisoning, and of course, drowning.

When I teach lessons on the structure and function of hemoglobin, I relate this textbook lesson but also link it to my real-life experience as a boy. A family friend had a similar model houseboat, and my brother and I would play and swim off this boat. I recall the headaches we would feel after visiting our secret breathing space under the boat, and then on some subsequent visit, the adults told us that under no circumstances were we to swim under the boat due to the exhaust trap. My brother and I didn't die, but I still remember the headaches; we were lucky. Students, including future doctors, benefit from real-life anecdotes that illustrate our lessons, and when appropriately placed they create long-lasting memories to allow future integration with more complex material.

My personal connection with CO poisoning injects a dose of reality to the lesson and creates poignancy.

While earning my BSc degree in biochemistry at Stony Brook, many professors treated the subject with love and affection. They told stories about the people who made the key discoveries which shaped modern chemical, physical, and biological theories. Those who could instruct with a personal touch were the strongest teachers. From there, the pedagogy naturally progressed to the next steps, including analysis of the concept, and how it interrelates with other aspects of science and society. I now attempt to frame my lessons in a similar way and recognize the importance of storytelling in the educational process.

Create Teachable Moments

A math lesson in early grammar school, where advice from a classmate moved me to change a correct answer to an incorrect one, helped me begin to develop confidence. Reflecting on this event many years later, I realize that this was an example of how my insightful teacher created a "teachable moment." I was upset about losing marks on my grade, but the teacher was able to take that negative reaction and convert it to a positive outcome. This is a simple example of how a good instructor can take negative feelings and develop something positive. When done properly, everybody learns.

Sometimes, in a formal classroom teaching environment, these "teachable moments" can be scripted in. For example, during a lesson on population genetics, I use a clicker question to ask students to calculate the square root of 25%. I tell them to do it fast and give only 15 or 20 seconds to answer. Of course, 90% of the students get it wrong, and answer 5% when the correct answer is 50%. Admitting that I also got it wrong when the question was posed to me in a similar context lets the students know that I have an understanding for their thought process. After all, their professor got it wrong as well! This story allows me to emphasize the importance of knowing the distinction of square roots and fractional numbers, and why this bit of elementary mathematics is important to the subject being taught.

Final Thoughts

Students ask their instructors for advice on the best way to prepare for their science classes; I teach biochemistry, genetics, cell biology, and molecular biology. Usually, I respond back that the best way might be different for each of us, and it is up to the individual to discover their own best way to prepare. However, I am always happy to describe what worked for me, and when appropriate, to share what I have learned about the learning process.

Crafting this essay helped me remember how I developed into the science teacher I am today. This process reminds me of important events in my formative years. If I expressed interest in a subject, my mother would quickly find books related to it; my father was always there to point out interesting things and discuss how they function. Recollecting early examples of learning, confidence building, successes, failures, and the development of metacognition have given me new motivation to strive towards improving my teaching, embracing technology, and supporting my students.

References

Andrews, M. (2010, 11 24). *https://www.edcan.ca/*. Retrieved 05 30, 2020, from https://www.edcan.ca/articles/learning-from-stories-stories-of-learning/

Bach, R. (1970). *Jonathan Livingston Seagull: A Story.* New York City: Macmillan Publishers.

Bordes, S. J., Walker, D., Modica, L. J., Buckland, J., and Sobering, A. K. (2021) Towards the Optimal Use of Video Recordings to Support the Flipped Classroom in Medical School Basic Sciences Education. *Medical Education Online*, 26(1), 1-8. doi: 10.1080/10872981.2020.1841406

Cook-Sather, A. (2002). Authorizing Students' Perspectives: Toward Trust, Dialogue, and Change in Education. *Educational Researcher, 31*(4), 3-14.

Craig, K. W. (2012). No Child Left Behind: Teaching the Metric System in US Schools. *International Journal of Applied Science and Technology, 2*(4).

Funk, R. C. (2002). Developing Leaders Through High School Junior ROTC: Integrating Theory with Practice. *The Journal of Leadership Studies, 8*(4), 43-53.

Hassumani, D., Cancellieri, S., Boudakov, I., Uphadhya, S., & Sobering, A. K. (2015). Quiz Discuss Compare: Using Audience Response Devices to Actively Engage Students. *Medical Science Educator, 25*, 299-302.

Hudson, A. (2012, 8 1). *https://www.bbc.com/news/magazine*. Retrieved 4 20, 2020, from Whatever happened to kids' chemistry sets? https://www.bbc.com/news/magazine-19050342.

Kay, R. H. (2009). A strategic assessment of audience response systems used in higher education. *Australasian Journal of Educational Technology, 25*(2), 235-249.

Kloosterman, P. (1988). Self-confidence and motivation in mathematics. Journal of Educational Psychology. *80*(3), 345–351. doi:https://doi.org/10.1037/0022-0663.80.3.345

MacGeorge, E. L., Homan, S. R., Dunning, J. B., Elmore , D., Bodie, G. D., Evans, E., . . . Geddes, B. (2008). *Education Tech Research Dev, 56*, 125–145.

Novak, J. D. (1990). Concept mapping: A useful tool for science education. *Journal of Research in Science Teaching, 27*(10), 937-949 . doi:https://doi.org/10.1002/tea.3660271003.

Pew, S. (2007). Andragogy and Pedagogy as Foundational Theory for Student Motivation in Higher Education. *InSight: A Journal of Scholarly Teaching, 2*(1), 14-25.

Ramnanan, C. J., & Pound, L. D. (2017). Advances in medical education and practice: student perceptions of the flipped classroom. *Advances in Medical Education and Practice, 8*, 63-73.

Shea, N. (2018). Metacognition and abstract concepts. *Phil. Trans. R. Soc. B, 373*, 1-7. doi:http://dx.doi.org/10.1098/rstb.2017.0133.

Siegle, D., & McCoach, B. D. (2005). Making a Difference: Motivating Gifted Students Who Are Not Achieving. *Teaching Exceptional Children, 38*(1), 22-27.

Spicer, D. B., Thompson, K. H., Tong, M. S., Cowan, T. M., & Fulton, T. B. (2019). Medical Biochemistry Without Rote Memorization: Multi-Institution Implementation and Student perceptions of a Nationally Standardized Metabolic Map for Learning and Assessment. *Medical Science Educator, 29*, 87-92. doi:https://doi.org/10.1007/s40670-018-00631-y

Wear, D., & Zarconi, J. (2007). Can Compassion be Taught? Let's Ask Our Students. *J Gen Intern Med, 23*(7), 948-953. doi:10.1007/s11606-007-0501-0.

White, H. B. (2012). Student-Centered Education: Visualizing the Perception Filter and Breaching It with Active-Learning Strategies. *Biochemistry and Molecular Biology Education, 40*, 138-139.

Yeager, D. S., Romero, C., Paunesku , D., Hulleman, C. S., Schneider, B., Hinojosa, C., . . . Dweck, C. S. (2016). Using design thinking to improve psychological interventions: The case of the growth mindset during the transition to high school. *Journal of Educational Psychology, 108*(3), 374-391.

Zielinski, S. (2012, 10 10). *https://www.smithsonianmag.com*. Retrieved 04 20, 2020, from https://www.smithsonianmag.com/science-nature/the-rise-and-fall-and-rise-of-the-chemistry-set-70359831/.

20

As I Grew Up

A Narrative Reflection with Colleagues' Responses

Kathleen Blake Yancey

The editors of this collection of essays invited us to post our drafts online and to comment on each other's chapters. Several colleagues responded to mine; the last one to respond, Kate Coleman, made an intriguing observation that I took as a suggestion: "What I have loved Kathi, is reading this with the digital marginalia, the sidebar as a beautiful addition to digital writing and reading." In response to Kate's suggestion, I have included a number of responses to the chapter in the hope that readers will, like Kate, find themselves in good company. The comments are added as footnotes throughout the chapter. In order to distinguish their comments from regular footnotes, the comments are in italics and begin with the name of the person who made the comment.

I first encountered the concept of critical incidents in Atul Gawande's (2002) *Complications*, the earliest of his many accounts and explanations of medical practice;[1] from that first encounter, I found it a compelling construct. I appreciated the multiple contexts it informs, from air traffic control to surgical practice; the way it can be used as an exigence for making change, as in surgical practice; the role dialogue plays in making sense of a critical incident, in medicine bringing together so-called hard data (e.g., blood test results) with a collective, human interpretation of events for a fuller representation and understanding of such incidents; the identification of reflection as a primary mechanism through which a critical incident can be understood—what it was, why it's critical, what it means, and what might be done about it as a consequence.[2] Indeed, I was so influenced by the concept that, working with colleagues, I've used it in my own research. Theorizing how students transfer writing knowledge and practice from one context to another, for instance, we developed a model of college students' *"use* of prior knowledge as they encounter new writing tasks, located in three practices," one of which is "a *critical incident* model where students encounter an obstacle that helps them

---

[1] All of Gawande's books are worth reading: see http://atulgawande.com/books/

[2] While I appreciate very much the Morbidity and Mortality (M&M) weekly meeting for attending surgeons, there are components of it, like the focus on error, that I think work well for surgical practice but not for learning more generally.

re-theorize writing in general and their own agency as writers in particular" (Yancey et al, 2014, p. 5).[3]

So: critical incidents? As a concept, they are very powerful and explain much. But upon reflection, it's clear that I had of course encountered critical incidents much earlier. Or: perhaps it's both wiser and more accurate to say that from an early age, I have *experienced* them.[4]

Critical Incident One: Thanksgiving in West Germany

When I was nearly eight, my family moved to Frankfurt-am-Main in what was then West Germany for an almost four-year residence. We lived in Bad Vilbel, outside of Frankfurt, in a small subdivision designed for military officers' families: it was quite odd, really, our fairly homogenous US community in the middle of rural German life. To the south of our subdivision was a German apple orchard where children weren't supposed to play but we did; to the north the town about one kilometer away; to the west a German cornfield; and to the east, just across the entrance to the subdivision, an apartment complex for Eastern European refugees just behind a small grocery shop featuring a large jar of gummy bears on the cashier's counter.[5]

In many ways, my life in 1958 West Germany—a mere 13 years after the conclusion of World War II and despite the fact that my father belonged to an occupying force—was very similar to my earlier life in the Virginia suburbs surrounding Washington, DC. I went to school, this one public rather than Catholic; played with my American friends, though some had German relatives, which made them simultaneously exotic and threatening; and read voraciously, though my reading preferences now began to include spy novels. In other ways, living in Germany contrasted starkly with life at home. We had no TV; consequently, we read and played and interacted like children did before there was television, and since none of our neighbors had TV, we didn't miss it. More soberly, we were living in a country where the price of war was expressed as much on people's bodies as on the landscape: as an eight-year-old, I didn't understand much about war, or World War II specifically, but I knew

---

3   Talar Kaloustian: I LOVE this. It really speaks to the messy, perhaps fragmented nature of our childhood - or just life experiences - as we are experiencing them. But then through reflection, we begin to add up the pieces, putting them together in an order and framework that speaks to us.

4   Talar Kaloustian: I really like how you label these incidents.
    Andrew Sobering: Yes, our lives are stitched together with critical events that impact our direction.

5   Talar Kaloustian: I imagine your own contexts will be coming up in subsequent sections. You are framing here, right? I simply LOVE this visual description. How strongly I feel that I am there, with you.
    Rohini Roopnarine: Dear Kathleen, this is fascinating. What type of reflection would you consider this to be as it applies to critical incidents in your context?

intuitively that something bad had happened and that somehow my country had something to do with it. It was not a comforting feeling.[6]

Still, living in a foreign country didn't feel all that different until our first Thanksgiving. We anticipated and prepared as usual, with pilgrim and Indian plays in school, with my grandmother's turkey stuffing at home. But as it turned out, and to my astonishment, Germans were not making paper turkeys out of handprints or baking pumpkin pie: they didn't celebrate Thanksgiving at all! How could that be? Although Germans weren't Americans, they looked like (most of) us; we all went to the same churches;[7] we ate (some of) the same foods. And I knew that they celebrated other (of our) holidays—Christmas and Easter. Why not Thanksgiving? As I sought to process this news, I apprehended pretty immediately that if Germans didn't celebrate Thanksgiving, people in other countries might not either.

This critical incident was a watershed moment for me. I began to understand something about cultural practices, about how they are often historically motivated: Thanksgiving was part of US history, not Germany's. I also began to understand such practices as situated. I began to wonder what cultural practices the Germans had that might be different than ours. One I fell in love with, not long after that first German Thanksgiving, is St. Nick's, when on the night of December 5th, children put their shoes outside the door and await St. Nick's visit during the night; in the morning, shoes are filled with tangerines and chocolate and perhaps a small present, *or* with a piece of coal. We brought that custom home with us when I was 12; we practiced it with my children growing up; we share it now with our three grandchildren.[8]

This critical incident, of course, occurred outside school. Inside school, there were other events, like when I was six and stayed out too long at recess and, along with 20 other children, was publicly punished, and when I was in eighth grade, and my boyfriend was loudly slapped across the face for rolling his eyes at the nun teaching us, and when I was in fourth grade and my drama teacher told my parents I was beautiful when I knew I was not. But none of those events re-wrote my sense of the world and thus my sense of myself the way living in Germany did. For me, this critical incident was Copernican: the

---

6 *Talar Kaloustian: These parenthesized parts add so much to the picture you are painting. They are very personal, and very much show how your young mind was perceiving your surroundings.*

7 At that point in my life, I had not met a Jew; the absence of active synagogues is a phenomenon I would notice much later.

8 *Rohini Roopnarine: Are you considering critical incident then as an event that has a turning point in your life assumptions?*

US, with its unique Thanksgiving, was no longer the centerpiece body among planets and stars, but rather one planet among others.[9]

Critical Incident Two: Two Courses, Geology and Victorian Lit, Related

As a student, I'd always done well in the subjects I cared for; alas, there were several—science, Latin, and math among them—that I did not. As a first-year student in college, I'd barely passed biology: the large, large lecture was tedious, decontextualized, and impersonal; the required drop-in lab prompted identifications of maple and oak leaves that looked completely, completely identical.[10] Since completing 12 hours of a lab science was required for my BA, I looked for another science, preferably *not* physics or chemistry, which seemed even more committed to science than biology. What's left? Geology! A science I knew nothing about, but that couldn't be worse than the others.[11]

And it wasn't. I didn't like it exactly, but during one quarter, we addressed what was basically a kind of history, which I like and which I identify as a strength, too; thus, I had a place to begin in terms both of geology-as-history and of my sense of self-efficacy. This science, in other words, was history, too, and approaching scientific change through history made a kind of intuitive sense to me. We learned more than historical geology, of course: we learned about kinds of rocks and about their relationship to the earth: about processes contributing to formations, like layers of sedimentation building up into mountains; about volcanoes and how they can mark earth-bound plates; about plate tectonics as a fundamental principle of changes in the earth. Moreover, unlike in biology, labs in geology were not self-directed, acontextual, pointless exercises—exercises in what learning theorists call inert knowledge, that is, the knowledge that is not used—but rather team-based tasks, oriented to real world situations, like identifying sites for oil exploration—not that I'd ever be involved in such work professionally, of course,[12] but the task provided a context for learning and a way of gauging what I was learning. Faculty now recognize that engaging students in such real-world, disciplinary tasks asks them to behave as experts and thus learn their way into expertise, a concept that wasn't

---

9 *Talar Kaloustian: I wonder how you must have felt when you saw the world map with the US on the left side (and not in the middle, with Asia cut in half, with half on the left and half on the right, and the US slap bang in the middle!) To me it seems more an incident that served to change your perspective at that period in your life, and not necessarily in your life assumptions. So I feel you are walking us through a moment that was watershed relative to where you were at that time in your life.*

10 Ironically, I have quite a green thumb and can now easily distinguish between leaves and plants: motivation and purpose matter.

11 *Talar Kaloustain: My nemesis, too.*

12 My assumptions about what I might or might not become were both very gendered and very much of my time.

yet popular when I was examining leaves in biology lab.[13] As *How People Learn*, a National Research Council compilation of what we know about how people learn based on multiple disciplines and learning contexts from kindergarten to graduate school, explains,

> Experts have not only acquired knowledge, but are also good at retrieving the knowledge that is relevant to a particular task. In the language of cognitive scientists, experts' knowledge is "conditionalized"—it includes a specification of the contexts in which it is useful (Simon, 1980; Glaser, 1992). Knowledge that is not conditionalized is often "inert" because it is not activated, even though it is relevant (Whitehead, 1929). (p. 43)

Although a science, geology seemed almost tolerable to me, in part because it offered me a familiar place to begin, in part because it offered me the opportunity to learn through conditionalizing or contextualizing knowledge. And learn I did.

During the same quarter, I was enrolled in several literature classes, among them Victorian literature, a survey course I liked in spite of the teacher, who seemed to be 150 at least and whose idea of teaching was repeating in class what we'd read for homework. Still, I loved the class. For one thing, I just loved the reading: Victorian poets Tennyson and Browning and Rosetti, non-fiction of the period by Carlyle and Arnold and Ruskin, and most of all, fiction by Dickens and Hardy and Thackeray and Bronte and Trollope and Eliot. For another, the time period itself is fascinating, its beginning often bookmarked by Queen Victoria's ascent to the throne in 1837 and her death in 1901. Its zeitgeist, characterized by rapid social, political, and cultural changes—as society shifts from a rural base to more of an urban one; from a political system dominated by the wealthy to one more egalitarian; from a population of low literacy to one of larger literacies, particularly for the middle class—is acutely rendered in the literature, especially in the novels, which often painstakingly and vividly portrayed both those advancing and those left behind, like David's family in *David Copperfield* and Tess in Hardy's *Tess of the D'Ubervilles*. For yet another thing, in depicting such widespread yet uneven social change, these 19th-century novels also, I thought, provided parallels to the rapidly changing contemporaneous US moment, with its civil rights legislation, its anti-war activities, and its nascent feminism. And for yet one more, the study of the novel at this time allows one to see how an artist translates a new genre for the public. In this case, the novel, as a relatively new genre, often distributed first in weekly "penny papers," transparently helped readers make sense of itself as

---

13 For a specific example of how this works in a given field, for students writing their way into writing expertise, see Nancy Sommers and Laura Saltz's "The Novice as Expert: Writing the Freshman Year."

a genre as it guided their reading. Often beginning by literally addressing the reader—the addresses "Dear Reader" and "Gentle Reader" were favorites—the narrator continued to direct the reader's attention as s/he enacted an intimate relationship between them. In sum, the course's literary materials, their historicity, their relevance, and their revelation of a genre-in-process were all compelling to me. Here, I'd found an intellectual home.

My studying habits in those days were spurt-like: I pulled all-nighters several nights a week, often in an empty dormitory lounge long since vacated by others then sleeping. One very early morning, I was reading the introductory text for the next day's assignment in Victorian Lit, its purpose to provide context for the Victorian Age, itself keyed (as suggested above) to Victoria's reign.[14] More specifically, it included some history, highlighting among other themes the beginnings of enfranchisement, acceleration of industrialization, and some significant changes in scientific thinking. Even more specifically on that last point, it referred to *Lyell's Principles of Geology, Being an Attempt to Explain the Former Changes of the Earth's Surface, by Reference to Causes Now in Operation*, published in several volumes, eight of which were printed or reprinted from 1830-1838. Lyell's research, demonstrating that changes in the earth were systematic and related and that the Earth wasn't a few thousand years old, as had been believed, but rather *millions* of years old, prompted something of an existential crisis for the Victorians. Much like Darwin's research but even earlier, Lyell's *Geology* evoked surprise, concern, and alarm, and in this case, considerable anxiety that earth, and thus life itself, was much different and older than had been understood. Among other questions unnerving Victorians was this central one: how could these findings align with biblical explanations of the earth's origins? Victorian literature, the introduction claimed, responded to and addressed such concerns.

And what I saw, by myself so early that morning in the dorm lounge, was that my beloved Victorian literature was directly connected to Lyell's new geological findings, that his findings had everything to do with the shape the literature took, the worlds it represented, the humans it depicted, the anxieties they experienced. That moment, showing me how seemingly unrelated intellectual areas can be part and parcel of each other, was intellectually defining for me.[15]

Given this critical incident, it's probably not surprising that one of my curricular, pedagogical, and research foci is portfolios, collections of work narrated by the portfolio composer. Not all portfolios invite students to draw connec-

---

14 Some, of course, call the end of the century Edwardian.

15 *Talar Kaloustian: Based on your intro and your reference to Atul Gawande, I have been waiting for this connection between two seemingly disparate realms of study. I read through this section hungrily.*

tions between different objects, contexts, disciplines, and themes, but integrative portfolios, especially ePortfolios, do, as Joseph Ugroetz (2019) explains in describing a capstone course at Macaulay Honors College called Springboard:

> The springboard course, as the first principle states, is designed to be integrative, to pull together the disparate pieces of a student's educational career (during college and before. And after). One way to help students make these connections, we have found, is to ask them to develop and post online digital, multimedia, educational timelines and to post those to their eportfolios. These digital timelines allow students to map out the course of their education from their earliest days (in elementary school and before) to the present and projecting into the future. (…) By building this assignment into the course curriculum and making the presentation of this wide-ranging timeline part of the presentation of the final project, we ask students to locate the final projects not only as culminations or final achievements of their education, but as connected pieces of the larger set of experiences. Students include classes and in-school activities and assignments in their timelines, but also life events and discoveries that are not connected directly to school. (p. 157)

Influenced by my own predispositions and by disciplinary boundaries enclosing each of two courses I was enrolled in, one in literature, another in geology, I assumed that they would be completely separate, that they would have nothing in common, that nothing in one would or even could contribute to the other. Such division had in some ways always defined my education. What I discovered in this critical incident, however, is that such courses, contexts, fields of inquiry, and intellectual issues may indeed *seem* to be different. However, if we look closely enough, we are likely to find that they are connected, and often in the most interesting, compelling, and creative ways. Perhaps not surprisingly, I often invite students to make such connections for themselves.[16]

Critical Incident Three: The Rhetoric Course in Communication Studies

I went to graduate school at Purdue, largely through a compromise with my husband: he wanted to complete his doctorate at Virginia Tech, where we were finishing our masters' degrees, while I wanted to study at SUNY Buffalo with a particular scholar.[17] Purdue was my husband's second choice, and it was mine as well; we agreed that this compromise choice would meet both our intellectual needs. My focal area was Rhetoric and Composition, a tricky field to specialize in at that time because the field was barely nascent, so I took a Ph.D. in the teaching of English with a specialty in Rhetoric and Composition. To complete this somewhat self-designed degree, I took relevant courses in the English department and other departments—for instance, a course in tests

---

16 See Arthur Koestler's work on juxtaposition and creativity, for example, in his The Act of Creation.

17 As it happens, the scholar left SUNY Buffalo the next year.

and measurement in Education, and another in rhetoric in Communication Studies. Getting to Communication Studies physically, given that it was right down the hall from English, was easy, and I expected the conceptual traverse to be likewise. Put another way, while I expected differences in Communication Studies' approach to language, medium, and text—which of course is why I signed up for the course--I also expected considerable overlap.[18]

Taught by Professor Burk, the course was a survey of modern rhetoric focusing on contemporaneous figures, among them Kenneth Burke, Henry Johnstone, and Lloyd Bitzer. Some of the readings, especially Bitzer's on rhetorical situation, changed my intellectual life forever. Bitzer's (1968) definition of rhetorical situation begins with "the context in which speakers or writers create rhetorical discourse" (p. 1). He continues by explaining:

Let us regard rhetorical situation as a natural context of persons, events, objects, relations, and an exigence which strongly invites utterance; this invited utterance participates naturally in the situation, is in many instances necessary to the completion of situational activity, and by means of its participation with situation obtains its meaning and its rhetorical character. (p. 5)

Moreover, a rhetorical situation is rhetorical to the extent that it brings about "the significant modification of the exigence" (Bitzer 1968, p. 6). What I have appreciated about Bitzer's theory, despite some provocative critiques by other scholars, is its capacity to describe multiple situations in multiple contexts, from the task facing any writer to the way we analyze events of nearly all kinds, on the screen and in pages and within politics. What, we can ask, is the exigence motivating this approach? What is the rhetorical situation the writer or speaker is seeking to change? Thus, the concept of the rhetorical situation acts as the first point of departure for me as I consider situations both in school and in life.

However, in this class on rhetoric, a theme dominating it was at least as influential—and unsettling. It was sounded, very gently, by Professor Burk at the beginning of *every* class in his single question "Where is meaning?" "In people," the class univocally replied. When he raised this question on the first day of class, I mistakenly took it for a genuine question and paused, waiting for a discussion to ensue. Where *is* meaning?, I thought. But immediately, the class replied in concert, "In people," which also immediately told me that rather than a response to an inquiry, this was an exclamation of faith. While I wasn't a heretic, I wasn't part of the fold, either.

---

18 *Talar Kaloustian: No kidding! I lived in West Lafayette and worked at Purdue for half a year - my sister was doing her grad studies there and I was between schools. Go boilermakers! And this is what we are doing with these reflections, is it not?*

Of course, as the only student from outside the Communications Studies department, I had understood that my views—as a person, as an English graduate student—-might be anomalous, but I hadn't appreciated how contrary they might be. The always-correct answer in an English department to that repeated question was—and mostly still is—that meaning is not in people but in *text*. Of course, the texts locating the two departments differed, with Communication Studies looking principally at non-fiction texts, and my department of origin, the English department, addressing fictional texts, but the contrast between the two was inflexible, telling. No one in the rhetoric class wanted to engage the idea that a source of meaning might be the text itself; no one in my English department believed that meaning could be generated outside of the text.[19] And me? I'm not sure where I thought meaning was: I had been schooled to understand the meaning of a text to be contained within it, but the weekly chorus called that understanding into serious question.

Over the next several months, I found the "In people" response less discordant, and in part because of this experience, I thought much more deeply about and reflected upon, sources of meaningfulness. Clearly, texts—articles, books, movies—are more or less meaningful: a good question is what accounts for such meaningfulness. At the same time, somewhat like art, meaning seems to be in the eye of the beholder: what are the processes allowing us to perceive—or is it construct?—meaning in one text but not in another? Just as important is how we create meaning, both through a text (as I am here, I hope) and in person, and how do we invite others to share the meaning we make of a text, an event, an experience? More generally, through the experience of the repeated question and class response, I became less certain about where meaning is, but more convinced that meaningfulness is central to more than texts, and more attuned to the idea of multiple sources of meaningfulness and the ways they might interact.[20]

I had signed up for a course in rhetoric; I completed a course in rhetoric, meaningfulness, and reflection. The class's weekly opening and response, articulating a meaning-in-persons so at odds with my own background in meaning-in-texts, provided an exigence, which is itself an opportunity to make meaning. Meaning itself, in other words, became a focus for me during that class, and

---

19 While focusing on texts as the sources of meaning still dominates literary practice, some theoretical models, like reader response, bring the reader into the transaction, as we see in the responses to the chapter here.

20 *Rohini Roopnarine: How would you link "meaning" in this case to an individual's epistemological and ontological positions? This differs widely in research [with] science based (positivist/objectivist) versus nonscientific (interpretivist/constructivist) orientations-would appreciate your opinion on this.*

Talar Kaloustian: In following the "connections across seemingly disparate realms" that serves as the overarching frame of this piece, I would add to my colleague's comment that this is connected to a quantitative-based orientation vs. qualitative-based as well.

reflection a mechanism for sorting out differences, for identifying alignments, for raising new questions, for thinking in terms of propositions to explore rather than claims to argue. It wasn't a passing fancy—meaning and meaningfulness became a primary focus in both my teaching and my research, especially as created and articulated through reflection.[21]

A Teaching Philosophy

My teaching philosophy, which conceptualizes learning developing through knowledge and practice in dialogue with each other, is defined by two distinctive features. The first feature is a definition and enactment of the curriculum as plural. The second is the reflective practice as the tissue articulates learning that takes place in different contexts.

Through my research on portfolios, reflection, curriculum, and pedagogy, I have theorized the classroom as the nexus of three interlocking curricula (e.g., Yancey, 1998, 2004). The first curriculum is the *delivered* curriculum expressed in catalogue copy, syllabi, assignments, and assessments. This curriculum is, of course, very important; critical for it is a set of key terms that students engage with; a set of practices inviting students to develop expertise along lines described in *How People Learn* (2000); and a set of readings and assignments I have scaffolded to support student development. Collectively, these terms, practices, readings, and assignments construct learning as a social and intellectual activity.

At the same time, as we know from work in assessment (e.g., Kuh et al., 2014), what students learn in our delivered curriculum doesn't always match our intent. What they actually learn is, in part, a function of the *experienced* curriculum, that is, the curriculum as constructed by students themselves in the process of completing a program, service learning project, or course of study.[22] We see the experienced curriculum in various texts, from student responses to readings to the ways they re-imagine our assignments to accommodate their own interests. I may be teaching a course in composition theory, for example, but as students' research projects attest, that more general focus is inflected by students' varying interests, from the role of media in composition and the influence of globalized English on written composition to a history of everyday composing and the relationship of composing in other fields (e.g., music, photography) to composing in writing.

Not least, learning is also influenced by what I call the *lived* curriculum, by the learning students bring with them to class, acquire during the term,

---

21 *Talar Kaloustian: This is apparent indeed, particularly in this very paragraph. "So meta" as the kids these days say :)*

22 My observation that the graduate course in rhetoric was for me a course in rhetoric, reflection, and meaning-making is also a statement about my experienced curriculum of the course.

and continue to develop in life after the term concludes; again, here, I am impressed by *How People Learn* as well as by what students have told me (see, e.g., Chapter Eight in my *Reflection in the Writing Classroom, 1998*). For students to learn, they need to connect the prior knowledge of their lived curriculum to new learning; to link concurrent life learning with class learning; and to make the transition to learning in future situations. One exercise bringing these three curricula into dialogue asks students to map their learning visually: they identify the key terms of a course (*delivered*); map them in relationship to each other (*experienced*); and link to other terms acquired outside school (*lived*).

For graduate students, especially, time contextualizes these curricula; the goal is to help students not only learn, but also *share* that learning in increasingly professional and peer-reviewed venues. To do that, students need to understand how our disciplinary making and sharing of knowledge "works," and my approach here is very Deweyian, which includes two interlocking components: experience and reflection. Because people learn through experience, as Dewey argued, my course design, from informal activities to final projects, requires that students engage in and make knowledge from those experiences. Specifically, I encourage students to share learning in class (in both f2f and blog settings); to present their learning at conferences; and to publish their learning in peer-reviewed journals. From this perspective, my graduate courses are exercises in experiences that are progressively shared; they culminate in a final project living and circulating both within and beyond the classroom--in the form of conference presentations, articles, and theses and dissertations—all of which my students have created, professionally shared, and/or published.[23]

In addition, I build in several kinds of reiterative reflection, not as an afterthought, but as a critical part of learning; as Dewey (1993) observed, "We do not learn from experience. We learn from reflecting on experience" (p. 33). I think of reflection as the tissue binding the three curricula: a Schonian (e.g., *Educating the Reflective Practitioner,* 1987) exercise of reviewing one's work, making sense of it in a social context, deciding what it means, assessing it, and planning how to move forward with it. Threaded throughout my graduate classes are opportunities to reflect, the theory that through multiple iterations of reflection, students *become* reflective learners, ultimately able to design, monitor, and shape their own meaningful learning.[24]

What do I make of the critical incidents biography, the teaching philosophy, and the dialogue between them? I'm not completely sure: despite my

---

23 *Talar Kaloustian: Hear, hear!*
  Brian Martin: I was just thinking this is very Deweyian!

24 *Talar Kaloustian: I have several Dewey quotes in my chapter. If it is alright with you, I hope to quote you (and/or quote you quoting Dewey) in my chapter.*

familiarity with critical incidents, there's a lot to process here. But I do have some observations.[25]

One: history is important to me as a person and as a teacher. I began college as a history major and was certified to teach history to students grades six–12; along with rhetorical situation, the historical context, perhaps in part because of my living, as an impressionable child, in such an intense historical context in post-war Germany functions as something of a standard intellectual framework for me. It's probably not surprising, then, that I begin every course I teach with history, more specifically with students' histories. I often open the first class period with an icebreaker focused on course content that taps students' prior experiences; my first homework assignment performs the same task more discursively. This term, I am teaching a special topics course, Writing across the Curriculum (WAC) and the Question of Writing Transfer, and the first assignment is what I've called The Snapshot Project:

> In 1-2 pages (single-spaced), identify three moments when your writing changed. For each moment,
>   a. describe it
>   b. analyze how your writing changed and why
>   c. consider whether this change was helpful or not
>   d. theorize about what this tells you about how writers may develop

Tracing our own histories, as my students did this week and I have done here, allows us to distance ourselves from them, see them from other angles, and begin to make meaning of them.

Two: Just as we're all similar, we're all different: that pattern in and of itself provides an occasion for learning. But as different as we-as-learners are, good teaching practices, regardless of pedagogical style, are similar in their underlying principles: they engage students where they are, ask real questions, pose actual tasks, and bring them together to make meaning. My own models of good teaching, ironically, are sometimes based on reactions to teaching situations and models I found negative: we don't examine leaves for the sake of examining leaves; we don't read students' homework assignments to them as an ersatz lecture. In my classes, I try to ensure that students are engaged

---

25 *Talar Kaloustian: I appreciate this candour. I too had/continue having a similar experience. Reliving, reflecting, re-feeling long since forgotten or pushed down emotions+experiences has left me in an unsettled and messy place.*

as meaning-making participants. In my current class on WAC and transfer, for example, students are interviewing writers to learn from them how they identify and understand the many contexts in which they write; students are also interviewing leaders of WAC programs to learn from them about WAC and its programs *and* to collaborate in creating a map, based on the interviews, of current WAC issues. However, a frustration I have with this approach is the difficulty of finding authentic ways for students to share what they are learning, the knowledge they are making.

Three: critical incidents (CIs) and threshold concepts (TCs) are in a relationship with each other that I'd like to tease out—but haven't yet. By definition, a critical incident is transformative, and so too a threshold concept, the latter defined as a key concept defining a field or discipline that once learned cannot be unlearned. TCs thus function as an assembleged portal into a discipline, whereas a critical incident can stand on its own and doesn't necessarily operate in a disciplinary context: the German Thanksgiving-that-wasn't isn't a disciplinary matter, although it was a meaning-making moment with implications for my teaching.

Four: making meaning, and meaningfulness itself, is a theme in my thinking, my teaching, my research. I'm always interested in the meaning we make through reflection, in the heretofore unobserved connections linking objects, practices, experiences, and humans that we articulate through reflection. Portfolios, of course, provide a site to trace and represent these connections and to make sense of them. Interestingly, I typically think of myself as initially interested in portfolios, in large part because I questioned the value of standard evaluative measures (aka, standardized tests), but what this exercise has also demonstrated to me is that I am drawn to them, also in large part, because I appreciate the story that others have to tell inside and across a portfolio. But yet another large part of it may have deeper roots: in the kind of portfolio model that I employ (see Yancey 2019, e.g.), students inquire, explore, consider. There isn't a standard guide or template for this, and I'm not sure that I want one. After all, as this reflection suggests, I had no standard guide as to how to make sense of post-war Germany, no standard guide as to what meaning to make of the connection between Lyell's *Geology* and Victorian literature, no standard guide as to find where meaning ultimately resides—that last, a task that I, quite obviously, continue to pursue. [26]

---

26 *Talar Taloustian: Full circle. I so enjoyed this candid, conversational, digestible and engaging read. The best part was hearing your voice through descriptions of your young self, descriptions of events and visuals, little asides, and humourous use of words in some places. The "alas" and the "most of" for example - those things made me smile.*

References

Bitzer, L. (1968). The rhetorical situation. *Philosophy and Rhetoric, 1*(1), 1-14.
Bransford, J., Pellegrino, J., & Donovan, M. S. (Eds.) (2000). *How people learn: Brain, mind, experience, and school: Expanded edition.* National Academy Press.
Dewey, J. (1993). *How we think* (2nd ed). D. C. Heath.
Gawande, A. (2002). *Complications: A surgeon's notes on an imperfect science.* Holt/Picador.
Koestler, A. (1964). *The act of creation.* New York: Penguin Books.
Kuh, G. D., Ikenberry, S. O., Jankowski, N. A., Cain, T. R., Ewell, P., Hutchings, P., & Kinzie, J. (2014). *Using student evidence to improve higher education.* Jossey-Bass.
Schön, D. (1987). *Educating the reflective practitioner.* Jossey-Bass.
Sommers, N.& Saltz, L. (2004). The novice as expert: Writing the freshman year. *College Composition and Communication, 56*(1), 124–49.
Ugroetz, J. (2019). Macaulay springboards: The capstone as an open learning portfolio." In Yancey, K. B. (Ed.). *ePortfolio-as-Curriculum: Models and practices for developing students' ePortfolio literacy* (pp. 149-69). Stylus.
Yancey, K. B. (1998). *Reflection in the writing classroom.* Utah State UP.
——, Robertson, L. & Taczak, K. (2014). *Writing across contexts: Composition, transfer, and sites of writing.* Utah State UP.
——. (Ed.) (2019). *ePortfolio-as-Curriculum: Models and practices for developing students' ePortfolio literacy.* Stylus.

21

Uncovering and Examining Three Distinct Paths to Educational Leadership

Laura Colket, Tracy Penny Light & M. Adam Carswell

Effective teaching involves modeling the practices that we ask of our learners. As such, we (the editors of this book) engaged in the same process that we asked of our contributing authors. At first, we did so informally, as a pilot, to ensure that what we were asking was reasonable and worthwhile. But as each of us began reflecting on, writing about, and discussing our experiences as learners in relation to our current teaching practices and philosophies, we decided to bring our distinct stories together into one chapter (this decision was also inspired by some of the other co-authors in this book who did the same). The three of us work together very closely so it was informative (though often not surprising) for us to read and listen to each other's stories of learning. Although our learning experiences were quite different, we quickly began to see the residue of our past experiences in our current teaching and leadership practices and philosophies—in other words, our unique commitments and idiosyncrasies became clearer as we learned more about each other's experiences as learners. As the reasoning behind our distinct approaches to teaching and leadership was coming to the surface, so too were the reasonings behind our similarities. It was fascinating to see how our unique experiences growing up led us to hold such similar philosophies of teaching and leadership. Laura recounts many unpleasant memories from her time in school, while her out-of-school learning experiences were much more positive; Tracy recollects *loving* the academic components of school, but not the social components; and Adam highlights the importance of context, as he had negative experiences in some school settings and very positive and influential experiences in other school settings.

Currently, the three of us work together very closely at St. George's University in Grenada, West Indies. Tracy is the director of the Leadership and Excellence in Academic Development (LEAD) division in the Department of Educational Services. Through LEAD, all three of us work together to design and lead faculty development experiences to support individuals, departments, and schools across the university. We all also work closely together as a teaching team in the Master of Education program, of which Laura is the director.

When the three of us first met, sparks flew. We often finish each other's sentences, our brainstorming sessions feel magical at times, and almost seamlessly, if one of us drops the ball, another one catches it mid-air. Through this experience of reflecting on and sharing our stories of learning, we learned why it is that we all work so well together. It seems as though our experiences as students, distinct as they were, led us to a very similar takeaway: when it comes to teaching and learning, relationships are key. On top of that shared foundational commitment, each of us has a unique (yet complementary) top layer because of our past experiences. For Laura, it is the importance of equitable learning environments guided by critical pedagogy; for Tracy, it is the importance of reflection and making connections in the learning process; and for Adam, it is the importance of a joyful and engaging learning environment. While each of us prioritize different areas, we all share and support each other's commitments. This allows us to work well together and also ultimately creates a more holistic learning experience for our students.

Laura Colket

My professional mission is to support the development of teachers and educational leaders who value and engage with multiple ways of knowing, thinking, and being in this world. This mission has guided me through much of my professional career and it is grounded in my personal experiences as a student in which I (far too often) was surrounded by teachers and educational leaders who were guided by a problematically narrow, constraining, and damaging notion of what it means to teach and learn. Of course, I didn't realize it at the time. At the time, I just felt like I wasn't "smart," wasn't a "good student," and didn't have what it took to succeed. I will come back to that point. First, I want to talk about how I also didn't realize that the stories I was taught to know and memorize were deeply problematic in that they were shaped by a grand narrative and thus perpetuated hegemonic beliefs and ways of being (Bartolomé, 2008; McLaren, 1993). I will provide two brief examples to illustrate these points and then I will provide some additional background about my educational experiences to further contextualize my current practice as a teacher and educational leader.

When I was in middle school, I took a required history/social studies class that made me think I hated history (it is now my favorite subject). We had to show that we had memorized dates, names, and places that defined history (read: White man's history) on our exams. From my recollection, we were not asked to think critically, just to regurgitate. We were not presented with different lenses or competing perspectives to process the "facts" that we were given. We were not taught that history is "the story of the powerful and how they use their power to keep them in positions in which they can continue to dominate others" (Smith, 1999, p. 34) and I didn't come to understand that the writing of history in and of itself is an act of power (Trouillot, 1994; Zinn, 2003). No, in that class, history was very clear cut. There were right and wrong answers. And one day, when I got many wrong answers on a test, the teacher publicly humiliated me in front of my classmates by announcing I had earned the lowest grade in the class. He told me to move to the back of the class, and stated that I would never be a good student if I continued on my current path (all I heard was that I would never be a good student). From that point on, I gave up on his class, and sadly, for many years, I gave up on history, too.

Fast forward to college. As a junior, I studied abroad and traveled to Cuba and met Fidel Castro. I sat and listened, for hours, to his stories. It wasn't until that point that I deeply, truly understood that what I had learned throughout all my years of schooling was a very limiting and problematic version of history (not just about Cuba, but literally about everything). It was in that moment that I began to understand that "To hold alternative histories is to hold alternative knowledges" (Smith, 1999, p. 34). It wasn't that I soaked in every word of every story that Fidel Castro shared and thus disregarded everything I had learned previously, but the experience led me to understand how complex history is and I began to wonder how it came to be that his stories were so vastly different from the "truth" that I had been told as a student in American schools. This opened Pandora's Box for me, in that it created many problems and inconsistencies that I was forced to contend with (which I see as a good thing). Very quickly, my curiosities were not only about American-Cuban relations, they became bigger and even more profound; I felt compelled to question, break apart, and re-learn all the "single stories" (Adiche, 2009) I had been exposed to in my schooling experiences to that point. I now believe that students can and should understand the complex nature of social history from an early age and that it should not require a privileged experience as a young adult for a student to understand what history is. Now, as an educator myself, and as someone who supports the development of future and current educators and educational leaders, I make it my mission to ensure the stories we share and learn from are more complicated, contradictory, complex, and transformative than the slew of hegemonic stories I was exposed to in my years of schooling.

Now on to a different story: the feelings of insecurity that I held on to tightly as a younger student. I still have a physical reaction when I think about some of the traumatizing learning experiences I had in school. I struggled significantly as a student. Much of my learning experiences from my formative years are blocked, but I know that I had deep anxiety about being called on to read aloud. When I was forced to do so, I would fumble over the words until one of my peers made fun of me and then I would shut down completely out of utter embarrassment. Getting asked to do a math problem out loud was equally as traumatizing and followed the same pattern. I hated school. I think it's likely that I have undiagnosed learning disabilities (my guess is dyslexia and dyscalculia), which added to my challenges as a student in a traditional school environment. I did not get the supports I needed, I often felt stupid, and I was regularly mocked by my peers. I am convinced that if I had been diagnosed and received the supports that I needed, I would have still been mocked by my peers, probably to a greater extent; I was already taunted for the thick glasses that I wore and because of my lisp. Both of these physical markers were a constant source of amusement for the other children in my classes. I still have the lisp today, but it was much more pronounced when I was younger. It wasn't until I was 22, learning to teach English to non-native speakers in Thailand, that I saw a diagram with tongue placements for different sounds and I was able to teach myself to lessen my lisp. When I was in elementary school, I remember going to a speech therapist, but it didn't seem to do anything except make me feel even more embarrassed. I didn't want to be singled out any more than I already was. There was an overall culture of bullying at my school, and this is something that the school leaders and teachers could have and should have addressed. I know, firsthand, that if a student is not feeling safe and secure in their home, community, and/or school environment, they are in no position to learn.

All of this is not to say that I had entirely negative learning experiences growing up. I did have many positive experiences as well. But the vast majority of those positive learning experiences came outside of a traditional school environment: summer camps where I made rocket ships and sandcastles, dance classes that I began taking at four years old, gymnastics competitions, swim lessons, building forts in the woods by my house, playing games with my siblings, school field trips that took us beyond the borders of our town, road trips with my dad where he stopped at every tourist attraction possible, traveling abroad in high school and college.

Throughout my formal schooling years, my negative in-school experiences could be off-set by the positive out-of-school experiences. I benefited a great deal from my father's salary as a combustion scientist; I was incredibly lucky to have been afforded with so many opportunities to explore and learn from the world beyond my school walls. I made it through the school day so I could get to my dance class after school. I made it through the school week so I could play with my siblings in our yard, in the woods, and around our neighborhood. I made it through the months so that I could go on a family vacation during a school break. And I made it through the year so I could get back to summer camp. Ultimately, the education I received outside of school is what stands out to me as powerful learning, not the "education" I received in school.

Students who are different, for any number of reasons, do not fare well in schools. That should not be the case. The fact that so many children experience their differences as a negative rather than a positive is deeply troubling to me. We can do better for our children. Growing up, I thought I was broken. Sadly, I had to go on to study education to realize it wasn't me; it was the system. It's also sad that I had to wait until I was an adult to realize that a different approach to teaching and learning could have helped me to thrive from the beginning. There still are so many children out there today who have low self-esteem, call themselves stupid, and believe they will never amount to anything. They don't realize the *school is failing them; they* are not failing school. If the schools I attended had been designed differently, if I had been exposed to project-based learning, experiential learning, inquiry-based learning, and if creativity had been at the core, rather than a *banking model* (Freire, 1996) focused on memorization and regurgitation, I believe I would have had an entirely different experience in school—a much more positive experience. I believe that my teachers would have come to know me better as a learner so that they could have better supported me. Looking back, one of the things that I find so troubling is that, with the exception of my sixth-grade teacher, Mr. Bush, and my two French teachers in high school, I cannot remember a single teacher reaching out to me and making me feel like they truly, deeply cared. Most of them either made me feel like I was doing something wrong (not trying hard enough), threatened me with a fail in their class, or somehow didn't even see me at all.

Importantly, all my educational experiences in elementary, middle, and high school were in public schools, but they were all *highly-resourced* public schools in a wealthy suburban town in Connecticut. My trajectory would have been entirely different if I had been in one of the many schools in the United States that are severely, horrifically, dangerously underfunded. I was able to get through, with just passing grades, in my well-resourced schools. I hated school, but I made it through. I am sure that part of the reason I could push through is because, in many ways, the schools I attended were designed for students with my identities (e.g., White, cisgender, English as a first language). I was already struggling a great deal in school, so if I had been in a school (and living in a society) where my identities were disregarded and destroyed, I wonder if/how I would have pushed through and what sort of a toll it would have taken on me. The fact that most students are forced to push through in school systems that aren't designed for them (and arguably, in many cases, are even designed to keep them down) is perhaps the most significant problem with our schools.

By the time I reached high school, I had virtually given up on academics and focused instead, almost entirely, on my social life. My social life was filled to the brim, and the academic part of school was just something I had to make it through. I was not motivated to learn. There are only three high school classes I have positive memories of. One was French, both because my teachers made the material fun (perhaps because they weren't as tied to the standardized tests) and made explicit efforts to get to know me as an individual, and also because I desperately wanted to visit France so I was motivated to learn the language. I was, ultimately, lucky enough to participate in an exchange program. I hosted a French student before my junior year of high school and then spent a summer living in Paris before my senior year. That was the most profound learning experience I had in all of high school. The second high-school class I enjoyed was Introduction to Psychology. It was the first time I felt truly curious to learn about the content, which motivated me to go to college to take more psychology classes. The third class I enjoyed was World History. I don't remember much about the class as a whole, but I do remember, for the first time, being given an assignment where I could *choose* what I wanted to focus on. I was blown away by this prospect. I chose to do a research project on the My Lai massacre. I am not entirely sure how/why I chose that topic, but perhaps there were a few sentences in our history book that shocked me into wanting to learn more. I dove into that project with all my heart. I stayed up all night the day before it was due—not because I waited until the last minute to work on it, but because I didn't want to stop working on it and I knew the deadline was fast approaching. It is amazing the difference that a seemingly little thing like a choice can make. I was so emotionally impacted by what I learned from that assignment that I felt compelled to travel to Vietnam. And four years later, I did, still holding on to all the details from that high school research project. Later, when I began to study education, it was no surprise to me that student choice is one of the biggest factors in motivation and engagement in learning (National Academies of Sciences, Engineering, and Medicine, 2018). That one assignment where I was able to choose a topic to research not only sparked motivation in me that I had lost long ago, but it also served as inspiration for years to come.

So how does this experience impact me as an educator? For one, I am significantly aware of the intersections between identity and learning. I am intentional about making sure students feel valued, see themselves in the curriculum, and feel safe to take risks. I am also deeply committed to providing students choice in what and how they are learning. I provide them with a variety of ways to learn the material and a variety of ways to illustrate what they have learned. I still help students to grow and stretch beyond their comfort zones, but always with support. I focus on experiential, project-based and inquiry-based approaches to learning so that students are actively involved in co-constructing knowledge and using critical thinking skills to explore their curiosities and to develop innovative solutions to the challenges they face. I also remind myself and my students of Paulo Freire's mantra: *we are always in the process of becoming*. That ongoing process of becoming is what makes us human beings.

I intentionally talk with my students about growth mindset (Dweck, 2016)—a concept I wish I had known about when I was younger—and I remind students that it is their effort that will make them learn and grow. When students want me to give them an answer or tell them how to do something, I refer them to Brown, Roediger, and McDaniel (2014) who argue that "productive confusion" is one of the most powerful ways to learn. I prioritize student inquiry and create space for students to experiment and make mistakes. I also follow the advice of John Dewey (1916) who argues we should "give the pupils something to do, not something to learn"; as he explains, through *educative experiences*, students are required to think and draw connections, and through this process, "learning naturally results" (p. 181). As such, I prioritize the learning experience, emphasize process over product, de-emphasize grades, and de-couple grading and feedback (Brown, Roediger and McDaniel, 2014; Kohn, 2011; Hattie and Timperley, 2007; Wiggins, 2012). If I had my way, I would follow the advice of Alfie Kohn and eliminate grades entirely so that students and teachers alike could focus solely on the learning experience. Perhaps one day I will.

Finally, I prioritize relationships with my students. I want to make sure the students feel connected to the material, connected to their peers, and connected to me as the teacher. If students feel connected, they will be in a much better place to explore learning. I start from the beginning by creating a brave space (Arao & Clemens, 2013) where we can share and listen to each other's stories, and through that process, learn more about ourselves as learners and teachers. I prioritize getting to know my students as individuals so I can help them make choices within our class assignments that will be relevant and meaningful to their lives beyond my classroom. If I see a student on the verge of giving up at any point in the course, I dive right in to figure out what is going on and help them climb back up. If a student is struggling there is always a reason, and it is rarely their fault (though often appears to be on the surface).

I want all my students to know that I deeply care about them. They may have missed a foundational concept and are struggling to keep up; they may have broken up with a significant other and are finding it hard to focus; they may have been experiencing microaggressions (Sue, 2010); they might have a mentally or physically ill family member; they may have a hidden learning disability; they might be struggling with depression or anxiety. There are any number of reasons a student might pull away from school, but I always try to help them to come back. I might not be successful 100% of the time, but I always try.

Ultimately, the reason I am now in teacher and leadership development rather than in a K–12 classroom is because I came to understand that the people I want to be teaching are the teachers and school leaders themselves. This makes me feel as though I can have a greater impact. Students should not have the experiences that I had in school. Educators can do better. Schools can do better. As I said at the beginning, my mission is to support the development of teachers and educational leaders who value and engage with multiple ways of knowing, thinking, and being in this world. This mission is grounded in my past experiences as a student and it is lived out in my current practice as the director of a Master of Education program. I might not be perfect, but this is the goal that I strive toward.

Tracy Penny Light

I love learning! This is the first sentence of my teaching philosophy and at the heart of all my teaching and research. I have also always loved being at school—I was the kid who hated summer holidays because I enjoyed being in a classroom environment. I thrived in the classroom, whereas I struggled on the playground to fit in and make friends, probably in part because I was so keen on academics while other kids were more interested in play. That isn't to say that I didn't enjoy socializing with the few close friends I had. Still, I was in my element in the classroom because the other kids seemed to recognize that I was a good person to have in their learning group—from an early age I could discern the best way to get a good mark. Looking back, I don't believe this was evidence of me being a strategic learner (Entwistle, 2008), but rather an integrative or deep one (Biggs, 1993). Regardless of why I approached learning the way I did, the natural flip-side of this was that I generally wasn't included on the playground and even recall being teased of because of my commitment to learning. One specific incident in grade 6 stands out—it wasn't an isolated event but reasonably typical of the kind of exchanges I had with my classmates throughout my elementary school years. It must have happened sometime in May or June because we were nearing our elementary school graduation (where I grew up, we attended a middle school for grades 7 and 8 before heading to high school) and prizes were awarded to some graduates for various achievements. I believed that I was in the running for some academic awards and was keen to receive them. During this incident, some kids reported that another female student wanted to "fight me." Apparently, she disliked something about me and was promoting a physical fight to settle things. The other girl was more popular than me and there were clear stakes involved in asserting myself. While I was definitely not interested in fighting (mainly because I was afraid of being hurt or getting into trouble, which I remember feeling like I was very likely to be), I used my chance at the awards as a rationale and excuse for not engaging with her. I remember telling one of the other children that I didn't want to "risk" losing out on the music award, and to tell the other girl that was the reason for not fighting her.

Looking back, I used my status as a good student to avoid having to engage in the fight but also to assert my position as someone who did not engage in such behavior. I remember being ridiculed for taking this stance—apparently the more socially acceptable thing to do was to physically assert myself—as a result, my "smart stance" served to reinforce that my domain was the classroom, not the playground, a space that was difficult to inhabit during a time when peer group membership is established (Newman, Lohman, & Newman, 2007; Goodenow, 1993). I had, as it were, chosen my place in the social hierarchy.

Given my identity development as a "good student," there was never any question (in my mind, at least) that I would go on to higher education after high school. I fast-tracked, giving up the opportunity of spare periods in high school in favor of more classes to finish sooner. While neither of my parents are university educated (my mother, one of the smartest people I know, did not even finish high school), they were both incredibly supportive of me pursuing higher education, even though we were not a wealthy family. Luckily, I grew up in Canada and my province then had a robust student loan program, so I could attend undergraduate and graduate school with support, some of which came in the form of grants. This meant that, while I had a substantial loan to repay upon completion of graduate school, it was far less than if I lived elsewhere.

And, as someone who has always strived to achieve, I have never regretted or resented having a debt to repay for the privilege of my education. I realize now, though, that this is a privileged perspective and not representative of all students' experiences, even those who identify as "smart". I have witnessed countless students struggle to afford their higher education throughout my academic career, both as a student and professor. As such, I regularly encourage my students to consider issues of power and privilege, even when in classes where this is not the explicit focus of the curriculum. For many students, a misstep in a class or on an exam can mean that their scholarships are rescinded. For others it might mean familial or community trauma. In my case, my parents, especially, supported my desire to pursue my education and there was never any question that their support would wane if I failed. And, yet, my identity was so connected to academic ability (for instance, I was the "smart" one where my sister was the "pretty" one) that my ability to achieve academically was never in question, at least in terms of others' perceptions of me. My first real academic "failure" came when I did not receive an offer of admission to law school at the conclusion of my bachelor's degree. Throughout my undergraduate studies, I know now, I did begin to employ strategic learning practices to ensure my success in certain contexts, choosing subjects that were suited to my learning preferences so that I could be successful—I quickly recognized that, even if I enjoyed learning a subject, the assessment strategies could make or break my success (I was really interested in psychology but did not feel I could be successful on multiple-choice tests). Such courses and even whole disciplines were avoided. Despite my focus on learning in disciplines both where I was able to engage in deep learning and which assessed my abilities in ways that made sense to me (I had an "A" average), the fact that I worked at a law office throughout my undergraduate studies, and earned a decent (albeit mediocre) LSAT score, it was a shock (yes, that is the correct word—I was absolutely shocked!) not to get into any of the law schools to which I applied. Lost, I took a job at a university in the student recruitment office. Despite being successful in my role, it was clear that they only desired recent graduates, so after one year, I figured that my next best option was graduate school—it was simply to obtain another degree to avoid choosing a career, rather than an intentional choice toward a particular career path.

 When I began graduate school, it was not clear to me what I could do with a bachelor's degree in history. While I'd previously always loved being at school, as a new graduate student, I was immediately made to feel by some male peers in my Master of Arts (History) program that I was stupid and inadequately prepared for graduate-level study. For instance, they made fun of me and told me I was a "closet Marxist" (an insult I didn't even understand at the time). They also made comments upon the return of our papers such as "it must be nice to get good marks because you have breasts or wear short skirts"—these comments always seemed amusing to me (more so than the one aimed directly at my intellect) because I am not particularly well-endowed nor did I wear short skirts. However, I was female, and I later learned that this was the root of their disdain with my presence in the program. Early on in my degree, however, a new professor joined the faculty and became my advisor. Not only did she teach me about doing history, but she also modelled what it meant to be an encouraging teacher by introducing me to academic conferences and being readily available to discuss teaching and research strategies. She was also a feminist and made quite sure that I understood the challenges of being a woman in academia and that I ought not accept the male derogatory "banter" through a desire to avoid any conflict (I'd learned early on in my education that it was easiest to smile and play nice, rather than to risk marginalizing myself further by fighting back). In short, she taught me about being a teacher/mentor and what it meant to be an educated woman. Later, I would equate these things with being an academic.

Despite all the personal and professional growth during my time as a Master's student, I was still unsure what to do next. As I'd done previously, I decided to pursue a Ph.D. and study with my M.A. Advisor's former Ph.D. advisor. This was not a conscious choice made to firmly place myself on the path to becoming an academic, but rather a move to buy time to figure out what to do for my career. Not surprisingly, my Ph.D. advisor was also a fantastic role model, mentor, and teacher who inspired me not only to strive but also to thrive in an academic environment. However, I also had my children during the early stages of my Ph.D., the timing of which meant that my grades were delayed (I took maternity leaves as my field courses were in progress) and by connection, funding opportunities became more limited (at the time, and perhaps still, grades are tied to funding). To supplement my family income, I took a graduate position in my university's Teaching and Learning Office. There I grew further as a teacher and loved the work of supporting the development of other graduate students' teaching initially, and then later that of faculty. I continued in academic development roles throughout my Ph.D., which eventually delayed its completion. And this began the root of my identity crisis—I constantly wondered whether I was an historian, or a teacher—the former was an academic identity, intimately connected to my "smart" identity, and the latter something lesser.

I'm not sure where the idea came from that working in academic development was a lesser career path (read, not smart) than a traditional academic job. Perhaps it was in part due to the appalled reactions I got from some fellow history faculty members when I suggested that, to learn how to do history, the best assessment might not be a full-blown research paper in a large introductory course with students unfamiliar with the discipline. Perhaps it was when, alongside my other academic colleagues while in a teaching and learning role, I was referred to as a "resource support person" rather than as a fellow academic. Or perhaps it was the acknowledgment by my mentor that the ceiling for me would be as an Associate Director of a Teaching and Learning Center; he advised that I would not be accepted by other faculty and senior administrators in the role of Director or beyond without having served as a "regular" faculty member—one who had successfully managed to jump through the hoops to earn tenure and (at a minimum) Associate Professor status. He advised (kindly) that only those professors would be taken seriously in an academic leadership role. I was particularly deflated by this realization, especially since I was the one training those "real" professors to be better teachers!! Luckily, I was able to land a tenure-track job (something that makes me far more privileged and frankly not necessarily any better than the countless colleagues undertaking precarious academic work), and I have published good (according to my peers) research in my discipline, as well as in interdisciplinary fields and education. I successfully earned tenure and climbed through the ranks as a professor while also serving as a university administrator at several levels and different universities. Why, then, have I continued to struggle with my academic identity, especially when it seems that I've done everything right? To be honest, I think the root is probably my ability to reflect on my learning and integrate not just what I know, but also what I still don't know. From an early age I recognized that part of my identity was tied to my ability to be successful because I was "smart" and yet I am acutely aware of all the things I do not know or have yet to learn.

Writing this story of learning has reinforced the importance of our own histories and the role they play in our thinking and beliefs about ourselves and others. My story of learning and teaching can really only be understood through the various lenses of my family history, my academic history, the history of my teachers and mentors. All of these histories are layers in my identity and form part of a complex, interplay of factors that, as a whole, is represented in and by my career. Reflecting deeply on my story as a teacher and learner helps me to recognize that all of our stories, and those of my students, are unique and these unique stories shape how we learn and move through the world. It also reinforces that our stories are not static—they are ever-evolving and shift and change over time with our experiences. As historian Joan Scott teaches us, "...narrative is a way of making human experience meaningful" (Scott, 2011, pp. 203-204). Rather than seeing my story as an identity crisis, I recognize in telling it that it holds deep meaning for me. And, it is a story I share with my students.

My teaching philosophy revolves around the importance of reflection and meaning-making to know oneself. In all learning contexts in which I am a teacher or facilitator, I work to provide opportunities for my learners to reflect on their own stories and to understand how that shapes their learning process, the research questions they ask, and how they interrogate their data/sources, or the learning experiences they design for their own students. In my view, without at least some self-awareness of our histories and how they shape who we are as learners and teachers, it is impossible to grow. I want my students to use their educational experiences to find ways to make a positive change in their own lives, those of their families, and in their communities. I hope the teachers I work with can leverage their own stories to design more engaging and effective learning experiences for the students they teach. It is my hope that sharing my stories here, and with my students and colleagues when I'm teaching them that it makes evident the importance of connecting our personal and professional identities to our work. And, I hope that it helps to reinforce the *value* of seeing each other as people, all of whom have our own stories and struggles that shape who we are and how we teach and learn.

Adam Carswell

Fostering joyful, engaging, and purposeful learning has remained a constant focus in my work at schools over the past quarter-century, regardless of geography or role. In response to this book's prompts, I feverishly wrote down my childhood and adolescent recollections of school experiences. When finished, I re-visited those memories through critical reflection to identify emergent themes. The process was enlightening, and I may have discovered why I have always prioritized the creation of joyful and engaging school climates, as well as the motivation for my obsession with purposeful learning and real-world application.

In general, I don't see myself as an academic; as much as I enjoy learning, school was not always easy for me. As I reviewed my educational autobiography, I saw cyclical patterns of success and disengagement. That said, I had a rather consistent *desire* to do well in school, even in "chapters" of my educational story where I was disengaged and less successful. Interestingly, the more successful years seem to be coupled with joyful and engaging school experiences shaped by teachers who cared, teachers who had a palpable interest in me as a person and student. Dewey (1938) wrote, "What avail is it to win prescribed amounts of information about geography or history, to win the ability to read and write if in the process the individual loses his own soul?" (p. 49). With this in mind, educators should strive to engage students in a way that will ignite their creativity, generate a state of flow, and make learning in school a joyful and authentic experience that will endure for a lifetime. Students who are given opportunities to develop their passions and engage in deep learning experiences are more apt to develop a true love of learning and lead lives of purpose where they inspire, lead, and make a difference in their own unique way.

I began my high school years with a disengaged mindset and mediocre academic standing, the product of a lackluster publicly funded school environment where individualism was muted. Sensing my frustration, my parents offered me the opportunity to attend Trinity College School (TCS), an all-boys' boarding school. As a new student, I felt overwhelmed with a new reality I had not yet encountered—academic rigor and high expectations across the board. I struggled academically at first, but where I struggled, there was a very intentional support structure in place. This was an important differentiator. I vividly recalled that teachers authentically cared about my well-being, which showed in their words and actions. Learning activities were engaging, rigorous, and strategically planned, while consequences for not putting forth sufficient effort were in plain sight. It was considered uncool by peers and faculty alike to be academically delinquent.

An important lesson I learned at TCS is that it is more meaningful when learning is relevant and exciting. The more meaningful the learning, the more likely it will be internalized and applied. I recall a geography unit on urban planning with an assignment requiring me to identify an underutilized parcel of public land, research gaps in the city's infrastructure or amenities, and then design and propose a land-use improvement project. The expectations were high and the work was beyond anything I had experienced in school. The process was as important as the product, and if I do say so myself, the product was pretty spectacular. Of course, all of this was joyfully facilitated by a keen and supportive teacher with whom I was able to freely dialogue about my ideas. He provided regular and encouraging feedback (even if constructively critical), and considered our work together of upmost importance. Our relationship, built on his authentic interest in my success and well-being, was the foundation for my success in that class, and that trickled into every aspect of my TCS experience.

Despite academic rigor and high expectations, TCS allowed plenty of leeway for boisterous boys to engage wholeheartedly in whatever passion or interest they found meaningful. Hughes and Gullo (2010) referenced the frightening reality that students are often deprived of the opportunity to construct knowledge how they are naturally inclined to do so—through play, social interaction, imagination, creativity, and problem-solving. Instead, they are frequently subjected to content-oriented, skills-based conventional teacher-directed learning where activities include listening, sitting still, and completing a never-ending stream of worksheets. When teachers create a climate that does not inspire positivity, inspiration, shared priorities, and collaboration amongst a school's stakeholders, joyful and authentic learning is less likely. At TCS, we were encouraged to be true to ourselves, to try new things, and explore opportunities that contributed to our development as human beings. Aside from academics, arts, and athletics, what little downtime we had was spent hatching some elaborate prank or getting into "trouble," although usually nothing too serious! Challenging beyond anything I had encountered in other schools, I truly enjoyed my experience at Trinity College School and will always be thankful to my parents for the opportunity to attend.

While at university, and in the midst of my quest to find a meaningful and productive life purpose, I was fortunate to have been a lifeguard and swim instructor at Northwood Easter Seals Camp. Easter Seals Canada, an organization that supports those living with disabilities, runs summer camps throughout Ontario. The enjoyment I realized while working with children could not be denied, and one particular summer, I somehow managed to relate that sense of fulfillment to my TCS experience. If I could become a teacher, I would dedicate my life to making a difference in children's lives—to making their learning experience engaging, personalized, joyful, and relevant. I would intentionally build meaningful relationships with students just as *some* teachers had done with me.

With that clear goal in mind, my teacher training in Australia was *purposeful and relevant*. The coursework was exhilarating, engaging, and most importantly pragmatic—it was preparing me to become a teacher! The first of two long-term practicums was in a grade two classroom at The Southport School, an all-boys' independent school, and I felt honored to be their first student-teacher. Furthermore, I was placed with a male grade two teacher, a rarity at the elementary level, and he was a fantastic mentor. My second practicum was in a grade seven class at the *only* school in Yeppoon, a tiny coastal town. Although very different in terms of demographics and resources, both practicum experiences provided invaluable opportunities to put what I had learned into practice—purposeful learning and real-world application.

It seems that despite having lived in three countries, working in public and independent schools with students ranging from kindergarten to graduate studies, I have retained consistency in my commitment to joyful, engaging, and purposeful learning as a teacher and school leader. Storytelling paired with critical reflection has helped me to understand why.

Concluding Thoughts

The three of us have quite distinct experiences, feelings and memories associated with our learning experiences, and we have each taken unique paths toward our current roles as educational leaders. Through this reflective process, we have gained clarity about why we work so well together, how we compliment each other, and also how we can best challenge each other in order to continue to grow together. We highly recommend other teaching teams to engage in this process, though it does not have to result in academic writing as it does here. Even just the process of sharing and listening to each other's stories of learning can help to strengthen a teaching team. We are lucky in that we already work well together, so for us it enhanced our understanding of how and why that is the case and gave us further inspiration for drawing out each other's strengths. This process could also work well in teams that are not functioning as effectively as the process of sharing and listening to each other's stories can help the team members to build empathy. And regardless of whether you are currently teaching or leading collaboratively, this process is helpful at the individual level. This work of excavating your learning stories strengthens your self-awareness, which allows you to enter into any new teaching and leadership experiences with greater clarity.

References

Adichie, C.N. (2009, July). *The danger of a single story*. [Video file]. Retrieved from https://www.ted.com/talks/chimamanda_ngozi_adichie_the_danger_of_a_single_story

Arao, B., & Clemens, K. (2013). From safe spaces to brave spaces. In L. M. Laundreman (Ed.), *The art of effective facilitation: Reflections from social justice educators* (pp. 135-150). Stylus.

Bartolomé, L. I. (Ed.). (2008). *Ideologies in education: Unmasking the trap of teacher neutrality*. Peter Lang.

Biggs, J. B. (1993). What do inventories of students' learning processes really measure? A theoretical review and clarification. *British Journal of Educational Psychology, 63*, 3–19.

Brown, P. C., Roediger III, H. L., & McDaniel, M. A. (2014). *Make it stick*. Harvard University Press.

Dewey, J. (1916). Democracy and education: An introduction to the philosophy of education. MacMillan.

Dewey, J. (1938). *Experience and education*. New York, NY: Collier.

Dweck, C. (2016). What having a "growth mindset" actually means. *Harvard Business Review, 13*, 213-226.

Entwistle N. (2008). *Taking stock: Teaching and learning research in higher education* [Conference Paper]. Ontario International Symposium on Teaching and Learning in Higher Education. https://www.researchgate.net/publication/234559483_Understanding_Student_Learning#fullTextFileContent

Freire, P. (1996). Pedagogy of the oppressed (revised). *Continuum.*

Kohn, A. (2011). The case against grades. *Educational Leadership, 69*(3), 28-33.

Goodenow, C. (1993). Classroom belonging among early adolescent students: Relationships to motivation and achievement. *Journal of Early Adolescence, 13*(1), 21-43.

Hattie, J., & Timperley, H. (2007). The power of feedback. *Review of educational research, 77*(1), 81-112.

Hughes, K., & Gullo, D. (2010). Joyful learning and assessment in kindergarten. *Young Children, 65*(3), 57-59.

McLaren, P. (1993). Multiculturalism and the postmodern critique: Towards a pedagogy of resistance and transformation. *Cultural studies, 7*(1), 118-146.

National Academies of Sciences, Engineering, and Medicine (2018). *How People Learn II: Learners, Contexts, and Cultures.* The National Academies Press.

Newman, B.M., Lohman, B.J., & Newman, P.R. (2007). Peer group membership and a sense of belonging: Their relationship to adolescent behavior problems. *Adolescence, 42*(166), 241-263.

Smith, L.T. (1999). *Decolonizing methodologies: Research and indigenous peoples.* Zed Books.

Sue, D. W. (2010). *Microaggressions in everyday life: Race, gender, and sexual orientation.* John Wiley & Sons.

Trouillot, M. (1994). Haiti's nightmare and the lessons of history. *NACLA Report on the Americas, 17*(4), 46-53.

Wiggins, G. (2012). Seven keys to effective feedback. *Educational Leadership, 70*(1), 10-16.

Zinn, H. (2003). *A people's history of the United States: 1492 - present.* HarperCollins Publishers.

Conclusion

Re-storying Education for Future Generations

Laura Colket & Tracy Penny Light

> "Professors who embrace the challenge of self-actualization will be better able to create pedagogical practices that engage students, providing them with ways of knowing that enhance their capacity to live fully and deeply" (hooks, 1994, p. 22).

We all have stories, yet sometimes, we do not explore them, let alone share them. As the book's contributors found, this is sometimes simply due to a lack of conscious effort, but sometimes it is because our stories highlight trauma and/or shame that we do not want to relive or reveal. Whether we engage with these stories or not, our own experiences of learning are reflected in our teaching and leadership philosophies, our pedagogical practices, and our relationships with students and colleagues. An archeological dive into our past experiences helps us to understand the connections between our past, our present, and our imagined futures.

The framework provided in this book enables educators to build connections between their stories of learning and their stories of teaching in order to enhance their ongoing professional growth. Importantly, our framework encourages educators to reflect on their stories (and by extension, the stories of their colleagues and their students) with the aim of creating more equitable and inclusive educational institutions and learning environments. This book is a starting point for that process, as it represents a collection of powerful stories that can help educators reimagine their practice. In this final chapter, we summarize and discuss the themes that emerged from the stories presented in each of the chapters. We also examine the key takeaways from our post-writing discussions with the authors. Finally, we reflect on the ways this work can contribute to our goal of using storytelling to create more equitable, inclusive, and accessible educational environments.

Themes from the Chapters

Across the chapters in this edited volume, five main interconnected themes emerged: trauma, shame, belonging, motivation, and relationships. It is notable that nearly all the authors experienced some form of trauma (either an isolated incident, multiple incidents, or a prolonged experience) during their time as a student, but they also all had experiences and/or individuals that helped them to re-ignite their motivation and passion for learning. As educators, we are able to help students create more hopeful and empowering stories; we can do this by creating spaces where they feel a sense of connection and belonging, spaces where they feel safe and brave enough to grow. This requires critical attention to the inequities that surround us so that we can do the work necessary to create more transformative and liberatory spaces for teaching and learning. As Freire (1992) reminds us: "One of the tasks of the progressive educator....is to unveil opportunities for hope, no matter what the obstacles may be" (p. 3). bell hooks shares this sense of optimism, despite the significant challenges that educators and students face. As she explains, "learning is a place where paradise can be created" (1994, p. 207). As educators, we must embrace this sense of hope as we contend with and respond to the current reality in which far too many students experience trauma.

It is easy for us to get stuck in and continue to perpetuate a cycle of trauma. If a parent experienced trauma as a child, if they do not do significant work to process that trauma, they are at risk of passing the trauma down to their children, often unknowingly. The same goes for educators. When we experience trauma as students, we are at risk of perpetuating that trauma if we do not identify and then interrupt the story. However, when we increase our self-literacy (Ravitch, preface), we increase our chances of interrupting intergenerational trauma and/or recovering from first-hand trauma. We need to do this work, both for ourselves and for future generations of students.

Throughout the stories shared in this volume, we also saw many examples of shame, an emotion that often results from trauma, though isn't always connected to a traumatic event. Burgo (2018) details four distinct types of shame: unrequited love, unwanted exposure, exclusion, and disappointed expectations. With the exception of unrequited love (which makes sense given the focus of these stories), we saw a plethora of examples of each type of shame identified by Burgo. As humans, these feelings of shame are unavoidable; despite our best efforts, we will all have times as students when we are exposed, excluded, and/or disappointed. However, as educators, we can learn more about how shame impacts learning and how we can help students to recover from, learn from, and ultimately re-story shame (and we can do the same for ourselves).

Brené Brown (2018) describes shame as "the intensely painful feeling or experience of believing that we are flawed and therefore unworthy of love, belonging and connection" (p. 69). We can help our students to understand that, even if they experience unwanted exposure, exclusion or disappointment, it does not mean that they are flawed and not worthy of love, belonging, and connection. If we start to foreground empathy for our students and our colleagues, we can start to combat shame. Currently, however, we have an education system that is flooded with shame. Brown conducted research on shame and saw how ubiquitous it is in our schools. She explains:

> ...85% of the people we interviewed could recall a school incident from their childhood that was shaming, it changed how they thought of themselves as learners.... on the flip side of that finding, the same data showed that more than 90% of the people we interviewed could name a teacher, coach, school administrator or faculty member who reinforced their ability". (p. 132)

In educational settings, feelings of shame can be seen through statements such as "I'm not smart enough," "I'm not good enough," "I am not worthy of being in this space." Many of the authors of this book told that story about themselves at some point in their journey as a student (or even still now in their professional life). Some of these stories originated from self-talk after a painful experience, some of them grew from a poisonous seed planted by a fellow student, a parent, or society more broadly, and some of these stories grew from seeds that were planted by a teacher, by a school's curriculum, and/or grew within a toxic school environment. These are things that we, as educators, have control over. We can help shape and reshape students' stories about themselves (as well as our stories about ourselves as educators). Shame should not be permeating our schools. We should not be shaming our students, and we should not allow others to shame them. We need to create spaces of learning where students can see themselves in the curriculum, where they can express themselves, where they feel like they belong and are cared for. While it is terrifying how one teacher's words can destroy a child's belief in themselves, it is also empowering to know that the words of a teacher can help rebuild a child's belief in themselves. We see evidence of this repeatedly in the stories of this book. The stories shared throughout echo Brown's findings: most of the authors revealed moments of shame, but they also discussed people or experiences that helped them to recover from that shame.

It is unfortunate that students carry an incredible amount of emotional weight with them, almost all the time. Some of that weight might help a child build muscle, but some of that weight is completely crushing. As educators, we cannot instantly change the broader cultural context in which our educational institutions are situated, but we do have the ability and responsibility to create mini cultures in our classrooms and schools that allow and encourage students not simply to exist, but to feel like they belong, and ultimately that they can thrive. Brené Brown (2018) explains:

> As I often tell teachers—some of our most important leaders—we can't always ask our students to take off the armor at home, or even on their way to school, because their emotional and physical safety may require self-protection. But what we can do, and what we are ethically called to do, is create a space in our schools and classrooms where all students can walk in, and for that day or hour, take off the crushing weight of their armor, hang it on a rack, and open their heart to truly being seen. (p. 13)

The need to be seen is an essential human psychological need, yet so many authors of the chapters in this book shared examples (some of which were prolonged) in which they were not only *not* seen, but where they felt "erased." They saw their culture erased in the history books; they felt their identities were erased from the discussion; they felt compelled to erase their home language to survive. As Browning (Section 1) states, "I walked in a world that challenged my being."

At some point in their educational journey, many of the authors did not feel welcome in their schools. They sometimes did not feel welcome because of subtle messages, and at other times they were explicitly told they were not welcome. Kapadia (Section 2) describes schools as carceral spaces because, far too often, they are designed to punish, control, and exclude students. Many of the authors of these chapters were left, as children, to manage stress, anxiety, depression, and feelings of inadequacy on their own. Their stories were privately held; many of their stories were not even told until they were shared in this book. Many of the authors were left to grapple with (and in some cases fight against) racism, colonialism, indoctrination, bullying and imposter syndrome on their own, *as children*. Take a moment to think about the weight of all the deeply harmful stories that our students are walking around with today, right now, as you are reading this book.

Despite the oppressive weight of the world that many of our authors had to bear as children and young adults, all of them found tools and supports to help them survive and even thrive. For many, it was a caring adult who influenced them, encouraged them, advocated for them, and equipped them with critical thinking skills that they could carry with them as they moved forward. For others, it was out-of-school experiences that helped them to build back their confidence and motivation for learning. For some, it was a new pedagogy or curriculum that finally allowed them to connect to the content and feel motivated to learn more. For others, it was a mindset instilled in them from their parents or grandparents that helped them push through, regardless of the obstacles before them. Each of the authors had something that helped them to unlearn and retell their harmful stories. As educators, we are in a perfect position to help our students with this process of re-framing their stories about themselves. But we must uncover and understand our own stories first.

Many of the authors in this edited volume are still in the process of unlearning some of the harmful stories they told themselves and were told about themselves when they were younger. As Freire and Greene explain, it is expected that this process is ongoing: as humans, we are always in the process of becoming, forever on our way. But we need to put in the effort to engage in that process. It can be arduous and painful, but it can also be liberatory. And through this process of engaging in an archeological dive into our learning foundations, we can, in time, transform education for future generations. Freire (1998) reminds us: "To the degree that the historical past is not 'problematized' so as to be critically understood, tomorrow becomes simply the perpetuation of today" (p. 102).

In their entirety, this book's stories represent an ongoing conversation we all have with ourselves as we continually develop professionally and personally and the need for and importance of regular reflection in our daily personal and professional lives. Importantly, this reflection is not for reflection's sake, but rather, it is so we can become transformative educators to create more powerful and equitable learning environments for our students. We must actively engage with this ongoing process. Angela Davis, an academic and political activist, underscored this in a lecture when she said: "You have to act as if it were possible to radically transform the world. And you have to do it all the time" (2014).

As we engage in this work to create more liberatory spaces for teaching and learning, we must prioritize relationships with our students. As bell hooks (1994) reminds us: "teach[ing] in a manner that respects and cares for the souls of our students is essential if we are to provide the necessary conditions where learning can most deeply and intimately begin (hooks, 1994, p. 13). Thich Naht Hanh (2004) also addresses the importance of relationships in schools as he describes his experience as a student:

> When I was in school, a teacher was like a father or mother, big sister or big brother, and there was love and communication between the teacher and the students. A school was a place where you learned how to live. Now, too often, it is only a place where you receive information or are put in danger. In too many schools, human relationships are no longer important and students no longer see themselves as brothers and sisters. This is a great loss. (p. 165)

We observed this focus on relationships throughout the chapters as well. Repeatedly, the authors reflected on moments in which they were lifted up, pushed forward, and brought back to life by a relationship with a teacher, a fellow student, or a mentor. Relationships matter. Positive relationships help create more space for joy, love, and belonging, which ultimately creates more space for motivation, learning, and growth. Through relationships, we can explore and reimagine our stories as students and teachers, and ultimately, imagine and then create more transformative and liberatory spaces for teaching and learning for the current and future generations.

Collaborative Reflection Process

One of the most powerful aspects of this book was the collaborative process of sharing, listening, and reflecting as we created it. In this section, we share what we (the editors and the contributing authors) learned through this collaborative reflection process in hopes of supporting others who want to engage in this work of excavation, storying, and re-storying in a similarly collaborative process. After each author wrote their chapter, they shared their stories with each other. Most of the authors had never met each other before and felt vulnerable sharing such personal stories. But also, through the process of reading, commenting on and discussing each other's stories, the author's felt connected, validated, and personally and professionally invigorated. It took a great deal of courage for our authors to engage in their archaeological dive, and then to share their experiences and perspectives with others. Because "courage is contagious" as Brené Brown (2018) reminds us, we are not only sharing the stories, but we are also sharing the process behind this book, in hopes that we might inspire others to be courageous enough to collectively embrace, or at least explore, the vulnerability that comes hand-in-hand with this autoethnographic work.

Through our collaborative post-writing reflections, several themes about this process emerged: (1) this process (perhaps productively) blurs the lines between public and private; (2) this process is both painful and therapeutic; (3) memory, culture, discipline, and audience shape this process (sometimes in yet to be identified ways); (4) this process helps create personal connections and builds community; and (5) this process has impacted our beliefs and our practices as educators. We discuss each of these themes below.

Private & Public Stories

Through our post-writing reflection, the authors noted the need to lean into their vulnerability as we surfaced and shared stories that were previously untold, revealing the often "secretive" side of ourselves. As one of our authors (Kapadia) noted, these private narratives are important for filling in the gaps for what is often not part of the public narrative. The more of these stories we hear, the more we can start to shift that larger public narrative. Importantly, some stories were still left untold. For some of those untold stories, the authors were not yet ready to dive that deeply into their soil; for other stories, the risk of sharing them publicly feels too great. Several of our authors also noted that they would not have felt safe sharing some of the stories presented here earlier in their career. It is an important reminder to all of us that we have colleagues, right now, who are holding onto stories they do not feel safe sharing. Our society has not yet created the space for some stories to be freely shared, and as Browning explains in his chapter (Section 1) "I am concerned that the stories unheard are the ones that hold the keys to fully understanding the world in which we live." Though there is still much work to do in this regard, in our post-writing reflections, one of our authors (Reynolds) noted feeling hopeful about this blurring of the public and the private when it comes to what stories we share, as it creates more space for educators and students alike to bring their whole selves into this work of teaching and learning.

Pain & Therapy

All the authors noted the cathartic power of telling their stories of learning and teaching as they re-remembered their own histories so that they could recover and reconnect to them. For some of the authors, this meant revisiting painful memories they had been avoiding. Several of the authors spent significant time reading through old journals and/or talking with family members to help surface some of the memories. It took a great deal of mental energy. In our post-writing discussions, the authors commiserated over how painful, yet powerful, the process was for them. Several of the authors (e.g. Kapadia, Browning, Kaloustian, MacDonald) also reflected on this in their writing, at the end of their chapters. In one of our post-writing discussions, one author described the process of writing and reading each other's stories as "digging deeper into our souls and the souls of others" (Ross). It takes strength, vulnerability and compassion to do this archaeological work. What is represented here is certainly not a complete project, but like therapy, it is part of an ongoing process.

Memory, Culture, Discipline & Audience

Another theme that came through in our post-writing discussions was that the stories we shared are undeniably shaped by culture, memory, theory, and audience. Our cultural perspectives shape what we experience, what we remember, and how we make sense of those memories. Memory also shifts and changes with time, with some details holding strong while others fade away. Memory theory tells us that the time and place in which stories are told shapes how the story is remembered. As such, if these stories had been told 20 years ago, they may have been different, or perhaps entirely different stories may have been told. Some of our memories have also been lost or buried, in some cases because of psychological survival strategies, and in other cases simply because we have become busy with life and have not been able to hold on to everything. On top of the role of memory, our academic disciplines also shape how we now process our memories. We now have access to theory that we did not have when we were younger, and the theories we ascribe to and are influenced by certainly shape how we process and make meaning of our experiences. Depending on our academic discipline, we have each been exposed to different theories and research, and thus our processing of our experiences has been uniquely impacted. Finally, the perceived audience also shaped which stories we told and how we chose to tell them. Some aspects of the stories may have been omitted while others were included or the first time because of the audience.

Our cultural traditions and academic traditions also shape our approach to storytelling, and this came through in each chapter of this book. Through our discussions and the feedback that authors provided to each other on their chapters, there were many moments of highlighting distinctions in cultural frameworks and disciplinary jargon. In many instances, contributors needed clarity because they weren't familiar with the disciplinary language or a cultural reference. They also noted the feedback process helped them clarify their story so it would connect with a broader audience. They were learning more and being exposed to different areas of literature and perspectives that were previously unfamiliar to them. It helped to build an academic community that extends beyond disciplinary and cultural boundaries. Many of the authors made changes to their chapter after receiving feedback from the other authors, and a few even brought this a step further by incorporating the actual comments into the text or making connections between their chapter and another through citations.

Connection & Community

The community aspect was, unexpectedly, one of the most powerful aspects of this entire project. One of the authors (Kaloustian) noted: "As transformative as the writing process has been, it is the community feedback that was most meaningful to me, I think. I am so grateful for this validating, supportive, compassionate community, and process." Through our shared storytelling, we became a community of educators and educational leaders who can continue to draw on each other's wisdom to broaden our own educational practices. Our hope is that, in your process of becoming, you will find ways to share your own stories, join our community, and build your own communities in your context.

We recognize how being vulnerable and self-aware enables us to gain empathy and compassion for others, whether it is our colleagues, students, family members, or even the broader community. There is great power in sharing stories in community. As Angela Davis notes, "It is in collectivities that we find reservoirs of hope and optimism" (2016, p. 46). And, as one of our author's (Roopnarine) noted, "other people's stories can bring light to our own." Throughout our discussion with the authors, there were repeated expressions of true empathy; even if authors did not share the same experiences, they understood the feelings associated with them. There were also many moments where authors noted shared experiences and felt connected that someone else, many metaphorical worlds away, had a similar experience to their own. The authors found this shared storytelling process to be one of looking through windows and into mirrors (Bishop, 1990), and through this they not only learned more about themselves but also built connections with each other. Many of the authors are looking forward to extending this work and finding further projects for collaboration.

Informing Practice

There were many exciting unintended outcomes of this project, but one of the things we set out to do from the beginning was to inform our own practice and the practices of other educators. We have already begun to see this happen. By telling our own and then reading each other's stories, the authors and editors alike gained new insights into their own positionality and experiences, and the ways those experiences (which are deeply informed by our social identities) shape our practice as educators. We also gleaned new ideas and faced important reminders from reading each other's stories. This process underscored that our humanness and our students' humanness have important reverberations for our practice as educators.

Several authors have already identified areas they plan to adjust in their practice as a result of this experience (e.g. weaving storytelling into their teaching, inviting students to share their stories, intentionally building more empathy for their colleagues and students, making a more conscious effort to lean into vulnerability in their teaching and leadership practice). One author (Sobering) noted that this experience better positioned him to shift to online teaching during this crisis while still maintaining connections with his students (which was particularly important during this time of social isolation because of the pandemic). He intends for his new approach to teaching (which is grounded in storytelling and building connections with students) to continue to shape his practice once he reverts back to teaching in person. All of the authors included in this book expressed a commitment to creating spaces that value all students' stories and find ways to leverage their, their colleagues, and their students' stories of learning to create more equitable, inclusive, and accessible spaces for teaching and learning.

Educators can be healers and agents of change (Emdin, 2016; Freire, 1992; Greene, 1997; Hahn, 2003; hooks, 1994; Paris, 2012; Rose, 1995). We have the power to reimagine pedagogy, curriculum, and school cultures. We can create safer, more loving, and more empowering spaces for students to learn and grow in. One of the ways we can do so is taking a more holistic and possibilities-oriented approach to education. Our stories can help us to reimagine what education can be. As Greene (1997) reminds us: "Imagination, after all, allows people to think of things as if they could be otherwise; it is the capacity that allows a looking through the windows of the actual towards alternative realities" (pp. 14-15). Our hope for a better future can provide us with fuel as we work toward creating radical change. Freire (1992) argues that this hope is a human need: "We need critical hope the way a fish needs unpolluted water" (p. 2). So, as we hold on to that critical hope, we can work on transforming education so that schools become more liberatory and filled with more connection, love, and belonging. We can create spaces where educators are inspired to embrace "the idea of multiple patterns of being and knowing, [a] regard for cultural differences, [an] attentiveness when it comes to voices never listened to before" (Greene, 1997, p. 15) and "confront the biases that have shaped teaching practices in our society and [create] new ways of knowing, different strategies for the sharing of knowledge" (hooks, 1994, p. 12).

When we value students' ways of knowing and expand our ways of knowing, we can create more liberatory spaces for teaching and learning, and we can experience education as "a paradoxical urgency to foster both a sense of place and a broadening of horizon" (Rose, 1995, p. 283). In *Possible Lives*, Mike Rose talks about how his work has been focused on "How to sharpen awareness of injustice and incompetence, how to maintain the skeptics acuity, yet nurture the ability to imagine the possible and act from hope" (p. 412). We hope that the stories weaved throughout this volume do just that: sharpen the lens on inequity while simultaneously providing hope for a better future.

Concluding Thoughts

When we first began this book, we had three main goals: (1) to compile a broad range of personal narratives about learning and teaching in order to better understand both diversity in experience and commonalities; (2) to better understand the connections between peoples' experiences as learners and their experiences as teachers and educational leaders; and (3) to offer a collection of narratives about learning and teaching to support the professional growth of educators and educational leaders. In this final chapter, we illustrate what we have learned in relation to each of these goals (and what we learned beyond those goals as well). The stories included in this volume were contributed by educators from all over the world, who teach in a variety of contexts. Their stories highlight the diversity of experiences of learning and teaching but, perhaps more importantly, the commonalities. This is an important finding, especially in a time of crisis. It points to the importance of amplifying all experiences to better understand how we are similar while also recognizing important contextual and cultural differences. This practice can build empathy and compassion in our lives and work, which will inevitably transform our learning spaces, making them inclusive and accessible for all.

This storytelling process is certainly not the entirety of the work that needs to be done, but it is an important starting point and a powerful way to build communities that we can learn and grow with. We have found that when individual critical reflection is coupled with collective critical reflection, the benefits are even more profound. No educator should feel like they have to go through this archeological dive on their own. You can certainly start the process on your own, but if you draw on the help of a professional therapist or a community of educators, you will be in a better position to process what you find.

Through this writing and reflection process, we have all been reminded that everyone carries stories with them into the teaching and learning space, and that it is worth the time and space to engage with those stories. We are now firm believers that critical storytelling pushes us as educators to authentically engage in the process of self-actualization, as described by hooks in the quote at the beginning so that we are better positioned to create spaces of teaching and learning that are grounded in "ways of knowing that enhance [our own, our colleagues', and our students'] capacity to live fully and deeply."

References

Bishop, R.S. (1990). Mirrors, windows, and sliding glass doors. *Perspectives*, 6(3), ix–xi.
Brown, B. (2018). *Dare to lead: Brave work. Tough conversations. Whole hearts.* Random House.
Burgo, J. (2018). *Shame: Free Yourself, Find Joy, and Build True Self-Esteem.* St. Martin's Press.
Davis, A. (2016). *Freedom is a constant struggle: Ferguson, Palestine, and the foundations of a movement.* Haymarket Books.
Davis, A. (2014). Lecture delivered February 13th at Southern Illinois University.
Emdin, C. (2016). *For White folks who teach in the hood… and the rest of y'all too: Reality pedagogy and urban education.* Beacon Press.
Freire, P. (1992). *Pedagogy of Hope: Reliving Pedagogy of the Oppressed.* Bloomsbury.

Freire, P. (1998). *Pedagogy of Freedom: Ethics, Democracy, and Civic Courage.* Rowman & Littlefield Publishers, Inc.

Greene, M. (2009). Teaching as possibility: A light in dark times. In *Critical pedagogy in uncertain times* (pp. 137-149). Palgrave Macmillan.

Hanh, T. N. (2004). *Creating true peace: Ending violence in yourself, your family, your community, and the world.* Simon and Schuster.

hooks, B. (1994). *Teaching to transgress.* Routledge.

Paris, D. (2012). Culturally sustaining pedagogy: A needed change in stance, terminology, and practice. *Educational researcher, 41*(3), 93-97.

Rose, M. (1995). *Possible lives: The promise of public education in America.* Houghton Mifflin.

About the Editors and Contributing Authors

Editors

Dr. Laura Colket, Associate Professor at St. George's University, is Director of the Master of Education program, Associate Director of Leadership and Excellence in Academic Development, and co-Founder of the Center for Research on Storytelling in Education. Laura is an educational leader with expertise in curriculum development and program design, and her work is focused on designing learning environments that lead us toward greater social justice and educational equity. She is a qualitative methodologist who focuses on narrative inquiry and participatory, action-oriented and practitioner-led approaches to research. She lives in Grenada with her two children and she is deeply passionate about teaching and learning.

Dr. Tracy Penny Light is Professor and Director of the Leadership and Excellence in Academic Development (LEAD) Division, and co-Founder of the Center for Research on Storytelling in Education at St. George's University, Grenada, West Indies. Tracy's ongoing educational research focuses on ePortfolio implementation and the ability for reflection in ePortfolios to transform the learner experience. Tracy works with institutions, faculty and staff who are using or wanting to use ePortfolios and regularly gives workshops and consults with campuses on ePortfolio implementation. She is President and Chair of the Board of directors for the Association for Authentic, Experiential and Evidence-Based Learning (AAEEBL) http://AAEEBL.org

Dr. M. Adam Carswell is a scholar-practitioner and school leader with over two decades of experience working to create joyfully engaging school climates for students and teachers. He has taught in Canada, Australia, the U.S., and the Caribbean and he currently resides in Canada with his family.

Contributing Authors

Dr. Debbie Devonish is an academic, teacher educator and a recent education researcher with a passion for unearthing the issues and factors impacting practices in the Jamaican education system. She has grown from an ordinary student with varied experiences in her schooling to become lecturer and Associate Professor at the University of Technology, Jamaica. As she defines her space in Academia she is reflective of her past experiences as a young pupil while she leverages her impact as an education practitioner. Debbie is a wife with two daughters and a son.

Dr. Melissa Kapadia (they/she) is a lecturer in the Critical Writing Program at the University of Pennsylvania, where they teach writing seminars on topics in Asian American Studies, Literacy Studies, and Ethnography. They are a community educator and organizer working with local Philadelphia organizations like the Radical Asian American Womxn's Collective (RAAWC), Philly South Asian Collective (PSAC), and Asian Arts Initiative; in addition, they work as a writing fellow and coach, supporting professional, graduate, and doctoral writers. Mel's research interests include workplace literacies, community and radical education, illness literacies, and collective storytelling.

Shaakira Olabisi Raheem is an American born to Yoruba parents. She works to develop critical literacy, positive body and self-image, emotional intelligence, connection to nature and self-actualization among youth and adults. She completed her Masters of Science in Education at the University of Pennsylvania in 2017, and her 200hr yoga teacher training through YogaWorks in 2019. Shaakira has worked in holistic and international education for over fifteen years. She has studied and worked in Ghana, Morocco, the United Arab Emirates, Palestine, the Dominican Republic, Canada and Tanzania. Her interests in education, individual and community development have led her to launch wellness initiatives that center strengthening our connections with self, community and God.

Dr. Candyce Reynolds is a Professor and Chair of Educational Leadership and Policy in the College of Education at Portland State University, Portland, Oregon, USA. She has an A.B. in Psychology and Social Welfare from the University of California at Berkeley, USA and an M.S. and Ph.D. from the University of Oregon, USA in Counseling Psychology.

Dr. Rohini Roopnarine is a Professor in Veterinary Public Health and Epidemiology at St. George's University in Grenada. Rohini is from Trinidad

& Tobago. She is on the University's Executive Committee for Teaching with Technology, and also active in accreditation efforts for the School of Veterinary Medicine (SVM). The SVM has dual accreditation with the American Veterinary Medical Association (AVMA) and more recently, the UK Royal College of Veterinary Surgeons (RCVS). She completed her Doctor of Veterinary Medicine and Doctorate in Higher Education at the University of Liverpool in the United Kingdom. She was also a clinical scholar at the Faculty of Veterinary Medicine, University of Glasgow, Scotland, UK. Her research interests have moved towards the exciting field of educational research with a focus on Interprofessional Education that incorporates "One Medicine, One Health" education for medical and veterinary students.

Dr. Kathleen Blake Yancey, Kellogg Hunt Professor of English and Distinguished Research Professor Emerita at Florida State University, specializes in writing studies and in portfolio theory and practice. She has served as president/chair of four major U.S. literacy organizations and has been active in national assessment efforts, including the AAC&U VALUE project and the WASC Assessment Leadership Academy. Author/co-author of numerous articles and book chapters, she is also the author/editor/coeditor of 16 scholarly books and a recipient of multiple awards, including the Purdue University Distinguished Woman Scholar Award and the Florida State University Graduate Teaching Award.

Dr. David B. Ross, a professor at Nova Southeastern University, teaches doctoral level courses in educational, organizational, and higher educational leadership. Learning from many perspectives and philosophies from mentors while attending Northern Illinois University, the University of Alabama, and Florida Atlantic University, has assisted him in guiding students in the learning process. Dr. Ross earned his Doctorate in Educational Leadership, Master of Justice Policy Management with an Executive Certificate in Public Management at Florida Atlantic University, and his Bachelor of Science Degree in Computer Science at Northern Illinois University. He has written articles and book chapters on leadership, power, narcissism, organizational stress, academic integrity, plagiarism and fraud, entitlement, mobbing/bullying, Gerontechnology, policy development, professional development, and areas of homeland security. Dr. Ross is a co-editor of a book titled *Higher Education Challenges for Migrant and Refugee Students in a Global World*.

Dr. Sonja Taylor is the Director of Senior Inquiry, a dual-credit first year seminar experience, at Portland State University (PSU). Senior Inquiry is the high school arm of Portland State's innovative general education program, University Studies. Dr. Taylor is a multi-disciplinarian and life-long learner. She has a B.S. in Biology, an M.S. in Conflict Resolution and an M.S. and Ph.D. in Sociology from Portland State University, USA. She brings her passion for social justice and authentic relationships to her work as an administrator, instructor, and researcher.

Andrew K Sobering is a Professor of Biochemistry at St. George's University where he manages the human genetics content for the integrated curriculum of the school of medicine. He graduated with honors from the State University of New York at Stony Brook with a bachelor degree in biochemistry. He earned a doctorate of philosophy from the Department of Biochemistry and Molecular Biology from the Bloomberg School of Public Health at Johns Hopkins University. Since 2004, he has been focused primarily towards teaching medical school education. His research interests include increasing the availability of genetic diagnostic services to underserved communities.

Dr. Browning M. Neddeau (he/him/his) is enrolled in the Citizen Potawatomi Nation. He is a jointly appointed Assistant Professor of Elementary Teacher Education and American Indian Studies at California State University, Chico located in Chico, California, USA. At the university, he is the Chair of the Ethnic Studies ad hoc subcommittee which created a new undergraduate General Education area concerning Ethnic Studies. He is the Chair of the National Art Education Association's Commission on Equity, Diversity & Inclusion. Furthermore, he holds a position on the National Advisory Council for the National Conference on Race and Ethnicity in American Higher Education (NCORE). He has three lines of research under the larger umbrella of student engagement: Native American culturally-appropriate representation in schools, agricultural education, and arts education. He explores issues, challenges, and misconceptions of content integrity and draws connections between the lines for interdisciplinary studies in education. His latest publications center on storytelling. In addition to publishing his work, Dr. Neddeau presents his research at international, national, state, and local conferences.

Brian Martin is a Senior Advisor, Technology (Students & Learning) at the University of Melbourne with focus on technology for teaching and learning. Brian is currently completing a Master of Education where he is immersed in understanding the educational experience of virtual spaces and the impact of deterministic learning environments on student learning and belonging.

Dr. Clare McNally (she/her) is the Academic Lead for Assessment and Evaluation at the Melbourne Dental School and the periodontics and dental hygiene coordinator for the Bachelor of Oral Health, University of Melbourne. Clare completed her PhD titled: *An exploratory investigation of the oral health of hospitalised older people* at the Adelaide Medical School in 2019. Clare also works as a senior dental hygienist in the Oral Medicine Department at the Royal Dental Hospital of Melbourne. She is a passionate, student-centred educator who uses ePortfolio and Storytelling pedagogy to encourage students to tell the story of their learning experience.

Dr. Kathryn Coleman (she/her) is a feminist, artist, researcher and teacher who lives and works in Kulin Nation. Her work focuses on the integration of digital pedagogies and digital portfolios for sustained creative practice, assessment and warranting of evidence across education sectors. She is a senior lecturer at the Melbourne Graduate School of Education at the University of Melbourne where her praxis includes taking aspects of her theoretical and practical work as a/r/tographer to consider how artists, artist-teachers and artist-students use site to create place in digital and physical practice. Kate makes a/r/t (visual, digital and textual) work to create new conversations with the germinal thinkers of theory, education, storying and creativities to create new discourses for contemporary art and design education.

Dr. Theresa Conefrey graduated from the University of Illinois with an MATESL from the Division of English as a Second Language and a Ph.D. from the Institute of Communications Research with a Graduate Minor in Women's Studies. She also holds a B.A. in German and Linguistics with a minor in Teaching English as a Foreign Language from the University of East Anglia, UK, and a Postgraduate Certificate in Education from the University of Reading, UK. She taught at the University of Hawaii, Hilo, before accepting a position at Santa Clara University, where she teaches oral and written communication courses and carries out research on undergraduate learning and ePortfolio implementation and usage. Through her research, she hopes to help all learners, especially those who are traditionally underrepresented in tertiary education, reach their full potential.

Dr. Thembelihle Makhanya is an academic / lecturer at the University of KwaZulu Natal, South Africa, in the Discipline of Social Work. Her doctoral research focused on (de) colonial South African higher education and (de) colonial Social Work programme. Her research interest includes teaching and learning in higher education; (de) coloniality and (de) colonialism; Social

Work education and fatherhood. Dr Makhanya offers her professional services to the Department of Correctional Services as a Victim-Offender Mediation Dialogue facilitator. She is also a chairperson of the NGO called Imbewu Youth Empowerment Centre which addresses psychological issues faced by young people. She has produced a number of publications in local and international journals. She has also presented papers in international, national and regional conferences.

Janay M. Garrett (she/hers) is an Assistant Dean of Student Affairs at Yale College, where she serves as the Director of the Office of Gender and Campus Culture, which houses the Communication and Consent Educators Program, the Alcohol and Other Drugs Harm Reduction Initiative, and also serves as the staff advisor to Yale University's Women's Center. Janay is also a Ph.D. candidate at the University of Pennsylvania, in Interdisciplinary Studies in Human Development, expected to complete her degree in December 2022. As a BlackChicana motherscholar with three children of her own, Janay's research agenda explores how Black birthing women who are first-time mothers story their transition to motherhood. With a focus on the developmental transition to motherhood, known as Matrescence, her dissertation integrates Matrescence and Motherwork frameworks to explore if and how first-time Black mothers experience and negotiate competing identity tensions within personal relationships *and community connection(s)*.

Lucas F. W. Wilson holds an MA in English from McMaster University, as well as an MTS from Vanderbilt University, with Certificates in Jewish Studies and in Religion in the Arts and Contemporary Culture. As a Dissertation Fellow through the Honor Society of Phi Kappa Phi, Lucas is finishing his interdisciplinary PhD in Comparative Studies at Florida Atlantic University. His work has appeared in Flannery O'Connor Review, Canadian Jewish Studies, and in edited collections published by The MLA and SUNY Press. Along with co-editing a multiauthor volume on third-generation Holocaust representation, he is currently a Sessional Lecturer at University of Toronto, where he teaches technical writing.

Raheem Jackson is Upper School History Teacher and Assistant Football Coach at Ransom Everglades School in Florida. He earned his Bachelor's degree from Amherst college and his Master's degree in Education from the University of Pennsylvania Independent School Teaching Residency Program.

About the Editors and Contributing Authors

Dr. Sharon M. Ravitch is a Professor of Practice at the University of Pennsylvania's Graduate School of Education. She is creator of flux pedagogy and has published 7 books on topics including applied qualitative research, educational leadership, and anti-racist pedagogical practice. She is Principal Investigator of Semillas Digitales, a school-based education program in the coffee-producing regions of Nicaragua that cultivates a holistic model of educational innovation focused on pedagogical and curricular enrichment, intensive inquiry-based teacher professional development, technology integration, digital literacy and community partnership. Dr. Ravitch is designated as a GIAN Scholar of the Government of India and is a Fulbright Fellow with Dr. BMN College in Mumbai, Maharashtra in an applied research project focused on pluralism and wellness for first-generation minoritized female students and their teachers.

Dr. Talar Kaloustian is Assistant Chair, ESL Unit and Assistant Professor of English as a Second Language at Community College of Philadelphia. Talar's professional career has centered around teacher training and language teaching. Her experience in adult education lies mainly in ESL/EFL curriculum development/instruction, international high school, graduate and undergraduate academic curriculum development/instruction, academic advising, student orientation, program coordination, and administrative setup.

Dr. Eliana Elkhoury is a STEM scholar who is focused on internationalization, student life, residence life, coaching, and mentoring. She is driven by understanding how we can build capacity and leadership in multiple situations thus igniting success in students.

Dr. Talia Guttin is an Assistant Professor within the Small Animal Medicine and Surgery Department in the School of Veterinary Medicine at St. George's University in Grenada. She is passionate about teaching and curriculum design and recently completed a master's degree in Curriculum, Pedagogy and Leadership from St. George's University.

Dr. Antonia MacDonald is Associate Dean, School of Graduate Studies and Professor, Department of Humanities and Social Sciences at St. George's University in Grenada. She is St. Lucian born, a LASPAU Fulbright scholar, and earned her Ph.D. from Ohio State University.